Theology
and Ethics in Paul

Theology
and Ethics in Paul

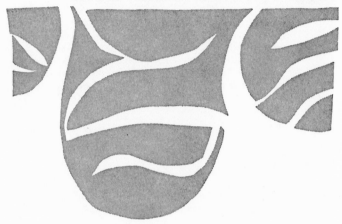

Victor Paul Furnish

Abingdon Press—Nashville & New York

THEOLOGY AND ETHICS IN PAUL

Copyright © 1968 by Abingdon Press

Library of Congress Catalog Card Number: 68-17445

SET UP, PRINTED, AND BOUND BY THE
PARTHENON PRESS, AT NASHVILLE,
TENNESSEE, UNITED STATES OF AMERICA

In honor of my Mother
Mildred Feller Furnish
To the memory of my Father
Reuben McKinley Furnish (1896-1961)

Preface

The present study is offered as a small contribution to a neglected area of biblical research. While the resurgence of interest in biblical theology which followed publication of Karl Barth's commentary on Romans opened the way for a mutually enriching dialogue between systematic theologians and biblical scholars, as yet there have been little effective communication and collaboration between biblical scholars and theologians working specifically in the field of Christian ethics. Only a few major critical studies of biblical ethics have been published in the last several decades, and most of the exegetical work on which Christian ethicists are forced to depend is sadly inadequate. Lamenting the "paucity of material that relates the two areas in a scholarly way," James M. Gustafson has called urgently for more work to be done on this topic,[1] and Thomas C. Oden suggests that "the simple task of honest and clear exegesis may be the undiscovered beginning point for contemporary Protestant ethics." [2]

It is not surprising that most writers on Christian ethics should feel obliged to devote some attention to the ethics of Paul, for

[1] "Christian Ethics" in *Religion*, ed. Paul Ramsey (1965), pp. 337-38.
[2] *Radical Obedience: The Ethics of Rudolf Bultmann* (1964), pp. 18, 21.

7

the apostle's place in the history of Christianity and his decisive
influence on Protestant thought in particular give his teaching
special prominence. But a glance at the rather different ways in
which these writers characterize Paul's ethic, and the problems
with it which they themselves raise, is enough to underscore
the need for a thorough review and reevaluation of the primary
sources. Paul Ramsey, for instance, reduces the Pauline ethic to
the formula, "Love and do as you *then* please," [3] while E. Clinton
Gardner imputes to Paul a concern for "the objective structure
of the moral order." [4] H. Richard Niebuhr argues that Paul's
imperatives are necessary because although the Christian's inner
moral transformation has begun, it is not yet complete; [5] Emil
Brunner calls the Pauline exhortations "pedagogical instructions
. . . not binding on the conscience"; [6] George F. Thomas describes
Paul's ethic as an "ethic of redemption, an ethic for the regener-
ate"; [7] Joseph Sittler invokes Paul's name in support of the view
that the Christian's ethical acts are to be "faithful re-enactments
of [Christ's] life." [8] And while Reinhold Niebuhr is bothered
by Paul's view of sin which "imperils and seems to weaken all
moral judgments which deal with the 'nicely calculated less and
more' of justice and goodness as revealed in the relativities of
history," [9] Joseph Fletcher calls on Paul to support the idea of
a Christian "situation ethic." [10] What, then, is the essential
character and structure of the Pauline ethic? In particular, what
are the theological presuppositions, if any, of Paul's ethic and
the ethical implications, if any, of his theology? These are the
concerns which have prompted the present investigation. The
ultimate objective here is not the compilation of a "Pauline

[3] *Basic Christian Ethics* (1953), pp. 75 ff.

[4] *Biblical Faith and Social Ethics* (1960), p. 83.

[5] "Introduction to Biblical Ethics" in *Christian Ethics*, ed. Waldo Beach
and H. Richard Niebuhr (1955), p. 42.

[6] *The Divine Imperative: A Study in Christian Ethics*, trans. Olive Wyon
(1937), p. 601, n. 8.

[7] "The Ethics of St. Paul" in *Christian Ethics and Moral Philosophy*
(1955), p. 87.

[8] *The Structure of Christian Ethics* (1958), p. 48.

[9] *The Nature and Destiny of Man* (1941), I, 219-20.

[10] *Situation Ethics: The New Morality* (1966); see esp. pp. 30, 49, 69, 81,
151-52.

code of ethics" but a better understanding of the structure of his ethical thinking, its ground, and its guiding convictions. Attention will not be focused on the "practical" content of the apostle's moral teaching (which other scholars have ably handled), but on its theological foundations and context.

Valuable help in approaching the task here undertaken is gained by examining the varied nineteenth- and twentieth-century attempts to interpret Paul's ethic. Some significant results of such a survey are reported in the appendix. The major conclusion to be drawn from that survey and thus one of the controlling presuppositions of this present study is that the relation of indicative and imperative, the relation of "theological" proclamation and "moral" exhortation, is *the* crucial problem in interpreting the Pauline ethic. Therefore, this fresh inquiry has, necessarily and simultaneously, two focuses. It must give attention to the origin, form, and character of the specifically "ethical" materials in Paul's letters (see especially Chapters I and II), and at the same time seek to discover how if at all these are related to the "theological" aspects of the apostle's preaching (see especially Chapter III). The question is not just whether doctrinal and moral concerns exist side by side in Paul. That coexistence is self-evident. Therefore, only to affirm that Paul never separates morals from religion does not yet speak to the real issue: Is there any inner, essential relationship between them? How is this question to be approached?

Previous interpretations of the Pauline ethic have usually begun with questions being raised about Paul's own past moral life and religious experience, and an examination of such topics as his presuppositions about man's nature, his Christian ethical ideal, the theological sanctions and motives of his ethical teaching, and so forth. The present study, however, will seek a different angle of vision. In the first place there will be no systematic attempt to chronicle the private religious and moral life of Paul. Despite claims to the contrary[11] his letters simply do not yield

[11] See especially the book by Mary Andrews, discussed below (Appendix, notes 33, 43, 44). Nygren has rightly seen that the attempt to reconstruct the apostle's psychological experience "is one of the chief errors of Pauline scholarship" (*Agape and Eros*, trans. P. Watson [1953], p. 109).

that kind of data. The apostle's preaching does not have the
character of "personal testimony," and he makes no specific attempt to interpret the "religious meaning" of his own conversion—to which he himself only briefly refers, and then in a
polemical context (Gal. 1:12 ff.). Deissmann's famous distinction between "letters" and "epistles" [12] is greatly overdrawn. He
was correct in saying that Paul's letters are not literary essays
("epistles"), but they are not "personal correspondence" in the
modern sense, either (not even the letter to Philemon). They
are apostolic communications to congregations, and they are all
(with the possible exception of Philemon) intended for public
reading, usually if not always in the context of the community's
worship. They are pastoral letters and have certain important
literary aspects.[13] It is inevitable that they should reveal some
things about the writer, but these revelations are incidental and
accidental and not integral to the writer's purpose. That purpose
is *evangelical:* to reaffirm the salient features of the gospel and
to expound its meaning to Christians who are in need of encouragement, exhortation, and instruction. The apostle's themes are
thus indisputably *theological* in the broad sense—related to the
cardinal tenets of the gospel to which his readers had been converted and in which he now seeks to help them be built up and
stand fast. One must therefore start with the theological ideas of
Paul's letters and abandon the attempt to start with "Paul the
man" and his "religious experience."

It is not to be presumed from what has been said so far that
Paul's letters exhibit anything like a *systematic* theology. Although virtually all the interpreters of Paul's ethic concede this,
there is often a tendency to overschematize the data which bear
on their topic. False systematizations are to be avoided, and to
facilitate this the present study will presuppose as little as possible about the structure of Paul's ethic. No attempt will be

[12] E.g. *The Religion of Jesus and the Faith of Paul* (1923), where Deissmann goes so far as to say that Paul's letters must be read as "confessions"
(p. 160).
[13] This is a major contribution of Paul Schubert's *Form and Function of
the Pauline Thanksgivings* in *BZNW*, 20 (1939). Dibelius acknowledges that
Schubert has demonstrated the "half literary character of the Pauline letters"
(*ThLZ*, LXVI [1941], col. 28).

made from the outset to inquire into its "principles," "norms," "ideals," "sanctions," "motives," and such. Rather, an attempt will be made to start where Paul starts in his preaching, insofar as this can be determined from his letters. Chapter III is thus devoted to an examination of what appear to be the central themes of his preaching and to whatever ethical impulses and dimensions they may have.

Finally, however, it is important to arrive at some overall judgment about the character of Paul's ethic and its decisive features. What is to be regarded as the touchstone of his ethic? Most interpreters have presumed it to be his view of the Spirit's presence and power in the Christian life; others regard the vital factor in his ethic as the concept of justification, baptism, the church, or the eschaton. Or is the clue to be found in some special "ethical doctrine" of "sanctification"? One's judgment on this matter inevitably determines his interpretation of the relation of indicative and imperative in Paul's thought and his estimate of the extent to which there are ethical dimensions to the apostle's theology and theological dimensions to his ethical teaching. These are the questions which finally must be tackled in Chapter IV.

The primary sources for this study are of course Paul's own letters, and the investigator's presuppositions in this matter also need to be stated. The Pastoral Epistles are here regarded as deutero-Pauline; the hypothesis that they contain fragmentary materials from Paul himself is too problematic to be of consequence in a study of his ethic. At various times and by various scholars the authenticity of Colossians, Ephesians, and II Thessalonians has also been questioned. It is not possible here to argue the cases pro and con for each of these, although the present writer is inclined to regard all three as deutero-Pauline. In any case, the soundest procedure methodologically is to limit oneself to the letters of indisputable authenticity: Romans, I and II Corinthians, Galatians, Philippians, I Thessalonians, and Philemon.[14] Any errors resulting from the omission of

[14] Statistical analysis of the vocabulary of the letters in the Pauline Corpus has recently called into question also the authorship of Philippians, I Thessalonians, and—less seriously—Philemon. See now esp. A. Q. Morton,

Colossians, Ephesians, and II Thessalonians will surely be less crucial than would be those resulting from their false inclusion as Pauline homologoumena.

A further problem of methodology is more complex. What allowance is to be made for the possibility of a change or "development" in Paul's thinking (for example, with respect to the eschaton or the law) during the course of his ministry? Dodd has argued forcefully for this,[15] and the question has recently been approached anew by John Coolidge Hurd, Jr., in his important analysis of the Corinthian correspondence.[16] Even under optimum conditions it is a difficult matter for interpreters of a given writer to reach agreement about the "development" of his thinking. (Note the recent controversies among scholars as to continuity and development in the thought of such men as Karl Barth, Rudolf Bultmann, and Martin Heidegger.) In the case of Paul, optimum conditions do not prevail; not only is the subject himself long deceased, but there is no certainty of the chronology, either relative or absolute, of his literary remains. Therefore, the possibility of reaching any kind of consensus about change and development in Paul's thought is not

---

"The Authorship of the Pauline Corpus" in *The New Testament in Historical and Contemporary Perspective, Essays in Memory of G. H. C. Mac-Gregor*, ed. H. Anderson and W. Barclay (1965), pp. 209 ff.; and Morton's (with James McLeman) *Paul: The Man and the Myth* (1966). It would be presumptuous to say that the employment of a statistical methodology can never help with these problems of authorship, for its effectiveness has been shown rather convincingly in other cases (see esp. Frederick Mosteller and David L. Wallace, *Inference and Disputed Authorship: The Federalist* [1964]). But it would be equally presumptuous to believe that this method can be used in isolation from other data or that, at this stage in the discussion, it has achieved results of such statistical probability as to be taken into account here. (For a critique of this methodology as applied to the Pauline letters, see Harvey K. McArthur, "Computer Criticism," *ET*, LXXVI [1965], 367 ff.) So far, then, the inclusion of Philippians, I Thessalonians, and Philemon among the "indisputably authentic" letters of Paul needs very little qualification.

[15] See "The Mind of Paul: II" in Dodd's volume of essays, *New Testament Studies* (1953), pp. 83 ff. This article was first published in 1934. A criticism of Dodd's developmental hypothesis is to be found in the article by John Lowe, "An Examination of Attempts to Detect Development in St. Paul's Theology," *JThS*, XLII (1941), 129 ff.

[16] *The Origin of I Corinthians* (1965).

very great, even though research must push ahead to some
eventual result. In the meantime other Pauline studies cannot be
postponed and are obliged to proceed with the presupposition
that the indisputably authentic letters, examined critically, can
yield meaningful even though always provisional glimpses of
something like "Pauline theology."

The thesis which finally emerges from this investigation is
that the apostle's ethical concerns are not secondary but radically
integral to his basic theological convictions. In a sense, therefore,
this study calls into question the very presupposition with which
it begins—that there is some identifiable "Pauline ethic" amenable to critical analysis in its own right. But perhaps readers
will agree that there are still some things to be learned along
the way to that conclusion.

Acknowledgments

Many persons have, in various ways, supported and contributed to this study of the Pauline ethic. My interest in Pauline theology was first kindled by Professor Paul Schubert at Yale, and under his guidance my doctoral dissertation—a first tentative venture into the subject of Pauline ethics—was conceived and completed. Although the present work is entirely new, there is a clear genetic relationship between these, most evident in Chapter II of the present study. It is also a pleasure to acknowledge the support of Dean Joseph D. Quillian, Jr., and numerous other colleagues of mine at Perkins School of Theology, Southern Methodist University.

Major portions of this book were completed during a year's research leave (1965-66) spent in residence at the Friedrich-Wilhelms-Universität in Bonn as a fellow of the Alexander von Humboldt-Stiftung. The courtesies extended to me by the von Humboldt staff and by many other persons in Bonn must not go unrecorded. Most especially am I indebted to Professor Wolfgang Schrage of the Protestant theological faculty there. He not only allowed me to sit in on his seminar on Pauline ethics, but in many additional ways exhibited his interest in my work on a topic to which he himself has made substantial contributions.

The tedious job of producing the final typescript was skillfully accomplished by Mrs. Bonnie Jordan and Mrs. Charlaine Brown. My wife, Jody, demonstrated concretely her interest in the whole project by assuming the awesome task of deciphering my original penned manuscript and converting it into a first typed draft.

Translations of biblical materials, unless otherwise specified, are my own. Other ancient writings, where possible, have been cited and quoted according to the texts and translations of "The Loeb Classical Library." Where English translations of secondary literature exist, these have been cited, although where I have deemed it relevant, the date of publication in the original language has also been indicated. Where no English translations exist, I have presumed to make and quote my own.

Contents

Abbreviations

I. Ancient Writers and Writings

Apoc. Bar.	The Apocalypse of Baruch
Epict.	Epictetus, Discourses
LCL	The Loeb Classical Library editions
LXX	The Septuagint, ed. A. Rahlfs
Test. XII P.	The Testaments of the Twelve Patriarchs
	(Ben., Benjamin; Jud., Judah; Lev., Levi; Reu., Reuben)

II. Secondary Literature

ABR	Australian Biblical Review
AThANT	Abhandlungen zur Theologie des Alten und Neuen Testaments
AThR	Anglican Theological Review
Bauer	W. Bauer, A Greek-English Lexicon of the New Testament
BEvTh	Beiträge zur evangelischen Theologie
BFChTh	Beiträge zur Förderung christlicher Theologie

BHTh	Beiträge zur historischen Theologie
BhEvTh	Beihefte zur evangelischen Theologie
Bibl	Biblica
Billerbeck	(H. L. Strack–) P. Billerbeck, Kommentar zum Neuen Testament aus Talmud und Midrasch
BJRL	Bulletin of the John Rylands Library
Bl–Deb–Funk	F. Blass–A. Debrunner, ed. R. Funk, A Greek Grammar of the New Testament
BZNW	Beihefte zur Zeitschrift für die neutestamentliche Wissenschaft
CNT	Commentaire du Nouveau Testament
ERE	The Encyclopedia of Religion and Ethics, ed. J. Hastings
ET	The Expository Times
Exp	The Expositor
FRLANT	Forschungen zur Religion und Literatur des Alten und Neuen Testaments
HNT	Handbuch zum Neuen Testament, begr. von H. Lietzmann
HNTC	Harper's New Testament Commentaries
HThR	The Harvard Theological Review
ICC	The International Critical Commentary of the Holy Scripture of the Old and New Testaments
IKZ	Internationale kirchliche Zeitschrift
IntB	The Interpreter's Bible
IntDB	The Interpreter's Dictionary of the Bible
JBL	The Journal of Biblical Literature
JewEnc	The Jewish Encyclopedia
JThC	Journal for Theology and the Church
JThS	The Journal of Theological Studies
KuD	Kerygma und Dogma

KEK	Kritisch-exegetischer Kommentar über das Neue Testament, begr. von H. A. W. Meyer
MNTC	The Moffatt New Testament Commentary
Moffatt	The New Testament in the Moffatt Translation
Moulton	J. H. Moulton, A Grammar of New Testament Greek
NEB	The New English Bible: New Testament
NKZ	Neue kirchliche Zeitschrift
NTD	Das Neue Testament Deutsch
NTS	New Testament Studies
RGG	Die Religion in Geschichte und Gegenwart
RSV	Holy Bible: Revised Standard Version
SAB	Sitzungsberichte der deutschen (until 1944: preussischen) Akademie der Wissenschaften zu Berlin
SAH	Sitzungsberichte der Heidelberger Akademie der Wissenschaften
SANT	Studien zum Alten und Neuen Testament
SBTh	Studies in Biblical Theology
SJTh	The Scottish Journal of Theology
StTh	Studia Theologica
ThBl	Theologische Blätter
ThEx	Theologische Existenz Heute
ThLZ	Theologische Literaturzeitung
ThR	Theologische Rundschau
ThW	Theologisches Wörterbuch zum Neuen Testament, begr. von G. Kittel, hg. von G. Friedrich [Eng. ed., Theological Dictionary of the New Testament, tr. by G. W. Bromiley]
ThZ	Theologische Zeitschrift

TU	Texte und Untersuchungen zur Geschichte der altchristlichen Literatur
UNT	Untersuchungen zum Neuen Testament
WMANT	Wissenschaftliche Monographien zum Alten und Neuen Testament
WUNT	Wissenschaftliche Untersuchungen zum Neuen Testament
ZNW	Zeitschrift für die neutestamentliche Wissenschaft
ZThK	Zeitschrift für Theologie und Kirche

I

The Sources
of Paul's Ethical Teaching

INTRODUCTION

It would be naïve to presuppose that Paul's ethical teaching is a completely new creation, like Melchizedek without progenitors, or like Athena sprung fully armed from the deity himself. Of course one must not discount the importance of unique factors or *hapax phenomena* which may have played a role in the apostle's conversion and in the formation of his message; he himself refers these to divine revelation (e.g. Gal. 1:15-16). Nor should one ignore those aspects of Paul's teaching which seem to be genuinely new and creative. Yet events of divine grace or supernatural revelation are hardly amenable to the methods of historical-critical research, and it is doubtful whether the vague concept of "creative genius" should be employed as a regular category of historical explanation. The historical investigator has his own work to do, partial and provisional though his results always are. In this particular case the task is to ascertain in what formal and material ways Paul is indebted to movements, traditions, and perspectives which do lie within the operative field of historical analysis.

There are at least three conceivable approaches to the broad topic of Paul's ethical and moral heritage. These must be clearly differentiated, although they are of course also significantly related. One, sociological and even psychological in its orientation, seeks to discern the various environmental influences upon the apostle's personality, attitudes, and concerns. Mary Andrews has purposefully identified herself with such an approach.[1] But, as already noted,[2] such questions cannot be directly studied, for Paul's letters do not yield the kind of data which are required for direct sociological and psychological analysis. Moreover, there is not even complete certainty about where or under what specific conditions Paul was reared, what formal training he had as a youth, or with what particular activities he was engaged prior to his conversion. While the interpreter of Paul's ethic must be ever alert to clues about social and psychological factors, this hardly seems to be the place for him to begin.

It is conceivable, secondly, that one could employ a "comparative" approach to the topic. If we view the Pauline ethic overall, against the background of what total thought-complex may it most illuminatingly be interpreted? Is it, for example, an ethic cut out from the Old Testament pattern, or has it more affinity with late Jewish and rabbinic ethics? Or with the ethical systems of Hellenistic popular philosophy? Or with the familiar motifs common to the syncretistic religious movements of the Hellenistic world? As appropriate as such questions are, the interpreter is here involved in a kind of "hermeneutical circle." While his overall estimate of the ideological background of Paul's ethic will determine his analysis and interpretation of individual Pauline concepts (e.g. righteousness, sin, obedience, salvation), it is really only *by means* of an analysis of such individual concepts that an overall estimate of the ideological background can be attained. Thus, the interpreter's judgment about the general ideological background of the ethic must always be tentative and open to correction in the light of his analysis of particular concepts, and vice versa. Moreover, a comparative approach always

[1] *The Ethical Teaching of Paul.* See Appendix, notes 33, 43, 44.
[2] See Preface, pp. 9-10.

requires expertise in several areas and demands that the scholar grasp clearly not only the character of Paul's ethic, but also, just as clearly, the character of those ethical perspectives and systems with which he seeks to compare it.[3] A comparative approach can do much, in the long run, to reveal the background of Paul's teaching, but it is neither the easiest nor the best approach with which to initiate such an investigation.

A third approach is, all things considered, the most practical beginning point, although it has its own difficulties and dangers. One may ask what similarities, formal and material, exist between Paul's ethical teaching and the various traditions to which he was exposed in the Hellenistic world of the first century. Thus the vague and difficult question of the "background" of Paul's ethic is converted into the more concrete and manageable question of the *sources* of his ethical teaching. Is one able to identify with any certainty the origins of the apostle's actual moral instruction? If so, it may then be possible to draw some tentative conclusions about its "background" in a more general sense.

This investigation of sources is not without its own problems. For instance, there is always the danger that discovered parallels will automatically be used as evidence for direct dependence, literary or otherwise, of one upon the other, whereas the possibility of a source on which the two are "independently dependent" is overlooked. And as Erwin Goodenough was fond of emphasizing to his students, a "parallel" consists, by definition, of "straight lines in the same plane, which never meet however far produced in any direction" (*Shorter Oxford English Dictionary,* 3rd ed., 1955). That is, parallels do not necessarily indicate actual genetic relationships.[4] Moreover, one must not presuppose that identification of the *origins* of Paul's ethical

---

[3] This was one of the points at issue in the spirited exchange between Bultmann and A. Bonhöffer concerning the similarities and differences between New Testament ethics and the ethic of Epictetus. See Bultmann's response to Bonhöffer's monograph, *Epiktet und das Neue Testament* (1911), "Das religiöse Moment in der ethischen Unterweisung des Epiktet und das Neue Testament" (*ZNW,* XIII [1912], 97 ff., 177 ff.), and Bonhöffer's reply, "Epiktet und das Neue Testament" (*ZNW,* XIII, 281 ff.).

[4] See Samuel Sandmel, "Parallelomania," *JBL,* LXXXI (1962), pp. 1 ff.

teaching is sufficient to explain its meaning and function within
the context of his own thought and letters. That is a question
deserving of discussion in its own right.[5]

Although considerable effort has been expended in the attempt
to trace the sources of Paul's ethical teaching, different conclusions have been drawn. Some scholars believe he was primarily
dependent upon and influenced by Old Testament and Jewish
traditions, others stress his use of Hellenistic materials, and still
others emphasize his dependence upon the teachings of Jesus.[6]
Obviously, a full-scale discussion of this topic is not possible
here, and it would be fruitless only to rehearse the arguments
and evidence already advanced in support of each of these posi-
tions. However, it is necessary for the sake of orientation and
perspective on subsequent topics to consider briefly the most
important data and to arrive at some general understanding
of Paul's sources. His use of Old Testament-Jewish and Hellenistic materials, and his dependence upon the teaching of Jesus
must be considered in turn.

1. THE OLD TESTAMENT AND JUDAISM

a. The Old Testament

That Paul's heritage is at least partly Jewish is beyond dispute.
In Phil. 3:4-6 he identifies himself emphatically with the people
of Israel and speaks of the Pharisaic attitude toward the law
which had characterized his preconversion life. His belonging
to Abraham's people is further stressed in II Cor. 11:22, and in
Gal. 1:13-14 he refers to his past zeal for the traditions of
Judaism. Indeed, the whole of Romans 9-11 is a poignant testimony to the extent to which, even as a Christian, the apostle
feels himself bound to the people of Israel. All Paul's letters
attest his indebtedness to the faith of the Old Testament and to
the traditions of this covenant people. Even though he often
sets himself over against those traditions and concepts, he does

---

[5] See Chapter II.
[6] See Appendix, pp. 252, 253, 259-60, 267-68, 274.

not abandon the fundamental conviction that the Christian community is the true Israel (e.g. Gal. 3:7, 29), that the patriarchs themselves played a key role in the proclamation of the gospel (e.g. Romans 4; Gal. 3:8-9), that the event of Christ's coming is integral to the history of Israel (e.g. Gal. 3:16 ff.; Rom. 9:5), and that in the economy of God's divine plan the Jews have an undiminished advantage over the Gentiles (e.g. Rom. 1:16; 3:1 ff.). It would be impossible to understand the Pauline gospel apart from the apostle's Jewish heritage.

But the special question to be considered here is whether, in his ethical teaching, Paul is actually dependent upon Old Testament and Jewish *sources*, whether the concrete ethical materials of Judaism are actually employed by him in his own moral instruction. At least with respect to the Old Testament the answer can be unequivocally affirmative. Harnack's reference to the importance of the Old Testament for the development of early Christian parenesis, and thus for the mission and expansion of Christianity itself,[7] may be amply documented from the Pauline letters. Near the close of the extended exhortations in Romans 12–15 Paul specifically says, after an Old Testament citation (Ps. 68:10, LXX), that "whatever was formerly written was written for our instruction [διδασκαλία], that by steadfastness and the 'encouragement and exhortation' [παράκλησις] of the scriptures we might have hope" (15:4). This, indeed, is one of the important presuppositions which guide Paul's use of the Old Testament, as seen also by other instances in which he specifically applies scriptural passages to the situation of his Christian readers (e.g. Rom. 4:23-24; I Cor. 10:6 ff.).

The so-called "parenetic sections" of Paul's letters provide sub-

[7] *The Mission and Expansion of Christianity*, trans. J. Moffatt (1908), p. 284. Harnack's contention that Paul, however, made no use of Old Testament materials as such in his initial missionary contacts in the Gentile world ("Das Alte Testament in den paulinischen Briefen und in den paulinischen Gemeinden," *SAB* [1928], pp. 124 ff.) is not fully supported by the evidence. See O. Michel, *Paulus und seine Bibel* in *BFChTh*, 18 (1929), 112 ff. The broad topic of Paul's use of the Old Testament falls outside the scope of the present discussion. On this see, in addition to the monographs by Harnack and Michel, E. E. Ellis, *Paul's Use of the Old Testament* (1957), and above all, Joseph Bonsirven, *Exégèse rabbinique et exégèse paulinienne* in "Bibliothèque de théologie historique" (1939).

stantial evidence for his hortatory use of Old Testament texts. Rom. 12:16, which cautions against preoccupation with one's own wisdom (μὴ γίνεσθε φρόνιμοι παρ' ἑαυτοῖς), seems to be a direct echo of Prov. 3:7 (LXX: μὴ ἴσθι φρόνιμος παρὰ σεαυτῷ); the specific citation in 12:19 is from Deut. 32:35 ("Vengeance is mine, I will repay, says the Lord," RSV); the exhortation to attend to the needs of the hungry, thirsty enemy (12:20) is almost a verbatim quotation of Prov. 25:21-22 (LXX); the Decalogue is cited in 13:9, and the commandment of neighbor-love which follows is drawn from Lev. 19:18; the exhortations of chap. 14 are supported by quotations from Isa. 45:23; 49:18 (vs. 11), and those at the opening of chap. 15 by a quotation from Ps. 68:10, LXX (vs. 3). In Gal. 5:14 the love-commandment of Lev. 19:18 is again quoted to summarize the law; in I Thess. 4:6 the words about the Lord being an avenger may well echo Ps. 93:1-2 (LXX), and in I Thess. 5:8 the metaphor of the Christian's moral armament undoubtedly derives at least in part from the same metaphor applied to Yahweh himself in Isa. 59:17.[8]

Paul's use of the Old Testament in his ethical appeals is also clear in contexts which are not "parenetic" in the same way as Romans 12–15, Galatians 5–6 and I Thessalonians 4–5. Thus, in Rom. 2:6, in connection with his argument (1:18–3:20) that "the whole world" is accountable to God (3:19), he invokes the words of Prov. 24:12: "[God] will render to every man according to his works." In the same context (Rom. 2:24) he specifically cites Isa. 52:5 against the Jews for themselves breaking the law: "For, as it is written, 'The name of God is blasphemed among the Gentiles because of you'" (RSV). And the whole argument of this section is concluded with a catena of biblical passages (Rom. 3:10 ff.) drawn from the Psalms (14:1 ff.; 53:2 ff.; 5:10; 10:7; 36:2) and Isaiah (59:7-8).

The employment of Old Testament materials in ethical teaching is again a prominent feature in the Corinthian correspon-

---

[8] The metaphor of Christian armament is also present in Eph. 6:14 ff. M. Dibelius, *An die Kolosser, Epheser, An Philemon* in *HNT* (3rd ed., rev. H. Greeven, 1953), believes this metaphor, popular in early Christianity, has several different "roots," among which is Isa. 59:17 (pp. 96-97).

dence, addressed to a congregation in particular need of concrete moral instruction. The apostle makes use, in I Corinthians 10, of motifs from the narratives of Israel's exodus from Egypt and wilderness wandering led by Moses, protected by Yahweh, and —according to Paul's typological interpretation of the "rock" (vs. 4; Exodus 17:6; Num. 20:11) —refreshed by Christ himself. The reminder that God's judgment came upon most of his children in the wilderness (vs. 5; Num. 14:29-30) is specifically applied to the Corinthians as a warning that they should not desire evil as Israel had (vs. 6). This warning is made more concrete in vss. 7 ff. which open with a citation of Exod. 32:6 ("The people sat down to eat and drink, and rose up to dance," RSV), but which also include allusions to Num. 25:1 ff.; 21:5-6; and 16:41, 49. The hortatory climax of the pericope occurs in vs. 12 ("Therefore let any one who thinks he stands take heed lest he fall," RSV) which encapsulates the moral lesson Paul wishes his readers to find in the Old Testament narratives.

Materials from the Old Testament also constitute a significant portion of the apostle's appeal that the Corinthians join in the raising of an "offering for the saints" (II Cor. 9:1). Regardless of what conclusion one reaches about the literary integrity of II Corinthians or the original relationship of chaps. 8 and 9,[9] the fact remains that in each chapter Old Testament citations and allusions occur. In an effort to have his readers contribute from their abundance, in 8:15 Paul quotes Exod. 16:18 ("He who gathered much had nothing in abundance, and thus he who gathered little had no want"). And in assuring the readers of his proper stewardship of the fund, in 8:21 (cf. Rom. 12:17) he draws upon the language of Prov. 3:4: "We have regard for what is honorable not only in the sight of the Lord but also in the sight of men." Similarly, the argument of chap. 9, especially vs. 7 ("God loves a gracious giver"), relies on scriptural teaching, first of all with an allusion to Prov. 22:8. Then in vs. 9 there is an almost verbatim citation of Ps. 111:9 (LXX), "He scatters abroad, he gives to the poor; his righteousness endures for ever" (RSV), and in vs. 10 verbal echoes of Isa. 55:10 and Hos. 10:12

[9] On these problems see, most recently, Günther Bornkamm, "Die Vorgeschichte des sog. zweiten Korintherbriefes," *SAH* (1961).

intended to support Paul's contention that the giver himself will
be bountifully enriched (vs. 11). The catena of Old Testament
passages in II Cor. 6:16 ff. (from Lev. 26:11-12 [Ezek. 27:37]; Isa.
52:11-12; II Sam. 7:14) is assembled in order to validate the
admonitions to separate oneself from unbelievers (vss. 14 ff.)
and to cleanse oneself "from every defilement of body and spirit"
(7:1 RSV).

There are further passages in I Corinthians where the apostle
makes fairly direct use of the Old Testament in his ethical
teaching. The Genesis text about man and woman becoming
"one flesh" (2:24 LXX) is quoted exactly in I Cor. 6:16 in
order to refute the notion evidently held by the Corinthian
"spiritists" that what one does with his body has no bearing
on his relationship to Christ. Almost as exact is the citation of
Deut. 25:4 (LXX) in 9:9, "You shall not muzzle an ox when
it is treading out the grain" (RSV). By this means Paul seeks to
remind his readers that scripture itself presumes the laborer deserves to live by his work, and that the apostles thus have every
right to expect support from their congregations. The same point
is made in vs. 13 by reference to the practice which obtains among
the temple priests (cf. Deut. 18:1), a precedent whose validity
for the Christian community Paul readily assumes. There are
other direct appeals to Jewish custom (10:18; cf. Lev. 7:6) and
to scripture (10:26) in the course of the exhortations about
shunning idolatry (10:14 ff.) and participating thankfully in all
the gifts of creation (vss. 23 ff.). The citation in vs. 26 ("the
earth is the Lord's and everything in it," RSV) follows verbatim
the LXX text of Ps. 23:1. Finally, the general exhortations which
stand near the end of the letter ("Be courageous, be strong,"
16:13 RSV) also seem to be drawn from the LXX (Ps. 30:25).

The passages examined here are sufficient to show the use
made of Old Testament texts in the Pauline ethical teaching.[10]
It is not surprising to find that slightly more than forty percent
of the scriptural texts Paul employs in ethical contexts are drawn
from the Torah. The remainder come, almost equally, from the

[10] Other passages could also have been mentioned. Among them: I Cor.
5:13 (Deut. 17:7; 19:19; 22:21, 24); I Cor. 15:32 (Isa. 22:13); I Cor. 13:5
(Zech. 8:17); Phil. 2:15 (Deut. 32:5).

prophets (virtually always Second Isaiah), the Psalms, and Proverbs. It is not possible to generalize about the subject matter of the contexts in which they appear. Some of them have to do with the responsibility of Christians to give of their "abundance," others with idolatry, personal morality, community relationships, church discipline, and one's relationship to "the world."

It is noteworthy that Paul never quotes the Old Testament *in extenso* for the purpose of developing a pattern of conduct. Except for a few instances in which a catena of passages from several different scriptural contexts is assembled, the citations are always brief. Moreover, and of even greater significance, they are never casuistically interpreted or elaborated.[11] In this connection it is significant, also, that Paul's use of ethical maxims and injunctions drawn from the Old Testament is relatively slight. For example, only about twenty percent of the instances in which Paul is demonstrably dependent upon scripture for ethical material comes from the book of Proverbs. Likewise, he makes surprisingly little specific use of the Decalogue and other statutory sections of the Torah. Michel thus overstates the case when he suggests that the Old Testament remains for Paul "a collection of divine norms for living which are also valid for the Christian." [12] There is no evidence which indicates that the apostle regarded it as in any sense a source book for detailed moral instruction or even a manual of ethical norms. Although in other ways his exegetical method is akin to that of the rabbis,[13] his ethical teaching, even when it takes a scriptural text as its starting point, does not resemble the moral tractates

[11] "Casuistry" here is used in the technical sense described by R. M. Wenley in *ERE*, III (1910), 241. It "presupposes (a) the existence of external rules, nomistic opinions, or systematic prescriptions (especially the last); and (b) individual cases, peculiar to separate persons at particular times, when the approved sanctions seem doubtful or silent, or require elucidation with a view to the justification of exceptions."

[12] *Paulus und seine Bibel*, p. 158. Schrage in *Die konkreten Einzelgebote in der paulinischen Paränese* (1961) also speaks of the "normative" character of the Old Testament for the content of Paul's ethic (pp. 228 ff.).

[13] This has been amply documented by Bonsirven, *Exégèse rabbinique et exégèse paulinienne*. See also H. J. Schoeps, *Paul: The Theology of the Apostle in the Light of Jewish Religious History*, trans. Harold Knight (1961; German ed., 1959), pp. 39 ff.

of the rabbinical tradition, or even the moral propaganda of Hellenistic Judaism (of which the epistle of James is a Christtianized example). Paul himself never seeks to assemble, codify, or interpret in a legalistic way the statutes or wisdom of the Old Testament.[14] It is not a "source" for his ethical teaching in this sense.

From these observations, however, one should not draw the conclusion that Paul uses the Old Testament only "in a 'talismanic' fashion" to "buttress" the points he wishes to make on other grounds.[15] He specifically *applies* the moral lessons of scripture to his congregations (Rom. 4:23-24; 15:4; I Cor. 9:9-10; 10:6 ff.) often enough that one must acknowledge the actual material influence it has exerted in his ethical teaching. In fact, Paul's use of the Old Testament in his ethical teaching is not to be radically differentiated from his use of the Old Testament overall. In connection with ethical admonition and instruction, as elsewhere, an important presupposition is that the Old Testament is scriptural witness to the history of God's dealings with his people, his claim upon them, and his promises concerning their future. That Paul believes God's promises to have been fulfilled in Christ is of course decisive for his interpretation of scripture, the truest and deepest meaning of which is now for the Christian fully disclosed in Christ (II Cor. 3:7 ff.). While the Old Testament, then, is not a "source" for Paul's ethical instruction in a narrow sense, it is a source for it in a more basic way. For the apostle draws upon it not only to support his admonitions, but also to gain an understanding of the Christian's concrete ethical responsibilities.

[14] In this connection note Michel's comment that, in their exegesis, the rabbis employed their erudition, while Paul employed his prophetic spirit (*Paulus und seine Bibel*, p. 102). Bonsirven, *Exégèse rabbinique et exégèse paulinienne*, also stresses the decisive ways in which Paul's exegesis differs from rabbinical procedures. S. E. Johnson, contrasting Paul's letters with the legalism of the Qumran materials, argues that "there would have been no place in the Pauline churches for Mishnah, a Manual of Discipline, or a Didache of the Twelve Apostles" (see "Paul and the Manual of Discipline," *HThR*, XLVIII [1955], 157).

[15] Morton S. Enslin, *The Ethics of Paul* (1930), p. 88.

b. The Apocrypha and Pseudepigrapha

Since the so-called "apocryphal books" were, in Paul's day, used in association with the more strictly canonical Old Testament books, one must ask whether the apostle did not also draw upon these for ethical teachings. The book of Tobit, a product of Diaspora Judaism dating from the second century B.C., contains, for example, two rich parenetic sections (4:3 ff.; 12:6 ff.). D. C. Simpson believes that Paul did in fact employ materials from exactly these portions of Tobit.[16] But the nature of the relationships between the passages in Tobit and Paul to which Simpson refers hardly permits the judgment that Tobit is an actual source of the apostle's ethical teaching. Tobit 4:7, 8, 16, for instance, deal with almsgiving and urge that one give liberally and ungrudgingly. The general idea is similar to Paul's when he is raising an offering in Corinth (I Cor. 16:2; II Cor. 8:12; 9:7), but this motif in Paul, insofar as it has any specific "source," clearly rests on Prov. 22:8, cited in II Cor. 9:7 (but not in Tobit). The admonition in Tobit 4:12a to flee from fornication (πρόσεχω σεαυτῷ, παιδίον, ἀπὸ πάσης πορνείας) certainly does have a parallel in I Thess. 4:3 (ἀπέχεσθαι ὑμᾶς ἀπὸ τῆς πορνείας) and also in I Cor. 6:18 (φεύγετε τὴν πορνείαν), but such admonitions are so common in the moral literature of the time that it is idle to suggest that Tobit specifically is Paul's "source." Other alleged instances of the apostle's dependence on Tobit are even less impressive (Tob. 12:9, cf. Rom. 6:23; Tob. 4:8-9, cf. Gal. 6:10).

Paul's acquaintance with the Wisdom of Solomon (first century B.C.) is more clearly demonstrable and has long been recognized by many scholars. Particularly significant are the parallels between Rom. 1:20 ff. and Wisd. of Sol. 13:1 ff. and Rom. 9:19 ff. and Wisdom of Solomon 10–11.[17] The first of these is of special

[16] See his introduction to Tobit in *The Apocrypha and Pseudepigrapha of the Old Testament in English,* ed. by R. H. Charles (1913), I, 199.

[17] The most detailed study of parallels between Paul and Wisd. of Sol. is that by Eduard Grafe, "Das Verhältnis der paulinischen Schriften zur Sapientia Salomonis," *Theologische Abhandlungen* (1892), pp. 251 ff. See also Sanday and Headlam, *A Critical and Exegetical Commentary on the Epistle to the Romans* in *ICC* (5th ed., 1902), pp. 51-52, and Samuel Holmes

interest to the student of Paul's ethic, for Paul's description of
the Gentile's sin and its consequences follows closely the corresponding passage in Wisdom of Solomon. Not only is the
apostle's terminology similar (cf. the vice lists in Rom. 1:26 ff.
and Wisd. of Sol. 13:22 ff.), but, more important, the type and
line of argument are significantly parallel in the two writings.
There is little question that Paul, at least in a few passages,
makes use of this apocryphal book, even though the similarities
are more formal than material.[18]

Within the wider field of intertestamental literature, R. H.
Charles has sought to document the Pauline use of both I Enoch
and the Testaments of the XII Patriarchs. The former of these
dates, in its present form, from the first century B.C. and attained
great popularity within the early Christian church. Yet it is
doubtful whether the parallels Charles cites between I Enoch
and the Pauline letters do more than show Paul's use of phrases
and concepts broadly current in his day.[19] Thus, the reference
to "angels of power and . . . angels of principalities" (I En. 61:
10) reminds one of the Pauline reference to "angels . . . principalities . . . powers" in Rom. 8:38; the description of God as
"blessed forever" is common to both (Rom. 9:5; I En. 77:1),
and both employ the apocalyptic figure of destruction coming
as travail comes upon a woman with child (I Thess. 5:3; I En.
62:4).[20] While I Enoch includes impressive sections of ethical admonitions, pronouncements of woes upon sinners, and assurances
for the righteous (especially chaps. 94–105), it is not possible
to say that the Pauline exhortations have in even the slightest
degree been drawn from here.

The attempt by Charles to demonstrate Paul's use of the Test.
XII P. is even less successful.[21] There are, indeed, some striking

---

in *Apocrypha and Pseudepigrapha*, I, 526. Both Michel (*Paulus und seine
Bibel*, pp. 14 ff.) and Bonsirven (*Exégèse rabbinique et exégèse paulinienne*,
p. 291), however, doubt that Paul's actual use of Wisd. of Sol. can be established.

[18] Grafe, "Das Verhältnis der paulinischen Schriften," pp. 285-86; Sanday
and Headlam, *A Critical and Exegetical Commentary on Romans*, p. 268.

[19] *Apocrypha and Pseudepigrapha*, II, 180-81.

[20] Cf. also I Cor. 6:11 and I En. 48:7; II Cor. 4:6 and I En. 38:4.

[21] *Apocrypha and Pseudepigrapha*, II, 292.

verbal similarities, most notably between Rom. 12:21, "Conquer evil with good" (νίκα ἐν τῷ ἀγαθῷ τὸ κακόν), and Ben. 4:3, "Doing good he conquers evil" (τὸ ἀγαθὸν ποιῶν νικᾷ τὸ κακόν). Unfortunately, however, the probability of significant Christian interpolations in the Test. XII P., and—even more basically— the dating of these documents, render all efforts to identify them as sources for New Testament writers highly problematic. Charles dated them in the late second century B.C.,[22] but a recent investigation, on good grounds, assigns them to A.D. 190-225.[23] L. Rost properly concludes that any decision on dating, especially since new evidence is coming to light in the Qumran scrolls, is still premature.[24]

Also difficult to assess because of problems of dating and literary dependency are Schrage's conclusions about the background in apocalyptic Judaism of the Pauline exhortations in I Cor. 7:29-31. Schrage argues that the apostle's words about conducting oneself in the world "as if not" are so strikingly parallel, both in form and in content, with the admonitions in IV Esd. 16:42-45 that Paul is here indebted to an apocalyptic motif.[25] There is general agreement, however, that the parallel Schrage cites dates, at least in its written form, only from the second or third century A.D.[26] The question becomes, then, whether IV (II) Esdras depends nevertheless on *pre*-Pauline apocalyptic motifs and perspectives, as Schrage maintains.

In summary, it is possible to detect some formal and material relationships between the ethical teaching of Paul and the ethical materials of apocalyptic Judaism, although direct *literary* de-

[22] *Ibid.*, pp. 282, 289-90.

[23] M. De Jonge, *The Testaments of the Twelve Patriarchs: A Study of Their Text, Composition and Origin* ("van Gorcum's Theologische Bibliotheek," XXV [1953]), p. 125.

[24] "Testamente der XII Patriarchen," *RGG* (3rd ed.), VI, cols. 701-2.

[25] "Die Stellung zur Welt bei Paulus, Epiktet und in der Apokalyptik. Ein Beitrag zu 1 Kor 7, 29-31," *ZThK*, LXI (1964), 125 ff., esp. pp. 139 ff. English editions (e.g. RSV) include the passage in question in II Esdras. It is also sometimes called VI Esdras.

[26] E.g. H. Duensing in E. Hennecke, *New Testament Apocrypha*, rev. W. Schneemelcher; trans. and ed. R. McL. Wilson, II (1965), 690; O. Plöger, *RGG* (3rd ed.), II, col. 700; N. Turner, *IntDB*, E–J, p. 142. Schrage, of course, acknowledges such judgments but does not find them convincing or decisive (pp. 139 ff.).

pendence is not always easy to establish. Nevertheless, it seems
clear that these particular intertestamental materials did not
exert the same kind of influence upon the apostle's concrete ethical instruction as the more established books of the Old Testament canon.

c. Rabbinic Judaism

One must also consider the possibility that Paul's ethical
teaching is in some measure dependent upon the traditions of
Rabbinic Judaism. W. D. Davies, for example, believes that the
apostle's "didactic habit" is influenced not only by the emerging
practical needs for discipline within his Christian congregations,
but also by the Jewish practice of catechetical instruction at the
time of baptism.[27] To describe Paul's churches Davies adopts
Carrington's phrase, "neo-levitical community," and suggests
that the apostle met the need for ethical regulations within his
congregations by framing for them moral codes using Jewish
hortatory materials.[28]

Davies' argument is initiated with a reference to Romans 1-2.
These chapters, he suggests, reflect the same concern for making
the Gentiles aware of and responsive to certain universally binding moral laws as that which produced the "Noachian Commandments" of Rabbinic Judaism.[29] Admitting that the form
of Romans 1-2 is Hellenistic, he insists that "their inner substance is also Jewish" and concludes that Paul is here using Hellenistic dress to clothe what is at its center a rabbinic concept.[30]
Davies' conclusion in favor of the rabbinic as opposed to the
Hellenistic "substance" of Romans 1-2 seems a bit arbitrary (he
says only that the substance is "*also* Jewish"). Yet there is no
denying the validity of his preliminary observation that a concern for identifying universal moral laws was no less operative

---

[27] *Paul and Rabbinic Judaism* (2nd ed., 1955), pp. 121 ff. Davies is here
dependent upon the work of G. Klein, *Der älteste christliche Katechismus*
(1909), and P. Carrington.
[28] *Paul and Rabbinic Judaism*, p. 130; P. Carrington, *The Primitive Christian Catechism* (1940), p. 21.
[29] *Paul and Rabbinic Judaism*, pp. 112 ff.
[30] *Ibid.*, pp. 116-17.

within rabbinic ethics than within, for example, Stoic thought. (The Noachian Commandments specifically forbid idolatry, blasphemy, cursing of judges, murder, incest and adultery, robbery, and eating flesh with the blood of life remaining in it.[31]) There is, however, no evidence that the Noachian Commandments themselves exerted any "normative" influence on Paul's ethical teaching, and Davies wishes to show only that they constitute part of the wider rabbinic background of Paul's teaching.[32]

No more impressive is Davies' appeal to Paul's imperatival use of unattached participles as evidence for his acquaintance with rabbinic materials. He appeals to the investigations of David Daube who has attempted to show that imperatival participles are a development of Tannaitic Hebrew and are therefore not of Hellenistic origin, as Moulton had held.[33] Since such participles are clearly present in Paul (notably Rom. 12:9 ff.), it would seem that the apostle was specifically acquainted with Jewish modes of exhortation and probably with Jewish moral codes as well. There are, however, two problems with the course of Davies' argument here.

First, there are more and clearer instances of the imperatival participle in Hellenistic papyri than Daube recognized or was willing to concede. Furthermore, the Tannaitic parallels he adduced are farther removed from Paul's actual usage than the Greek examples. This has been effectively established, in refutation of Daube, by A. P. Salom.[34]

Second, Davies, employing Daube's results, wishes to push the argument even further, claiming that Paul was not only acquainted with, but actually "drew upon" and purposefully

[31] George Foot Moore, *Judaism in the First Centuries of the Christian Era* (1927), I, 274-75; cf. p. 453.

[32] *Paul and Rabbinic Judaism*, p. 119.

[33] "Participle and Imperative in I Peter" in E. G. Selwyn, *The First Epistle of St. Peter* (1955), pp. 467 ff.; and further remarks in his own book, *The New Testament and Rabbinic Judaism* (1956), pp. 90 ff. See also E. Lohse, "Paränese und Kerygma im I Petrusbrief," *ZNW*, XLV (1954), 77, n. 46, who adduces further examples from the Qumran "Manual of Discipline."

[34] "The Imperatival Use of the Participle in the New Testament," *ABR*, XI (1963), 41 ff.

"uses" Jewish codes in the composition of his ethical exhortations.[35] Specifically, he discusses the Jewish *derek 'eretz* (literally,
"way of the world") literature and says "the probability . . .
would be very great that Paul would naturally have turned to
this missionary ethical material in dealing with his converts." [36]
The principal documents involved here are the two tractates
Derek 'Eretz Rabba and *Derek 'Eretz Zuta,* the first commonly
dated A.D. 160-220, the second in the ninth century, A.D., although
both doubtless have assembled and incorporated earlier traditions.[37] Here as elsewhere Davies follows G. Klein, holding that
these collections of moral sayings, proverbs, and precepts represent Judaism's interest in mediating a basic morality to those
outside the law. The material collected here presumably reflects
the same fund of Jewish ethical teaching the apostle also employs, and for similar purposes. Davies believes, then, that Paul's
moral instruction stands within the rabbinic tradition and that
Paul himself may be aptly described as a "Christian Rabbi." [38]

Although there are significant rabbinical elements within
Paul's ethical teaching (especially his Old Testament exegesis),
it is too much to say that the rabbinical tradition finds a Christian representative in him. Two notes of caution must be raised
with respect to Davies' conclusions. The first Davies himself
acknowledges, viz. that it is not possible to demonstrate Paul's
use of the *derek 'eretz* material as a "source" in any strict sense.
Not only are the documents as they stand of relatively late compilation (the earliest no earlier than the second half of the
second century A.D.), it also happens that in these particular
derek 'eretz tractates the participial imperative, according to
Davies the most impressive formal link between Paul's teaching
and Jewish catechesis, rarely occurs! All that can be safely concluded, Davies admits, is "that there was a tradition well defined
and familiar within Judaism of ethical exhortation, which *would*

[35] *Paul and Rabbinic Judaism,* pp. 130, 131.
[36] *Ibid.,* p. 134.
[37] See the articles on these two tractates by Louis Ginzberg in *JewEnc,*
IV, 526 ff.
[38] *Paul and Rabbinic Judaism,* p. 145.

and *probably* *did* supply precedents for the early Christian leaders in their work of moral education." [39]

This conclusion in itself seems modest and restricted enough. The problem is that it becomes the foundation for Davies' bolder and considerably less restricted characterization of Paul's ethical style and method as essentially rabbinic. Moreover—and here is the second point which calls for caution—Davies, precisely in this formulation of his conclusion about Paul's presumed rabbinical sources, leaves one crucial presupposition unexamined. His presupposition is that Paul was motivated by concerns and anxious to achieve objectives significantly similar to those of the rabbis and Jewish catechists. The conclusion that Jewish materials *"would* and probably did supply precedents for the early Christian leaders" is not possible apart from this presupposition. But is there, at least in Paul's case, such a correspondence of concerns and objectives as Davies supposes? Are the Pauline exhortations thoroughly at home in the stream of rabbinic catechesis? These are exactly the points at issue.

The questionableness of describing Paul's ethical teaching as rabbinic may be underscored by noting Daube's perceptive description of the *Sitz im Leben* of the rabbinic form of instruction, specifically the Tannaitic form of the participial imperative. The teacher or lawgiver who employs it "addresses an elite among whom the right thing, provided only it is known, is done—or at least is supposed to be done—as a matter of course. There is no need of exhortation or warning. He appeals to the self-respect of his public." Indeed, "this form of legislation is a result of the change from revelation to interpretation and stabilization of custom, from prophet to scholar and compiler." [40] Applied to the present discussion, this description of the *Sitz im Leben* of Jewish catechetical instruction suggests the following pointed questions: Is Paul, as an ethical teacher, more a "scholar" than a "prophet," more a "compiler" and interpreter than an "apostle"? Are his congregations accurately described as "neo-levitical communities" [41] or assemblies of the morally "elite"?

---

[39] *Ibid.*, p. 135 (italics added).
[40] *The New Testament and Rabbinic Judaism*, pp. 94, 97.
[41] See above, n. 28.

In short, is Paul so much a "servant" of tradition that he can justifiably be called a "Christian rabbi"? The evidence assembled by Davies is hardly of the type to permit affirmative answers to these questions, and Klaus Wegenast's recent study of Paul's relation to tradition leads to the opposite result. His conclusion as it relates to Paul's dependence on the parenetic traditions of late Judaism is amply documented and pertinent here. The apostle, Wegenast finds, is not a self-conscious "servant of the tradition" in the rabbinic sense, but employs tradition with quite "unrabbinic" freedom when it happens to serve his purpose of exhortation.[42] That there are elements of rabbinism, both formal and material, in Paul's ethical teaching cannot be denied. But it is going too far to say that Paul is a self-conscious and consistent bearer and interpreter of that tradition, and that his ethical instruction is best described as a continuation, albeit in a Chrstian context, of it.[43]

d. Summary and results

To what major results does the investigation of possible Old Testament and Jewish sources for Paul's ethical teaching lead? For one thing it is clear that the apostle makes use of Old Testament materials, although not in a narrow, copybook fashion. His sparing use of, for example, the wisdom literature and his relatively infrequent appeal to the Decalogue significantly distinguish his letters from the rabbinic as well as the *derek 'eretz* traditions. The Old Testament is not a source for his ethical teaching in that it provides him rules, aphorisms, maxims, and proverbs. Rather, it is a source for his ethical teaching in that it provides him with a perspective from which he interprets the

[42] *Das Verständnis der Tradition bei Paulus und in den Deuteropaulinen* in *WMANT*, 8 (1962) , 93 ff.; esp. p. 120.

[43] While numerous scholars have been concerned with discussing theological and ethical *motifs* in the Qumran scrolls which have parallels in the Pauline letters, the possibility of any direct Pauline literary dependence upon these materials is remote and therefore need not be considered here. Millar Burrows notes: "Parallels have been found also in the ethical sections of the Epistles, but they are no closer than the many contacts with other Jewish and Hellenistic sources" (*More Light on the Dead Sea Scrolls* [1958], p. 122) . Cf. the quotation from S. E. Johnson above, n. 14.

whole event of God's act in Christ, and the concomitant and consequent claim God makes on the believer.

Further, while Paul's letters reflect his familiarity with and use of various rabbinic modes of thought, forms of teaching, and ethical motifs, there is no evidence which demonstrates any deliberate or self-conscious association with the rabbinic tradition on his part. In particular it is not possible, without making some premature assumptions about the character and function of the apostle's ethical teaching, to maintain that he "must have" relied directly on Jewish *derek 'eretz* materials.

One's final evaluation of the Old Testament and Jewish background of Paul's ethic need not be negative, but it must be qualified in three respects.

First, although the themes and concerns of Old Testament and Jewish ethics still find expression in Paul's ethical teaching, the specific collection, collation, and casuistic application of ethical rules, wisdom, and maxims seem not to be a part of his purpose.

Second, one must therefore take care not to use the manifest presence of Old Testament and Jewish *influences* in Paul's ethical teaching as evidence that his teaching is identical in character, function, and objective with Jewish materials.

Finally, the presence of Jewish influences does not exclude the possibility that Paul's ethical perspectives and teachings were also nourished by other religious and cultural sources, for example, Hellenistic. It is important to recognize that the Jewish materials most often compared with Pauline parenesis (Wisd. of Sol., Test. XII P., the didactic poem of the Pseudo-Phocylides,[44] etc.) are precisely those which themselves bear the unmistakable impress of the *Hellenistic* ethos and style. Indeed, the rabbinic tradition itself, in certain of its didactic methods, is indebted to Greek and Hellenistic precedents.[45] And even Davies acknowl-

---

[44] A precise dating of this Hellenistic-Jewish parenesis is not possible. Vetschera dated it in the last half of the second century B.C. (*Zur griechischen Paränese* [1912] p. 14), but Easton has more recently assigned it to the Christian era ("Pseudo-Phocylides," *AThR*, XIV [1932], 222). A particularly helpful discussion of this interesting document (a full English translation of which Easton provides) is to be found in Emil Schürer, *Geschichte des jüdischen Volkes im Zeitalter Jesu Christi* (4th ed., 1911), III, 617 ff.

[45] Daube, *The New Testament and Rabbinic Judaism*, pp. ix, 86 ff.

edges that Paul's first-century environment was complex and variegated. "In particular has it become clear that the traditional convenient dichotomy between Judaism and Hellenism was largely false. In the fusions of the first century the boundaries between these are now seen to have been very fluid." [46] This insight suggests that no investigation of the sources of Paul's ethical teaching is complete which does not attend also to the possibility of Hellenistic influence.

2. THE HELLENISTIC WORLD

Paul's Judaism was itself of the Diaspora, thoroughly ventilated by the pervasive influence of Hellenistic concerns, concepts, and modes of expression. Not only the religious views of the Old Testament and Palestinian Judaism find expression within it, but the style and views of Hellenistic popular philosophy as well.[47] One must not minimize the significance of the fact that Paul read a Greek Bible which already bore the impress of Hellenistic piety,[48] that he himself wrote in Greek and labored among Gentile people. The very fact that Paul on occasion finds it necessary to emphasize and document his Jewishness perhaps suggests that at least some of his readers would not think of him first of all against that background. It is too extreme to say that no important Hellenistic influences are to be discerned in Paul's thought[49] and that, remaining throughout his life "a Jew to the finger tips," [50] he may have borrowed some Hellenistic terms and forms, but always with "entire unconcern for their original meanings." [51] No one really concerned about *communicating* to his contemporaries can afford to ignore or remain indifferent to the jargon of his day or the meaning of

---

[46] "Paul and the Dead Sea Scrolls: Flesh and Spirit," *The Scrolls and the New Testament,* ed. K. Stendahl (1957), p. 157.

[47] As shown, e.g., by H. Thyen's study, *Der Stil der jüdisch-hellenistischen Homilie* in *FRLANT,* n.F. 47 (1955); see esp. pp. 117 ff.

[48] Schoeps, *Paul: The Theology of the Apostle,* pp. 27 ff.

[49] James T. Cleland, *The Religious Ethic of St. Paul* (1954), p. 130.

[50] Enslin, *The Ethics of Paul,* p. xxiv (Apex ed.).

[51] *Ibid.,* p. 102. Cf. L. Dewar, *An Outline of New Testament Ethics* (1949), pp. 143, 168.

established terms and concepts. More reasonable is F. W. Beare's insistence that the literature of earliest Christianity, which took shape within and was addressed primarily to the Hellenistic world, "should be interpreted in terms of its meaning for that world, and that due weight should be given to the positive influence of Hellenistic thought" upon the New Testament.[52]

a. Hellenistic terminology and style

The presence of Hellenistic influences in Paul's ethical teaching cannot be demonstrated by the identification of specifically Greek "sources" he has employed. The attempts which have been made in this direction have not been very successful.[53] Even the one line in the apostle's letters which can be definitely traced to a Greek writer ("Bad company ruins good morals" [I Cor. 15:33 RSV]; see Menander *Thais*, Fragment 218) is probably known to Paul not directly from any literary source, but as an everyday proverb in common use.[54] Explicit references to secular sources are of course not to be found in the Pauline letters.

Paul's ethical teaching is, however, indebted to Hellenistic "sources" in a more general sense. Numerous scholars have pointed out Pauline phrases, metaphors, and terms which are familiar and frequent in Hellenistic circles as represented by

[52] "New Testament Christianity and the Hellenistic World," *The Communication of the Gospel in New Testament Times* (1961), p. 60.

[53] See, e.g., the whole series of articles produced by J. Rendel Harris: "St. Paul and Epimenides," *Exp*, 8th series, IV (1912), 348 ff. [Tit. 1:12]; "Did St. Paul Quote Euripides?" *ET*, XXI (1919–20), 36-37 [Acts 21:39]; "Pindar and St. Paul," *ET*, XXXIII (1921–22), 456-57 [II Tim. 2:7]; "St. Paul and Aristophanes," *ET*, XXXIV (1922–23), 151 ff. [Col. 2:18, 23]; "St. Paul and Aeschylus," *ET*, XXXV (1923–24), 151 ff. [Phil. 4:4]. See also D. John, "St. Paul and Empedocles," *ET*, XXXIX (1927–28), 237-38 [I Cor. 2:9]. Richard Reitzenstein sought to demonstrate the Hellenistic background of Paul by examining, especially, the relationship of his thought to concepts familiar in Hellenistic mystery religions and cultic practices. See, e.g., his excursus, "Zu Porphyrius und Paulus" *Historia Monachorum und Historia Lausiaca* in *FRLANT*, 24 (1916), pp. 242 ff., replied to by R. Corssen, "Paulus und Porphyrios," *ZNW*, XIX (1919–20), 2 ff.

[54] Enslin, *The Ethics of Paul*, p. 205, n. 22; Lietzmann, *An die Korinther* I, II, in *HNT* (4th ed. supplemented by W. G. Kümmel, 1949), p. 83. Otherwise, J. Weiss, *Der erste Korintherbrief* in *KEK* (10th ed., 1925), p. 367.

the broad and pervasive movement of Stoicism.[55] These include
the metaphors of life as warfare (e.g. II Cor. 10:3 ff.; I Thess.
5:8) or as an athletic competition (I Cor. 9:25); descriptions of
God as "all in all" (I Cor. 15:28) and as the one of, through,
and unto whom all things are (Rom. 11:36); the term τὸ ἀνῆκον
(RSV: "what is required," Philemon 8); the concept of "spend-
ing" and "being spent" for others (II Cor. 12:15) and disregard
for the external circumstances of one's life (II Cor. 6:8 ff.; Phil.
4:11-12). Moreover, it is impossible to deny the clear Hellenistic
ring of Phil. 4:8. Two of the qualities Paul commends there are
mentioned nowhere else in the New Testament (προσφιλής
[RSV: "lovely"], εὔφημος [RSV: "gracious"]), and εὔφημος is also
absent from the LXX. Other terms in this verse, above all ἀρετή
(RSV: "excellence") and ἔπαινος (RSV: "worthy of praise"),
have a firm and significant place in Greek ethical materials. It
is beyond question that Paul's terminology in this verse is drawn
from the vocabulary of Hellenistic popular philosophy.[56]

Although it is true that Paul's handling of scriptural texts
must be seen primarily against the background of rabbinic
exegesis, at another point of form his indebtedness is first of all
to the Greek world. Bultmann's monograph on Paul's style has
impressively documented the extent to which the apostle, in
his oral preaching, was influenced by the diatribe form as prac-
ticed and popularized by the Cynic and Stoic street preachers
of his day.[57] This form is apparent in the less "epistolary" portions of his letters where, as in the diatribe, he enters into "dialogue" with those addressed by expressing for them what they
could be expected to say or ask (e.g. I Cor. 15:35; Rom. 9:19;
11:19; II Cor. 10:10), by posing rhetorical questions designed to
give his point greater effect (οὐκ οἴδατε and ἀγνοεῖτε ["Don't you
know?"]; e.g. Rom. 6:16; 11:2; I Cor. 3:16; Rom. 6:3; 7:1), by

[55] See, e.g., J. B. Lightfoot's noted essay on "St. Paul and Seneca" in his
St. Paul's Epistle to the Philippians (1896), pp. 270 ff., and Enslin, *The
Ethics of Paul*, pp. 34 ff.

[56] See Dibelius, *An die Thessalonicher I, II, An die Philipper* in *HNT*
(3rd ed., 1937), p. 95; S. Wibbing, *Die Tugend-und Lasterkataloge im Neuen
Testament* in *BZNW*, 25 (1959), 101 ff.

[57] *Der Stil der paulinischen Predigt und die kynisch-stoische Diatribe* in
FRLANT, 13 (1910).

framing false conclusions introduced by the provocative τί οὖν ("What, then?") and subsequently proceeding to refute them (e.g. Rom. 6:1, 15; 7:7), and by many other devices commonly employed wherever Hellenistic teachers could draw some hearers.[58]

b. Hellenistic concepts

The detection in Paul's letters of Hellenistic terminology and elements of style is not enough to warrant the conclusion that his teaching stands in the tradition of Hellenistic popular philosophy, any more than the presence of rabbinic elements places him in that tradition. Bultmann points out that even in some formal matters the apostle has decisively altered and broken through the Hellenistic patterns: "To be sure, the cloak of the Greek speaker hangs over the shoulders of Paul, but Paul has no faculty for skilful drapery, and the lines of his foreign figure are apparent everywhere." [59] This is even more true with respect to some of the major concepts of Hellenistic popular philosophy which, while formally present in Paul, are often endowed by him with quite a different meaning. The concepts of "freedom" (ἐλευθερία) [60] and "contentment" (αὐτάρκεια, see Phil. 4:11 ff.) [61] are cases in point—Hellenistic ideas which, within the context of the Pauline letters, are decisively redefined.

Yet there are some ways in which the apostle has been influenced materially as well as formally by the Hellenistic world. One of the clearest instances happens also to be particularly relevant for the interpretation of the Pauline ethic: the concept of *conscience*.

The Greek word for "conscience" (συνείδησις) [62] has no equivalent in Hebrew, and thus it is not surprising that συνεί-

[58] *Ibid.*, esp. pp. 64 ff.

[59] *Ibid.*, p. 108.

[60] See Bultmann, *Primitive Christianity in Its Contemporary Setting,* trans. R. H. Fuller (1956), pp. 185 ff., and Enslin, *The Ethics of Paul,* pp. 39-40, 305-6.

[61] *The Ethics of Paul,* p. 38.

[62] The literature on this topic is enormous. The most recent extended discussions are by C. A. Pierce, *Conscience in the New Testament* in *SBTh,* 15 (1955), and C. Maurer in *ThW,* VII (1964), 897 ff. Maurer provides a good bibliography of preceding books and articles.

δησις rarely occurs in the LXX. Paul can only have received the term from the Greek world, and this is supported by the fact that the sole instance in the LXX where συνείδησις means what it does for Paul is in Wisd. of Sol. 17:10, a book itself influenced by Greek philosophy.[63] The earliest and most frequent New Testament occurrences of the word are in Paul's letters, and considering its prominence in I Cor. 8:7 ff. and 10:25 ff., it was probably a term current among the apostle's Corinthian opponents.[64] The precise way in which Paul himself uses συνείδησις is better reserved for another place.[65] It is enough here to note that its primary meaning is "a man's knowledge ('consciousness') of his conduct as his own" which also exercises the function of approval or disapproval, condemnation or acquittal.[66] Although a recognition of this *capacity* and *function* of man's self-consciousness is not absent in the Old Testament and Judaism, the development of the concept of "conscience" as such, as the studies of Maurer and others have shown, is a phenomenon of the Greek world, particularly from the third century B.C. forward. Not only in connection with the question of idol meats at Corinth, but in other contexts as well (Rom. 2:15; 9:1; 13:5; II Cor. 1:12; 4:2; 5:11), this concept of conscience plays a role in the Pauline ethic. At least to this extent, one must say, the apostle is materially dependent upon Hellenistic sources in his ethical teaching.

It is much less clear whether Paul is also materially dependent upon the Hellenistic concept of a "natural law" which accords to all men a solemn sensibility of right and wrong. The passage in question is Rom. 2:14-15:

When Gentiles who do not possess the law do by nature [φύσει] what the law prescribes, they—though not having the law—are a law to them-

[63] G. Bornkamm, "Gesetz und Natur," *Studien zu Antike und Urchristentum* in *BEvTh*, 28, II (1963), 113, n. 49.
[64] Pierce, *Conscience in the New Testament*, pp. 60 ff.; Maurer, *ThW*, VII, 912.
[65] Below, pp. 228-29.
[66] Bultmann, *Theology of the New Testament*, trans. K. Grobel (1951), I, 216-17. Cf. Maurer, pp. 912 ff.; Enslin, *The Ethics of Paul*, pp. 101-2; Schrage, *Die konkreten Einzelgebote*, pp. 153-54; Bornkamm, "Gesetz und Natur," pp. 111 ff.

selves [ἑαυτοῖς εἰσιν νόμος]. They show that what the law requires is written in their hearts, their conscience bearing witness [συμμαρτυρούσης αὐτῶν τῆς συνειδήσεως] and their inner thoughts accusing, or perhaps also commending one another [καὶ μεταξὺ ἀλλήλων τῶν λογισμῶν κατηγορούντων ἢ καὶ ἀπολογουμένων].

G. Bornkamm argues that the contrast Paul draws here between φύσις ("nature") and νόμος ("law"), his concept of the Gentiles' being "a law to themselves," his reference to the requirements of the law being "written in their hearts," and, of course, his mention of their conscience as an inner judge—that all these elements are un-Jewish but thoroughly and specifically Greek.[67] The most impressive support for Bornkamm's conclusion is the fact that so many Hellenistic motifs are present here in the same context and even arranged in a way which has a Hellenistic ring. On the other hand, it can be argued that φύσει here is not used as a technical term but only with the meaning "instinctively" or "spontaneously," and that, therefore, the law which the Gentiles sometimes obey is none other than God's law (the Torah), not a universal "law of nature." At any rate, as Bornkamm also acknowledges, the application and point of Paul's argument in this passage are specifically his own and "fully un-Greek."[68]

c. Summary and results

One must conclude that Paul's Jewish background does not fully account for the manner, or even the substance, of his ethical teaching. That teaching is in various ways dependent upon Hellenistic forms and concepts even though there is nothing in the least way analogous to his specific citation of the Old Testament. And yet the familiar controversy about whether Jewish or Greek influences have contributed more to the apostle's thought neglects to recognize the essential point—that Paul's Judaism was itself already substantially modified by Hellenism

[67] "Gesetz und Natur," pp. 101 ff. Others who support the view that the background of Rom. 2:14-15 is Hellenistic are cited by Bornkamm on p. 101, n. 11.

[68] *Ibid.*, p. 117. See also John L. McKenzie, S.J., "Natural Law in the New Testament," *Biblical Research,* IX (1964), 3 ff.

and that his thought does not reflect his own fusing of two backgrounds so much as it reflects the syncretistic culture of his day.[69] The fact that the question: "More Jewish or more Greek?" can be raised not only with respect to Paul's letters, but also with respect to many other writings of the period (for example, the didactic poem of the Pseudo-Phocylides), is but one indication of the extent to which syncretistic tendencies were taking effect. A one-sided decision about Paul's background, whether in favor of his Jewish (e.g. Enslin) or Greek (e.g. Andrews) heritage, is bound to result in a one-sided interpretation of his ethic. This ethic can be brought into sharper focus when it is acknowledged that Paul was a Jew of the Diaspora—of the Hellenistic world.

There is, however, a further and decisive factor in Paul's "background." Both Jewish and Greek influences upon his life and thought are in an important sense secondary to the fact of his conversion to Christianity. Although there are rabbinical aspects to his thought and to his ethical teaching specifically, he is not a rabbi. And although there are both formal and material similarities between his teaching and that of Hellenistic popular philosophy, he is not a Cynic or Stoic street preacher. His message is the gospel of Christ, his mission is to be an apostle, and —whatever else must be said—his ethical teaching stands in the broad context of this message and mission. To remember that Paul was a *convert to* Christianity involves the recognition that he was converted by and to a movement which was already beginning to have and to protect its own traditions and forms. Paul was converted to a movement which was already in possession of liturgical, homiletical, and catechetical materials, and in which the rudimentary lines of an ecclesiastical structure were already becoming visible. It is therefore logical and important to ask whether, in his ethical teaching, the apostle has made use of materials which can be identified as specifically Christian.

---

[69] Thyen's study of the Jewish-Hellenistic homily illustrates the way in which this interpenetration of Jewish and Greek elements was present in the Diaspora synagogues themselves. See *Der Stil der jüdisch—hellenistischen Homilie,* esp. pp. 119-20 where he compares the same amalgamation of elements in Paul's letters.

This question can be more sharply focused by dealing with the problem of the relation of Paul's ethical teaching to the teaching of Jesus.

3. THE TEACHING OF JESUS

Scholarly opinion is by no means unanimous in its evaluation of the relation Paul's ethic bears to the message of Jesus. Whereas Alexander and C. A. A. Scott view Paul as interpreting and applying Jesus' ethical teaching,[70] John Knox believes the apostle "seriously distorts" it.[71] Although Dibelius insists that Jesus' teachings were so outmoded in the context of Paul's Hellenistic society that the church had to turn elsewhere for ethical guidance, Davies insists with equal vigor that the sayings of Jesus constituted the "primary source" in Paul's work as an ethical teacher.[72] This topic clearly demands some further attention.

a. Paul's citations of "the Lord"

It is clear beyond question that Paul was the recipient, and in turn bearer, of Christian traditions. This is evident when he "hands on" creedal formulations or liturgical material he himself has "received" (I Cor. 15:3 ff.; 11:23). The words he uses in these two passages (παραλαμβάνειν ["receive"], παραδιδόναι ["hand on"]) are, in such contexts, technical terms referring to the mediation of tradition.[73] That the "traditions" Paul received had to do with matters of conduct, at least with matters of church discipline, is not only a priori probable, but specifically indicated in I Cor. 11:2 ff. There his commendation of the Corinthians for maintaining the "traditions" (παραδόσεις) he has "handed on" (παρέδωκα) to them introduces a discussion of the propriety of women's head coverings in church.

Further, it is easily established that Paul's "traditions" included sayings of Jesus, for on occasion he specifically cites these. His exhortation to the married that they should not divorce (I

[70] See Appendix, pp. 253, 269.
[71] *The Ethic of Jesus in the Teaching of the Church* (1961) , p. 75.
[72] See Appendix, pp. 259, 274.
[73] See F. Büchsel, *ThW,* II (1935) , 173 ff. [ET: pp. 171 ff.].

Cor. 7:10-11, although the possibility of such is nonetheless acknowledged in vs. 11a) is specifically identified as coming from "the Lord" and reflects similar traditions incorporated in the Synoptic Gospels (Matt. 5:32; 19:9; Mark 10:11-12; Luke 16:18). "The Lord" is again specifically cited in I Cor. 9:14 to strengthen the argument that apostles are entitled to financial support from their congregations: "the Lord commanded that those who proclaim the gospel should get their living by the gospel" (RSV). This is perhaps a formulation of the saying contained in Luke 10:7, "the laborer deserves his wages" (RSV; cf. Matt. 10:10). And in I Cor. 11:23 ff. the "words of institution" are cited (cf. Matt. 26:26 ff.; Mark 14:22 ff.; Luke 22:17 ff.). The apostle also refers to sayings of "the Lord" in I Cor. 14:37 and I Thess. 4:15, although in these cases convincing parallels from synoptic sayings are not to be found.

While no other specific citations of dominical words stand in Paul's letters, there are some instances which one may fairly judge to be allusions to teachings of Jesus. Since, however, the identification of "allusions" or "echoes" is always a particularly subjective matter, one must tread carefully here and not lay too great a strain on the imagination or too great an emphasis on the results.

Certainly guilty on both counts was Alfred Resch who claimed to have located, in nine Pauline letters, no fewer than 925 parallels with the Synoptic Gospels. He found 133 more in Ephesians, 100 in the Pastoral Epistles, and 64 in the Pauline speeches in Acts.[74] On the one hand Resch's massive effort was directed polemically against the "ultrapaulinism" of F. C. Baur and the Tübingen school,[75] and on the other hand it seems to have been motivated by a desire to prove that, already in the first decades of the church's life, there existed a written collection of Jesus' sayings (the "main source" of Paulinism) which served as an "authentic corrective" to the church's sacramental teaching and oral traditions.[76] This written *Logia* source, Resch

---

[74] *Der Paulinismus und die Logia Jesu in ihrem gegenseitigen Verhältnis untersucht* in *TU*, xxvii (1904), p. xxvii.

[75] *Ibid.*, pp. 21 ff.

[76] *Ibid.*, p. 635.

maintained, is employed by both Paul and the Evangelists. In this way the hundreds of alleged parallels between the Pauline Corpus and the Synoptic Gospels are to be explained.[77]

A more cautious search, however, and one limited to the ethical teaching of Paul, turns up only eight convincing parallels to the Synoptic Gospels—and therefore possible "allusions" to Jesus' teaching.

Most of these eight occur in the latter chapters of Romans. In 12:14 Paul admonishes, "Bless those who persecute you; bless and do not curse them" (RSV), a likely echo of Jesus' command, "Love your enemies and pray for those who persecute you" (Matt. 5:44 RSV). The related exhortation, "Repay no one evil for evil" (Rom. 12:17 RSV), also seems to reflect the synoptic traditions about loving the enemy (above all, Matt. 5:39 ff.). Moreover, the Pauline instruction to give all men their due, including as it does mention of taxes and revenue (Rom. 13:7), could possibly be based on the traditional words of Jesus about rendering Caesar's things (taxes) to Caesar (Matt. 22:15-22). Also notable are the exhortations of Rom. 14:13, 14. The first prohibits judging others lest a "stumbling-block" fall in a brother's way. The striking image of a "stumbling-block" [σκάν-δαλον], which appears with similar meanings in synoptic logia (Matt. 18:7; Mark 9:42; Luke 17:1-2), may well be enough to suggest that Paul has been influenced in this verse by those or similar traditions. Rom. 14:14 ("I know and am persuaded in the Lord Jesus[78] that nothing is unclean in itself; but it is unclean for any one who thinks it unclean," RSV) recalls the synoptic saying that it is not what goes into a man's mouth but what comes out of it which defiles him (Matt. 15:11; Mark 7:15).

Three additional allusions may fairly easily be found in I Thessalonians. The remark in 5:2 that the Lord will come like

---

[77] *Ibid.*, pp. 635 ff.

[78] This is the preferable translation here for ἐν κυρίῳ Ἰησοῦ, although it is sometimes interpreted as an instrumental dative. Thus, "I know and am persuaded *by the Lord Jesus*" (e.g. Davies, *Paul and Rabbinic Judaism*, p. 138). But against this instrumental interpretation is the fact that parallel phrases (forms of πείθειν with ἐν κυρίῳ) in Gal. 5:10 and Phil. 2:24 (cf. II Thess. 3:4) can hardly be so interpreted.

a thief in the night probably depends on an image also used in the Synoptics (Matt. 24:43; Luke 12:39). Also, the wording of 5:13 ("Be at peace among yourselves," RSV [εἰρηνεύετε ἐν ἑαυτοῖς]) is impressively close to that of Mark 9:50 ("Be at peace with one another," RSV [εἰρηνεύετε ἐν ἀλλήλοις]). And finally, the admonition in 5:15 (to repay no one evil for evil) again seems to rest on teaching traditions about nonresistance (Matt. 5:39-47).

It is not possible, in connection with a study of the sources of Paul's ethic, to explore the larger and complex problem of the relation of Paul's preaching as a whole to that of the earthly Jesus.[79] But it is important to consider, on the basis of the evidence already presented, what legitimately may be concluded about Paul's use, in his ethical teaching, of Jesus' sayings.

First, it is certain, because of the specific citations, that the apostle was familiar with traditions about Jesus' teaching and had possession of certain elements of that teaching. Even Dibelius is convinced of this,[80] although he also believes that Jesus' ethic was inadequate as a moral guide for the church in a Hellenistic society. Indeed, this second point of Dibelius finds some support in I Cor. 7:25 where Paul expresses disappointment that, "concerning those who are not married," no word of the Lord is available to him. Yet the same remark, and also the apostle's care to distinguish his own opinion from the charge of the Lord (I Cor. 7:12), suggests the value and importance Paul could, at least in some instances, ascribe to dominical sayings.

The question whether such sayings had been committed to writing by the time Paul's letters were written should probably be left open (Dibelius: "orally or fixed in writing"). Synoptic research has, for a number of decades, been enamored of the hypothetical "Q" source, described as a written collection of *Logia* of Jesus, and it is tempting to suppose that Paul perhaps had access to this very "document." But recently the Q hypothesis itself has come under heavy attack,[81] and some of the

---

[79] On this topic see my article, "The Jesus-Paul Debate: From Baur to Bultmann," *BJRL*, XLVII (1965), 342 ff.

[80] *From Tradition to Gospel,* trans. B. L. Woolf (1935), p. 242.

[81] See e.g., A. M. Farrar, "On Dispensing with Q," *Studies in the Gospels: Essays in Memory of R. H. Lightfoot* (1955), pp. 55 ff.

arguments advanced against Q could also be used to question Resch's conclusion that Paul did in fact have a written *Logia* source. But of Paul's familiarity with *some* traditions of Jesus' sayings in *some* form there can be no doubt.

Second, however, one must concede the relative sparsity of direct references to or citations of Jesus' teachings in the Pauline letters. The argument that he could *presuppose* his readers' familiarity with these because he had already passed them on in his missionary preaching is not convincing. He could and does presuppose knowledge of the Old Testament, but this in no way deters him from constantly and specifically citing it in the course of his ethical teaching. Moreover, when Paul himself summarizes the content of his missionary preaching in Corinth (I Cor. 2:1-2), there is no hint that a narration of Jesus' earthly life or a report of his earthly teachings was an essential part of it. And in Romans, a letter which cannot presuppose the apostle's missionary preaching and in which he attempts to summarize its main points, there is not one direct citation of Jesus' teaching.[82] One must record with some surprise the fact that the teaching of the earthly Jesus seems not to play as vital, or at least as obvious, a role in Paul's concrete ethical instruction as the Old Testament.

Third, not once does Paul refer to Jesus as a "teacher," to his words as "teaching," or to Christians as "disciples." The word "disciple" is never used by him, and while many related ones are ("teacher," "to teach," "teaching," "to learn" [διδάσκαλος, διδάσκειν, διδαχή, διδασκαλία, μανθάνειν]), they are never applied to Jesus himself, his message, or his mission. One apparent exception is I Cor. 4:17 where Paul speaks of his "ways in Christ" which he "teaches" in all his churches.[83] But precisely here, in the phrase "my ways in Christ (τὰς ὁδούς μου τὰς ἐν Χριστῷ), the categories of teacher, pupil, teaching—and also the category of "sources"—are broken through and transcended. The reference is not to "the way of Jesus" (ἡ ὁδὸς τοῦ ᾽Ιησοῦ). Instead, it is the pregnant Pauline formula "in Christ" which is used, and the "ways" (plural) are Paul's ways (αἱ ὁδοί μου) which, however,

[82] On this question see my article, "The Jesus-Paul Debate," pp. 375-76.
[83] Other possible exceptions (Rom. 6:17; 16:17) are discussed below.

are the ways of a man "in Christ" who believes that he has "the Spirit of God" (I Cor. 7:40).

It is of the greatest significance that when Paul cites "sayings of Jesus," they are never designated in this way. Rather, his references in such instances are, without a single exception, to "the Lord" (ὁ Κύριος: I Cor. 7:10; 9:14; 11:23a [although in vs. 23b, doubtless because it is part of the liturgical tradition, the title is "Lord Jesus"]; 14:37; I Thess. 4:15; and also in I Cor. 7:12, 25). Paul does not appeal to Jesus as an earthly teacher or to his sayings as the instruction of a distinguished rabbi. His appeals are to the risen, reigning *Christ,* the church's *Lord.* The "words of the Lord" carry authority not because they can be identified as the *ipsissima verba* of a particularly wise or important figure from the past. Rather, their "authority" and "authenticity" inhere in the believer's encounter with them in the context of his whole life in faith, in the Spirit, in the community of believers—"in Christ."

b. Other alleged "allusions" to Jesus' teaching

There are those, however, who still seek to defend Resch's conclusion that Paul's primary source is some kind of collection of Jesus' words. Davies goes even farther, arguing that Paul's mind was not only "steeped in" and "permeated with" Jesus' sayings, but that the apostle himself "must have shared in and contributed to" the attempt to preserve those sayings, an attempt which probably eventuated in some such *Logia* source as "Q." [84] Such conclusions, obviously, require a broader base of evidence than the handful of specific citations and allusions discussed so far. Davies, in fact, is one who believes the evidence is more abundant. Although conceding that Resch "has overstated his case," Davies follows him in the view that a good many significant parallels with the Synoptic Gospels are to be found in Paul and that these indicate the apostle's use of a sayings source.[85] Davies lists twenty-five of these from Romans, I Thessalonians, and Colossians.[86] The eight references to Colossians

[84] *Paul and Rabbinic Judaism,* pp. 140, 142, 144.
[85] *Ibid.,* p. 137.
[86] *Ibid.,* pp. 138 ff.

will not be discussed here, in keeping with the methodological presuppositions governing the present investigation.[87] The possible validity of eight others (Rom. 12:14, 17; 13:7; 14:13, 14; I Thess. 5:2, 13, 15) has already been noted, but the nine remaining instances are not as convincing.

1. *Rom. 12:21* ("Conquer evil with good"). To this saying Davies lists no synoptic parallel, but simply refers to the whole of "Jesus' teaching on non-resistance." Paul's thought here is certainly in keeping with the nonresistance theme (e.g. Matt. 5: 39 ff.), but this hardly warrants listing the verse as an "allusion" to that teaching. Moreover, note the parallel in Test. XII P., Ben. 4:3.[88]

2. *Rom. 13:8 ff.* At first glance this Pauline summation of the commandment to love seems clearly dependent on Jesus' summation as handed down also by the Evangelists (Matt. 22:34 ff.; Mark 12:28 ff.; Luke 10:25 ff.). Yet the double commandment of the synoptics—love of God, love of neighbor—is reduced in Romans 13 (cf. Gal. 5:14) to the single command to love the neighbor. Dodd dismisses this difference as insignificant, saying that "there is no real contradiction." [89] That there is no necessary material contradiction between these two summaries is true enough. Nevertheless, the formal difference presents a grave difficulty to those who, like Davies, wish to see Paul reverently dependent upon Jesus' words. Moreover, there are also parallels in the rabbinic literature, for example *Sifra Kedoshim,* to Lev. 19:18: " 'And thou shalt love thy neighbor as thyself'—R. Akiba [2nd cent. A.D.] says: 'This is a comprehensive rule in the Torah.' " [90] Rom. 13:8 ff., therefore, does not necessarily represent an instance of Paul's dependence on Jesus.

3. *Rom. 14:10* ("Why do you pass judgment on your brother?" RSV) is indeed similar to the saying "Do not judge lest you be judged" (Matt. 7:1), but there are also significant and early parallels in the rabbinic tradition. Compare, for example,

[87] See above, p. 11.

[88] Cited above, p. 37.

[89] "ΕΝΝΟΜΟΣ ΧΡΙΣΤΟΥ," *Studia Paulina* (1953), p. 101, n. 1.

[90] See Billerbeck, I, 358. The English translation above follows that by Max Kadushin, *Worship and Ethics: A Study in Rabbinic Judaism* (1964), p. 31.

R. Hillel (ca. 20 B.C.): "Do not judge your neighbor until you have gotten into his condition." [91]

4. *I Thess. 4:8* ("Therefore, whoever rejects this [God's call to holiness, vs. 7] rejects not man but God"). Davies wishes to see an allusion to Luke 10:16 ("Whoever hears you hears me, and whoever rejects you rejects me, and whoever rejects me rejects the one who sent me"). While the verb "reject" (ἀθετεῖν) is common to both passages,[92] the contexts and meaning of the two sayings are quite different. It is improbable that Paul is alluding to the dominical word.

5. *I Thess. 4:9*b ("You yourselves are taught by God to love one another"). Davies himself lists no synoptic parallel, and presumably he only wants to suggest that such a statement would be in the "spirit of Jesus." [93] This hardly qualifies as "evidence."

6. *I Thess. 4:15-16* ("This we say to you by the word of the Lord, that we who are alive, who are left until the Lord's coming, shall by no means precede those who have fallen asleep. For the Lord himself will come down from heaven accompanied by a cry of command, an archangel's voice and a trumpet-call ordered by God.") Davies does not indicate where a synoptic parallel is to be found, nor even in which verse (15 or 16) the allusion is to be located. As Dibelius notes, the use of the first person plural makes it unlikely that Paul is mediating a word of Jesus in vs. 15; and on the other hand the only two possible parallels to vs. 16 (Matt. 24:30-31; John 6:39-40) are not impressive. Moreover, "the Lord himself" is hardly a phrase that would stand in a logion of Jesus, and Dibelius prefers to interpret both verses against the background of parallels in Jewish apocalyptic literature.[94]

---

[91] See Billerbeck, I, 441 ff. (to Matt. 7:1) for this and other instances.

[92] Dibelius suggests the possibility that ὁ ἀθετῶν is a familiar parenetic expression employed in concluding warnings. Luke 10:16 could thus be seen as a parenetic recasting of Matt. 10:40 (*Thessalonicher*, p. 22). In this case, Paul's use of the expression in I Thess. 4:8 would reflect a parenetic style and would not be evidence for his allusion to a traditional saying of Jesus.

[93] *Paul and Rabbinic Judaism*, p. 139.

[94] *Thessalonicher*, pp. 25 ff. P. Nepper-Christensen's attempt to solve the problem by reference to John 11:25-26 and I Cor. 15:51-52 is not very convincing. See "Das verborgene Herrnwort. Eine Untersuchung über 1. Thess. 4, 13-18," *StTh*, XIX (1965), 136 ff.

7. *I Thess. 5:3* ("When people say, 'There is peace and security,' then sudden destruction will come upon them as travail comes upon a woman with child, and there will be no escape," RSV). Admittedly, the suddenness of God's coming and judgment in the eschaton is also an element in the traditions of Jesus' sayings (Davies refers to Luke 12:39 ff.; 21:34), but there are also many similar passages in the literature of Jewish apocalyptic. Nothing in the present verse demands a reference to synoptic traditions in particular.

8. *I Thess. 5:6* ("So then let us not sleep, as others do, but let us keep awake and be sober," RSV). The synoptic parallel (Matt. 24:42: "Therefore be awake, because you do not know on what day your Lord is coming"; cf. Mark 13:37; Luke 21: 36) is real enough, but admonitions to watchfulness and sobriety are frequent in Oriental-Hellenistic Gnosis and other literature of the day.[95]

9. *I Thess. 5:16* ("Rejoice always" RSV). Davies cites the admonitions to rejoice ("in that day"; "that your names are written in heaven") in Luke 6:23 and 10:20, but one must certainly exercise great imagination if he is to see any kind of an allusion to Jesus' teaching here.

Ultimately, nothing is going to be gained by continuing the quest for Pauline "allusions" to Jesus' teaching. Resch long ago proved that, with imagination and patience, the possibilities can be multiplied like loaves and fishes. But the really convincing instances are fewer than a dozen and cannot, in themselves, constitute solid evidence that the "primary source" of Paul's ethical teaching is a collection of dominical *Logia*.

c. Paul and the "law of Christ"

Also adduced as evidence by those who believe Jesus' teaching constitutes the major source of Paul's ethical instruction is the apostle's mention (Gal. 6:2) of "the law of Christ" (ὁ νόμος τοῦ Χριστοῦ). This is then related to his statement in I Cor. 9:21, "To those without the law I became as one without the law— not being without the law of God, but rather 'in-lawed' to

[95] For examples and the literature see *Thessalonicher,* p. 29.

Christ [ἔννομος Χριστοῦ]—in order that I might win those without the law." (Sometimes, too, Paul's striking references to
"the law of the Spirit of life in Christ Jesus" [Rom. 8:2] and
"the law of faith" [Rom. 3:27] are brought into the discussion.)
C. H. Dodd, for example, contends that Paul is referring in
Gal. 6:2 and I Cor. 9:21 to "a new Torah," the nucleus of which
is a group of traditional sayings of Jesus.[96] Dodd's argument
is principally dependent upon three points.

(1) There are many "reminiscences" of Jesus' teachings in
the Pauline letters, especially in Romans 14, and hence one may
conclude that traditional sayings played a large role in Paul's
ethical instruction.[97] As demonstrated above, however, convincing echoes of Jesus' teaching are not as numerous in the Pauline
Corpus as is sometimes supposed, and identification of them
is often a highly subjective process. This aspect of Dodd's argument needs to be considered with great caution.

(2) I Cor. 9:21 and Gal. 6:2 both stand in contexts where
Paul is issuing specific commands and exhortations which are to
be fulfilled.[98] Thus, in I Corinthians he has already explicitly
cited commands of the Lord forbidding divorce (7:10) and
commending payment for services rendered (9:14). Such commands, Dodd believes, are in Paul's mind when he speaks of
being "in-lawed to Christ" (9:21). But how credible is this conclusion? The phrase ἔννομος Χριστοῦ is difficult to interpret, for
it occurs nowhere else in the New Testament. In this context,
however, it is clearly antithetical to the preceding ἄνομος θεοῦ.
The RSV treats θεοῦ here as if it were an objective genitive and
construes it with ἄνομος to obtain the translation "without law
toward God." But it is more probable that θεοῦ should be re-

---

[96] "ΕΝΝΟΜΟΣ ΧΡΙΣΤΟΥ," pp. 107, 110. In a later article ("The Primitive
Christian Catechism and the Sayings of Jesus," *New Testament Essays:
Studies in Memory of Thomas Walter Manson*, ed. A. J. B. Higgins [1959],
pp. 106 ff.) Dodd does not describe the church's collection of Jesus' sayings
as "the law of Christ." Instead, he employs the reference in Rom. 6:17 to a
"pattern of teaching" (τύπος διδαχῆς). On this expression see below, pp. 196 ff.
In explicit agreement with Dodd about "the law of Christ" is Jürgen Roloff,
who describes it as the "Christusparadosis" in *Apostolat—Verkündigung—
Kirche* (1965), p. 94.

[97] "ΕΝΝΟΜΟΣ ΧΡΙΣΤΟΥ," pp. 106-7.

[98] *Ibid.*, pp. 100, 107-8.

garded as a subjective genitive linked to νόμος as such, "without
the law of God." [99] This second translation is supported by
Rom. 2:12-13, where the adverb ἀνόμως clearly refers to God's
law. Therefore, Dodd's point that the antithetical phrase
ἔννομος Χριστοῦ at least "implies the existence" of a "law of
Christ" may be granted. [100]

But what does Paul *mean* by his reference to the "law of
Christ" in I Cor. 9:21? The general point of the context is clear:
although the apostle considers himself free from the legalism of
the Jewish law and even emphasizes this freedom in the course
of his mission to the Gentiles, he is not therefore to be regarded
as a libertinist insensitive to concrete ethical responsibilities.
Paul's reference to the "law of Christ" is thus not the principal
matter in the context, but is inserted to guard against a possible
misunderstanding of the preceding remark that to those "outside the law" he was himself as one "outside the law." For this
very reason it is farfetched to think, as Dodd does, that the relative proximity of cited commands of the Lord (7:10; 9:14)
shows that they are "conceived as in some sort constituent elements in the 'law of Christ.' " [101]

The reference to "the law of Christ" in Gal. 6:2 also occurs
in a context where the apostle is seeking to define the true meaning of Christian freedom (5:1 ff.). In this case Dodd is quite
correct in noting that the reference stands in a passage where
Paul is exhorting ("Bear one another's burdens, and so fulfil
the law of Christ," RSV). Yet there is not, in the whole of Galatians, a single explicit citation of the Lord's words, and it is
doubtful if Paul is thinking of the exhortations in 5:26 ff. as com-
prising in any cohesive sense a body of material attributable to
Jesus. Rather, these exhortations follow and serve as the elucidation of the words about living and walking in the Spirit (5:
16 ff.). This is the primary motif in the context, and it is with
reference to this motif that the meaning of the phrase "law of

[99] On the construction see Moulton, I, 236; II, 307; and Bl-Deb-Funk,
182, 3.
[100] "ΕΝΝΟΜΟΣ ΧΡΙΣΤΟΥ," p. 99.
[101] *Ibid.*, p. 108.

Christ" should be sought. But a third point in Dodd's argument seems designed to meet this objection:

(3) Discernible in Paul's thought is a distinction between "living by the Spirit" and "walking by the Spirit." [102] These two are not fully identical, and the latter, says Dodd, must be regarded as a "consequence" of the former. Thus, when Paul refers to the "law of the Spirit of life" (Rom. 8:2), he uses νόμος to mean, in the Greek sense, "regulative principle," and is referring to the Spirit by which the Christian *lives*. But in the phrase "law of Christ" νόμος is used to indicate a body of regulative precepts analogous to the Torah according to which the Christian is obliged to *walk*. This means that Dodd would relate the "law of Christ" in Gal. 6:2 not primarily to Gal. 5:25a (*living* by the Spirit) but to vs. 25b (*walking* by the Spirit). The difficulty is that such an exegesis overlooks, and tends even to contradict, the very point Paul is trying to make—that the life in the Spirit which the Galatians themselves claim to experience (cf. 3:2, 5) *in and of itself* lays upon them moral imperatives; that the freedom to which they have been called is a freedom to *obey* (5:13-14). It is precisely the *unity* of "living" and "walking" by the Spirit which the apostle seeks to formulate in 5:25 ("Since we live by the Spirit, let us also walk by the Spirit"). The integrity of these two is further expressed when Paul speaks of the believer's concrete obedience as the Spirit's "fruit" (5:22). Therefore, Dodd's interpretation of "the law of Christ" in Gal. 6:2 not only imposes an idea not clearly present in the context (viz. the idea of a body of dominical precepts), but also runs the danger of ignoring the controlling thought in the context which (to anticipate a later topic) may be identified as the integrity and indissolubility of indicative and imperative.

It should be observed that Dodd himself tries carefully to avoid the idea that Paul's "law of Christ" constituted "a code of regulations" demanding legalistic obedience. Rather, he insists, it was concerned primarily with the quality and direction of human action, and its precepts were meant to stir the imagination and arouse the conscience.[103] But W. D. Davies goes farther than his

[102] *Ibid.*, pp. 102-3, 104.
[103] *Gospel and Law* (1951), pp. 74 ff.

teacher in several respects.[104] He believes that the words of
Jesus constitute for Paul "a kind of Christian Halakah" and
that the apostle himself may be regarded as "a Christian Rabbi"
who applies, expounds, and transmits it. Davies believes that in
Gal. 6:2, as elsewhere, Paul must be understood primarily
against the background of rabbinic thought. The rabbis assumed
that the Torah would remain unchanged in the messianic age,
but that it would be more accurately studied and interpreted.[105]
Hence, the phrase in Gal. 6:2, ὁ νόμος τοῦ Χριστοῦ, should be
rendered "the Law of the Messiah," in conformity with the Jewish anticipation that the Messiah would be the law's true interpreter.[106]

The difficulties of accepting Davies' portrait of Paul as a
Christian rabbi have already been noted,[107] and his related interpretation of Gal. 6:2 is no more convincing. In the first place,
it is significant that only one certain rabbinic reference to "the
law of the Messiah" can be adduced.[108] This is not impressive evidence for the kind of precedent Davies insists lies behind Gal.
6:2. Second, if Paul holds such a specific view of the "law of
Christ" and places such high value on it (Davies), then it is
remarkable that he does not refer to it in many other contexts
where he is exhorting and appealing to the authority of the
Lord. That the phrase as such is used by Paul only once lends
plausibility to Friedrich's suggestion that the apostle has in fact
taken a concept over from the tradition and used it for his own
purposes. It should not, in this case, be used as evidence that
Paul himself is referring to a body of teaching derived from
Jesus.[109]

---

[104] *Paul and Rabbinic Judaism*, pp. 144-45.

[105] See Davies' study, *Torah in the Messianic Age and/or the Age to Come*
("*JBL* Monograph Series," VII [1952]), esp. pp. 72-73.

[106] *Ibid.*, p. 92.

[107] See above, pp. 40 ff.

[108] Midr. Qoh. 11, 8 (52a): "The Torah which a man learns in this world
is vanity in comparison with the Torah of the Messiah" (Billerbeck, III,
577).

[109] G. Friedrich, "Das Gesetz des Glaubens Röm. 3, 27," *ThZ*, X (1954),
407-8. With respect to Davies' conclusion that ὁ νόμος τοῦ Χριστοῦ should
be translated "the Law *of the Messiah*," attention should also be given to
W. Kramer's impressive argument that Χριστός, even with the definite

While it is true that Paul's reference to "the law of Christ" is used by later writers to support the idea of a "new law" valid for Christians, the actual phrase "new law" is not Pauline, and the concept is not developed until the second century (see Barn. 2:6; Herm. sim. V, 6, 3; VIII, 3, 2, etc.).[110] It could perhaps be argued that the idea of a new law is nevertheless foreshadowed in the Pauline letters, for example when the apostle comments on love as the fulfilling of the law (Rom. 13:8 ff.; Gal. 5:14). But in these passages love is not singled out as some principle according to which a new code of responsibilities may be fashioned. Rather, the emphasis is upon love as fulfilling the one law which has already been given. ,

Indeed, it is with reference to the love commandment that the phrase "law of Christ" in Gal. 6:2 is to be interpreted. Earlier in the same context love has been described as the fulfilling of the law (5:14). For Paul, living and walking in the Spirit (5:25) means living and walking in love. In Rom. 5:5 Paul speaks of the Spirit as the mediator of God's love, and then in the next verses identifies the death of Christ as the constitutive event of God's love (Rom. 5:6 ff.; cf. Rom. 8:9, 10). Therefore, while the phrases "law of Christ" (Gal. 6:2) and "law of the Spirit of life in Christ Jesus" (Rom. 8:2) probably ought not to be absolutely identified, they are both in contexts which speak of God's act of divine love by which the believer is given life and claimed for obedience in love. The "law of Christ" is, then, the law of love.[111] When Paul exhorts the Galatians, "Bear one an-

---

article, almost never has, in the Pauline letters, the primary meaning "Messiah." See *Christ, Lord, Son of God* (*SBTh,* 50), trans. Brian Hardy (1966), pp. 203 ff. (Sects. 60-65).

[110] See Kümmel's addendum to the notes on I Cor. 9:21 in Lietzmann, *Korinther,* p. 180. Also Wahlstrom, *The New Life in Christ* (1950), p. 166, and G. Friedrich, "Das Gesetz des Glaubens," p. 406.

[111] Among those who so interpret Gal. 6:2 are Schrage, *Die konkreten Einzelgebote,* pp. 99-100, 250; Schweitzer, *The Mysticism of Paul the Apostle,* trans. W. Montgomery (1931), p. 303; Bultmann, *Theology,* I, 262, 268; W. Gutbrod, *ThW,* IV (1942), 1069. More in agreement with the views of Dodd and Davies are T. W. Manson, *Ethics and the Gospel* (1960), pp. 69, 78; C. T. Craig (in comments on I Cor. 9:21), *IntB,* X (1953), 104; R. N. Longenecker, *Paul, Apostle of Liberty* (1964), p. 187; E. DeW. Burton, *A Critical and Exegetical Commentary on the Epistle to the Galatians* in *ICC* (1920), p. 329 (hesitantly).

other's burdens, and so fulfil the law of Christ" (RSV), he is
not commending obedience to a body of traditional sayings.
He is directing attention to a concrete way in which God's gift
and demand of love revealed in Christ may be expressed in the
Christian's life. This love is at once the "fruit" of the Spirit
("of life in Christ Jesus"!) and the fulfilling of the law of God.

If these preliminary observations about Paul's use of the concept of "law" in Christian contexts have any validity,[112] then
it is apparent that the phrases ἔννομος Χριστοῦ (I Cor. 9:21) and
ὁ νόμος τοῦ Χριστοῦ (Gal. 6:2) cannot be used to support the
hypothesis that he conceived of the traditional words of Jesus
as constituting a new Torah or a Christian Halakah.

CONCLUSION

This chapter has been concerned with the background of Paul's
ethic only in a restricted sense, for attention has been focused on
the particular question of the sources of the apostle's concrete
ethical teaching. It has been seen that this teaching shares many
of the formal and material characteristics of the ethical literature and traditions of the Hellenistic world at large. Paul himself
does not hesitate to employ current forms, concepts, and standards, even secular ones, already familiar to his readers. Two of
his specific sources, the Old Testament and the "words of the
Lord," are explicitly identified by him and have in his teaching
a special priority. Beyond these, however, important parallels
and relationships may also be discerned between his ethical
instruction and that of the rabbis, the Jewish apocalypticists,
and the Hellenistic popular philosophers.

The base on which this investigation has proceeded has not
been broad enough to permit any general conclusion about the
ideological roots of Pauline theology as a whole. With respect
to this larger question the present narrower inquiry permits only
the modest conclusion that the apostle's background is pluralistic
and complex. But with respect to the interpretation of the

[112] For a more extensive discussion of "law" and "Spirit" within the
structure of the Pauline ethic, see below, pp. 126 ff., 135 ff.

Pauline ethic in particular, several somewhat more specific points
have emerged.

First, the interpreter of Paul's ethic must learn to distinguish
between the more and less "original" elements in the apostle's
teaching. Paul had predecessors, and his ethical teaching, in
many of its aspects, had precedents. By these predecessors he
was, unquestionably, influenced, and on these preceding materials he felt free to draw. Nothing is gained, and much is lost
by ignoring the various ways in which the Pauline ethic is indebted to earlier and contemporary movements and perspectives.

Second, it is wrong to emphasize, one-sidedly, Paul's "Jewishness" over against his "Hellenism" or vice versa. In the Hellenistic society which formed the setting of his ministry and
whose culture was broadly and significantly diffused throughout
the Mediterranean world, philosophical, ethical, and religious
movements of many origins and varieties were constantly en-
gaging and interpenetrating one another. Elements of both
Jewish (rabbinic and apocalyptic) and Greek ethics are to be
found in Paul's teaching. To say that he was Jewish and not
Greek, or Greek and not Jewish, or even *primarily* one or the
other, is to miss the essential point. Insofar as he looked for
ethical wisdom wherever it was to be found and expressed this
in forms appropriate to his own time, he was very much a man
of the *Hellenistic* age.

But third, and in another sense, Paul was, theologically expressed, a man of the age to come, a citizen of the "heavenly"
world (Phil. 3:20). Neither the category of "rabbi" nor that of
"ethical philosopher" describes Paul very accurately. His employment of the Old Testament in his ethical teaching is not,
when considered in the broadest perspective, rabbinic. Nor does
he, like the typical Hellenistic pareneticist, attempt to gather
and sort the ethical wisdom of the centuries. He writes always
as an apostle, as a man in Christ. The structure of the Pauline
ethic is not yet laid bare when only its several specific "sources"
are uncovered. Already in these initial stages of the investigation
of Paul's ethic this much is clear. Not even the recognition that
one of Paul's sources is the teaching of Jesus—though this is probably not his "primary" one—requires a modification of this

judgment. For the sayings which he cites are regarded and described by him as "words of the Lord." Their authority derives from the fact that they are the words of a risen and reigning Sovereign. It is of this Lord that Paul is an apostle, and it is in the perspective of the whole redemptive event of Christ that this apostle frames his ethical exhortations.

II
The Pauline Exhortations

INTRODUCTION

A clarification of the sources of Paul's ethical teaching is not by itself sufficient. There remains the task of observing the manner in which he has employed these materials and the ways in which he may have adapted them to serve his own purposes. In short, it is also necessary to explain the form and function of the Pauline exhortations as they stand within the context of the apostle's letters.[1] Four important insights emerge from such a study, the validity of which the succeeding sections attempt to demonstrate. First, in his ethical exhortations Paul is not trying to be original, but concrete, relevant, inclusive, and persuasive. Second, the apostle usually assimilates traditional ethical material so thoroughly into the total context of his letters that its function, if not always its form and content, may be said to be significantly transformed. Third, Paul's exhortations are by no means confined to the so-called "parenetic sections" of his letters, but are expressed in a variety of ways throughout each

---

[1] I have dealt with this topic at length in my Yale doctoral dissertation, "Paul's Exhortations in the Context of His Letters and Thought" (1960), on which the present chapter is largely dependent.

letter. And finally, in the light of these facts, one must conclude that the Pauline letters cannot be neatly divided into doctrinal and ethical sections at all, and that the distinction between *kerygma* and *didache,* at least when applied to Paul, is more misleading than it is helpful.

1. THE USE OF TRADITIONAL MATERIAL

If Paul's use of traditional ethical materials is to be correctly understood, it is important to acknowledge from the outset that the apostle himself does not claim to be original in his ethical teachings. Quite the contrary, he appeals to traditions—Christian and non-Christian, biblical and nonbiblical—precisely in order to show that his concrete expectations for the Christian life are *not* necessarily new or novel. This, as Dibelius and others have emphasized, is a characteristic concern of the parenetic writer who consciously and intentionally employs the wisdom of the ages, and sometimes even emphasizes this. Isocrates (436-338 B.C.), or perhaps an early imitator, writes that just as the bee settles on all the flowers, "so also those who aspire to culture ought not to leave anything untasted, but should gather useful knowledge from every source" (*To Demonicus,* 51-52 [*LCL*]) ; and in the parenesis to his son, Cicero claims that "the subject of this inquiry is the common property of all philosophers" (*De Officiis* I. ii. 5 [*LCL*]) .[2]

Nowhere does Paul make such a blanket reference to or commendation of universal wisdom. One should hardly expect this from the apostle who calls worldly wisdom "foolishness" in comparison with God's and who declares that the wisdom of "this age" has no place in his preaching (I Cor. 1:20 ff.; 2:6-7) . On the other hand, in numerous subtler ways Paul does not hesitate to acknowledge the traditional character and therefore the commonly accepted validity of his concrete ethical teachings. There are first of all those instances in which he employs Chris-

---

[2] A pseudo-Plutarchian tract (*Moralia* 8, B) advises that acquiring the works of earlier writers does for moral education what the collection of tools does for good farming.

tian traditions—dominical, liturgical, ecclesiastical, or scriptural. Paul's use of dominical traditions (words of the Lord), already examined in another connection,[3] provides a very obvious instance of his concern to deny the originality of his moral instruction in order to win for it the support of a greater authority (I Cor. 7:10 ff.; 14:37; I Thess. 4:15). Also noteworthy are the passages in which he seeks authoritative support by appealing to liturgical traditions with which, he can readily assume, most of his readers are familiar. His reference in I Cor. 11:23 to the words of institution should probably be listed here, although it is also an appeal to a dominical word, and certainly also Paul's specific reliance on the creedal tradition (παράδοσις) in I Cor. 15:3 ff.: "For I handed on [παρέδωκεν] to you as of first importance that which I also received [παρέλαβον]." While other probable instances of the use of liturgical materials are not acknowledged by the apostle in this same way (e.g. the Christ-hymn in Philippians 2 and the creedal excerpt in Rom. 1:3-4), Paul's dependence on them would have been clear to his readers.

In I Corinthians, at least, Paul also appeals to what may be described as "ecclesiastical" traditions, customs, or ways of doing things which, because they are accepted by "all the churches," have a certain binding authority in each particular congregation. These are doubtless the kind of "traditions" (παραδόσεις) to which he makes reference in I Cor. 11:2 as himself having "handed on" to the Corinthians. In the discussion concerning women's head coverings in church which follows, the apostle is not promulgating anything new, but appealing to custom. This is reflected also in his closing comment (vs. 16) that "if any one is inclined to be contentious, we simply have no other custom, nor do the churches of God." The appeal of I Cor. 14:33 is similarly supported: "It is for prophets to control prophetic inspiration, for the God who inspires them is not a God of disorder but of peace, as in all communities of God's people" (NEB, margin[4]). Even in some instances in which Paul appeals to his

---

[3] See above, pp. 51 ff.

[4] G. Fitzer has argued convincingly that the instruction about women remaining silent in church (I Cor. 14:34-35) has all the marks of an un-Pauline interpolation. See "'Das Weib schweige in der Gemeinde': Über den

own rules or advice, he seems to regard these as helping to constitute that body of church traditions which, because it is acknowledged and adhered to by "all the churches," has gained an
authority of its own. To this authority even the apostle himself
can appeal (I Cor. 7:17; 16:1). But most obvious and most frequent are the many instances in which Paul explicitly cites scriptural passages in support of his teaching and exhortations (e.g.
I Cor. 9:8-9). Scripture he considers to have been written "for
our sake" (Rom. 15:4; cf. 4:23-24; I Cor. 9:10; 10:6 ff.), to be
the essential core of "Christian tradition" (it "preaches the gospel," Gal. 3:8), and because it embodies God's own words to his
people (e.g. II Cor. 6:16; cf. vs. 2), to be of special, unquestion-
able authority.

Paul's dependence upon traditional teaching is not, however,
restricted to that which may be called "Christian," [5] and his
admonition to the Thessalonians to "test *everything*, hold fast
to what is good, abstain from every form of evil" (I, 5:21-22)
seems in his own case to have a wide application. He never supposes that "what is good and acceptable and perfect" (Rom.
12:2) has an exclusively Christian provenance. Thus, for example, he does not hesitate, in exactly the same context as that
in which he appeals to the Christian creedal tradition and to
the church's scripture (I Cor. 15:3 ff., 45 ff.), to appeal also to
a quite secular proverb, "Bad company ruins good morals" (I
Cor. 15:33; cf. Menander *Thais*, Fragment 218). Similarly, Paul's
listing of particularly repulsive vices (Rom. 1:29-31; 13:13; I Cor.
5:10-11; 6:9-10; II Cor. 12:20-21; Gal. 5:19-21) and of particularly
commendable virtues (II Cor. 6:6; Gal. 5:22-23; Phil. 4:8) shows
the extent to which his ideas of "good" and "bad" are in accord
with those of contemporary ethical writers. He does not seek
to distinguish between the content of his ethical advice and
theirs, but supports his own exhortations by relating them to
what, on other grounds, his readers are already willing to ac-

---

unpaulinischen Charakter der mulier-taceat-Verse in I Korinther 14," *ThEx*,
n.F. Nr. 110 (1963). Paul's reference to "all the churches" (vs. 33*b*) must then
be construed with vs. 33*a*. As Fitzer has shown, this presents no problem.
Consequently, the NEB marginal reading is to be preferred and is the one
cited here.
[5] See Chapter I.

knowledge. The "works of the flesh," he writes to the Galatians, are "obvious" (φανερά),[6] and the vices he then lists are typical of those condemned by secular writers (5:19-21). On the other side, the qualities commended in Phil. 4:8 are representative of the best secular morality of the day.

Such examples make it clear enough that Paul's concern is not to be "original" or to foster a morality of exclusively "Christian" content. He readily appeals for support to any sources—pagan, Jewish, or Christian—which uphold the kind of conduct he wishes to commend and attack the vices he wishes to condemn. By doing this he is taking quite seriously his own advice to "test *everything*, hold fast to what is good, abstain from every form of evil."

a. The concern to be concrete and relevant

If originality is not the apostle's chief concern in his ethical teaching, what are his concerns? What particular purposes are served by the ethical materials he has taken over? Above all, his use of traditional material reflects his concern, perhaps one might say even his "pastoral" concern, to be *concrete* and *relevant*. He is not willing to leave the identification of specifically "good" and "evil" deeds to the Christian's own imagination or intuition.

It is true that exhortations of a very fundamental, even "timeless" kind, have a place in Paul's letters: "Present yourselves to God as those who have been brought from death to life, and your members to God as instruments of righteousness" (Rom. 6:13); "Present yourselves to God as a living sacrifice, holy and acceptable, your spiritual worship; and do not be conformed to this world but be transformed" (Rom. 12:1-2); "Glorify God in your body!" (I Cor. 6:20 RSV); "Whether you eat or drink, or whatever you do, do everything to the glory of God" (I Cor. 10:31). There is a sense in which such exhortations may be

---

[6] E. Kamlah (*Die Form der katalogischen Paränese im Neuen Testament* in *WUNT*, 7 [1964], 19-20, n. 5) believes that φανερά in Gal. 5:19 is to be interpreted, on the basis of Rom. 1:18 and I Cor. 3:13 ff., as a reference to the "eschatological exposure" of these deeds as evil. This possibility cannot be excluded, but neither is there anything in the immediate context in Galatians which makes it necessary or certain.

classified as "basic principles" or described as "general truths," but this does not mean that the Pauline ethic is devoid of specific content. On the one hand, these "general" exhortations are themselves directed to concrete situations and problems in Christian congregations.[7] And on the other hand, they stand side-by-side with other Pauline admonitions—indeed, the majority of Pauline admonitions—which are quite specific.

Concreteness is no less a characteristic of the apostle's exhortations in his letter to the Roman Christians, about whom he probably has little specific information, than it is of those in his letters to the Corinthians, with whose problems he has had firsthand experience. The Roman Christians are to employ their God-given *charismata* to the fullest and are to be zealous in rendering aid and cheerful in showing mercy (Rom. 12:3 ff.). They are to be loving, forgiving, faithful in prayer, hospitable, humble (Rom. 12:9 ff.), good citizens of the state (Rom. 13:1 ff.), and understanding and supportive of those whose opinions differ from their own (Rom. 14:1 ff.). The Corinthian brethren are to put away jealousy and strife (I, 3:3), arrogance (I, 4:18 ff.), all forms of sexual immorality (I, 5:1 ff.; 6:9, 12 ff.). They are to exercise discipline within their own community (I, 5:4 ff.) and refrain insofar as possible from bringing legal judgments against one another in civil courts (I, 6:1 ff.). There is to be no greed, idolatry, drunkenness, or thievery among them (I, 5:11; 6:9-10), and they are to be responsible in all matters pertaining to marriage (and celibacy!) (I, 7:1 ff.). They are to be concerned for the brother's conscience (I, 8:1 ff.), they are to be orderly when assembled for the Lord's Supper and for worship (I, chaps. 11-14), and they are to abound in the Lord's work (I, 15:58) —for example in their material contributions for the Christians of Jerusalem (I, 16:1 ff.). Such examples of *concrete* exhortations, immediately *relevant* for the Christians to whom Paul writes, are to be found throughout his letters.

[7] This point is effectively made by Bultmann, "Allgemeine Wahrheiten und christliche Verkündigung," *ZThK*, LIV (1957), 244 ff. Compare W. Baird who believes that such exhortations (e.g. I Cor. 10:31) make only an "elusive demand" (*The Corinthian Church—A Biblical Approach to Urban Culture* [1964], quoted below, p. 278).

The importance of these concrete commandments has been stressed by Schrage,[8] who sees correctly that precisely *in* them the Christian is confronted by the claim of God upon *his* life in the world. The self-styled "spiritists" (πνευματικοί) in Corinth, for example, had evidently thought themselves "above" mundane considerations of right and wrong, but in his Corinthian letters Paul seeks in the most urgent way to demonstrate their concrete ethical responsibilities. The believer is "in Christ" or "in the Lord," but he is at the same time "in the world" (ἐν σαρκί, Gal. 2:20; Philemon 16). This means not only that he is still subject to worldly cares, pressures, and temptations (e.g. I Cor. 5:9-10), but also that he is still obliged to act responsibly in the world, in accord with the new master whom he has pledged to serve. The Christian's life in Christ is not divorced from his life in this world, and because the Christian himself stands, as it were, where these two orders meet, his concrete actions have important ramifications.

In I Corinthians 6 Paul pleads with his readers to recognize the truth of this. What one does with his body is not a matter of indifference; being "one spirit" with Christ (vs. 17) does not mean that somehow one is relieved of responsibility for the way he disposes his life in the world. Since the believer's whole being (σῶμα) has been claimed by the Lord (vss. 13, 15, 19), the "general exhortation" to "glorify God in your body [σῶμα]" (vs. 20) has concrete implications which the apostle does not hesitate to point out (vss. 15 ff.).

In the same way, in Galatians 5 Paul does not stop with the exhortations to "love" (vss. 13-14) and to "walk by the Spirit" (vs. 16), but describes concretely what these exhortations require the Christian to do and to avoid (vss. 17 ff., 26; 6:1 ff.). Also in I Thessalonians 4 he makes concrete the demands of "sanctification" (vs. 3) and "love" (vs. 9) by speaking of a man's relationship to his wife (vss. 4 ff.) and his brethren (vss. 10 ff.), and in the next chapter illustrates Christian "sobriety" (5:5 ff.) with reference to the concrete responsibilities of respect, community order, industriousness, brotherly concern and helpful-

[8] See Appendix, pp. 276-77.

ness, patience, prayer, thanksgiving, etc. (vss. 12 ff.). Even in
his letter to the Roman church which he has not personally
visited, his exhortation to "be transformed" and "seek out the
will of God" (12:1-2) is given added force and meaning in the
long series of specific admonitions which follow in chaps. 12–14.

Whether these teachings about specific problems and situations
are best characterized as "examples," "paradigms," and "illustrations," or, on the other hand, as "norms" and "principles" is a
question which need not be decided here.[9] In any case they are
self-evident attempts by the apostle to confront his readers in-
escapably with the relevance, in their concrete choices and relationships, of the gospel to which they are committed. He wishes
to make it clear that the new life in Christ is not some vague
experience of detachment from the world, but manifests itself in
multiple and concrete engagements in and with the world. The
Christian must know about the "ways in Christ" (I Cor. 4:17),
and concerning these Paul teaches and gives directions in all
the churches (I Cor. 4:17; 7:17; cf. 11:34). In so doing he does
not hesitate to use traditional material drawn from a wide variety
of sources.

b. The concern to be inclusive

Paul's intentions are misread if the concreteness of his exhortations is interpreted as an attempt to define the precise extent of
what the Christian is to do. He clearly does not regard his concrete exhortations as supplying an exhaustive catalog of moral
responsibilities. Quite the contrary, one effect of his use of a wide
variety of traditional ethical materials is to underscore the
virtually unlimited extent and breadth of those responsibilities.
He is concerned that no good work or noble deed should be
excluded from the Christian's life. *Inclusiveness,* then, is one
of the objectives of the apostle's concrete ethical teaching. He
tries to avoid giving the impression that there are ever any
limits either to the good that is required or to the evil that is
possible. The following examples illustrate the point.

In Phil. 4:8 he commends *"whatever [ὅσα] is true, whatever*

* See below, pp. 91-92, 229-30.

is honorable, *whatever* is just, *whatever* is pure, *whatever* is lovely, *whatever* is gracious" (RSV). Not only the content of this list, much of which is traditional, but also the rhetorical emphasis achieved by the repetition of the ὅσα gives material emphasis to the apostle's point. He is intent on making the range of the appeal and the field of the Philippians' ethical responsibility as inclusive as possible. It is incorrect to say that Paul is here referring to "a few settled principles on which one always acts";[10] it is much more accurate to describe this as "a comprehensive exhortation covering all possible virtues." [11]

Paul's use of the so-called "vice lists" provides another example of his concern to be inclusive. After listing fifteen commonly recognized vices in Gal. 5:19 ff., he quite deliberately adds, "And others *such as* these" (καὶ τὰ ὅμοια τούτοις), warning that those who do "things *like these* [τὰ τοιαῦτα] shall not inherit the kingdom of God." Another series of vices is presented in Rom. 1:29 ff. and concluded with a similar remark. Those who do "things *like* these [τὰ τοιαῦτα] deserve to die" (vs. 32). It is apparent that such lists are intended to be only representative of evils to be avoided. Paul simply offers, in such instances, a "handful" [12] of vices as examples. This is confirmed by the fact that, in six "vice lists" in the Pauline homologoumena, forty-two different terms appear relating to thirty-nine distinct vices. No term appears in all six lists; only two are in as many as four (ἔρις, μέθη/μέθυσις) ; five appear three times (πορνεία [but also μοιχεία and κοίτη, once each], ἀσέλγεια, εἰδωλολατρία, ζῆλος, and πλεονεξία) ; eight twice each; and all the rest (twenty-five) in only one list.[13] It is quite illegitimate, then, to subject the Pauline ethical catalogs to minute exegesis as if they could yield deep insights into Paul's own thought or "ethical ideals." [14] Every indication is that the

[10] E. F. Scott, *IntB*, XI (1955), 118.

[11] Marvin R. Vincent, *A Critical and Exegetical Commentary on the Epistles to the Philippians and to Philemon* in ICC (1906), p. 139.

[12] H. Schlier, *Der Brief an die Galater* in KEK (13th ed., 1965), p. 251.

[13] See S. Wibbing, *Die Tugend- und Lasterkataloge im Neuen Testament,* pp. 86 ff.

[14] Both Enslin (*The Ethics of Paul,* pp. 161 ff.) and Wahlstrom (*The New Life in Christ,* pp. 218 ff., pp. 281 ff.) correctly warn about the dangers of over-exegeting these ethical lists. Wibbing (*Die Tugend- und Lasterkata-*

apostle himself presents these only as a typical, and for the most part random, sampling of the deeds and traits which are to be espoused and avoided.[15]

There is always a danger that concrete exhortations to specific actions will be taken as defining the limits of one's moral responsibility, that they will be regarded as maximum rather than minimum requirements. But, as shown by the examples cited above, Paul's exhortations are *inclusive* at the same time that they are concrete. He employs traditional material in such a way that the scope of the Christian's ethical responsibility is indefinitely extended. Paul's ethic is by no means provincial. He admonishes his congregations to espouse every conceivable moral excellence, to be open to every possible good and closed to every possible evil. His ethic is not *indeterminate,* if by this one means that its content is problematic or elusive. But it is *indefinite,* in the sense that it sets no limits (and therefore no neatly definable or readily attainable "goals") to what is required. The apostle's adoption of material from many varied sources shows his concern to broaden the concept of Christian ethical responsibility without thereby sacrificing anything of its concreteness.

c. The concern to be persuasive

Finally, but by no means of least importance, Paul's use of traditional material helps to lend *persuasiveness* to his ethical exhortations. The apostle does not represent himself as a sponsor of a "new morality," and insofar as he can make use of ethical concepts, counsels, and even hortatory formulations already familiar to his readers, his chances for success in the task of persuasion are increased. In this regard one may speak of (1) his appeals to heed a higher authority and (2) his appeals to heed what is generally accredited as right and proper.

The first of these is the most obvious. Paul constantly makes use of the Old Testament and on occasion applies a "word of

---

loge, pp. 81 ff.) has demonstrated the way in which rhetorical and stylistic considerations have often been determinative in the particular arrangement of the various items in the lists (e.g. Rom. 1:29 ff.) .

[15] This judgment, particularly with respect to the catalogs of "virtues," needs some important qualification. See below, pp. 84 ff., 86 ff.

the Lord." Both the apostle and his readers recognize both of these as authoritative in matters of faith and practice. An appeal to either lends the most effective kind of persuasiveness to any ethical exhortation. This is clearly the case when the words of the Lord are brought to bear on the questions of divorce (I Cor. 7:10) and of support for the apostles (I Cor. 9:14). The instances in which Old Testament materials are cited in order to persuade are, of course, much more numerous. It is necessary to mention only one of these instances here because it illustrates the point so well. Again in speaking of the apostles' right to expect financial subvention by the churches, Paul asks: "Do I say this *personally?*" (κατὰ ἄνθρωπον, I Cor. 9:8: literally, "according to man"; RSV translates, "on human authority"; NEB, "Do not suppose I rely on these human analogies.") No, he has a higher authority. "Does not the law say the same?" (RSV), he asks, and then cites Deut. 25:4 in support of his point (vs. 9).

On other occasions Paul's appeal is to heed what is more generally accredited as right and proper. His references to what is customary "in all the churches" should probably be mentioned here (I Cor. 11:16; 14:33; cf. 11:2) as also his employment of such creedal traditions as that cited in I Cor. 15:3 ff. It is too much to say that Paul ascribes either to the church's customs or to its liturgical or creedal formulations any "higher authority" even approaching that of scripture or the Lord. On the other hand, insofar as the practice and confession of Paul's churches have become generalized, the appeal to such may be presumed to lend persuasiveness to any corresponding exhortation. The appeal is thus to what is, among the Christian brethren, generally regarded as right and proper.

There are other instances in which the apostle calls upon materials which have a yet broader, one might even say universal, accreditation. On the one hand are the vices which are "obvious" (φανερά) to all (Gal. 5:19 ff.; cf. Rom. 1:29 ff., etc.).[16] On the other hand are the universally respected "virtues" listed in Phil. 4:8. Again, the quotation of the saying "Bad company ruins good morals" (I Cor. 15:33) is surely prompted because its wisdom

[16] See above, p. 72.

would be everywhere acknowledged. And even more striking is the appeal of I Cor. 11:14-15: "Does not nature itself teach you that for a man to wear long hair is degrading to him, but if a woman has long hair, it is her pride?" (RSV).

This last example is of special interest because the appeal is associated with the admonition in vs. 13: "Judge for yourselves" (RSV). It is unquestionably true that Paul's ethical exhortations, especially those which refer to generally accredited concepts of right and wrong, are often based on the presupposition that reason plays a part in the Christian's moral discernment and decision.[17] "I speak as to sensible men [φρονίμοις]," he says to the Corinthians, adding: "You decide about what I'm saying" (I, 10:15). Again to them: "We do not write anything to you except what you can read and understand, and I hope that you will understand fully just as you have already understood us in part" (II, 1:13-14). Paul's frequent rhetorical question, "Do you not know?" (οὐκ οἴδατε; Rom. 6:16; 11:2; I Cor. 3:16; 5:6; 6:2, 3, 9, 15, 16, 19; 9:13, 24; ἢ ἀγνοεῖτε; Rom. 6:3; 7:1) which, as in the Cynic-Stoic diatribe, prefaces ideas with which the readers are presumed to be familiar and in agreement (e.g. Epict. Discourses I. xii. 12; II. v. 26), represents nevertheless another, though subtler, form of this appeal to reason. It is an appeal which is already implicit in the apostle's admonitions to examine one's own life (I Cor. 11:28; II Cor. 13:5; Gal. 6:4) and to "test everything" (I Thess. 5:21).

If this is examined from another point of view, we can see that the persuasive weight of traditional materials is summoned by Paul to aid him in achieving a variety of specific objectives: to instruct, promise, warn, encourage, and illustrate or exemplify. Examples of each are easily found.

Traditional materials are often simply *instructional*. This is manifestly the case with the words of the Lord (I Cor. 7:10; 9:14) and many Old Testament texts, for instance the command to love the neighbor (Rom. 13:8 ff.; Gal. 5:14).

---

[17] See M. Dibelius, " 'Επίγνωσις ἀληθείας," *Botschaft und Geschichte*, II, 1 ff., and G. Bornkamm, "Glaube und Vernunft bei Paulus," *Studien zu Antike und Urchristentum*, pp. 119 ff. A shortened English version of Bornkamm's article, "Faith and Reason in Paul," may be found in *NTS*, IV (1958), 93 ff.

In II Cor. 9:6 ff. Old Testament materials are used (vss. 7, 9, 10) to support the *promise* that generous contributions to Paul's collection for Jerusalem will greatly enrich the contributors (e.g. vs. 11).

Very often scriptural passages (e.g. Rom. 12:19; 14:10 ff.; I Cor. 10:1 ff.) or vice lists (e.g. Rom. 1:29 ff.; I Cor. 6:9 ff.; II Cor. 12:20 ff.) are used to lend persuasiveness (in the case of the vice lists, by adding vividness) to the apostle's *warnings*. Such warnings may have to do with Paul's own disciplinary action against offending brethren (II Cor. 12:20 ff.), but most often they are warnings about the wrath of God which shall come upon the wicked (e.g. Rom. 14:10 ff.).

Sometimes traditional materials are called upon to assist Paul in *encouraging* his readers to stand fast in a particular line of action or style of life. Although the creedal material of I Cor. 15:3 ff. is employed initially to correct a mistaken notion of resurrection, it ultimately stands in the service of the exhortation to remain "steadfast," always abounding in the Lord's work (vs. 58). The objective here is that the Corinthians should "stand" in the gospel and "hold it fast" (vss. 1-2), and the encouragement to do this is supported by the content of that gospel itself.

More specific than encouragement, and yet not instructional in the strictest sense, are the passages in which traditional materials are used for the sake of *illustrating or exemplifying* the proper course of action. In Rom. 15:3 an Old Testament verse is applied to Christ's giving of himself for others in his death on the cross, though the crucifixion is not specifically mentioned here. The "picture" thus evoked is intended to support the exhortation that the believer should not try to please himself but the neighbor (vss. 1-2). Even clearer is the use of the Christ-hymn in Phil. 2:6 ff. Christ's humbling of himself, his laying aside of every claim to status, his obedience even to death, exemplifies the humility (vss. 3-4) and obedience (vss. 12-13) to which the Christian himself is called. The larger question raised by such passages as Rom. 15:3 and Phil. 2:6 ff. is the meaning of Paul's appeals to "imitate" Christ or follow his example.[18] Here, how-

---

[18] See below, pp. 218 ff.

ever, it is enough to recognize that traditional materials (e.g. scriptural citations, Christian liturgical forms) are sometimes used as persuasive ways of commending a particular style of life.

2. THE ASSIMILATION OF TRADITIONAL MATERIAL

Without detracting from the importance of the insight that Paul's concrete ethical teachings are in large measure derived from traditional sources, both Christian and non-Christian, it must also be emphasized that he has, in most cases, exercised his own critical judgment in selecting these materials and has assimilated them into significantly new contexts. He has not been simply a collector and curator of miscellaneous moral advice; the impress of his own interests, perspectives, and objectives has been left upon them to a greater extent than Dibelius, for example,[19] was inclined to acknowledge.

a. Selection and integration

It must be recognized, first of all, that Paul was *selective* and *critical* in his taking over of non-Christian materials. As Schrage points out, it is important not only to notice what Paul accepted of these materials, but also what he rejected, or at least chose not to accept.[20] Only once, for example (Phil. 4:8), does the apostle employ the term ἀρετή ("moral excellence") which was an important theme not only of secular Greek ethics (e.g. Plato, Aristotle, Plutarch), but also of the moral tractates of Hellenistic Judaism (Wisdom of Solomon, II, III, IV Maccabees, Philo, etc.). Nor does the important term ὕβρις ("insolence," "overweening pride") have any place in his vocabulary—with the exception that the adjective ὑβριστής is among the vices listed in Rom. 1:30. Although pride, arrogance, and self-esteem are roundly

---

[19] See Appendix, pp. 261-62. This same objection to Dibelius' work is registered by L. Goppelt, "Tradition nach Paulus," *KuD*, IV (1958), 227, n. 44. See also H. Preisker, *Das Ethos des Unchristentums* (2nd ed., 1949), pp. 186-87.

[20] *Die konkreten Einzelgebote*, p. 202. See also H. Preisker, *Das Ethos des Urchristentums*, p. 190.

condemned by Paul in many places, he has other ways of identifying these, most significantly with the term φυσιοῦν (I Cor. 4:6, 18-19; 5:2; 8:1; 13:4) and φυσίωσις (II Cor. 12:20) —which appear rarely in secular Greek literature, hardly ever with the Pauline meaning "arrogance" or "conceit." [21] Paul also omits discussion of the Greek "cardinal virtues" as well as many other favorite topics and concepts of the Hellenistic parenetic tradition.[22] The specifically Christian theologoumena aside, Paul is already distinguished from the secular and Jewish traditions of his day to some extent by the topics, themes, and vocabulary of his concrete ethical teaching. In his use of commonly circulating moral ideas he has been critical and selective.

Equally important, Paul has assimilated these materials into the framework of his own thought and letters and used them for the attainment of his own special objectives. Here particularly the views of Martin Dibelius need to be modified. Although it is clear that Paul's ethical teaching is not a *creatio ex nihilo,* neither is it a simple continuation of the Hellenistic parenetic tradition[23] or a mechanical and superficial "Christianization" of it, as Dibelius' student, Weidinger, held.[24]

Paul's thorough assimilation of *Old Testament and Jewish concepts* and materials is so obvious as to require little specific documentation. The law, for example, is now defined solely in relation to the decisive Christ-event (Gal. 3:23 ff.), and for Paul its function is thus significantly altered (e.g. Rom. 7:7 ff.). The word νόμος itself can now be used in association with the Spirit (Rom. 8:2), Christ (I Cor. 9:21; Gal. 6:2), and even faith (Rom. 3:27). The apostle's use of Abraham as the prototype of faith (Romans 4; Galatians 3) is another example of the way Old Testament materials have been thoroughly taken up into his own thought and applied in new ways.

---

[21] See the entries on these words in Bauer. Paul also uses the concept of καύχησις (e.g., Rom. 3:27).

[22] Schrage mentions some of these in *Die konkreten Einzelgebote,* p. 202, and refers to the additional ones listed by A. Bonhöffer in *Epiktet und das Neue Testament* (1911), pp. 218 ff.

[23] Correctly Schrage, *Die konkreten Einzelgebote,* pp. 197, 200.

[24] *Die Haustafeln. Ein Stück urchristlicher Paränese* in *UNT,* 14 (1928), 51 *et passim.*

While Paul's assimilation of *secular materials* is less massive and dramatic, it is no less significant. A few examples must suffice to make the point. Three times he employs the familiar parenetic expression, "Do not be deceived" (μὴ πλανᾶσθε; cf. James 1:16; Epict. IV. vi. 23) to introduce traditional ethical material. In each case, however, this traditional material has been thoroughly assimilated into the total context. In I Cor. 6:9b the formula introduces a vice list with quite conventional contents. But this list stands between two solemn warnings that perpetrators of such vices will not inherit the kingdom of God (vss. 9a, 10). Moreover, that this is not a completely random sampling of vices is shown by the fact that the first ones listed (fornication, idolatry, adultery, homosexuality, vs. 9c) are specifically applicable to and undoubtedly suggested by the situation Paul is addressing in Corinth (5:1: "There has been an actual report of fornication in your midst").

In Gal. 6:7 μὴ πλανᾶσθε introduces a proverblike saying which includes the familiar parenetic image [25] of sowing and reaping ("God is not mocked, for whatever a man sows, that he will also reap," RSV). In itself this proverb lacks a specific reference and may be employed as a very general motto, but Paul here applies it in a particular way. "For he who sows to his own flesh will from the flesh reap corruption; but he who sows to the Spirit will from the Spirit reap eternal life" (vs. 8 RSV). It is thus assimilated to the point of the whole section. Since there is a constant warfare between the flesh and the Spirit (5:17), the Galatians should not use their freedom in Christ as an occasion for the flesh (5:13) but should "walk by the Spirit" (5:16). The assimilation to the context of yet another proverb ("Bad company ruins good morals," I Cor. 15:33) is perhaps less complete but hardly less clear. It is evidently quoted to "neutralize" the preceding saying ("Let us eat and drink, for tomorrow we die," I Cor. 15:32b RSV) which Paul had employed to express the *reductio ad absurdum* of denying the resurrection of the dead.[26]

[25] Schlier lists parallels from Greek authors, the LXX, Hellenistic Jewish tractates, and from elsewhere in the New Testament (*Galater*, p. 277, n. 1).

[26] The attempt of Weiss to relate the proverb about bad company ruining good morals to Paul's discussion in chap. 10 is not very convincing (*Der erste Korintherbrief*, p. 367).

b. The vice lists

The apostle's integration of more or less traditional lists of virtues and vices into particular contexts is particularly striking. The earlier observation that such lists represent "a typical, and for the most part random, sampling" [27] from commonly identified virtues and vices now needs to be qualified. One instance in which at least some members of a vice list are specially relevant to the situation being addressed has just been noted (I Cor. 6:9). This is also true of I Cor. 5:9-10, which stands in the same general framework and like the list in chap. 6 emphasizes the vice of fornication (πορνεία, cf. 5:1) and its attendant evils. The list in II Cor. 12:20-21 is entirely tailored to the situation in Corinth. The three vices of impurity, fornication, and licentiousness (ἀκαθαρσία, πορνεία, ἀσέλγεια, vs. 21) all reflect Paul's problems with sexual immorality there (I, chaps. 5, 6), and the eight vices enumerated in vs. 20 all pertain to the infighting, jealousies, and disruptive arrogance which so much of Paul's Corinthian correspondence is devoted to combatting. Four of these eight vices are dealt with elsewhere in relation to specific situations (ἔρις [discord], I, 1:11; 3:3; ζῆλος [envy], I, 3:3; cf. 13:4; φυσιώσεις [conceit], I, 4:6, 18-19; 5:2; 8:1; cf. 13:4; ἀκαταστασίαι [unruliness], I, 14:33). The remaining four are closely related in meaning (anger [θυμοί], selfish ambition [ἐριθεῖαι], slander [καταλαλία] and talebearing [ψιθυρισμοί].

Although it is not possible to draw such clear lines of connection between the lists of Rom. 1:29 ff. and Gal. 5:19-21 and their epistolary contexts, it is noteworthy that these lists, like those in I and II Corinthians, are heavily weighted with "social vices," vices which disrupt the life of the community (covetousness, malice, envy, murder, strife, deceit, etc.—Rom. 1:29 ff.; enmity, strife, jealousy, anger, selfishness, etc.—Gal. 5:19-21). Thus Paul's vice lists, unlike those of the Hellenistic world in general which emphasized "personal" vices, are particularly formed for the life of the community. Paul was not a wandering street preacher, but an apostle and a leader of congregations, and his ethical lists reflect this function.[28]

[27] See above, p. 77.
[28] See further, Wibbing, *Die Tugend- und Lasterkataloge,* pp. 95 ff.

Even when attacking the more "traditional vices" of the parenetic tradition, for example, fornication, this distinctively community concern of Paul's exhortations is manifest. The admonition to "shun fornication" (φεύγετε τὴν πορνείαν, I Cor. 6: 18a) is almost identical with one in the Hellenistic-Jewish Test. XII P. (λοιπόν, φεύγετε τέκνα μου τὴν πορνείαν, Reu. 5:5). But unlike the treatment of this vice in most Hellenistic moral tracts, the apostle elaborates neither the causes nor the attendant circumstances of fornication. For example, in the Test. XII P. the vice is discussed as a particular threat to the inebriated man (Jud. 14:2-3) and to the one who succumbs to the deceitful wiles of dangerous women (e.g. Reu. 5:3). At other times the exhorter speaks about the "spirit of fornication" (e.g. Lev. 9:9; Jud. 13:3; Reu. 3:3). None of these typically parenetic interests appears in Paul. In I Corinthians 5–6, at least, the apostle's first concern is not with the effects of the vice upon the guilty individual (contrast Reu. 6:1 ff.), but with its effects in the community as a whole. The larger issue is how the church is to respond to evil in its midst. And Paul is chiefly alarmed at the Corinthians' continuing arrogance (5:2; cf. vs. 6) and moral complacency. For him, the viciousness of prostitution (I Cor. 6:15 ff.) is not that it pollutes the purity of one's mind (Reu. 6:1 ff.), but that it violates the body of Christ and perverts the community of brethren.

Some attention should also be given to Paul's words about fornication [πορνεία] in I Thess. 4:1-8, for at least one scholar has described this as a typical parenetic topos on sexual morality.[29] But a comparison with the discussion of πορνεία in the testament of Jud. 13:1 ff. shows how atypical of the general parenetic tradition Paul's discussion really is. First, in Jud. the writer's entire attention is focused on the vice per se and with the two related vices of drunkenness (μέθυσις) and passion (ἐπιθυμία). The repugnancy of these three is related with a repetitiveness which verges on monotony. Paul, however, refrains from the detailed description of individual vices. A mere mention of πορνεία (I Thess. 4:3) is enough. Moreover, in Jud. the

chief vice is drunkenness, for from it, the writer claims, both
passion and fornication spring. While Paul does mention ἐπιθυμία ("passion") here (vs. 5), and μέθυσις ("drunkenness") in
the next chapter (5:7, but applied metaphorically), he never
suggests that one is the origin of the others, for within the context of his thought they are all manifestations of man's refusal
to heed the call of God (4:7). Finally, in Jud. the admonitions
are almost all negative; they are prohibitions, not exhortations:
"Do not commit fornication; do not boast" (13:2); "Do not
become drunk" (14:1); "Do not touch wine at all" (16:3). Paul's
remarks, in contrast, constitute a positive appeal to the Thessalonians to remember that to which and in which they were
called: "holiness" or "sanctification" (ἁγιασμός). I Thess. 4:1 ff.
is not a moral treatise after the fashion of Hellenistic parenesis,
then, even though some of the elements of such are undeniably
there. And it is by no means accurate to say that this whole
section is given its Christian character only because the exhortations are issued "in" or "through the Lord Jesus." [30]

c. Lists of "virtues"

Even more fully influenced by and assimilated to a distinctively
Christian context are the so-called "virtue lists" in Paul's letters.
Whereas Paul uses forty-two different terms relating to thirty-
nine distinct vices, he uses fewer than twenty terms relating to
sixteen distinct "virtues," a difference which also holds when
looking at the New Testament as a whole.[31] Thus, the range
of "virtues" is, for Paul as for the New Testament in general,
approximately only one third as wide as the range of vices, and
these tend to cluster around the three central themes of love
(ἀγάπη, II Cor. 6:6; Gal. 5:22; cf. longsuffering, kindness, peace,
gentleness, goodness, self-control, etc.), purity (ἁγνότης, II Cor.
6:6; ἁγνός, Phil. 4:8), and truthfulness (ἀλήθεια, II Cor. 6:6;
Phil. 4:8; cf. knowledge, faithfulness, etc.). The most important
of these lists is in Gal. 5:22-23 and amply documents the extent
to which the "virtues" Paul enumerates have their context within
his own thought and purpose.

[30] Dibelius, *Thessalonicher*, p. 20.
[31] See Wibbing, *Die Tugend- und Lasterkataloge*, pp. 99 ff.

In the first place, the "virtues" of Gal. 5:22-23 are identified
collectively as "the fruit of the Spirit" (ὁ καρπὸς τοῦ πνεύματος).
Not only does the apostle avoid describing these qualities as
"works" (ἔργα, cf. the "works of the flesh," vs. 19) ; he also avoids
speaking of them as separate, individual traits of character. They
are not to be regarded as qualities which may be successively
achieved by human effort ("works") but as manifestations of
the gift of God, hence "fruit of the Spirit." Paul also uses the
singular "fruit" in Phil. 1:11 (καρπὸς δικαιοσύνης). There it
contrasts sharply with the plural "fruits of righteousness" in
Prov. 13:2 and also with the remark of Epictetus that "the
greatest fruit of righteousness" is "calm disinterest" (ἀταραξία).[32]
The various qualities of Gal. 5:22-23 are not listed as moral
"duties" (καθήκοντα) in the secular Hellenistic sense, but describe, first of all, something of the nature of the Christian's
new life in the Spirit. It is misleading, then, to say that Paul is
here seeking "to paint in words the portrait of the good man,"
"to set out the various ingredients in the recipe of goodness,"
or to specify the "quite definite adornments of the Christian
character," [33] if these phrases are allowed to suggest that he is
presenting an ideal toward the accomplishment of which the
Christian should aim. In the context of his thought as a whole
this "virtue" list has quite a different function.

Moreover, there is a "threefold rhythm" [34] discernible within
this list, three groups with three members each (love, joy, peace;
longsuffering, kindness, goodness; faithfulness, gentleness, self-
control) . Each triad manifests not only a greater or lesser degree
of rhetorical balance, but also a certain similarity of content. It
is hardly accidental that love heads the opening triad and thus
stands first in the whole list. The two terms which follow next,
"joy" and "peace," are frequently eschatological terms,[35] and
their close connection here with "love" seems to echo the thought
of vss. 5-6: life in the Spirit is a waiting in hope and in faith,

[32] Fragment 519, cited by Dibelius, *Der Brief des Jakobus* in *KEK*, "Ergän-
zungsheft," ed. H. Greeven (8th ed., 1957) , p. 20.
[33] William Barclay, *Flesh and Spirit: An Examination of Galatians 5:19-23*
(1962) , pp. 63, 102.
[34] Schlier, *Galater*, p. 256.
[35] Bultmann, *Theology*, I, 339.

and this faith manifests itself in love. The triad of "love, joy, peace" is thus not unrelated to that other, more famous, triad of "faith, hope, love" (I Cor. 13:13; I Thess. 1:3; 5:8; cf. Col. 1:4-5). Indeed, it is "love" which embraces and includes all the other "virtues" which follow so that, no less than I Cor. 13:4 ff. with which it is strikingly parallel, this list may be regarded as a description of the concrete ways in which love is expressed. While Gal. 5:22-23 bears certain superficial similarities to the traditional "virtue list," in fact it must be regarded as a genuinely Pauline creation.

The same is true of Phil. 4:8: "Finally, brethren, whatever is true, whatever is honorable, whatever is just, whatever is pure, whatever is lovely, whatever is gracious, if there is any excellence, if there is anything worthy of praise, think about these things" (RSV). On the one hand, this list is one of the most thoroughly Hellenistic passages in the Pauline Corpus, employing several ethical terms derived from the vocabulary of popular philosophy.[36] On the other hand, these terms do not stand in the service of a "character ethic," but, representing as they do a distillation of the highest ideals of the Hellenistic secular ethic, they must be read here in the light of Paul's exhortation to conform to the apostolic tradition (vs. 9).

Dibelius' comment that the imperative "consider these things," in vs. 8 indicates that Paul is here moving quite within the bounds of a rationalistic Greek ethic cannot be supported.[37] The passage from Marcus Aurelius (*Meditations* X. viii) which Dibelius cites as evidence really supports the contrary conclusion: the context in Paul is quite different from that in the ethics of popular philosophy. M. Aurelius appeals to man's nature as a rational creature (ὡς ὑπὸ φύσεως μόνον διοικουμένου, X. ii). There are, he says, certain characteristics (ὀνόματα) which man should assume: goodness, modesty, truth, etc., and the accompanying exhortation is "Take heed thou be not new-named" (πρόσεχε μήποτε μετονομάζῃ, X. viii). In contrast, Paul's appeal is not "to observe what thy nature as a living creature asks of thee," but to "stand in the Lord" (vs. 1) and "rejoice" in him

---

[36] See above, p. 46.
[37] *Thessalonicher*, p. 95.

(vs. 4). Moreover, while M. Aurelius refers to "these *few* characteristics" which define the virtuous life so completely that their loss might well commend suicide (X. viii), the effect of Paul's enumeration of the excellences in vs. 8 is to broaden the Christian's responsibilities, not to restrict them (ὅσα). The exhortation to "consider these things" is not, therefore, just an admonition to thoughtful contemplation. As the same imperative (λογίζεσθε) at Rom. 6:11 shows, it is an admonition to action; the excellences of Phil. 4:8 are to be made manifest in one's life, just as is the fact of one's death to sin and life to God in Christ Jesus (Rom. 6:11). The exhortation to "consider" in Phil. 4:8 is alternately expressed in the exhortation to "do" (πράσσετε) in the verse which follows.

d. The Pauline context

From just these few examples it is easy enough to see that the traditional ethical materials Paul uses have been set within an important new context. While the apostle does appeal to the "reason" and "understanding" of his readers,[38] he is not a philosopher-moralist addressing "secular" men, but an apostle bearing a gospel to men who have been baptized "into Christ." It is false to say that he exhorts his readers "to use their logical powers and recognize that a high ethic is the only possible conclusion that can be drawn from the premises of the Christian faith." [39] Paul's exhortations, unlike those of the secular traditions on which he admittedly draws, do not presume that the power of the good life is resident in man's "right reason," [40] but presume that it is given, rather, by what God has done for men in Christ. Hence, Paul does not exhort the Christian to live "according to nature" (κατὰ φύσιν),[41] but "according to the Spirit" (κατὰ πνεῦμα, Rom. 8:4 ff.). The apostle's exhortations not only

[38] L. H. Marshall, *The Challenge of New Testament Ethics* (1946), p. 315.
[39] *Ibid.*
[40] See the *Greek Anthology* (*LCL*) X, 109, 115; Menander Fragment 617; Epict. *Discourses* I. xxvi. 6-7; M. Aurel. *Meditations* III. vi. *a;* cf. IV. xxxvii. In Hellenistic Judaism this idea of man's "reason" was transformed into the notion of an "inspired Reason" (ὁ εὐσεβὴς λογισμός) which rules the passions. See IV Macc. 18:1-2.
[41] E.g., Epict. *Discourses* IV. v. 6.

take account of the Christian's present life "in the flesh" (ἐν σαρκί), but also of his life "in Christ" (ἐν Χριστῷ). Even the admonition to "test everything, hold fast to what is good" (I Thess. 5:21-22) presupposes that this testing is done by one who is committed to the doing of "God's will in Christ Jesus" (vs. 18).[42]

In summary, while Paul's concrete ethical teachings owe something in form and in content to commonly accredited traditions and ideas, these materials have, within the context of the apostle's letters, a significantly different function. The popular moralists of the day liked to think of their works as "storehouses" of helpful precepts and directives, to be drawn on as needed by those for whom they wrote.[43] The attempt to view Paul's exhortations in this way, as a "bag of answers to meet recurring problems and questions common to the members of different early Christian communities," [44] is not successful. There are few passages in the Pauline letters which cannot be related in some significant way to particular problems and needs the apostle is confronting. He is not self-consciously compiling miscellaneous bits and pieces of ethical wisdom.

Moreover, Paul bears a unique relationship to those he addresses. Although he sometimes uses typically parenetic forms of address ("my children" [τέκνα μου], Gal. 4:19; cf. I Cor. 4:14; II Cor. 6:13; Philemon 10; "babes" [νήπιοι] [ἐν Χριστῷ!] I Cor. 3:1; cf. I Thess. 2:7), more often he uses the distinctively Christian expressions "brethren" [ἀδελφοί] (Rom. 1:13; I Cor. 15:58; Phil. 3:1; 4:1; I Thess. 1:4) or "beloved" [ἀγαπητοί] (Rom. 12:19; I Cor. 10:14; 15:58; II Cor. 7:1; 12:19; Phil. 2:12; 4:1). He is more than an "advisor" or "wise counsellor" to those whom he writes. It is true that he calls himself their "father," which is a familiar appellation in parenesis; but Paul is "father" in a different sense. The metaphor does not just designate his superior

[42] In his essay on I Cor. 6:1 ff. ("Zum Problem der Ethik bei Paulus," *ZThK*, XLIX [1952]), Erich Dinkler makes a similar point (p. 200).

[43] E.g. (pseudo-?) Isocrates *To Demonicus* 44; Menander Fragment 714; Seneca *Epistulae morales* 94. 35. Cf. the idea of a moral "inheritance" in the *Test*. XII P., e.g. Ben. 10:4-5.

[44] D. G. Bradley, "The *Topos* as a Form in the Pauline Paraenesis," *JBL*, LXXII (1953), 246.

wisdom and experience, but is related to the fact that the congregations he addresses are of his own "begetting" (I Cor. 4:15);
they are of his apostolic founding. He writes as an apostle to
the churches of Christ, not as a private moral advisor recording
and commending collected ethical wisdom.

In both Greek and Hellenistic-Jewish parenesis the purpose
had been essentially pedagogical; the goal was education (παι-
δεία), defined as learning to adapt oneself to nature, to fulfill
the responsibilities (τὰ καθήκοντα) appropriate to one's own
characteristics (ὀνόματα) according to the guidance of right
reason or (in Hellenistic-Jewish parenesis) "Inspired Reason."
This goal is succinctly stated by Seneca: "The happy life consists in upright conduct; precepts guide one to upright conduct;
therefore precepts are sufficient for attaining the happy life"
(Epistulae morales 95. 4). Similarly, M. Aurelius insists that
maxims and precepts lead to the "salvation of life" (σωτηρία
βίου, Meditations XII. xxix) or "revivification" (ἀναβίωσις, VII.
ii). But in the Pauline letters the concrete ethical teachings are
assimilated to an evangelical, not a pedagogical, purpose and
context. It is hardly possibly that Paul would have defined the
purpose of his own ethical instruction in terms of Seneca's syllo-
gism about the sufficiency of moral precepts for attaining the
happy life.[45]

What, then, is the intended function of the Pauline exhortations? Certainly not to provide a full-fledged code of ethics or
even the major norms and principles of such, either for the
apostle's own day or for the future. No ethical system can be
extracted or extrapolated from Paul's admonitions. They are
appeals which presuppose that those addressed are, first, baptized
into Christ and belong to him, and second, faced with resolving
specific moral problems and conflicts in the world, though their
worldly existence be only temporary and conditional. Paul's
exhortations are not just his own personal "opinions" of what
the Christian should do; yet neither are they legalistic rules
designed either to interpret or in themselves to constitute some
new "Christian law." Sometimes they take the form of commands

[45] Against A. J. Gross, "The Development of Pauline Paraenesis on Civil
Obedience" (1947), p. 2.

which Paul, as an apostle, expects his congregations to obey. In many other instances they are appeals to the brethren to discover for themselves the practical daily implications of their new life in Christ. But in either case, Paul's intention is to emphasize the reality of that new life by insisting on the multiple and often varied concrete ways in which the gospel impinges on the believer's existence while still "in the flesh." [46]

3. THE VARIED MODES OF EXHORTATION

It is not adequate to restrict one's investigation of the Pauline exhortations to the specifically imperatival and concretely instructional passages in his letters. One of the essential points to notice is that the apostle's exhortations are expressed in a very wide variety of ways. Variety of exhortation is, to be sure, characteristic of parenesis in general, and most of the standard means of admonition are also to be found in Paul's letters. He employs not only direct imperative forms in both the second and third person, but also the imperatival infinitive (Phil. 3:16; Rom. 12:15), adjective (Rom. 12:10, 11), and participle (e.g. Rom. 12:9 ff.). There are also numerous instances of the hortatory subjunctive (Rom. 13:12, 13; 14:13, 19; II Cor. 7:1; Gal. 5:25-26; 6:9, 10; Phil. 3:15; I Thess. 5:6) and of verbs of entreaty: παρακαλῶ, παρακαλοῦμεν (I Cor. 4:16; 16:15; II Cor. 10:1; I Thess. 5:14; Philemon 10; with an infinitive construction, Rom. 12:1; 15:30; cf. 16:17; II Cor. 2:8; 6:1; Phil. 4:2 [twice]; I Thess. 4:10; with a ἵνα construction, I Cor. 1:10; I Thess. 4:1), δέομαι,

---

[46] Schrage has discussed in some detail the particularity and generality of the Pauline exhortations, as well as the extent to which they are intended to be binding on his congregations (*Die konkreten Einzelgebote*, Chaps. IV, V, VI). It should be observed that Schrage does not regard the concrete exhortations as in themselves "norms," but as having certain Christian norms (the "highest" of which is love) as their basis. Thus, he insists, the concrete exhortations are given a unity and consistency (Chap. VIII) and are genuinely (not "only") paradigmatic for Christian conduct (see p. 127). He argues persuasively that the Pauline exhortations are not just random and occasional. It should be pointed out, however, that they are nevertheless (with only a few exceptions) *ad hoc* exhortations, directed to particular situations and not *necessarily* intended for general application without modification.

δεόμεθα (II Cor. 5:20; 10:2; Gal. 4:12), ἐρωτῶ, ἐρωτῶμεν (Phil. 4:3; I Thess. 4:1; 5:12), θέλω, οὐ θέλω (I Cor. 7:7, 32; 10:20; 14:5; cf. Gal. 3:2 and numerous instances in which Paul says, "I want you to understand," e.g. I Cor. 11:3, or "I do not want you to be ignorant," e.g. I Cor. 10:1), ἐνορκίζω (I Thess. 5:27), and even λέγω (Rom. 12:3). The parenetic practice of asking questions which have a hortatory force is also apparent in the Pauline letters, especially the frequent query, "Do you not know?" (οὐκ οἴδατε or ἢ ἀγνοεῖτε) followed by reference to something the apostle would like his readers to espouse or repudiate (e.g. Rom. 6:3; I Cor. 6:3, 16; 9:24).

Paul, however, goes beyond these standard forms of exhortation. Not only his questions introduced by the parenetic οὐκ οἴδατε, but many others as well have an essentially imperative objective. This is obvious in the cases where the apostle answers his own question with a firm "By no means!" (μὴ γένοιτο! Rom. 6:2, 15), but it is also clear where he allows the question to stand by itself. "How can we who died to sin still live in it?" he asks (Rom. 6:2 RSV), and the force of the question is to affirm that the Christian must not continue in sin. Later in Romans he asks, "Who are you to judge the servant of another?" (14:4), clearly an exhortation to judge no man. The question "What do you have that you have not received?" (I Cor. 4:7) is, interpreted in its context, an exhortation to stand humbly before God and in the service of the brethren. The question "Do you not have houses in which to eat and drink?" (I Cor. 11:22a) exhorts the disorderly and thoughtless Corinthians to keep the Lord's supper what it ought to be. And the successive questions in II Cor. 6:14-15 have the effect of admonishing the readers to dissociate themselves from all forms of iniquity.[47]

The Pauline exhortations are expressed in even subtler ways. When the apostle refers to the obedience of other churches, he often, as I Cor. 16:1 shows, means for his present readers to

[47] The use of questions with imperative force is characteristic of the diatribe form. See Bornkamm, "Faith and Reason in Paul": "Paul's style is not that of revelational speech. It is that of the diatribe, with its pointed statements, questions and rejoinders, a speech that treats the hearers as partners in a dialogue and never loses sight of them for a minute" (pp. 97-98).

follow the example (Rom. 15:26-27; II Cor. 8:1 ff.). He expresses his "fear" about how his congregation at Corinth is behaving (II Cor. 11:3; 12:20 ff.), and that is already in itself a warning admonition to stand firm. The mention of God's judgment, even without the actual employment of imperative forms, has the same effect (Rom. 2:2 ff.; 14:10 ff.; I Cor. 3:10 ff.). Another common form of exhortation is to commend the former obedience of the readers in order to encourage them to live up to their own past performance. "As you have always obeyed, so now," he writes to the Philippians (2:12) and attempts to rally the Thessalonians to continuing steadfastness by reference to the favorable report Timothy has brought about them (I, 3:6 ff.). A similar appeal is present in Gal. 4:12b ff.

Related to the commendation of his readers' past performance is Paul's expression of his present confidence in them. Such expressions regularly have a hortatory force, as at Gal. 5:10, "I am confident about you in the Lord, that no one will take a view other than mine." When he tells the Corinthians it is superfluous for him to write them about an "offering for the saints," for he has boasted to others of their readiness to give (II, 9:1 ff.), this is the strongest kind of admonition to do just that. So is his remark to Philemon, that he is "confident" of that brother's obedience and knows he will do even "more" than Paul has explicitly requested (Philemon 21). A special form of this mode of exhortation is the formal section of "thanksgiving" with which most of the letters open. Schubert quite correctly notes that "all Pauline thanksgivings have either explicitly or implicitly paraenetic function." [48] The most impressive example of this is the letter to Philemon where the apostle's commendation, in the thanksgiving section (vss. 4 ff.), of Philemon's love (ἀγάπη, vss. 5, 7) and "partnership of faith" (κοινωνία τῆς πίστεως, vs. 6) corresponds to his later appeal to Philemon "on the basis of love" (διὰ τὴν ἀγάπην, vs. 9) and as a "partner" (κοινωνός, vs. 17). Moreover, the reference in the thanksgiving to the "hearts" (σπλάγχνα, vs. 7) of the saints which Philemon has already refreshed is certainly not unrelated to the subsequent request

[48] *Form and Function of the Pauline Thanksgivings,* p. 89.

that Paul's own "heart" (σπλάγχνα, vs. 20) be refreshed; and
Paul had already indicated that his heart was Onesimus, the
slave on whose behalf the whole letter is written (vs. 12). Thus
the indicative statements in the opening verses of Philemon
point forward to the imperatives which are expressed further
on, giving the whole thanksgiving section a hortatory function.[49]

Even the Pauline benediction forms have imperatival force,
as at Rom. 15:5-6 where the prayer that God may grant the
readers to live in harmony with one another and in accord with
Christ Jesus is no less an admonition to them to do so. Similarly,
the benedictions at I Thess. 3:11 ff. and 5:23 recapitulate and
reinforce the themes of the exhortations which precede them.
The apostle is also exhorting, though indirectly, when he tells
the Corinthians that he prays to God that they shall do right
and no wrong (II, 13:7 ff.; cf. similar "hortatory prayers" in
Phil. 1:9-11 and Philemon 6). Another form of exhortation is
the use of the first person singular pronoun. When Paul says,
"Therefore, if food is a cause of my brother's falling, I will
never eat meat, lest I cause my brother to fall" (I Cor. 8:13
RSV), he thereby admonishes his readers to adopt this as a practice in their own dealings with the brethren. The first person
pronouns in I Cor. 13:1 ff., 11-12, and 14:19 are likewise hortatory in effect.[50]

Paul sometimes admonishes by telling or referring to a story,
what may thus be described as a "hortatory narrative." Biblical
narratives are readily at hand, and Paul sometimes uses them in
this way—for example, the appeal to the story of Abraham in
Romans 4 and Galatians 3. The hortatory use of the Abraham
narrative is especially clear in Romans 4 where it is specifically
applied to the readers (vss. 23 ff.). The allegorization of the
patriarch's two wives (Gal. 4:22 ff.) is another instance, for even
without the citation of the actual scriptural imperative in vs. 30
the narrative itself, read in the context of Galatians 4–5, already
contains impressive imperatival force. The typological use of the
Old Testament in I Cor. 10:1 ff. should perhaps also be classified
as an instance of the "hortatory narrative."

---

[49] Knox makes some similar observations, *IntB*, XI (1955), 563-64.
[50] So also H. Thyen, *Der Stil der jüdisch-hellenistischen Homilie*, pp. 104-5.

The apostle is also able to employ autobiographical narratives imperatively. The clearest instance of this is the report of his meeting with Cephas in Antioch (Gal. 2:11-14). Paul relates how Cephas and "even" Barnabas submitted to the pressures of the "circumcision party," separating themselves from some of the Antioch brethren and thus deserting "the truth of the gospel" (vss. 12-14). Since it is the actual or threatened perversion of the gospel which has prompted Paul to write the Galatians (1:6-9), it is clear that he is using Cephas and Barnabas as illustrations of those who, knowing the truth of the gospel, are yet coerced into yielding on fundamental points and thus perverting the whole. Paul is not just reciting a story here. He is using the Antioch incident to exhort his readers, represented in the persons of Cephas and Barnabas, to remain faithful to the gospel they have received. The words addressed to "Cephas" in 2:14b are in fact uttered for the benefit of Paul's opponents: "If you, being a Jew, nonetheless live like a Gentile, how can you compel the Gentiles to live like Jews?" This question— which, like the narrative as a whole, has a hortatory function— is the one Paul wishes to put to his readers who, acknowledging themselves to be freed from the law, betray their own convictions by forcing those who never were in bondage to it to undergo the rite of circumcision.

Satire, which often makes use of caricature and ridicule, has by its very nature an imperatival effect. To whatever precise literary category one assigns I Cor. 4:8-13, it exhibits at least some of the traits of satire, and its intention is clearly to exhort the Corinthians to divest themselves of spiritual arrogance and complacency. Their pretentious religious claims make even the apostles look like a sorry lot. The Corinthians act like kings, affecting great wisdom, strength, and honor, but the apostles, in contrast, of whom the Corinthians themselves are so eager to boast (3:3 ff., 21), must appear foolish, weak, disreputable, the lowest of the low. The style in this passage is close to what Bultmann has called the "ironic imperative," [51] and the hortatory objective is manifest. This is explicitly confirmed by Paul

[51] *Der Stil der paulinischen Predigt und die kynisch-stoische Diatribe*, pp. 32-33.

in vs. 14: "I do not write these things to shame, but to admonish you as my beloved children."

Finally, and of greatest importance, is the apostle's use of indicative statements in order to exhort. His indicatives so frequently have imperatival force that they must be regarded as one of Paul's primary means of exhortation. For example, in Gal. 4:31 he concludes his allegorization of Abraham's two wives with the simple affirmative statement, "So, brethren, we are not children of the slave but of the free woman" (RSV). The introductory particle (διό) and address (ἀδελφοί) give this verse two of the stylistic characteristics of a closing hortatory summary, and yet no hortatory subjunctive or imperative form occur. None is needed. Paul's meaning is clear. His readers are being admonished to conduct their lives in keeping with their status as children of the free woman (cf. 5:1). The same is true of the affirmations in Gal. 3:25-29: "We are no longer under a custodian; for in Christ Jesus you are all sons of God, through faith" (Gal. 3:25b-26 RSV); "you . . . have put on Christ . . . are all one in Christ Jesus" (Gal. 3:27-28 RSV); "heirs according to promise" (Gal. 3:29 RSV); and 4:1-9: "You are no longer a slave but a son, and if a son then an heir" (4:7 RSV). Sometimes indicative statements like these are used as protases of conditional sentences and followed by apodoses which do have an actual imperatival form (e.g Gal. 5:25: "Since [εἰ] we live by the Spirit, let us also walk by the Spirit"). But even where the indicative is not formally converted into an imperative, it often has a hortatory effect.

The Pauline letters are replete with examples of the "imperatival indicative." Rom. 5:1 ff. is a classic instance. Even though it is probably best to read the indicative ἔχομεν ("we have") and not the hortatory subjunctive ἔχωμεν ("let us have") in vs. 1,[52] the whole series of affirmations about rejoicing, endurance, character, and hope has an admonitory dimension, more subtle but hardly less effective than the formal imperatives about rejoicing, patience, love, and hope in chap. 12. Similarly, the hortatory appeal of Romans 6 does not just begin in vs. 11, but is

[52] See Otto Michel, *Der Brief an die Römer* in *KEK* (13th ed., 1966), p. 130, n. 2.

already clearly present in the indicative statement of vs. 4 ("We were buried therefore with him by baptism into death, so that as Christ was raised from the dead by the glory of the Father, we too might walk in newness of life," RSV). Equally obvious is the imperatival force of Rom. 7:4 where the hortatory introduction, "So then, my brethren," is followed by an indicative: "You have died to the law through the body of Christ, so that you may belong to another, to him who has been raised from the dead in order that we may bear fruit for God" (RSV) and the hortatory function of the affirmation at I Thess. 4:7: "God has not called us for uncleanness, but in holiness" (RSV). Among the other instances Rom. 13:10; 14:8; I Cor. 2:14 ff.; 6:11; 12:27; and II Cor. 6:16 are particularly noteworthy.

Although still but a sampling, the evidence assembled here is sufficient to demonstrate the varied modes of exhortation Paul employs. This suggests, in turn, that a study of his exhortations must not be confined to those passages which make use of such obvious grammatical forms as imperatives, hortatory subjunctives, and verbs of entreaty. In many subtler and less direct ways the apostle urges his congregations to action. If this elementary conclusion is valid, then it follows that an interpretation of Paul's ethic dare not restrict itself to the so-called "ethical sections" of his letters, just because the obvious forms of exhortation are clustered there.

4. THE PROBLEM OF "KERYGMA" AND "DIDACHE"

a. The letter to the Romans

The evidence in Paul's letters clearly demands a broadened and flexible conception of what "exhortation" is and involves. Consequently, the usual division of the letters into "theological" and "ethical" parts and the tendency to make a similar distinction within Paul's preaching as a whole are rendered highly questionable.[53] In fact, an examination of the letters which does

---

[53] Scholars who presume such distinctions are numerous. Already in the

not prejudice the issue by first presupposing a twofold division along these lines discloses the impossibility of neatly distinguishing between dogmatic and moral themes. Romans is a good test case because it has been cited most of all as typical of Paul's separate handling of theology and ethics. "Nowhere else," writes Knox, "not even in Galatians and Colossians, is the transition from doctrine to exhortation so definite and, one might almost say, so abrupt as here." [54] But is this really so?

It must be acknowledged that the *explicit* exhortations of Romans are concentrated in chaps. 12–15; for example thirty-one of the forty-two imperative forms of the letter are in this section,[55] and there are also examples of imperatival infinitives, adjectives, and participles, as well as of the hortatory subjunctive. These chapters also exhibit other parenetic features: the use of traditional sayings and proverbs, a tendency for ethical topics to be rather loosely strung together, and, overall, a fairly general applicability. Yet Bradley goes too far when he literally "dissects" these chapters into thirteen unconnected *topoi* on assorted subjects, and then further divides chap. 14 into six sub-*topoi*.[56] And although Lietzmann, for example, is not able to find any "principle of arrangement" for the exhortations in these

---

nineteenth century Weizsäcker's discussion of the "ethical motives" in Paul stood completely apart from his exposition of Pauline "theology" (*The Apostolic Age of the Christian Church*, trans. James Millar [2 vols., 1894; 1st German ed., 1886]). Later, Martin Dibelius stressed the independence of the "parenetic sections" of the letters (e.g. *From Tradition to Gospel*, pp. 238-39; *Jakobus*, p. 19; but see already Bultmann, *Der Stil der paulinischen Predigt*, pp. 99-100), and Dodd popularized a relatively inflexible distinction between the apostle's "kerygma" and "didache" (e.g. *The Apostolic Preaching and Its Developments* [new ed., 1944], pp. 7 ff.).

[54] *IntB*, IX (1954), 578-79. See also P. Wernle, *Der Christ und die Sünde bei Paulus* (1897), 113: "The attached ethic in chaps. 12-13 is completely removed from the striking accent of Rom. 8"; and Davies, "Ethics in the New Testament," *IntDB*, E-J, p. 175: "Most of the letters reveal a twofold structure: a first part, dealing with 'doctrine,' is followed by a second, dealing with ethics. Romans is typical."

[55] These figures exclude chap. 16 but include the eight imperative forms contained in Paul's citations from the LXX. Of those eight imperatives, six are in chaps. 12-15.

[56] "The Origins of the Hortatory Materials in the Letters of Paul," pp. 141 ff.

chapters,[57] neither are they to be judged as a typical parenetic miscellany connected only by accidental "catchwords."

Catchwords are to be found in this section, and the verb διώκειν which appears twice in 12:13-14 is a notable instance. In vs. 13 it is used in the admonition to "*practice* hospitality" (RSV; τὴν φιλοξενίαν διώκοντες), but in the following verse it is quite differently employed: "Bless those who *persecute* you" (RSV; εὐλογεῖτε τοὺς διώκοντας). Bradley concludes that "we have a clear example of the use of a *Stichwort,* i.e. two words with a similar sound linking two sentences which have no logical connection" and thus also two separate parenetic topics. This assumes that Paul has here associated two unrelated exhortations simply because, in the tradition from which he has "drawn" them, they contained phonetically similar words. But the exhortations in this section are not so conglomerate, nor their connection so artificial as this view suggests. Vss. 3-8 discuss the varied "gifts" bestowed by God on the Christian community for the common good, to be used for mutual upbuilding. Thus, love is the principle which governs them all, and Paul's exhortations to love (vss. 9-14) do not, as Bradley claims, constitute a new topic, but simply extend what has already been said about the relationship of Christians within the congregation. The sequence of thought is exactly the same as in I Cor. 12-13 and is thoroughly Pauline.

Nor are the admonitions in vss. 14-21 completely miscellaneous and unrelated to what has gone before. Here the love-commandment is further extended and radicalized. It applies, says Paul, not only within the church but also in the Christian's dealings with outsiders, even his enemies. Viewed in this way, the catchword of vss. 13-14 (διώκοντες, διώκοντας) is not just an artificial link between two separate topics, but constitutes a play on words which illuminates the writer's thought. Moffatt tries to capture this verbal trick in an English paraphrase: "Make a practice of hospitality. Bless those who make a practice of persecuting you." Put another way, the apostle emphasizes that love has responsibilities also for those who "pursue" the "pursuers of love." Simi-

[57] *An die Römer* in *HNT* (3rd. ed., 1928), p. 107.

lar lines of connection between the various exhortations may be discerned in chap. 13 and especially in chaps 14–15, where, indeed, it is possible that Paul is addressing some specific problems in Rome.[58]

Even if Romans 12–15 can be shown to be less a typical "parenesis" than is often argued, the more important question is whether the objective of these latter chapters is significantly different from the objective of those which precede. In order to demonstrate that this is not the case and that Romans has, almost from the beginning, a hortatory aspect of which chaps. 12–15 are only, so to speak, the denouement, several crucial passages from earlier chapters must be examined. But first it is necessary to comment on the important transitional verses, 12: 1-2.

In 12:1-2 Paul beseeches his readers to give themselves up, wholly and entirely, to God; this is their true "spiritual worship" (RSV). Bultmann's exposition of Paul's concept of σῶμα ("body" or "self") [59] helps to show that the appeal of the present verse is for nothing less than the whole person, for every dimension and capacity of his being. And what Paul means by "presenting" (παριστάναι) one's self to God is at least partly clarified in vs. 2 (the introductory καὶ has an epexegetical function): avoiding conformity to this age (τῷ αἰῶνι τούτῳ), being transformed (further described as the "renewal" of one's whole character, ἀνακαινώσει τοῦ νοός), and committing one's self to the discovery and doing of God's will (εἰς τὸ δοκιμάζειν τί τὸ θέλημα τοῦ θεοῦ).

The question is frequently raised whether the introductory οὖν ("therefore") of vs. 1 is only transitional and thus points to no important logical or inner connection between what precedes and what follows it,[60] or whether it refers "to the result of the whole preceding argument."[61] Also in dispute is the

[58] The example of chap. 12 must suffice here, but the succeeding chaps. are also discussed in my dissertation, "Paul's Exhortations in the Context of His Letters and Thought," pp. 232 ff.

[59] *Theology*, I, 192 ff. See also C. E. B. Cranfield, *A Commentary on Romans 12–13* ("SJTh Occasional Papers," No. 12), 1965, p. 8.

[60] So Knox, *IntB*, IX, 579.

[61] So Sanday and Headlam, *A Critical and Exegetical Commentary on*

significance of the fact that Paul appeals διὰ τῶν οἰκτιρμῶν τοῦ
θεοῦ. Has the διά here a causal force ("on the basis of God's
mercies") or an instrumental force ("through God's mercies")?
Does the reference to "mercies" link the present verses to all
the preceding chapters in which the apostle has spoken of such
"mercies of God" as grace, resurrection, forgiveness, the Spirit,
election, and faith? [62] Or does it refer more specifically to chaps.
9–11 where emphasis has been laid upon God's mercy to the
disobedient (e.g. 11:3 ff.)? [63] This phrase, unfortunately, offers
as little help in defining the relationship of chaps. 1–11 and 12–15
as the introductory οὖν. Not only is Paul's word for "mercy"
different in chaps. 9–11 (ἔλεος, ἐλεεῖν), but the phrase in 12:1
reflects a familiar biblical description of God (cf. II Cor. 1:3;
James 5:11, and many passages in the LXX [64]). Moreover, considerations of Hellenistic Greek usage and a comparison of the
Pauline appeals in Rom. 12:3; 15:30; I Cor. 1:10; II Cor. 10:1,
each supported by a διά-phrase, suggest that in all of these, Rom.
12:1 included, the preposition is used instrumentally. It thus
expresses Paul's consciousness of being the means by which God
himself exhorts the believers; the apostles are "ambassadors for
Christ, God making his appeal through us [παρακαλοῦντος δι'
ἡμῶν]" (II Cor. 5:20; cf. I Thess. 4:1).[65] And when the causal
interpretation of διὰ τῶν οἰκτιρμῶν τοῦ θεοῦ in Rom. 12:1 is
abandoned, the possibility of finding therein a substantive link
with chaps. 1–11 disappears.

Yet there are other ways in which the appeal at 12:1-2 does

Romans, p. 351. Cf. C. K. Barrett, *A Commentary on the Epistle to the
Romans* in *HNTC* (1957), p. 230, and Cranfield, *A Commentary on Romans
12-13,* pp. 4-5. In this case Rom. 12:1 would provide a further example of
what Nauck calls the "οὖν-paraeneticum" ("Das οὖν-paräneticum," *ZNW,*
XLIX [1958], 134-35), binding together a systematic-theological discussion
with a concluding ethical exhortation.

[62] Karl Barth, *The Epistle to the Romans,* trans. from the 6th German ed.
by Edwyn C. Hoskyns (1933), p. 427.

[63] Michel, *Römer,* p. 291; Barrett, *A Commentary on the Epistle to the
Romans,* p. 230; Sanday and Headlam, *A Critical and Exegetical Commentary
on Romans,* p. 352.

[64] See Bultmann, *ThW,* V, 161-62.

[65] See Heinrich Schlier, "Vom Wesen der apostolischen Ermahnung, nach
Römerbrief 12:1-2," *Die Zeit der Kirche* (2nd ed., 1958), p. 80.

significantly recapitulate and focus earlier motifs in Romans. The "theme" of this letter is sounded in 1:16-17: the gospel, for those who receive it through faith, reveals the righteousness of God and is the power of God for salvation. In 1:18-3:20 Paul shows that the revelation of God's righteousness is at the same time the unveiling of his wrath, for the divine righteousness also discloses itself as judgment against sin, under whose power man apart from God is held captive. In 1:18 ff., with the Gentiles particularly in mind, the apostle is anxious to show that knowing God (vs. 21) does not necessarily mean that one honors him as God or gives thanks to him. Knowledge by itself establishes no claim upon God, and to glorify and give thanks to him as God is the abdication of all personal claims upon him. God's righteousness demands the surrender of all those human pretensions and "claims" which constitute, in Paul's view, man's bondage to sin. The consequences of sin are vividly presented in vss. 24 ff. God "gives up" the sinners to the dishonoring (ἀτιμά-ζειν) of their bodies (σώματα, vs. 24); though they seek to be wise (σοφοί), they become fools (vs. 22); their "knowledge" becomes a lie, and they end up worshiping (σεβάζεσθαι) and serving (λατρεύειν) the creature rather than the creator (vs. 25). They are given up to a reprobate mind (ἀδόκιμος νοῦς) and to "improper conduct" (ποιεῖν τὰ μὴ καθήκοντα, vs. 28).

The correspondence in vocabulary and concern between Romans 1 and 12 is striking. In 12:1-2 Paul is calling the brethren to a new life exactly opposite that which he has previously described. They are to "present" their σώματα to God, not "dishonor" them; they are no longer to serve (λατρεύειν) the creature, but are to offer "spiritual worship" (λογικὴ λατρεία) to God. The ἀδόκιμος νοῦς has been transformed; hence Paul in 12:2 can speak of the ἀνακαίνωσις τοῦ νοός. And "improper conduct" (ποιεῖν τὰ μὴ καθήκοντα) must now yield before the exhortation to "find out what God's will is" (δοκιμάζειν τί τὸ θέλημα τοῦ θεοῦ) and do it. Rom. 12:1-2 is but the restatement, now to be sure, in an explicitly hortatory mode and context, of the theme which had already been emphasized in 1:16-17. True knowledge of God is at the same time man's recognition of his own creatureliness and "his situation of being one to whom God has laid claim." [66] The revealing of God's righteousness is both the revealing of who God is and the revealing of who man, put right and claimed by God, therefore is. In chap. 1 Paul illustrates the way in which the ἀδόκιμος νοῦς leads to disobedience; in chap. 12 he suggests the way in which the ἀνακαίνωσις τοῦ νοός gives the capacity for finding out God's will to do it. That this transformation can take place is due to the gospel, God's power for salvation.

The appeal of 12:1-2 is also related to what Paul has said about the Jews in 2:17 ff. There the "Jew" is defined as one who relies on the law, boasts in God, knows his will, and therefore certifies what is excellent (vss. 17-18). All this is possible because the Jew, unlike the Gentile, is "instructed by the law." Relying upon this, he is enabled to know God's will, to be confident in his understanding of what is required of him, and thus to boast in God. For the Jew the law is in fact "the embodiment of knowledge and truth" (vs. 20 RSV). But repose in the law and prideful confidence that one somehow possesses the full knowledge of what God demands are, for Paul, as serious an idolatry as any other. As he will show in chaps. 3 and 7, especially, there is no security in the law, for it is impotent to bring about the obedience it requires, and thus ultimately becomes man's accuser, not his redeemer (e.g. 7:7 ff.). In contrast to the Jew who "knows God's will" because he has the law (which then becomes his real boast), Paul beseeches his readers to make their "boast" in God through the Lord Jesus Christ (5:11); or, as he exhorts in chap. 12: "Present yourselves to God as a living sacrifice." This no longer allows reliance on the written code; no longer does one "know surely" (δοκιμάζειν, 2:18) what is required. Now, in Christ, he must commit himself to "seeking it out" (δοκιμάζειν, 12:2). [67] In Paul's view the Jew's obedience is not radical enough.

---

[66] Bultmann, *Theology*, I, 228-29.

[67] Knox (*IntB*, IX, 582) believes that δοκιμάζειν . . . τί τὸ θέλημα τοῦ θεοῦ in 12:2 should be translated, "to *know surely*" or "to *have trustworthy knowledge* of the will of God." If so, it would correspond to the use of δοκιμάζειν in 2:18 where it is parallel to the remark that the Jew has a secure knowledge of God's will because he is "instructed by the law." But applied to Christians (Rom. 12:2; Phil. 1:10), the verb has a slightly—though significantly—different meaning. This is apparent in Phil. 1:10 where

He places himself at the disposal of the law, but the new man in Christ must place himself, repeatedly, at the disposal of God, whose claims are broader and deeper than any prescribed code of requirements.

Of special significance are the relationships between chap. 6 and the appeal of 12:1-2. As early as 3:8 Paul had acknowledged the possibility of a libertinistic misinterpretation of his gospel of grace ("Why not do evil that good may come?" RSV), and now in chap. 6 ("Are we to continue in sin that grace may abound?" vs. 1 RSV) he attempts to respond. He reiterates the proposition that the Christian is "under grace" and no longer "under law" (vs. 14), but emphasizes that freedom from the law also means freedom from the power of sin (vss. 6 ff.) and freedom for obedience (vss. 16 ff.). In developing this theme special use is made of the concept of "presentation," the verb (παρι-στάναι) occurring five times in this chapter (vss. 13 [twice], 16, 19 [twice]). The Christian is called upon to present himself to God for obedience, righteousness, and sanctification. The metaphor of Rom. 7:1-6 makes the same point. Freedom from the old (one's former husband, the law concerning monogamy) involves the responsibility to effect a new relationship, to "belong to another," Jesus Christ (7:4 ff.). This metaphor is used again by Paul when reminding the Corinthians that he had "betrothed" them to Christ, to "present" them to Christ (παραστῆσαι τῷ Χριστῷ) as a pure bride is presented to her one true husband (II, 11:2).

When the Pauline exhortations of Romans 12–15 are introduced by the solemn appeal to "present [παραστῆσαι] your whole

---

δοκιμάζειν is used with τὰ διαφέροντα ("the excellent things") as in Rom. 2:18. For the Christian, the ability to know these excellent things is not dependent upon instruction in the law (Rom. 2:18), but upon abounding in love with knowledge and all discernment (αἴσθησις, Phil. 1:9). Nor is there any appeal to the law in Rom. 12:1-2. Paul refuses to define the law and God's will as coextensive entities or to think that his will has been once and for all revealed. It is continually being revealed to the man in Christ, and the Christian's responsibility is to be ever open to God's command addressing him. This openness to God's will requires the placing of one's whole being, every capacity for learning, understanding, and doing, at the disposal of God. In the context of Paul's thought, Goodspeed's translation of δοκιμάζειν in 12:2 is the most satisfactory: to "find out."

beings as a living sacrifice, holy and acceptable to God, your spiritual worship," the appeals made already in chap. 6 are simply being recapitulated and reemphasized. Moreover, chap. 6 itself is an integral part of the whole "doctrinal" argument of Romans 1–8 (11). God's righteousness, revealed in the event of Christ's coming, death, and resurrection, made real for the Christian in the event of his baptism into Christ, is also revealed in the claim God makes for the believer's obedience. This obedience is expressed as man places himself at God's disposal, "presents" himself for service. The exhortation of Rom. 12:1-2 and the specific appeals which are thus introduced summarize and focus the whole preceding argument. The first verses of chap. 12 offer a fresh statement, now in the imperative mood, of what it means to receive by faith the revealing of God's righteousness (1:16-17). Romans 12–15 is not, therefore, just an appendix on Christian morals. These exhortations not only presuppose the "theological" assertions of chaps. 1–11, but supply a further and needed explication of that one gospel (God's power for salvation) which both "theology" and "ethics" seek to unfold.[68]

b. "Kerygma," "didache," and "paraclesis"

An understanding of the way Paul has employed parenetic materials, of the extent to which they have been adapted to serve his apostolic objectives, of the variety of ways in which his exhortations are expressed, and of the close relationships between the so-called "theological" and "ethical" sections of his letters (illustrated here by even the "difficult" case of Romans) shows the impossibility of making tidy distinctions between "kerygmatic" and "didactic" themes in his preaching. This is further confirmed by noting the ways in which Paul himself uses the two terms κήρυγμα ("preaching") and διδαχή ("teaching"), the way in which he describes the functions of his fellow workers and his use of the word παράκλησις (*paraclesis* ["exhortation"]).[69]

---

[68] See also Paul Althaus, *Der Brief an die Römer* in *NTD*, 6 (7th ed., 1953), p. 111.

[69] The following is adapted from my article, "*Kerygma* and *Didache* Reconsidered," *Perkins School of Theology Journal*, XIV (1961), 31 ff.

First, in the apostle's vocabulary κήρυγμα ("preaching") and
εὐαγγέλιον ("gospel") are closely identified. Thus, Rom. 1:16-17,
which speaks of the "gospel" bringing salvation to those who
believe, has a parallel in I Cor. 1:21, where Paul says it is
"preaching" which saves those who believe. And just as in Rom.
1:17 he speaks of the "gospel" as "the power of God," so does he
in I Cor. 2:4-5 speak of "preaching" as "the power of God."

The meaning of both terms is seen in a third, virtually synonymous with the first two, "word of God" (λόγος τοῦ θεοῦ), which
in Paul's letters is never a description of scripture per se. In I
Cor. 2:4 he couples λόγος and κήρυγμα, and then describes both
as "the power of God." This conception of God's word as
"power" owes a great deal to the Old Testament. Second Isaiah,
for example, speaks of God's word as being like the rain and
snow which come down to water the earth; it actually accomplishes what God purposes and prospers in the thing for which
he has sent it (55:10-11). Just so Paul can speak of God's word
which is *"at work* among you believers" (I Thess. 2:13) and
which does not "fail" (Rom. 9:6). The apostle does not conceive
of the word of God, the gospel, or the *kerygma* as a series of
theological propositions or religious truths. These terms designate the *event* of preaching and God's coming to men in the
preached word, not the verbal substance of that preaching.

It is likewise misleading to use the term *didache* (διδαχή) as
a designation for moral instruction as contrasted with theological
proclamation. The term in itself means only "that which is
taught," and this may be theological doctrine as well as moral
instruction.[70] Two of the four occurrences of the noun in Paul's
letters are suspect, on other grounds, of being non-Pauline, redac-
tional additions (Rom. 6:17; 16:17).[71] The two remaining occurrences are in I Cor. 14:6, 26 where, along with revelations, knowl-

---

[70] Even Dodd acknowledges this when he observes that sometimes,
"especially in the Johannine writings, [*didache*] includes the exposition of
theological doctrine" (*The Apostolic Preaching*, p. 7).

[71] For the view that the whole of Romans 16 is by a later hand see Knox's
introduction to the letter in *IntB*, IX, 365 ff. Bultmann holds Rom. 6:17
to be a non-Pauline interpolation ("Glossen im Römerbrief," *ThLZ*, LXXII
(1947), col. 202). For additional comments on these passages see below,
pp. 196 ff.

edge, prophecies, hymns, speaking in tongues, and interpretations, "teaching" is listed as one part of the community's worship. In these lists διδαχή is probably used to describe the exposition of scripture, thus, in a sense, "preaching." These passages, then, do not support the attempt to define kerygma and didache as, respectively, the theological and ethical aspects of Paul's ministry.

Nor, secondly, is such a distinction supported by the passages in which Paul describes the ministry of his fellow workers. In I Cor. 4:17 he refers to his sending of Timothy to Corinth to "remind" the Christians of Paul's "ways in Christ" as they are taught "everywhere in every church." Timothy's mission is "didactic" in Dodd's sense: to issue the moral instruction and exhortation of which the Corinthians are in need (vs. 14). Consistent with this description of Timothy's didactic function is the remark in Phil. 2:20 that he will soon be sent to the Philippian congregation to exercise responsibility for certain unspecified "things" among them; and also the words to the Thessalonians: "We sent Timothy . . . to establish you in your faith and to exhort you" (I, 3:2 RSV).

This much might suggest that Paul conceives of his own ministry as kerygmatic (preaching the gospel to those outside the church) but of Timothy's ministry as didactic (the instruction and exhortation of those within the church). But such a distinction does not hold even here. For one thing, it must be noticed that Paul writes of his own teaching "everywhere in every church" (I Cor. 4:17), a fact for which the mere existence of any one of Paul's letters would be sufficient evidence. Moreover, in each of the other passages there is reference to Timothy's serving in and for the *gospel* (εὐαγγέλιον) which, as already ncted, is but an alternate expression for kerygma. "Timothy's value you know, how as a son with a father he has served with me for the sake of the gospel," he writes the Philippians (2:22); and in I Thess. 3:2 he refers to Timothy as a "brother" and "a fellow worker for God in the gospel of Christ." It is perfectly consistent, then, for Paul to declare that Timothy is "doing the Lord's work *just as I am*" (I Cor. 16:10), and in another letter to Corinth (II, 1:19) to refer to the work of himself, Timothy, and Silvanus under the one comprehensive slogan, *"preaching the Son of God, Jesus Christ."*

The untenability of a strict distinction between kerygma and didache is further demonstrated by Paul's use of the noun παρά-κλησις and its verb παρακαλεῖν. Dodd, for example, assumes that *paraclesis* is a synonym for didache and designates "moral instruction." [72] While it is true that often the best translation for the word is "exhortation," it may also mean "comfort" or "encouragement." Thus, Phil. 2:1 is most appropriately rendered, "If there is any *encouragement* in Christ" (RSV). As this passage shows, the "encouragement" which is in Christ is moral encouragement, namely, the exhortation to "have this mind among yourselves, which you have in Christ Jesus" (vs. 5 RSV). The word παράκλησις itself embraces the twin aspects of Paul's preaching: the gift of God's love in Christ and the consequent demand of God upon men. [73]

This is further documented in I Thessalonians. Paul refers to his prior visit in Thessalonica when, despite great opposition, he had had the courage "to declare . . . the gospel of God" (2:2 RSV). It is clear from the context that Paul and his fellow workers have been attacked and that the apostle seeks to defend the purity of their motives in preaching the gospel. He continues: "For our appeal is not motivated by envy or uncleanness, nor is it made with guile; but just as we have been certified by God to be entrusted with the gospel, so we speak, not to please men but God, who tests our hearts" (vss. 3-4). Here the terms "gospel" (εὐαγγέλιον, vss. 2, 4) and "appeal" (παράκλησις, vs. 3) are parallel. For the apostle, "exhortation" and "gospel" can be used interchangeably, so closely are they identified in his own mind.

But does there not remain some validity to the kerygma-didache distinction insofar as it perceives a difference between the church's "missionary preaching" (kerygma) and its ethical instruction to those already baptized (didache)? This distinction, also, is contradicted by the evidence of Paul's letters. For in-

---

[72] *The Apostolic Preaching*, p. 8.
[73] See Schrage, *Die konkreten Einzelgebote*, pp. 182-83, and especially Schlier, "Vom Wesen der apostolischen Ermahnung," pp. 76 ff.

stance, the whole discussion of apostolic "salaries" in I Corinthians 9 (especially vss. 12 ff.) has no meaning unless this
preaching of the gospel (vss. 16, 18) is to organized Christian
congregations. Moreover, it is to an *existing Christian church*
that Paul writes, "I am eager to preach the gospel to you also"
(Rom. 1:15 RSV). This preaching of the gospel, as Rom. 1:11-
12 indicates, will have the character of spiritual encouragement
and moral exhortation: "For I long to see you, that I may impart
to you some spiritual gift to strengthen you, that is, that we
may be mutually encouraged [συμπαρακληθῆναι] by each other's
faith, both yours and mine" (RSV). This passage further supports the conclusion that Paul can describe his exhortation
(παράκλησις) as "preaching the gospel."

In summary, when applied to Paul's letters the categories of
"theological" and "ethical" tend to confuse rather than clarify.
The apostle's ethical exhortations are expressed in a wide range
of stylistic forms and appear in virtually every chapter, from
first to last. It is inaccurate to say either that his concern is
primarily theological and secondarily ethical, or the reverse,
that it is primarily practical, secondarily theoretical. His concern
is, in a word, *evangelical:* to preach the gospel. There is, for example, no indication that he feels it either less or more urgent
to admonish the Romans to "love one another with brotherly
affection" (12:10) than he does to declare to them that believers
"are justified by [God's] grace as a gift, through the redemption
which is in Christ Jesus" (3:24 RSV). Neither "theology" nor
"ethics" nor a combination of the two is to be equated with "the
gospel." Rather, the good news Paul preaches finds expression
now in theological statements, now in ethical exhortations.
Moreover, it begins to appear that just as the exhortations gain
their context and some of their content from the apostle's
"theological" affirmations, so the theological declarations may
already carry within themselves the moral imperative.

This possibility suggests a further investigative task: the examination of the so-called "theological" themes of Paul's preaching to see what "ethical" dimensions they may have. Just as
French and Italian engineers, digging from opposite sides, even-
tually joined their respective tunnels deep in the heart of Mont

Blanc, so the interpreter of Paul's ethic is called upon to work not only from the side of his ethical exhortations toward his theology, but also from the side of his theology toward his exhortations. Hopefully, the two approaches may thus converge on and illumine the problem of indicative and imperative which lies deep in the heart of the Pauline gospel.

III
The Themes of
Paul's Preaching

INTRODUCTION

It has been shown that Paul's concrete exhortations and moral instruction cannot rightly be assessed without attention to the theological context in which they stand. It is also possible to demonstrate, working from the "theological" side of Paul's preaching, that the relationship between proclamation and exhortation is not just formal, or only accidental, but thoroughly integral and vital to the apostle's whole understanding of the gospel. Just as his ethical teaching has significant theological dimensions, so do the major themes of his preaching have significant ethical dimensions.

Some preliminary matters, however, deserve consideration. Paul's "preaching" as such, the content of his oral proclamation of the gospel in such places as Ephesus, Philippi, Athens, and Corinth is not directly available for examination. The "Pauline speeches" of Acts are certainly not verbatim reports of that preaching, but creations of the Third Evangelist. They serve as a source for Lukan, not Pauline, themes and perspectives.[1] Nor

[1] See esp. M. Dibelius, *Studies in the Acts of the Apostles*, ed. H. Greeven (1956); E. Haenchen, *Die Apostelgeschichte* in *KEK* (13th ed.), esp. pp. 81 ff.,

should Paul's own letters be regarded as "sermon transcripts" or "notes" in any sense. They are addressed to already established Christian congregations, occasioned by specific historical situations and, although they were undoubtedly orally dictated by Paul and read aloud for the hearing of the addressees, belong more to the category of written than oral communication.

It is, however, both reasonable and necessary to presume that Paul's letters in general reflect the themes and perspectives of his "preaching" as such. One important function of his letters is to remind his congregations of the gospel he had preached to them and to reaffirm its essential points. This purpose he quite explicitly states in I Cor. 15:1-3 ("Now I would remind you, brethren, in what terms I preached to you the gospel," RSV), and there makes use of an apparently fixed creedal formulation (vss. 3 ff.). Moreover, in I Cor. 2:1 ff. he refers directly to his original mission in Corinth and the content of his preaching there: "Jesus Christ and him crucified" (vs. 2 RSV). It has already been shown that a clear-cut distinction between the Pauline "kerygma" and "didache" cannot be sustained,[2] and now it must be added that a sharp distinction between Paul's missionary preaching (kerygma) and his subsequent pastoral letters (didache) is equally misleading. Not only do the letters serve to reaffirm, defend, and clarify the preaching, but—as the apostle himself specifically says in I Thess. 2:11-12 and 4:2—his original evangelizing activity already included exhortation, encouragement, and instruction. Therefore, while the preaching of Paul does not lie immediately at hand, its scope and content may be validly inferred from his letters.

There have been various suggestions as to the controlling motif or central concept of Pauline theology. If Romans is taken as a guide, then *the righteousness of God* (1:16-17) would seem to be the correct starting point, as Peter Stuhlmacher, on the grounds of an investigation of all the major passages relevant to this theme, has argued.[3] Other exegetes, to cite a second example,

---

99 ff.; P. Vielhauer, "On the 'Paulinism' of Acts," *Studies in Luke-Acts*, ed. L. E. Keck and J. L. Martyn (1966), pp. 33 ff.

[2] See above, pp. 106 ff.

[3] *Gerechtigkeit Gottes bei Paulus* in *FRLANT*, 87 (1965), 203 ff.

have been impressed with the possibility of understanding the whole of Pauline theology as an "interpretation" of *baptism*.[4] Or again, one could note that the apostle himself singles out *Jesus Christ crucified* as the heart of his gospel (I Cor. 2:1-2), or, the corollary to this, "Christ Jesus as Lord" (II Cor. 4:5). None of these by itself, of course, nor any number of others which could also be mentioned (justification by faith, love, the Spirit, the church, the law), can be understood in isolation from the remaining ones, so fully and subtly do the themes of the Pauline preaching interpenetrate one another. Whiteley goes so far as to say that Paul's theology is so "closely integrated" that it could "be made to center equally well" upon almost any individual theme.[5] Yet even this would not justify Whiteley's own decision to fall back upon a traditional dogmatic organization of Pauline theology, and to discuss it under such completely artificial headings as "creation," "fall," "morality," and—of course saved for the last—"eschatology." Such a method utilizes too many categories with which Paul himself was unfamiliar and thus distorts his own distinctive theological profile. Moreover, it particularly obscures the feature of Pauline theology which Whiteley himself has clearly recognized, the interrelatedness of its several themes.

In the discussion of Paul's preaching which follows, the traditional "chronological-dogmatic" approach has been abandoned altogether. Instead, it is suggested, at least as a working hypothesis, that the heuristic key to Pauline theology as a whole, the point in which his major themes are rooted and to which they are ultimately oriented, is the apostle's eschatological perspective. Eschatology, therefore, is properly the *first*, not the last, section in an exposition of Paul's theology.[6]

  [4] E. Fuchs, "The Theology of the New Testament and the Historical Jesus," *Studies of the Historical Jesus*, trans. A. Scobie, *SBTh*, 42 (1964), 173; E. Lohse, "Taufe und Rechtfertigung bei Paulus," *KuD*, XI (1965), 318.
  [5] *The Theology of St. Paul*, p. xiv.
  [6] This has been effectively shown by H.-D. Wendland, "Ethik und Eschatologie in der Theologie des Paulus," *NKZ*, XLI (1930), 757 ff., 793 ff. See also Henry M. Shires, *The Eschatology of Paul in the Light of Modern Scholarship* (1966).

1. THIS AGE AND THE AGE TO COME

a. The powers of this age

Characteristic of the writings of apocalyptic Judaism, as it had not been of the Old Testament, is the distinction between the present age ("aeon") and that which is to come (see especially II Esd. 4:2; 6:9; 7:13, 47, 122-23; 8:1; 9:19) .[7] Although Nygren's attempt to schematize the whole of Pauline theology in accord with these categories must often force the evidence,[8] there is no question but that this doctrine of apocalyptic Judaism has exerted its influence in Paul's thought. Repeatedly he speaks of "this age" (Rom. 12:2; I Cor. 1:20; 2:6 [twice], 8; 3:18; II Cor. 4:4), and while the corresponding phrase "the coming age" is never used by Paul himself (but see Eph. 1:21), the contrast between "this age" and "the age to come" is nevertheless implicit, particularly when he contrasts "things present" with the "things to come" (Rom. 8:38; I Cor. 3:22) . "This age" may also be described as "this *world*," as shown by I Cor. 3:18, 19 where the two phrases are used interchangeably. Also synonymous is the expression "the present time," employed in the New Testament only by Paul (Rom. 3:26; 8:18; 11:5; II Cor. 8:14), but later also in Barn. 4:1.

The present "age," "world," or "time" is characterized by its transitoriness ("the form of this world is passing away," I Cor. 7:31 RSV) , by tribulation and suffering ("For it is my view that the sufferings of the present time are in no way comparable with the coming glory to be revealed to us," Rom. 8:18), and by its pervasively evil aspect ("the present evil age," Gal. 1:4 RSV) . In this same connection one may note Paul's use, in Phil. 2:15, of the phrase "wicked and perverse generation" which in Deut. 32:5 had referred to Israel, but is now applied by the apostle to the world in which the church must live, a "world" filled with immorality of all kinds (I Cor. 5:10) .

In particular, the present age is viewed as being held captive

---

[7] Sasse, *ThW*, I, 206-7 [ET: *ibid.*].
[8] See his *Commentary on Romans,* trans. Carl C. Rasmussen (1949) , esp. pp. 16 ff.

by powers which are alien to God and hostile to his purpose.
The apostle does not deny that God himself has created "this
world" (see Rom. 1:20), and he would certainly have subscribed
to the apocalypticist's judgment that "the Most High has not
made one age but two" (II Esd. 7:50). Yet, as the apocalypticists
also held, the present age had fallen victim to "evil cosmic
forces . . . bent on the destruction of mankind and of the world
itself." [9] Thus, Paul speaks of the *rulers* of this age who are
"doomed to pass away" (I Cor. 2:6 RSV), the *god* of this world
(II Cor. 4:4), and the *elemental spirits* of the cosmos (Gal. 4:3).
While these rulers and powers cannot finally frustrate the purposes of God (Rom. 8:38) and will at last be destroyed by him
(I Cor. 15:24), their power still has its effect in the present
world. The hostility of these alien powers is expressed not only
in their attempt to enslave man to their own purposes (Gal.
4:3), but also in their blinding him to the gospel of Christ and
thus to the true God himself (II Cor. 4:4) and, ultimately, in
their crucifixion of "the Lord of glory" (I Cor. 2:8).

Man's "possession" by the evil powers of this age,[10] and his
own alienation from and hostility to God, is further described
by reference to his bondage to the powers of *sin* and *death*. On
occasion—and this is also characteristic of apocalyptic thought [11]
—Paul speaks of these powers as if they were personal forces
exercising their dominion over men. Man stands "under sin's
power" (ὑφ' ἁμαρτίαν, Rom. 3:9; cf. Gal. 3:22); he has been
"sold" as a slave is sold to a new master and thus is "under sin"
(ὑπὸ τὴν ἁμαρτίαν, Rom. 7:14). Sin is not an original part of
the world but "infiltrates" itself into the world (εἰσέρχεσθαι,
Rom. 5:12) to take it captive and subject men to its reign
(βασιλεύειν, Rom. 5:21; 6:12; κυριεύειν, Rom. 6:14). Sin "deceives" man (Rom. 7:11); it demands his obedience and then
enslaves him (Rom. 6:16-17, 20; 7:14, 25), and it finally "kills"
him (Rom. 7:11; 8:10).

Paul's view that death is the inevitable consequence and

[9] D. S. Russell, *The Method and Message of Jewish Apocalyptic, 200
B.C.–A.D. 100* (1964), p. 267.
[10] *Ibid.*, p. 176.
[11] *Ibid.*

punishment of sin is held in common with Judaism.[12] The concept of "death," when it is applied by the apostle to the total annihilation of man's self by sin's power (Rom. 7:11), becomes a designation for the ultimate extent of man's alienation of himself from God. Death, like sin, is a demonic power which "reigns" in this age (βασιλεύειν, Rom. 5:14, 17) and is in fact the manifestation of sin's reign (Rom. 5:21), the "enemy" power which still holds out when all others have been conquered (I Cor. 15:26).

Associated with the powers of this age, but not strictly identified with them by Paul, is man's flesh (σάρξ) with its passions and desires (Gal. 5:24; cf. Rom. 13:14; Gal. 5:16-17).[13] Paul's linking sin with the flesh stems, like his linking of it with death, from the Old Testament.[14] Insofar as man is mortal, insofar as he, like the present age, is destined to "pass away," he is "flesh" and subject to the weaknesses and tribulations of mortality (cf. Rom. 6:19; I Cor. 7:28; II Cor. 4:11). But more than that, flesh becomes the "subject" of sin in a double sense: obedient to sin's ruling power (Rom. 7:14, 25) and in turn striving to fulfill its own goals (Gal. 5:16-17, 24; Rom. 13:14). The flesh thus seeks to exercise control over man's life, and while it is not a power *outside of* and *over against* man in the same way as are sin and death,[15] it threatens always to become the quisling tyrant, holding man in bondage to the demonic forces of the world. Since this quisling power itself provides death its opportunity, it is no less God's enemy, "hostile" to him (Rom. 8:6-7) and to his Spirit (Gal. 6:8). In and of itself the flesh is not sinful, as numerous "neutral" references in the Pauline letters show clearly. But when it "sells out" to sin and is thus taken over by sin, it allies itself with the evil forces of the present age and represents all that is "worldly" and "material" as opposed to what is divine and "spiritual" (cf. Rom. 15:27; I Cor. 3:1; 9:11; II Cor. 1:12;

[12] See Bultmann, *ThW*, III, 15, n. 67 [ET: *ibid.*].

[13] A. J. Bandstra's attempt to identify σάρξ directly with the στοιχεῖα τοῦ κόσμου (Gal. 4:3, etc.) is not persuasive (*The Law and the Elements of the World. An Exegetical Study in Aspects of Paul's Teaching* [1964]). See my review in *JBL*, LXXXIV (1965), 192-93.

[14] Schweizer, *ThW*, VII, 132.

[15] *Ibid.*, p. 133; also Schweizer's comments on πνεῦμα, *ThW*, VI, 427.

10:4). For this reason the flesh may be described as a "quisling" power seeking to rule man's life.

b. The "transcendent power" of God

While the powers of the present age seek to annihilate what is and to enthrone death as sovereign, it is God's power which "summons into being things that are not" and "makes the dead to live" (Rom. 4:17). There is, then, a fundamental and inalterable opposition between the powers of this age and "the transcendent power" (ἡ ὑπερβολὴ τῆς δυνάμεως, II Cor. 4:7 RSV) of God. It is an opposition between the "spirit of the world" and the "Spirit of God" (I Cor. 2:12), between "the flesh" and God's Spirit (e.g. Rom. 8:4-5, 12-13; Gal. 4:29), between sin and righteousness (Rom. 6:16-23), and ultimately between life and death (I Cor. 15:26).

God alone is able to destroy the alien forces which are ranged against him, but this will occur only in the future; it is one of those things still "to come" (cf. Rom. 8:38; I Cor. 3:22). The power of God is not, therefore, a this-worldly power, but is transcendent of this age and will have its full effect only in the age to come when the present powers are finally subdued and abolished. An emphasis on the might and power of God and on his final triumph over evil is of course one major characteristic of apocalyptic, both Jewish and Christian. A primary manifestation of this power is the judgment of God against all unrighteousness and his commendation and reward of those who are faithful and obedient. It is perhaps correct to say that the doctrine of *the last judgment,* understood as an attempt to describe the absolute transcendent power of God over all men and the whole course of history, "is the most characteristic doctrine of Jewish apocalyptic." [16] And this doctrine still has a place in Pauline theology.

Already Paul's reference to the "revealing" (ἀποκαλύπτειν) of God's *wrath* against all ungodliness and wickedness of men (Rom. 1:18; cf. 2:5) shows his appropriation of apocalyptic categories, as do the several other passages where he speaks of the

---

[16] Russell, *The Method and Message of Jewish Apocalyptic,* p. 380.

wrath (ὀργή) of God and its judgment of evil. That God's wrath
is an expression of his power is explicitly stated in Rom. 9:22
(RSV): "What if God, desiring to show his wrath and to make
known his power, has endured with much patience the vessels
of wrath made for destruction?" This passage also shows that
God's wrath is not conceived of as contradictory to his mercy
and justice, but as a corollary of them.

The apostle's references to the wrath which is to come (e.g.
Rom. 2:5, 8; 5:9; 12:19; cf. I Thess. 5:9) [17] correspond to his
conviction that the same power of God which will one day
destroy the powers of this age also reveals itself in the final judgment of men. The Jewish doctrine of recompense is by no means
absent from Pauline teaching.[18] Every man will be judged ultimately by his works, and for those who please God there will be
"eternal life" while for those who are disobedient there will be
"wrath and fury" (Rom. 2:6-10). On the day of judgment each
man's work will be disclosed for what it really is, and he whose
work is well founded will receive a reward (I Cor. 3:13-15).
Christ himself will sit in the judgment seat (Rom. 2:16), and
each man who stands before him will receive good or evil according to whether he has "pleased God" (II Cor. 5:9-10).

Some interpreters of the Pauline ethic have regarded this
teaching about eschatological recompense as in basic tension
with the doctrine of justification by faith alone apart from works
of the law.[19] Its survival in Paul despite this is, in turn, sometimes ascribed to its utilitarian value as a prod to morality, and
the "eschatological motive" is thus listed along with a number
of others as one "sanction" for the apostle's ethical exhortations.[20] The concept of divine recompense, however, has a far
more fundamental place in Pauline thought than such conclu-

---

[17] I Thess. 1:10 could also be listed here. Even though it is likely that
Paul is employing in vss. 9-10 a theological formulation of the pre-Pauline
church, as G. Friedrich has persuasively argued ("Ein Tauflied hellenistischer
Judenchristen, I Thess. 1:9 ff.," TZ, XXI [1965], 502 ff.), he is nonetheless
the willing recipient of this theologoumenon.

[18] See, e.g., F. V. Filson, St. Paul's Conception of Recompense in UNT, 21
(1931).

[19] E.g. J. Weiss, The History of Primitive Christianity, pp. 561-62.

[20] Ibid., pp. 559 ff.

sions presuppose. On the one hand, the doctrine grows out of
the conviction that God wills the good and is aggressively opposed to what is evil. His wrath, his punishment of evil, is thus
a dynamic, personalistic expression of his holiness.[21] Therefore,
it may not be too much to say that "the first thought of Paul
about God" is that he wills the good and separates himself from
the evil.[22]

On the other hand, the doctrine of recompense is also rooted
in the conviction that all men are ultimately and individually
accountable to God for their actions. This is particularly clear in
Romans 1-3. The recompense passage of this section (2:6-16)
is an important part of the total argument, the conclusions to
which may be found in 3:19-20 (cf. 3:23). Gentiles (1:18 ff.)
and Jews (2:1 ff.) alike stand under the judgment ("wrath")
of God. The "whole world" is held accountable to him (3:19).
It is man's ultimate responsibility to God for which Paul is here
arguing,[23] or described from the other side, God's active concern
for good and opposition to evil—not only in the world as a
whole, abstractly, but in the individual life of every man, concretely. The same point is made in Rom. 14:10-12 which concludes a citation of Isa. 45:23 with the emphatic assertion: "Thus
each one of us shall give an account of himself to God."

It is also important to observe that Paul does not speak of
specific, material rewards which can be counted and calculated
like "wages." [24] What awaits the righteous is, instead, God's
"praise" (ἔπαινος, Rom. 2:29; I Cor. 4:5; cf. Rom. 13:3), his
"honor" (τιμή, Rom. 2:7, 10), and his "glory" (δόξα, Rom. 2:7,
10; 5:2). The traditional concept of "eternal life" is also used
in this connection (Rom. 2:7; 5:21; 6:22-23; Gal. 6:8; cf. "im-

---

[21] H.-D. Wendland, "Ethik und Eschatologie," p. 763. C. H. Dodd's attempt to interpret the Pauline view of God's wrath in terms of the immediate consequences of sin itself (the "inevitable process of cause and
effect in a moral universe," *The Epistle to the Romans* in *MNTC* [1932], p.
23) is an unwarranted psychologizing of a concept which has to do basically
with God's own purposes and actions.

[22] Wendland, "Ethik und Eschatologie," p. 764.

[23] See G. Bornkamm, "Die Offenbarung des Zornes Gottes, Röm. 1-3,"
Das Ende des Gesetzes in *BEvTh*, 16 (1963), esp. p. 27.

[24] G. Bornkamm, "Der Lohngedanke im Neuen Testament," *Studien zu
Antike und Urchristentum,* pp. 90-91.

mortality" [ἀφθαρσία], Rom. 2:7; I Cor. 15:42 ff.) but without
the sort of concerted effort to define—or *redefine*—it which one
finds in the Fourth Gospel. Also employed with a more or less
traditional meaning is the idea of God's "kingdom" which only
the righteous shall "inherit" (I Cor. 6:9-10; Gal. 5:21)—for it
is the immortal (I Cor. 15:50) realm of "righteousness, peace
[cf. the mention of the reward of "peace" in Rom. 2:10], and
"joy" (Rom. 14:17), the realm of God's glory (I Thess. 2:12)
and power (I Cor. 4:20).

The categories thus used to describe the "rewards" awaiting
the righteous show that the apostle's objective is to emphasize
man's status as the servant of a sovereign God. Man is called
to be obedient to his Lord, and the end result of his obedience
is participation in God's own kingdom when the power of God
shall have abolished the alien princes of the present age (I Cor.
15:24). The good works Paul commends are not regarded as
having value in and of themselves. They have value only as
responsible acts of obedience to the sovereign Lord.[25] The reward
of eternal life is not correlated with obedience in the same way
that "wages" are correlated with the laborer's achievements.
Rather, eternal life, participation in the Lord's victorious reign
over all things, inheritance of his kingdom, is bestowed as a
free gift from God himself (Rom. 6:23). But it is never forgotten
that this God is always man's Sovereign, the Judge before whom
each individual is at last called to account.

It must be emphasized that Paul conceives of the power of
God as basically *creative* and *redemptive* (Rom. 4:17), even
when it is exercised in judgment and wrath. For him the decisive
manifestation of divine power is in the gospel, specifically described as "the power of God for salvation" (Rom. 1:16). The
content of the gospel is Jesus Christ the crucified Lord (I Cor.
2:2; II Cor. 4:5), by whose death and resurrection God's ultimate
victory is accomplished (I Cor. 15:57). For this reason there is
"power" in the cross (I Cor. 1:17); Christ himself may be called
"the power of God" (I Cor. 1:24), and what is finally wrought
through him is referred to as "salvation" and God's "new
creation."

[25] *Ibid.,* pp. 71 ff.

c. Salvation and "the new creation"

The victory of God's "transcendent power" over the powers of this age is accomplished through the death and resurrection of his Son (cf. Gal. 1:3-4) who at length yields the reign to God (I Cor. 15:24). Paul's overall descriptive term for the final victory of God in the coming age, when the last enemy shall have been destroyed and God shall reign as the unchallenged Sovereign above all, is *salvation*. Salvation comes from God (Phil. 1:28) through the gospel (I Cor. 15:1-2) which speaks of Jesus Christ as "crucified" (I Cor. 2:2) and as "Lord" (II Cor. 4:5). The death and resurrection of Christ is thus the decisive salvation event in which God's power is operative (cf. I Cor. 1:17, "lest the cross of Christ be emptied of its power," RSV). For Paul the "gospel" *is* the "word of the cross," as shown when he describes now one, now the other as "the power of God" ("for salvation," Rom. 1:16; "to us who are being saved," I Cor. 1:18).

The concept of salvation belongs unquestionably to the apostle's eschatological perspective, and its basic reference is futuristic.[26] It is significant that the Old Testament image of the "helmet of salvation" (Isa. 59:17) is altered by Paul to make it clear that salvation is still to come. He speaks, instead, of the helmet of "the *hope* of salvation" (I Thess. 5:8). With only a single exception in the Pauline homologoumena, the tense of the verb "to save" is always either present or future. The one exception is only grammatical, not material, and serves to confirm the primacy of the future dimension of "salvation" in Paul's thought. "We were saved," he says, *"in hope"* (τῇ γὰρ ἐλπίδι ἐσώθημεν, Rom. 8:24). Whatever present dimensions salvation may have,[27] it is first of all something *to come* and is granted to those who survive the refining "fire" of judgment at the last day (I Cor. 3:13, 15). For the wicked this coming day will be one of "wrath" (Rom. 2:5), but for the righteous it will be a day of "salvation" (Rom. 13:11-12).

This salvation has, as Paul speaks of it, both a negative and a positive aspect.[28] Negatively it means man's deliverance from

[26] See W. Foerster, *ThW*, VII, 992, 993.
[27] See below, pp. 126 ff.
[28] Foerster, *ThW*, VII, 993.

bondage to the world with its transitory powers whose only fruit is decay and corruption. This accounts for the antithetical position of the concepts "salvation" and "death" in II Cor. 7:10: "For godly grief involves repentance, leads to salvation and brings no regret, while worldly grief produces death." Salvation from the tyrannous power of death means, as a consequence, that man will also be saved from God's wrath on the day of judgment. This negative aspect of salvation is particularly clear in Rom. 5:9 ("Through [Christ] we shall be saved from wrath") and I Thess. 5:9 ("For God has not destined us for wrath, but to obtain salvation through our Lord Jesus Christ," RSV). In such formulations Paul stands fully within the tradition of the earliest church. This is well demonstrated by the probably pre-Pauline formulation he employs in I Thess. 1:9-10 [29] which concludes with reference to "Jesus who rescues us from the wrath to come."

In its positive aspect salvation has to do with the total transformation of man's life and being by God's sovereign power at work in Christ. In Rom. 8:23 this is called "the redemption of our bodies," and it is evidently the same concept, slightly elaborated, which is articulated in Phil. 3:21. There Paul speaks of the Christian's expectation that the "Savior" Christ will come from heaven to "transform our lowly bodies to be like his glorious body, through the instrumentality of the power which enables him to subject all things to himself." Positively, then, salvation means "glorification." When Paul writes the Thessalonians that God has "destined" them for "salvation" (I Thess. 5:9), that is but an alternate way of saying that God "calls" them into his own "kingdom and glory" (I Thess. 2:12). Although the present age is one of tribulation (Rom. 5:3; II Cor. 4:17; cf. Rom. 8:18), the Christian can still rejoice in his hope of "[sharing] the glory of God" (Rom. 5:2), that "eternal weight of glory" (II Cor. 4:17 RSV) which is being prepared for him and which will one day be "revealed" (Rom. 8:18).

Often in the LXX God's "glory" is associated with his "might." [30] So also for Paul. The Christ into the likeness of

---

[29] See above, n. 17.
[30] Kittel, *ThW*, II, 247-48 [ET: p. 244-45].

whose "glorious body" the Christian's body will be transformed
is the agent of God's power by which the transformation occurs
(Phil. 3:21). It is Christ's face which is incandescent with God's
glory (II Cor. 4:6; cf. vs. 7 and the reference there to "God's
transcendent power"). God's power is particularly and specifically effective in resurrection, first of all Christ's, but then
through him also those who believe in Christ. Abraham knew
that God could give life to the dead (Rom. 4:17), and consequently he had faith that the one who had promised to bring
forth life from the "dead" bodies of himself and Sarah (vs. 19)
"also had the power to do it" (δυνατός ἐστιν καὶ ποιῆσαι, vs. 21).
Christ was "crucified in weakness but lives by the power of God"
(II Cor. 13:4). Those who believe in Christ, confident that as
"God raised the Lord" he "will also raise us up by his power"
(I Cor. 6:14 RSV), hope one day to experience the power of
Christ's resurrection (Phil. 3:10). The hope to be "glorified with
Christ" (Rom. 8:17) is thus the hope to be resurrected and live
with him. This means, in turn, the hope for participation in
that age to come which shall be the reign of God's power. As
the parallelism of I Cor. 15:43 indicates, to be "raised in glory"
means to be "raised in power."

Resurrection with Christ is for Paul, like salvation itself, first
of all a hope for the future. Those who are united with Christ
in his death "shall" also be united with him in his resurrection
(σύμφυτοι . . . καὶ τῆς ἀναστάσεως ἐσόμεθα, Rom. 6:5) and
"shall" live with him (συζήσομεν αὐτῷ, Rom. 6:8). Resurrection
life is before them as a possibility (Phil. 3:11); those who are
open to God's grace "shall" reign in life through Jesus Christ
(ἐν ζωῇ βασιλεύσουσιν, Rom. 5:17). In this life there is hope
for something beyond (I Cor. 15:19), when all "shall" be made
alive in Christ (ἐν τῷ Χριστῷ πάντες ζωοποιηθήσονται, I Cor. 15:
22). The apostle is sharply critical of the Corinthians who think
that there is no future resurrection (I Cor. 15:12) and that
already in this present age they "reign" in life. "And would
that you did reign," he writes them with poignant irony, "that
we might share the rule with you!" (I Cor. 4:8.)

Essentially, the hope for salvation, understood as resurrection
from the dead and sharing God's glory, is the hope that man's

alienation from God, represented by his bondage to the "present evil age," will be ultimately overcome. Christ is "Savior" because in him the veil which separates men from God is lifted, and they are at last able to behold the transforming glory of God (II Cor. 3:12 ff.). In the present age one sees only the dim and shadowy likeness of God, but in the age to come he shall see with all the clarity of a direct confrontation (I Cor. 13:12a). All that is present is imperfect, "but when the perfect comes, the imperfect will pass away" (I Cor. 13:10 RSV). Probably once more in criticism of "Corinthian theology," which held that true and saving knowledge is already present for the believer, Paul emphasizes that even "knowledge" (γνῶσις) belongs to the realm of the imperfect (I Cor. 13:1-2). But what is now partial knowledge shall, in the age to come, pass away. Then man shall know God with a completeness and intimacy comparable to that by which he has all along been known by God (I Cor. 13:12b). No longer in bondage to the death-dealing powers of this age, the believer, through God's victory over death, shall find his whole being transformed (I Cor. 15:51 ff.) as he takes his place within the kingdom where God rules (I Cor. 15:28).

The present age is so fully enthralled by the hostile powers that something far more than its fulfillment, renewal, or renovation is required. It is significant that neither Paul nor any other early Christian writer ever refers to God's future rule as "the new world," for the term κόσμος in itself suggests alienation from God.[31] Instead, the salvation of the world is seen to require a transformation so radical and total that, expressing himself negatively, Paul is constrained to speak of the world's *crucifixion* (Gal. 6:14). Expressed positively, God's saving power is said to effect a "new creation" (Gal. 6:15; II Cor. 5:17), one which bears a fully new relationship to its creator.[32]

Upon examining Paul's concept of the new creation, one is struck by the apostle's most decisive conviction concerning "this age and the age to come." While God's power stands "beyond" the present age and over against the powers to which it is in

[31] Sasse, *ThW*, III, 885 [ET: *ibid.*]; cf. Schrage, "Die Stellung zur Welt bei Paulus," p. 130. Nor does Paul speak of "the new *age*."
[32] Cf. Foerster, *ThW*, III, 1033 [ET: p. 1034].

bondage, and while the salvation which God effects is first of all
an object of hope, God's power is nevertheless *already* effective
for men in Christ. The two ages "meet," as it were, in him
through whom God is even in the present reconciling the world
unto himself (II Cor. 5:19). Thus, Paul sees the "eschatological"
power of God as already operative and says that the man "in
Christ" *is* "a new creation," and that for him the old *"has* passed
away" (παρῆλθεν) and the new *"has* come" (γέγονεν, II Cor.
5:17). Salvation, then, is not unambiguously "future," and it
is not only a "hope." Even in the present age the "first fruits"
of salvation may be savored and the authenticity of hope confirmed.

d. The "first fruits" of salvation, the "guarantee" of hope

Those to whom the gospel is proclaimed, even those who accept it in faith, still belong to the present age, to "this world"
(e.g. I Cor. 5:10). They are still "in the flesh" (ἐν σαρκί, e.g.
Gal. 2:20). Therefore, already when Paul speaks of the gospel
as "God's power for salvation for every one who believes" (Rom.
1:16), it is implied that this saving power is operative in the
present. Moreover, when he proceeds to say that the gospel
simultaneously "reveals" God's righteousness and wrath, his verb
is in the present tense (ἀποκαλύπτεται, Rom. 1:17, 18). The
present-ness of salvation is also indicated by his use of the present
participle: the word of the cross is the power of God for "those
of us *who are being saved"* (τοῖς σῳζομένοις, I Cor. 1:18); the
apostles "are the aroma of Christ to God among those *who are
being saved"* (ἐν τοῖς σῳζομένοις, II Cor. 2:15 RSV). Whereas
in general Paul speaks about the "hope of glory," even this seems
to have a present dimension, as another present tense form
suggests: "We all *are . . . being transformed* from glory into
glory" (μεταμορφούμεθα ἀπὸ δόξης εἰς δόξαν, II Cor. 3:18).[33]
To be mentioned above all is the declaration of II Cor. 6:2. After
quoting Isa. 49:8 with its reference to the "day of salvation,"
Paul applies the text with emphasis: "Behold, *now* is 'the day
of salvation.'" He does not mean that salvation has now been

---

[33] See Kittel, *ThW*, II, 254 [ET: p. 251].

manifested in all its aspects (apparently the "Corinthian error") but that the decisive event of salvation—the death and resurrection of Christ [34]—has already occurred and is already effective.

The dialectic of present and future is deeply and broadly imbedded in Pauline thought and is expressed in many different ways.[35] For example, in I Thessalonians 5, after noting that the future "day of the Lord" will come swiftly and suddenly (vss. 2-3), he adds that his converts in Thessalonica "belong to the day" (vs. 8), are "sons of the day" (vs. 5). Their present life is already qualified by their ultimate destiny ("to obtain salvation" vs. 9). Although "the day" itself is still to come they do not live in the world's "darkness" and therefore will escape the travail and ultimate destruction it is to suffer (vss. 3-4). The metaphor of Phil. 3:20 is different but the meaning is essentially the same: the manifestation of Christ as "Savior" is still future ("we *await* a Savior") but already in the "waiting" those who believe in him know that they are citizens of a "commonwealth in heaven." Although still in the world they are not oriented toward "earthly things" (τὰ ἐπίγεια, vs. 19) but toward the age which is to come (cf. Rom. 12:2).

Another way in which the apostle expresses the dialectical relationship between this age and the age to come is his use of the metaphor of "inheritance." It is not the teaching of Jesus however, which offers the foundation for Paul's development of this metaphor. Where the apostle does speak of inheriting "the kingdom of God," the phrases have a formal, traditional ring, and the metaphor of "inheritance" is not itself exploited (I Cor. 6:9-10; 15:50; Gal. 5:21). Rather, Paul has retrieved the concept from the Genesis accounts of the promise to Abraham, and it is in connection with the Abraham narrative that he develops it for and applies it to the believers (Rom. 4:1 ff.; Gal. 3:6 ff.). God's "promise" to Abraham was that in him "all the nations shall

---

[34] This decisive salvation-event constitutes another major theme of Paul's preaching and is discussed below, pp. 162 ff.

[35] Somewhat analogous, on the negative side, is the tension between present and past with respect to "the world." In I Cor. 7:31 he uses the present tense to speak of the world's form passing away (παράγει), but in II Cor. 5:17 he says that "the old *has* gone" (παρῆλθεν) and, in Gal. 6:14, that the world "*has been* 'crucified'" (ἐσταύρωται).

be blessed" (Gal. 3:8, citing Genesis; cf. 12:3; 18:18). Paul understands this "blessing," or promised "inheritance" (Gal. 3:18),
to be *righteousness*, and the two major passages in which the
Abraham narrative is exposited open with appeals to the text
of Gen. 15:6: "Abraham believed God and it was accounted
to him as righteousness" (Rom. 4:3; Gal. 3:6). Abraham's true
"heirs" are those who, like the patriarch himself, "believe" (cf.
Rom. 4:13-14). The object of this faith is Christ; so if one "belongs to Christ," then he also belongs to Abraham and stands
to inherit what has been promised (Gal. 3:29).

This metaphor is a uniquely appropriate vehicle for convey-
ing the characteristically Pauline dialectic of present and future.
An "heir" is, by definition, one who is "in the line to receive"
and waits for the receipt of something which is not yet given.
The inheritance itself is still to come, but the one who is designated as an "heir" thereby has a new status already. In that
sense the "future" has decisively entered the present. Now in the
case of God's promise to Abraham, the primary heir is Christ.
He is the one "offspring" (Gal. 3:16), the "one righteous man"
(cf. Rom. 5:17-18). All other heirs can only be "co-heirs," and
then only if they belong to Christ (*"Then* you are Abraham's
offspring, and consequently heirs according to the promise," Gal.
3:29). "Belonging to Christ" means being united with him in
his death and resurrection.[36] Thus, believers are "heirs of God
and co-heirs with Christ" *only because* (εἴπερ) they share his
sufferings and hope to share his glory (Rom. 8:17).

Since a father's heir is normally his son, Paul also speaks of
believers as "children" or "sons" of God. In several passages these
terms are fully interchangeable with the idea of being "heirs"
(Rom. 8:17); the believer is not just a household "slave" but
the Father's "son, and if a son, also an heir" (Gal. 4:7). It is also
in keeping with the idea of a future inheritance by which the
Christian's present life is already conditioned (see Phil. 2:15)
that he speaks of believers as "children of promise" (Gal. 4:28),
and if children of promise, then the true "children of God"
(Rom. 9:8; cf. Rom. 8:16, 21; Gal. 3:26; 4:6; Phil. 2:15).

[36] See below, pp. 171 ff.

This metaphor of sonship, like that of an awaited inheritance, is developed particularly in relation to the Abraham narrative (Rom. 9:6 ff.; Gal. 3:6 ff.; but not in Rom. 4:1 ff.). Paul takes advantage of the fact that Abraham's two sons were by different wives, Hagar the slave (cf. Gen. 16:15) and Sarah the free woman (cf. Gen. 21:1 ff.). Since the slave son has no rights of inheritance (Gal. 4:30, citing Gen. 21:10 ff.), God's promise concerning Abraham's descendants is effective only for those born to the family of Isaac, the son of the free woman (Rom. 9:7, citing Gen. 21:12). Only Isaac's descendants are "children of promise" (Gal. 4:28), and that means, according to Paul, only those who are free from slavery to the law and live by faith: "Those who live by faith are the sons of Abraham" (Gal. 3:7). The object of this faith is always Jesus Christ; thus the apostle can say further that "in Christ Jesus you are all sons of God through faith" (Gal. 3:26 RSV). As Christ is the primary heir and believers are "co-heirs" only as they belong to him, so Christ is God's true Son, who was sent as "Son" in order that "we might receive adoption as sons" (Gal. 4:4-5 RSV). Believers thus participate in sonship only insofar as they heed the call "into the fellowship of [God's] Son" (I Cor. 1:9) and thereby hope to be "conformed to the image of his Son" (Rom. 8:29 RSV).

Closely related to all these themes is Paul's view of the Spirit, a power representative of the coming age which is already operative in the present. It is significant that he can identify God's promise as "the promise of the Spirit" (Gal. 3:14) and that those who receive the promise as "sons" are said to be recipients also of "the Spirit of [God's] Son" (Gal. 4:6; cf. "the Spirit of sonship" [πνεῦμα υἱοθεσίας], Rom. 8:15). It is the Spirit, then, who "bears witness" as to who God's children are (Rom. 8:16); all "who are led by the Spirit of God are sons of God" (Rom. 8:14 RSV).

Although Paul does not simply equate God's "Spirit" with his "power," [37] it is nevertheless true to say that the Spirit works with divine power and that the two concepts are thus closely

---

[37] For a discussion of the problem see K. Stalder, *Das Werk des Geistes in der Heiligung bei Paulus* (1962), pp. 29 ff.

allied in the apostle's thinking. This is evident, for example, in I Thess. 1:5 where it is said that the gospel came to the Thessalonians "in power and in the Holy Spirit" (RSV; ἐν δυνάμει καὶ ἐν πνεύματι ἁγίῳ) and also when the Corinthians are reminded that Paul's preaching among them was "in demonstration of the Spirit and power" (I Cor. 2:4 RSV; ἐν ἀποδείξει πνεύματος καὶ δυνάμεως). In the benediction of Rom. 15:13 and again in vs. 19 the apostle speaks explicitly of "the power of the [Holy] Spirit," and not only in the latter verse, but also in Gal. 3:5 a reference to miraculous "signs and wonders" stands in close association with the idea of God's powerfully operative Spirit. As in late Judaism and even already in the Old Testament itself (e.g. Joel 2:28-29) the sign of the inbreaking of the eschaton was to be the coming of the Spirit in power, with attendant wonders, so also in Paul the Spirit signifies the coming of the new age. What Paul says about the Spirit does not, however, qualify in any way the dialectic of present and future in his preaching. Rather, it contributes to that dialectic and even sharpens it.

On the one hand, the Spirit represents the actual entry of the eschaton into the present age. For Paul, one might say, the Spirit is *the operative presence of God's love* with men. "God's love has been poured into our hearts through the Holy Spirit which has been given to us" (Rom. 5:5 RSV). The declaration of Gal. 4:6-7 provides an illuminating parallel: "God has sent forth the Spirit of his Son into our hearts crying, 'Abba, Father.' Hence, you are no longer a slave, but a son; and if a son, then an heir, through God." By receipt of the Spirit into his heart, the believer is encountered and claimed by God's love which makes him a son, thus an heir to the promise of salvation. The effective working of the eschatological power of God already in the present is further emphasized by reference to the Spirit's *life-giving* power. The Spirit "gives life" (II Cor. 3:6; ζωοποιεῖ, present tense) and can be described appropriately as "the Spirit of life in Christ Jesus" (Rom. 8:2) because it is in the event of Christ's death and resurrection that the coming age, with the Spirit and power, has broken in. The apostle speaks alternately of the Spirit and Christ "in you" (ἐν ὑμῖν, Rom. 8:9, 10), and in II Cor. 3:17 he says explicitly that "the Lord *is* the Spirit." [38]

In particular God's Spirit is associated, like God's power, with Christ's death and resurrection. Even if, as is probable, a traditional formulation lies behind Rom. 1:3-4,[39] the reference there to Christ's resurrection "in power according to the Spirit of holiness (='Holy Spirit') " conforms to the apostle's thought as a whole. In his own way he makes the same connection. Having spoken of the Spirit as the means by which God's love is given and made real (Rom. 5:5), he proceeds to elaborate this by considering immediately the event of Christ's death and resurrection (vss. 6 ff.). The character of God's love is revealed in the cross (vs. 8) which justifies the ungodly and reconciles them to God (vss. 9-10). In turn, Christ's resurrection from the dead, his "life" (vs. 10), means salvation for the believer, that is, his own "resurrection" and "life" (Rom. 6:4 ff.). In Paul's thinking, therefore, the work of the Spirit does not stand apart from the total "eschatological event" of Christ's death and resurrection. The Spirit's presence signifies that God's "power for salvation" (the gospel, Rom. 1:16) is already operative and effective in its mission to "give life."

On the other hand, the Spirit is a harbinger of that which is to come, and thus *the ground of hope*.[40] While, as already noted, Paul can describe the Spirit as a power already at work "giving life" (II Cor. 3:6), he can also employ the verb in the future tense: "If the Spirit of the one who raised Jesus from the dead dwells in you, he who raised from the dead Christ Jesus *will give life* [ζωοποιήσει, future] also to your mortal bodies through his Spirit dwelling in you" (Rom. 8:11). The Spirit is present (note the present tenses, "dwells" and "dwelling" [οἰκεῖ, ἐνοικοῦντος]), but it points to something ahead. The verb "to make alive" (ζωοποιεῖν), which occurs more often in Paul's letters than in the rest of the New Testament combined, is also applied

---

[38] See the discussion of these and related passages in Neill Q. Hamilton, *The Holy Spirit and Eschatology in Paul* ("SJTh Occasional Papers," 6), 1957, pp. 3 ff.

[39] Schweizer, *ThW*, VI, 414-15; Michel, *Römer*, pp. 38-39; Barrett, *A Commentary on the Epistle to the Romans*, pp. 18 ff.

[40] Schweizer, *ThW*, VI, 420 ff.

to Christ himself with reference to the Christian's anticipated future resurrection with him: "For as in Adam all die, so in Christ all *shall be made alive*" (ζωοποιηθήσονται, I Cor. 15:22). The parallel declaration refers to Christ as "the last Adam" who became "a life-giving Spirit" (πνεῦμα ζωοποιοῦν, I Cor. 15:45). The apostle's description of God himself as one "who makes the dead to live" (ὁ ζωοποιοῦντες τοὺς νεκρούς, Rom. 4:17) and also his references to God's "life-giving Spirit" are indebted to the apocalyptic image of the eschaton when, in his power and by his Spirit, God will "give life" (cf. Ezek. 37:14, "And I will put my Spirit within you, and you shall live" [RSV]; LXX, καὶ δώσω τὸ πνεῦμά μου εἰς ὑμᾶς, καὶ ζήσεσθε).[41]

In other passages Paul specifically identifies the Spirit as the ground of hope. For instance, in the benediction of Rom. 15:13 the "power of the Holy Spirit" is invoked in order that the recipients may "abound in hope." Even more striking is Rom. 5:1 ff. The hope of sharing God's glory (vs. 2) is authenticated and survives even the stresses of suffering because "God's love has been poured out into our hearts through the Holy Spirit which has been given to us" (vs. 5). Precisely because God's love is already powerfully present and active in his Spirit, there is hope for something more, namely, the fulfillment of salvation, the completion and perfection of God's redemptive activity. Similarly, when Paul contrasts the "dispensation of death" (the law) with the "dispensation of the Spirit" (II Cor. 3:7-8 RSV), he regards the Spirit itself (identified with "the Lord," vs. 17-18) as giving validity to, and actually constituting, the "hope" (vs. 12) for a future glory (vs. 18). The Spirit, then, is the *presentation*—construed literally, the "making-present"—of that which belongs to another "age" and which, in spite of its "presentation," continues to belong to that age. The Spirit thereby becomes the certification of what is still to come. The dialectic of present and future thus finds its focal point in Paul's concept of the Spirit.

Two related metaphors assist the apostle in his articulation of this dialectic. In Rom. 8:23 he writes that "not only the crea-

---

[41] See Michel, *Römer*, pp. 193-94.

tion, but we ourselves, who have the *first fruits of the Spirit* [τὴν ἀπαρχὴν τοῦ πνεύματος], groan inwardly as we wait for adoption as sons, the redemption of our bodies" (RSV). The word ἀπαρχή is not infrequently employed in the LXX, with its literal meaning, as a designation for the first part of the harvest, theoretically the best of the yield (cf. Num. 18:8 ff.; Deut. 18:4; 26:2, 10, etc.). The ἀπαρχή is to be dedicated to God, for it represents the whole, and that all has been given by God.[42] By Paul the concept is employed metaphorically to describe the Spirit as itself part and parcel of that which is to come. It does not just *precede* the coming age but actually *bears* it and represents the power of that age (i.e. of God himself) already at work. The same metaphor is applied with the same meaning to Christ. In his resurrection he is "the first fruits of those who have fallen asleep" (I Cor. 15:20 RSV); in him the resurrection of believers is proleptically present. Yet the future is not dissolved into the present, for "each in his own order: Christ the first fruits, then at his coming [παρουσία] those who belong to Christ" (I Cor. 15:23 RSV).

The second metaphor likewise describes the Spirit in its dialectical position as the presence in this age of the power of the age to come. In II Cor. 1:22 and 5:5 Paul speaks of the Spirit as an ἀρραβών given by God. This is a Semitic term brought over into Greek from the vocabulary of business and commerce[43] and means literally a "down payment," the first installment of what has been promised. It is by the payment of an ἀρραβών that a business contract is certified and—in that sense—"concluded." The down payment is not reckoned apart from that which is still to come but belongs to it, even though as that which is "advanced." This makes the metaphor fully appropriate for application by the apostle to his concept of the Spirit. With reference to his and Timothy's commissioning, Paul says that God is "the one who has 'sealed' us and has given the Spirit in our hearts as a 'down payment' [ἀρραβών]" (II Cor. 1:22). The Spirit which is placed in the believer's heart is "the Spirit of

---

[42] On the concept see Delling, *ThW*, I, 483-84 [ET: pp. 484 ff.].
[43] Behm, *ThW*, I, 474 [ET: p. 475].

[God's] Son" (Gal. 4:6), that is, God's own "love" (Rom. 5:5). As such it is the first installment of the promised future inheritance. That inheritance is to be "salvation," "life" in the fullest sense. While still in this age, in the flesh, the believer longs for his mortality to be "swallowed up by life" (II Cor. 5:4), and the "guarantee" of this hope is the presence of the Spirit which God has bestowed as an ἀρραβὼν (vs. 5).

It is necessary to emphasize, in conclusion, that Paul's views about "this age" and "the age to come" do not have to do, first of all, with a specific chronological scheme, one age following sequentially upon the first.[44] Any such schematization is already rendered problematic by the central declaration of his gospel, that in the event of Christ's death and resurrection, where God's Spirit is present and effective, and in the present dwelling of the Spirit with the believers themselves, the power of the coming age, that is, "God's transcendent power," has already broken in. Man does not, precisely stated, stand "between" the ages, but at the point where they interpenetrate. Paul does not deny or neglect the temporal aspects of these two ages, but these are definitely subordinated, in his thinking, to their qualitative aspects. The coming age is *future* precisely because it is the realm of God's power, *transcendent* of the world which God has brought into being and which he purposes to redeem from the hostile forces which hold it in bondage. Paul's eschatology is by no means reducible to anthropology; the categories and perspectives of apocalyptic theology are still present in his own.[45] On the other hand, the apostle does not remain within the categories of apocalyptic but decisively breaks through them, just as he says that the "eschatological" power of God has deci-

[44] Correctly, Stalder, *Das Werk des Geistes*, pp. 240 ff. Contrast Shires, who, following Cullmann, holds that central to Paul's eschatology is the concept of a "progression" or "succession" of ages (*The Eschatology of Paul*, e.g. p. 222).

[45] See E. Käsemann, "An Apologia for Primitive Christian Eschatology," *Essays on New Testament Themes* in SBTh, 41 (1964), 182; "Die Anfänge christlicher Theologie," *Exegetische Versuche und Besinnungen*, II, (1964), 102-3; "Zum Thema der urchristlichen Apokalyptik," *ibid.*, esp. p. 130; "God's Righteousness in Paul," *JThC*, I (1965), esp. 109-10; also Stuhlmacher, *Gerechtigkeit Gottes bei Paulus*, pp. 203 ff., and Schrage, "Die Stellung zur Welt bei Paulus," esp. p. 127.

sively broken through into the present. And because the present is where man stands, enslaved by the powers of this world and yet confronted by the liberating power of God, the nature of man's situation, the possibilities for his future and his responsibilities for the present, play a major role in Paul's preaching.

2. THE LAW, SIN, AND RIGHTEOUSNESS

a. Sin and its "reign" through the law

Sin is one of the powers of the "present evil age." Like death, with which it is closely associated, it is representative of those forces which are in rebellion against the power of God and which seek continually to alienate themselves from his sovereign presence. Paul's view of sin, therefore, is conditioned first of all by his conviction that the powers of this age stand over against the power of God in the age to come. Yet Paul never speaks of sin as a completely abstract force or power. Its power has effect in the lives of men; where there is "sin," there are "sinners." Because man is a *creature*, he belongs to "this world," and his creatureliness may be exploited by the powers of the world. But because man is a creature *of God*, he belongs, ultimately, to another domain, to the kingdom of God. In Pauline theology, therefore, eschatological and anthropological categories are indissolubly related. As a creature whose destiny, however, transcends the world, man is seen as the focal center of the struggle between the forces of evil and the power of God.[46]

This is seen particularly in the relationship which Paul presumes between sin and *the flesh*. The flesh, he says, serves "the law of sin" (Rom. 7:25), and anyone who gives himself over to the "passions and desires" of the flesh (Gal. 5:24; cf. vss. 16-17; Rom. 13:14) has thereby set himself over against the coming age, against God himself. This is shown already when the apostle contrasts the "flesh-oriented" life (κατὰ σάρκα, Rom. 8:4-5, 12-13) with the "Spirit-oriented" life (κατὰ πνεῦμα, Rom. 8:4-5,

---

[46] Stuhlmacher has made this same point in *Gerechtigkeit Gottes bei Paulus*, esp. pp. 228-29.

12-13). Moreover, he can refer to Isaac, Abraham's son by Sarah, either as born "through promise" (Gal. 4:23) or born "according to the Spirit" (Gal. 4:29), and in each case the contrast is with the slave son born to Hagar "according to the flesh." For Paul, "the flesh" itself, man's creatureliness and mortality, may come so to dominate his life as to alienate him from God's promise and Spirit. Through this quisling tyrant, sin gains entry into man's life and there exercises its own tyrannical power.

There are other passages which confirm this, notably Romans 7.[47] Insofar as man lives "in the flesh" (vs. 5; here ἐν τῇ σαρκί = κατὰ σάρκα), "the sinful passions" (τὰ παθήματα τῶν ἁμαρτιῶν) are at work in him bringing "death." Thereby sin can actually be "resident in" man (ἐνοικεῖν, vss. 17, 20) with its power to kill (vs. 11; cf. Rom. 8:10). This chapter of Romans also indicates that the effect of sin's power is to turn man against God (the "Spirit," the "promise") and to alienate him from his true destiny as a child of God, an heir of God's kingdom. To be an heir means to live with the certified hope of attaining "life" in the fullest sense.[48] But, as Paul stresses in Romans 7 (vss. 5, 11; cf. 5:12 ff.; 6:16, 21, 23; 8:6, 10; I Cor. 15:55-56), sin leads to death. Sin, therefore, is given a very radical meaning in Paul's thought. It is not just life's perversion, but ultimately its negation. For him sin means hostility to God's purposes and rebellion against his rule, an *alienation* from God so serious and (from man's side) so irremediable that only the concept of "death" is finally appropriate to describe it.

It is important to note, however, that Paul does not subscribe to the Gnostic idea of the flesh as something sinful in and of itself.[49] Discarding the flesh is by no means regarded by him as

[47] W. G. Kümmel (*Römer 7 und die Bekehrung des Paulus* in *UNT*, 17 [1929]) and Bultmann ("Romans 7 and the Anthropology of Paul" in *Existence and Faith*, pp. 147 ff. [originally published 1932]) have both made important contributions to the understanding of this crucial passage. In the present discussion it is assumed that the "I" of this chap. is not biographical but general, and that Paul is describing the situation of man under the law, although seen from the perspective of his new life in Christ.

[48] See above, pp. 127-28.

[49] See, e.g., E. Schweizer, *ThW*, VII, 133.

a prerequisite for obedience to God,[50] even though man's "flesh-liness" represents his existence in its mortal, creaturely aspects. Rather, the flesh becomes "sinful" when it is accorded status as the regulative principle of man's life, when its standards, values, and desires become determinative of man's actions. Man's aliena-tion from God is not automatically consequent upon his life *"in* the flesh" (ἐν σαρκί, Rom. 2:28; II Cor. 10:3; Gal. 2:20; Philem. 16; at Rom. 8:8-9 the expression is used negatively, how-ever, [cf. ἐν τῇ σαρκί, Rom. 7:5, 18]) but is associated with his living *"according* to the flesh" (esp. II Cor. 10:3 where ἐν σαρκί and κατὰ σάρκα are contrasted; cf. also Rom. 8:4, 12-13). Flesh-liness takes on a negative, sinful aspect when man becomes so oriented to its demands that he becomes *dis*oriented to the claim of God and thus incapable of "pleasing" God (Rom. 8:8-9). To put it another way, the flesh becomes the host to sin, its "quis-ling" power within man's own existence, when man makes "the flesh" rather than *God* the object of his confidence and hope. The believer, on the other hand, is one who places "no con-fidence in the flesh" (Phil. 3:3 RSV).

What does the apostle mean by putting one's "confidence" in the flesh? The answer comes in Phil. 3:4 ff. where he enumer-ates the "reasons" he himself has for such confidence: his be-longing to Israel, his zealous persecution of the church, and his moral righteousness. Putting "confidence in the flesh" means regarding one's own status and accomplishments as the highest good and the ground of hope. It means regarding oneself as an *achiever* and in effect declaring one's independence of God. For Paul sin is, in a word, "boasting" (καύχησις, καύχημα, καυχᾶσθαι; φυσίωσις, φυσιοῦν). This "boasting" is not simply identified with "conceit" or "egotism" in the relatively superficial psychological sense, although it also manifests itself as conceit in relationships

[50] Paul's view thus stands radically opposed to the pervasive Hellenistic view of man's physical existence as inherently evil, as summed up in an epigram which was still current in the fifth century A.D. (attributed to the Alexandrian Palladas): "The body is an affliction of the soul, it is Hell, Fate, a burden, a necessity, a strong chain and a tormenting punishment. But when the soul issues from the body as from the bonds of death, it flies to the immortal God" (*The Greek Mythology,* IV in *LCL,* trans. W. R. Paton, p. 49).

with others (e.g. I Cor. 4:6). Rather, it refers to man's turning away from God "to the creation and to one's own strength." [51] Sin (boasting) thus means "a misconstruing of the human situation," [52] a refusal to recognize that life is a gift from God (I Cor. 4:7). Hence, Paul bids his readers not to boast in men (e.g. I Cor. 1:29; 3:21) or "in your flesh" (Gal. 6:13), but only "in the Lord" (I Cor. 1:31; II Cor. 10:17-18) or "in the cross of our Lord Jesus Christ" (Gal. 6:14).

The idea of sin as man's alienation from the Creator also finds expression in Rom. 1:21 ff. The context shows that Paul is thinking particularly of the Gentiles. Although they themselves claim to know God, they do not *acknowledge* him as such ("they did not glorify him as God or give thanks to him," vs. 21). Rather, they make their own "wisdom" their god (vs. 22) and end up serving "the creature rather than the Creator" (vs. 25 RSV). But equally severe are the apostle's words about the false boasting of the Jews (Rom. 2:1 ff.). They are guilty of an idolatry no less serious, although of a different kind. Their "boast" is in the law (vs. 23) and in the privileged relationship to God that they believe themselves to have by virtue of their status as recipients of the law (cf. vs. 17). Their boasting, like that of the Gentiles, really separates them from God; such boasting has no place in the life of the man who lives by faith (Rom. 3:27).

Not only Paul's conception of "the flesh," but also his view of the law is closely related to his understanding of sin. If the flesh is sin's "host," then the law is sin's "agent." In most instances the apostle means by "law" (νόμος) either the Old Testament Torah in particular or else the whole Old Testament—conceived, of course, primarily as that which contains the law.[53] The apostle explicitly and emphatically repudiates the idea that the law itself is to be identified with sin (Rom. 7:7), but holds nevertheless that it plays an important role in sin's "reigning" in the world. Three major passages require examination in this connection: Rom. 5:12 ff.; 7:7 ff.; Gal. 3:19 ff.

---

[51] Bultmann, *Theology*, I, 241.

[52] *Ibid.*, p. 242.

[53] See Gutbrod, *ThW*, IV, 106 ff.; Bultmann, *Theology*, I, 259 ff.

1. *Rom. 5:12 ff.* Bultmann is quite correct in holding that the subject under consideration here is not sin and its "origin" but the origin of the new life.[54] Nevertheless, the passage is important for an understanding of Paul's view of sin and of its relationship to the law. Sin entered the world through Adam's "trespass" (vss. 12, 15) and thus was in the world already in the pre-Mosaic period before the law had been given (vs. 13). With sin came death's tyrannical "reign," not only over Adam, the primeval man and representative of the whole race, but also over all men (vs. 14). Yet Paul discerns, in this pre-Mosaic period, a difference between Adam's trespass and the sin of mankind in general. Death reigned from Adam to Moses, he says, "even over those whose sins were not like the transgression of Adam, who was a type of the one who was to come" (vs. 14 RSV). The apostle presumes that the difference is readily apparent and thus does not spell it out. Perhaps he has two points in mind: first, that Adam was the archetypal man, not only the original man but in himself the embodiment of all mankind;[55] second that he himself was immediately responsible for transgressing a specific commandment he had been given.

The first point is already suggested in vs. 14 when Adam is described as "a type of the one who was to come." Adam's status as a "universal man" is really only comparable (and then not completely) with Christ's. Adam's trespass has an originative and universal significance which cannot be ascribed to Adam's progeny. The second point is not less clear. It is suggested in vs. 13 where Paul observes that in the pre-Mosaic era sin is present (for all men, because through Adam they had "all sinned," vs. 12), but is "not tabulated where there is no law." While

---

[54] "Adam and Christ According to Romans 5," *Current Issues in New Testament Interpretation,* ed. W. Klassen and G. Snyder (1962), p. 152.

[55] For discussions of Adam as the "original man" (*Urmensch*) see, e.g., K. Rudolph, *RGG* (3rd ed.), VI, cols. 1195 ff.; E. G. Drower, *The Secret Adam* (1960), and "ADAMAS—humanity: ADAM—mankind," *ThLZ,* LXXXVI (1961), cols. 173 ff.; Egon Brandenburger, *Adam und Christus, exegetisch-religionsgeschichtliche Untersuchung zu Röm. 5, 12-21 (1. Kor. 15)* in *WMANT,* 7 (1962). The Gnostic background of Paul's Adam speculation is disputed by Robin Scroggs in *The Last Adam: A Study in Pauline Anthropology* (1966), who seeks to demonstrate that Paul is dependent on Jewish Adam myths.

Adam's sin is in direct violation of a commandment he has
been given, the sin of mankind in general, following Adam's
trespass, contravenes no given law. Adam's sin has a dimension
of personal guilt and responsibility which the sin of his progeny
does not have.

Yet all of this changes with the giving of the law through
Moses. The implication of vs. 13 is that when the law *is* given,
then the sins of men *are* "tabulated." The originative and universal effect of Adam's sin, also a doctrine of late Judaism (see,
e.g. II Esd. 3:7, 21-22; 7:118; Apoc. Bar. 17:3; 23:4; 48:42; 54:15,
19), is not denied, but to this is added the conviction that those
who "inherit" Adam's sin also become their own Adams (a
motif also present in apocalyptic Judaism, e.g. Apoc. Bar. 54:
19).[56] The recognition of personal guilt and responsibility is,
to be sure, already present in the comment that "death spread
to all men because [57] *all men sinned*" (vs. 12 RSV). But it is the
giving of the law which makes sin a personal factor in each
man's existence and individualizes guilt. In vs. 20 the result of
the law's coming into the world is described as "multiplication
of the trespass." Where before there was just "one" (Adam's),
now there are "many" (cf. εἷς—πολλοί in vs. 15). It is in fact
the law's *function* in coming into the world (παρεισῆλθεν ἵνα, vs.
20) to multiply Adam's sin by making each man his own Adam.
Now it is clear what Paul has in mind when he speaks of sin's
being "tabulated" (vs. 13): each man's experience of his own
guilt and responsibility as a *sinner*. Through the law sin is concretized, and guilt is individualized; this is its "multiplication."

2. *Rom. 7:7 ff.* Here Paul specifically denies that the law itself
is sinful (vs. 7). Already the comment of 5:13, that sin was present in the world before the giving of the law, had shown his
refusal to equate the two. The law may "multiply" sin, but the
law does not "bring" it. Nevertheless, the law does bring "the
knowledge of sin." So much Paul had said in an earlier phase
of his argument (3:20). Now in chap. 7 the same point is picked
up and developed. "I should not have known sin," he declares,

---

[56] See Michel, *Römer*, p. 139.
[57] ἐφ' ᾧ must certainly be so translated. See, e.g., Michel, *Römer*, pp. 138-39.

"except through the law" (7:7a). As Adam primevally had been personally confronted with God's commandment, so in the law of Moses each of Adam's "children" is personally addressed by the claim of God: "I should not have known covetousness had the law not said, 'Thou shalt not covet'" (vs. 7b). It is clear, especially in the light of 5:12 ff., that Paul does not mean *simply* that the law brings a "recognition" of sin and thus assists in identifying it (though it does that, too). More important, the "knowledge" of sin spoken of in 3:20 and 7:7 is also its "multiplication" (5:20), each man's encounter with and experience of it.

The correctness of this interpretation is confirmed in the following verses of chap. 7. Sin is not just revealed in the commandment but actually *works* by means of it. Sin is already "in the world" (ἐν κόσμῳ, 5:13), but taking advantage of the opportunity presented in the law, it establishes itself specifically "in me" (ἐν ἐμοί, vs. 8a). Through the law sin becomes present for each man and there exercises its destructive power ("wrought in me all kinds of covetousness," vs. 8a RSV). For this reason it is appropriate to say that "the power of sin is the law" (I Cor. 15:56 RSV). The law brings sin to "life" for man (Rom. 7:8b, 9) and is thus indirectly responsible for man's death (vs. 10). Sin's work *is* the work of death (κατεργαζομένη θάνατον, vs. 13), and sin is revealed as sin precisely where the commandment makes man "sinful beyond measure" (RSV). While the apostle is careful to explain that the law provides only the "opportunity" (vs. 11; cf. vs. 8) and that sin itself remains the real culprit who "deceives" and "kills" (vss. 11, 13), it is also clear that this happens through the instrumentality of the law's commandment (δι' αὐτῆς ["by means of it"], vs. 11), "by means of what is good" (διὰ τοῦ ἀγαθοῦ, vs. 13).

It is possible, however, to say still more precisely how the law functions as the agent of sin. The clue is offered in the much discussed section of Romans 7 in which Paul speaks of "willing" the right but not "doing" it. A consideration of all the detailed problems of these verses (14 ff.) is not possible here, and in any case Bultmann's persuasive exposition has already supplied the key to Paul's meaning.⁵⁸ It is essential to observe that the law does not serve as sin's agent only when it is transgressed, but also when it is fulfilled. Insofar as the law is *served*, insofar as man stands under the law at all, it becomes for him the agent of sin. This Bultmann has correctly shown with a reference to Rom. 7:6.⁵⁹ Man serves the law because it promises "life" (vs. 10), and it is life which man seeks to gain ("what I want" [ὃ θέλω], vs. 15; "to want the right" [τὸ ... θέλειν ... τὸ καλόν], vs. 18; "the good I want" [ὃ θέλω ... ἀγαθόν], vs. 19; "wanting to do right" [τῷ θέλοντι ἐμοὶ ποιεῖν τὸ καλόν], vs. 21). But precisely in the "seeking to do the law" in order to find life, life is lost. Through the law sin "deceives" man and kills him (vs. 11); not life, but death is wrought (vss. 13, 24); not what is sought, but what is shunned (vss. 15 ff.); not what is "right," but what is "evil" (vs. 21); not the "law of God," but the "law of sin" (vs. 25).

The law affords sin the opportunity for perpetrating its act of deceit because the commandments of the law tempt man to think that by fulfilling them he will have "life." The law thus asks for obedience in the sense of *achievement*. As already seen, however, Paul regards man's reliance upon himself as an "achiever" to be reliance upon "the flesh" as opposed to God. That is the essence of sin. Service to "the law" then turns out to be the service of sin (vs. 25). The law, according to Paul's view, does not release man from his bondage to sin but confirms him in it, makes him "sinful beyond measure" (vs. 13). It is no accident that the apostle's polemic against "works of the law" (cf. Rom. 3:20) finds its climax in the emphatic assertion that faith, which stands over against those works, fully excludes "our boasting" (Rom. 3:27). Similarly, when in another polemical passage the apostle cites Deut. 27:26 ("Cursed be every one who does not abide by all things written in the book of the law, and do them," Gal. 3:10 RSV), it is clear that for him the law's "curse" consists in its demand for *performance* in the sense of personal accomplishment. Because the law says, "He who *does*

---

⁵⁸ See above, n. 47.
⁵⁹ "Romans 7," pp. 154-55.

them shall live by them" (Gal. 3:12 RSV; cf. Lev. 18:5), it
shows that it is not based on faith but on the premise that life
can be achieved "according to the flesh," apart from the power
of God.

3. *Gal. 3:19 ff.* As in Rom. 7:7, so in Gal. 3:19 the apostle explicitly raises the question of the law's function. His answer:
"It was added because of transgressions" (RSV; τῶν παραβά-
σεων χάριν προσετέθη). A clue to Paul's meaning here is afforded
by the important statement of Rom. 4:15: "The law works wrath,
and where there is no law there is no transgression" (οὗ δὲ οὐκ
ἔστιν νόμος, οὐδὲ παράβασις). "Because" in Gal. 3:19 is therefore not to be interpreted to mean that God gives the law to
serve as a *check* on transgression, but the reverse. It is given to
bring transgression forth. The thought here is fully consonant
with what is said in Rom. 5:12 ff. and 7:7 ff.: through the law
the trespass (τὸ παράπτωμα, Rom. 5:20) is actually "multiplied"
and made a factor in each man's own existence. Paul's view of
the law's function does not at all conform to that implicit in I
Tim. 1:8 ff. where it is said that the law was given "for the law-
less and disobedient, for the ungodly and sinners" (RSV), given
in order to hold immorality under restraint. Quite different is
the apostle's view that the law itself prods sin into activity.
Moffatt's translation of the key phrase in Gal. 3:19 expresses
the point accurately: "[the law] was interpolated for the purpose of *producing* transgressions." (Italics added.)

b. Righteousness and justification

Paul's view of the law cannot be understood fully apart from
a consideration of his views of the righteousness of God and
justification by faith. As the course of the argument in Romans
and Galatians demonstrates, these themes are closely related.

The concept of God's righteousness (δικαιοσύνη θεοῦ) has an
especially prominent place in the letter to the Romans. There
it figures already in the "thematic" statement of 1:16-17. The
gospel, which is God's "power for salvation," is the means by
which "the righteousness of God is being revealed." The association of God's "righteousness" with his "power," as well as the
comment that it is something "revealed" (ἀποκαλύπτεται), sug-

gests Paul's indebtedness to apocalyptic categories.[60] The apocalyptic-eschatological background of his thinking on this point is further reflected in his understanding of God's righteousness as his faithfulness to the covenant he has established with his people. This comes to expression in several passages in the same letter.

In Rom. 3:3 ff. Israel's "unfaithfulness" (ἀπιστία) to the covenant is contrasted with God's "faithfulness" (πίστις) to it (vs. 3). In spite of Israel's apostasy, however, God remains "true" (ἀληθής, vs. 4), and thus his "righteousness" is confirmed (vs. 5). It is clear that for Paul the righteousness of God has to do with his faithfulness and truth as expressed in his establishment and maintenance of a covenant relationship with his people. In accord with this is the more fully traditional formulation of Rom. 3:25 which identifies God's righteousness with the "divine forbearance," his forgiveness of sins, and thus his continuing fidelity to the covenant he has given.[61] The most extended discussion of God's relationship to his covenant people occurs, however, in Romans 9–11. Here, once more, the concept of God's "righteousness" plays an important role.[62] Especially significant is Rom. 10:3 which characterizes Israel as being "ignorant" of God's righteousness and not "submitting" to it. The contrast is again between the faithfulness of God and the unfaithfulness of his people.

Implicit in this understanding of the divine righteousness as covenant "faithfulness" and "truth" is the notion of God's creating, sustaining, and redeeming *power*. It was to this power of righteousness that Israel had refused to "submit" (οὐχ ὑπετάγησαν, Rom. 10:3). God's righteousness is the power which has established the covenant and which seeks ever to uphold it. It is the power of God's mercy and God's call which, as Romans 11

[60] It is the thesis of Stuhlmacher in *Gerechtigkeit Gottes bei Paulus* that the phrase "righteousness of God" represents a fixed, technical concept of apocalyptic Judaism. Whether or not that be so, his detailed examination of the relevant Pauline texts and his comparison of them with apocalyptic materials have demonstrated the prominence of apocalyptic concerns in the apostle's thought.

[61] *Ibid.*, pp. 86 ff.

[62] *Ibid.*, pp. 91 ff.

emphasizes, has been continuously extended to God's people and is never rescinded. Moreover, God's righteousness expresses itself as power in his redemptive activity. This is seen in Romans 4 which may be regarded as the apostle's scriptural "proof" of the thesis that righteousness has been decisively given to believers in Christ (3:21 ff.).[63] Abraham's faith is "accounted as righteousness" (vs. 4), and the object of his faith is the God who has the power to fulfill what he has promised (δυνατός ἐστιν καὶ ποιῆσαι, vs. 21). God's power is further characterized (perhaps with reliance on a traditional formulation) as that which raised Christ from the dead (vss. 24-25); it is, indeed, in keeping with God's own being that he bestows life where there is death and gives being to that which previously had no existence (vs. 17). In other words, the meaning of God's righteousness is manifested preeminently in Christ's death and resurrection, the decisive expression of God's power. Because Christ himself has been made "righteousness" (I Cor. 1:30), it is appropriate to say that God's grace exercises its powerful rule (βασιλεύειν) "through righteousness for eternal life through Jesus Christ our Lord" (Rom. 5:21 RSV). And the gospel is "the power of God for salvation" to believers because by means of it "the righteousness of God" is revealed to them (Rom. 1:16-17 RSV).

From these representative passages it may be concluded that Paul understands God's righteousness to consist in his power, truth, and faithfulness as expressed in creation, the covenant, and—decisively—in the raising of Christ from the dead for man's salvation. The righteousness of God has to do not only with his own "character" but with his relationship to men and his acting on their behalf. It is significant that the apostle says Christ was made righteousness "for us" (I Cor. 1:30) and that he speaks of Abraham's faith in God "who establishes the ungodly in righteousness" (Rom. 4:5). Paul's doctrine of the righteousness of God (δικαιοσύνη θεοῦ) is thus not to be isolated from his doctrine of justification by faith (δικαιοσύνη ἐκ πίστεως).[64] This latter, contrary to the insistence of Wrede,

---

[63] Bultmann, *Theology*, I, 279.

[64] The English translation of the Greek verb δικαιοῦν as "justify" obscures the fact that this is the cognate verb of the noun "righteousness"

Schweitzer, and others,[65] stands not just at the periphery of
Pauline thought, giving it a polemical edge. Rather, because
his concept of justification is related first of all to his affirmation
of the righteousness and power of the covenant God who creates,
upholds, and redeems, it stands at the very center of his gospel.

The Pauline doctrine of justification, no less than the conception of God's righteousness, must be understood first of all in
terms of *relationships*. God's righteousness consists in the particular relationship he bears to his people, a relationship created,
sustained, and redeemed by his power, effective as faithfulness
and truth. So also man's "righteousness" has to do with his relationship to the covenant and the covenant God. When by man's
apostasy and willful disobedience that relationship is perverted,
then it is by God's power that it must be restored. By his faith
in such a God, says Paul, Abraham gained righteousness, was
"rightwised." [66] The meaning is not that he attained some particular *quality* of life. In Paul's thought the concept of righteousness is not "moralized" as it is, for example, in the Pastoral
Epistles (e.g. Titus 2:12 where the adverb δικαίως ["righteously"]
refers to a particular kind of moral conduct in the world).
Rather, for Paul, to be "rightwised" means to be restored to a
proper relationship with God.

Illustrative of the apostle's meaning is Ps. 51:6 (LXX) which
he quotes in Rom. 3:4 (RSV):

> "That thou mayest be justified in thy words,
> and prevail when thou art judged."

Here, to be "justified" means to "prevail" when judged, to "win
out" in legal action. Righteousness is a *standing* accorded, a particular relationship into which one is brought by reason of a
"verdict" pronounced over him.[67] Justification thus has a basically "forensic" aspect [68] and may be described as receipt of the

---

(δικαιοσύνη). Kendrick Grobel, the translator of Bultmann's *Theology*, has
sought to circumvent this problem by rehabilitating the obsolete Anglo-
Saxon verb "rightwise" (see his editorial note, *Theology*, I, 253), and this
precedent will be followed also in the present study.

[65] See below, pp. 258-59.
[66] See n. 64.
[67] On this see Bultmann, *Theology*, I, 271 ff.
[68] *Ibid.*, p. 272.

verdict of "acquittal" (in Rom. 5:18 this is an appropriate translation [RSV] for the noun δικαίωσις). Moreover, Paul associates this verdict of righteousness with God's *eschatological* judgment. The term "righteousness" may be employed alongside the terms "salvation" and "life" to describe the object of man's longing and hope (see e.g. Gal. 5:5, "the hope for righteousness," and Rom. 14:17 where God's kingdom [his rule in power!] is described as "righteousness and peace and joy in the Holy Spirit," RSV). The eschatological dimension of righteousness-justification is also reflected in such a passage as Rom. 2:13 which looks to the future judgment of God ("For it is not the hearers of the law who are righteous before God, but the doers of the law who will be justified," RSV).[69]

This basically forensic-eschatological nature of the Pauline concept of justification accords with the background of the term in Judaism. But its polemical application against the Jewish doctrine of justification shows that in some crucial regard the apostle's teaching is different. In contrast to Judaism, it is decisive for Paul that the eschatological judgment of God is *already* breaking in and that righteousness is *already* given to those who belong to the crucified and resurrected Christ. "In *him* [Christ]," says Paul, *we* may become "the righteousness of God" (II Cor. 5:21 RSV), and he finds it appropriate to speak not only of the believer's "being rightwised" (present tense, e.g. Rom. 3:24, 26; 4:5; 8:33; Gal. 3:11), but even of his *"having been* rightwised" (aorist, Rom. 5:1, 9; 8:30; I Cor. 6:11; cf. the perfect, Rom. 6:7). This means that the νυνὶ δέ ("But now") of Rom. 3:21 has profound theological significance. "Now"—in Christ—"God's righteousness has been manifested" and, as the subsequent development of the argument shows, has its effect in the life of the believer who is himself "rightwised." Christ reveals the "righteousness" of God (δικαιοσύνη θεοῦ) because his coming (above all his death and resurrection) is itself a "righteous act" (δικαίωμα, Rom. 5:18) which saves the believer from "condemnation" (κατάκριμα) and grants him "acquittal" (δικαίωμα, Rom. 5:16). Bearing a similar theological weight are the νυνὶ δέ formu-

⁶⁹ *Ibid.,* p. 273.

lations introducing Rom. 6:22 and 7:6, each of which serves to describe further what Paul means by justification: "But now . . . you have been set free from sin and placed in bondage to God"; "But now we have been released from the law, having died to that by which we were imprisoned, in order to serve in the new life of the Spirit and not under the old written code."

These latter passages show that the doctrine of justification presupposes not only the righteousness of God, but also, of course, man's need to be "rightwised," his need for salvation. It presupposes that man apart from Christ, outside faith, remains in bondage to the powers of the present evil age (sin and death), to sin's "host" (the flesh), and to sin's "agent" (the law). This slavery to sin and its retinue of related powers means that man is alienated from God, that he does not stand in a "right relationship" to his Creator. And this is why he is in need of "rightwising." The Pauline doctrine of justification expresses the confidence that, by the powerful initiative and persistence of his faithfulness and love, God overcomes the estrangement and hostility which characterizes man's bondage to alien powers. The concept of δικαιοσύνη ("righteousness," "justification") is therefore not a purely formal one, but has a specific content and meaning. In relation to God δικαιοσύνη connotes the divine faithfulness, love, and will to redeem, and in relation to men it connotes the *effects* of these: "salvation," "life," or— as the apostle once says—"peace with God" (Rom. 5:1). Each of these terms, like δικαιοσύνη itself, refers first of all to a hope for the future. Yet each of them may also be used to refer to the present effect of the saving work of God in Christ.

That God's act of justification in Christ has to do with the restoration of man to a proper relationship with God and overcoming the estrangement and hostility between them is also indicated when Paul employs the concept of *reconciliation* (καταλλαγή, καταλλάσσειν; the only New Testament occurrences of these words are in the Pauline letters). The theme, as applied to the relationship between God and men (for its application in the human sphere see I Cor. 7:11), appears in two major passages (Rom. 5:6 ff.; II Cor. 5:17 ff.) which serve to elaborate the meaning of the reference to God's "reconciliation of the world" in Rom. 11:15. These passages show, first of all, that "reconciliation" is but an alternate way of expressing the reality of what has occurred in "justification." [70] This is established not only by the parallelism of the expressions in Rom. 5:9, 10 (cf. vs. 11), but particularly by II Cor. 5:19 where reconciliation is described as God's "not counting" (μὴ λογιζόμενος) men's trespasses against them. Such a statement is parallel to the remark of Rom. 3:26 that God's righteousness is shown in his "passing over" of sins, and it is the corollary of passages which identify God's act of rightwising as his "counting" (λογίζεται) man's faith as righteousness (e.g. Rom. 4:5). Also to be noted is II Cor. 5:21: the result of God's reconciling act in Christ (vss. 17 ff.) is that "in him" the believer becomes "the righteousness of God."

Above all, this parallel metaphor of "reconciliation" emphasizes the point that man's estrangement from God is overcome solely because of God's initiative. It is not *God* but *men* who stand in need of reconciliation; the subject of the reconciliation is God; its object is "the world" (II Cor. 5:19; "us," vs. 18). "Everything is from God," says Paul as he introduces the thought of God's reconciling activity (II Cor. 5:18), and in Rom. 5:11 he refers to reconciliation as that which is "received." Of course, the metaphor presupposes that man's prior alienation had the aspect of *hostility*. This demands God's initiative: *"while we were enemies* we were reconciled to God" (Rom. 5:10 RSV, italics added). The parallel expressions, "while we were still helpless" (vs. 6) and "while we were still sinners" (vs. 8) further identify the extent of man's estrangement and the absolute priority of God in overcoming it. The emphasis on the need for the initiative of God's grace springs from Paul's conviction that man is so helplessly enslaved to the powers of the present evil age that his salvation can come only from "beyond," from the "transcendent power of God."

The contours of the apostle's argument take on yet sharper definition when he directs his doctrine of justification polemically against the teaching of Judaism. This polemical edge is apparent when he speaks of the rightwising, reconciling grace of God:

[70] *Ibid.*, pp. 285 ff.

"But if by grace, then not at all on the basis of works, for in that case 'grace' would no longer be *grace*" (Rom. 11:6); "I do not set aside the grace of God; for if rightwising were through the law, then Christ died gratuitously, in vain" (Gal. 2:21); "You who would be rightwised by the law . . . have fallen away from grace" (Gal. 5:4). Involved in Paul's insistence that the righteousness of God is already breaking in through the saving work of Christ—in itself the decisive departure from Judaism—is the conviction that the law is thereby shown to be ineffective as the way to salvation. "But now the righteousness of God has been manifested *apart from law*" (Rom. 3:21 RSV, italics added). The law's promise of life (Rom. 7:10) is empty because the promise rests on grace (Rom. 4:16), and law and grace are representative of entirely different ways to salvation (Rom. 6:14). Grace points to the initiative and power of God as the one who "gives" righteousness and to man (in his helplessness, sinfulness, and enmity) as the receiver. But the law seems to presuppose that man is in his own right an "achiever," and it may lead him to suppose that by his performance of the works which the law commends, he is himself enabled to win the verdict of "righteousness" from God.

This criticism of the law has its basis in Paul's insight that reliance on "the flesh," the orientation of one's life in terms of the values, goals, and possibilities of "this world," only drives one ever further away from God, in relationship to whom true life is found. Man's alienation from God and "boasting" in the flesh is the essence of his sin,[71] and since the law encourages reliance on "worldly" accomplishment, the law itself becomes sin's agent.[72] It is true that the "works of the law" (ἔργα νόμου) are never identified with such "works of the flesh" (ἔργα τῆς σαρκός) as are enumerated in the vice list of Gal. 5:19 ff. (cf. "the works of darkness" [τὰ ἔργα τοῦ σκότους], Rom. 13:12). Nevertheless, they are works of the flesh insofar as their performance becomes an occasion for man's taking pride in his own achievement. Had Abraham been rightwised by "works," says

[71] See above, pp. 137-38.
[72] See above, pp. 138 ff.

the apostle, he would have had "something to boast about" (Rom. 4:2 RSV), a basis upon which he could presume to claim a favorable standing before God as his "due" (cf. κατὰ ὀφείλημα, vs. 4). But Abraham was rightwised on the basis of his faith (vss. 3, 9, etc.), a gift of God's grace (vs. 4). Precisely because righteousness is founded in the promise and power of God, man's ground for boasting is taken away (Rom. 3:27), and the alienation which such boasting represents is overcome. That is why, in Paul's view, justification cannot possibly come through reliance on works of the law (Rom. 3:21, 28; 4:6; 11:6; Gal. 2:16, etc.). The impossibility of achieving righteousness by reliance on the law is also clear if one remembers that the effect of the law's coming is to "tabulate" sin ("sin is not tabulated [οὐκ ἐλλογεῖται] where there is no law," Rom. 5:13), whereas the essence of God's rightwising, reconciling grace is that man's sin is *not* "charged" against him ("in Christ God was reconciling the world to himself, not charging [μὴ λογιζόμενος] their trespasses against them," II Cor. 5:19).

It was previously observed that Paul does not conceive of "justification" in a purely formal way. He regards it as having a specific "content" and "meaning," viz., "peace with God," reconciliation with him and hence "salvation" or "life." [73] This point now needs to be stated in a new way, and thus reemphasized. The (correct) understanding that justification is a "forensic" category referring to a "verdict of acquittal" must not obscure the fact that it is a verdict which works an actual *change* in the situation of the one rightwised. When God "rightwises" the

[73] The tendency of many interpreters to regard the concept of justification as a more or less formal one, devoid of the more richly salvific content of the concept of reconciliation, may be observed in Büchsel's discussion of the latter in *ThW*, I, 254 ff. [ET: pp. 255 ff.]. While acknowledging a certain parallelism between reconciliation and justification (p. 255 [ET: *ibid.*]), he insists nevertheless that the meaning of reconciliation must not be reduced to that of justification. Reconciliation speaks of "the kindling of love," while justification involves only "the removal of guilt in forgiveness" (p. 258 [ET: *ibid.*]). But against this, the present interpretation suggests that the parallelism of the two concepts is much more thoroughgoing than Büchsel acknowledges, and that it is no less false to "reduce" the apostle's idea of *justification* to mean a formal verdict, "Not guilty," than it is to reduce his idea of reconciliation to that meaning.

sinner, he not only "declares" him "right" but "puts" him right.
As Paul uses it, the verb δικαιοῦν has not only a declarative but
also a causative meaning.[74] This double aspect of justification
is missed if the apostle's courtroom metaphor is elucidated only
on the basis of criminal proceedings. Paul emphasizes that it is
the sinner, the ungodly who is "declared right." But when an
acknowledged criminal is "found innocent" by a court, does that
make him innocent? Rather, is not one then confronted with
a legal fiction? Expounded in this way the metaphor is indeed
open to the kind of criticism levelled against it by John Knox,
who argues that being placed "in a legally right position" affects
only the sinner's standing in the eyes of the law (i.e. freedom
from it) and does nothing with respect to the sinner's own life.[75]

But Knox's criticism does not hold, for Paul clearly *does*
intend that justification should mean more than a legal declaration. Since righteousness and justification deal with relationships
and not "qualities," [76] the legal metaphor is perhaps better expounded if one thinks not of a criminal case which concerns a
specific past offense, but of a *juvenile* case. Let it be supposed
that the court waives its rights to prosecute for an acknowledged
crime and decides, instead, to deal with the offender as a delinquent in need of rehabilitation. In such a case the court's
objective is neither to execute nor accuse, but to reorient the
acknowledged delinquent to society. On the one hand, the
court's decision not to prosecute may be regarded as tantamount
to a verdict of acquittal. On the other hand, the court is empowered to place the "acquitted offender" in the setting which
can afford him the needed redemptive relationships—perhaps
his own home, a foster family, a "training school," or some other.
By this means the court does not just make a "declaration" concerning the delinquent (which, in effect has been acquittal),
but causes an actual change in his situation. The court does not
ignore the delinquent's disorientation and estrangement from
society, but moves to overcome it. His acquittal does not involve
a legal fiction, but presupposes that the new relationship which

[74] See, e.g., Stuhlmacher, *Gerechtigkeit Gottes bei Paulus,* pp. 217 ff.
[75] *The Ethics of Jesus,* pp. 77 ff.
[76] See above, pp. 146 ff.

is being established can be reconciling and redemptive. Perhaps along these lines one may begin to discern the meaning of justification in Pauline thought. By the power and initiative of another, by grace which includes both judgment and forgiveness, the believer is brought back from his alienation and estrangement, reconciled with his God and thus returned to "life." [77]

Once the various facets of this doctrine of justification have been grasped and its importance for the apostle's thought as a whole has been acknowledged, several special questions and problems arise. If, for example, it is precisely the *sinner* who is rightwised, and that through faith, not works, does the justified man then *remain* a "sinner"? If so, what meaning does it have to say that he is "freed" from sin and the law, as Paul often does? On the other hand, if he does not continue to sin, why is Paul himself constantly admonishing, warning, imploring, exhorting, and instructing his congregations ("the saints"?) in ethical matters? Or, further, if where sin is rampant, grace abounds all the more (Rom. 5:20), what possible grounds are there for the apostle's emphatic denial that sin and grace are therefore fully compatible (Rom. 6:1)? The answers to such questions will unfold as the discussion proceeds, especially in connection with the Pauline view of faith, love, and obedience. There is, however, one other related question which is most appropriately handled in the present context—the relation of justification to "sanctification."

The specific question which needs to be considered here is whether "sanctification" may accurately be described as the *development* or *actualization* of justification in the life of the believer. Such a definition of the relationship of these two concepts has often been defended (e.g. Ernesti, Jacoby, Goguel, Whiteley; but also many others). To be sure, the word order of I Cor. 6:11 is in itself enough to make such a neat distinction exegetically precarious ("But you were washed . . . sanctified . . . rightwised in the name of the Lord Jesus Christ and in the

[77] Stalder also speaks of Paul's doctrine of justification in terms of being brought back from death (*Das Werk das Geistes*, pp. 185-86). This theme must receive fuller attention later (below, pp. 183, 195, 217).

Spirit of our God"), as well as the fact that even the Corinthians can be addressed as those who "have been sanctified in Christ Jesus" (I Cor. 1:2). But there are even more serious difficulties with saying that justification represents the initiation of salvation and sanctification its realization in the believer's life.

On the one hand, a distinction formulated in these terms fails to understand that the Pauline doctrine of justification refers not only to a formal declaration about the believer, but also presumes an actual change in his standing and therefore in his life.[78] To be rightwised means to be claimed and encountered by the power and love of God which reconciles and makes new. God's righteousness, with its twin aspects of judgment and grace, is met and received in Christ who is righteousness "for us" (I Cor. 1:30). Therefore, to be "in him [Christ]" is to become the "righteousness of God" (II Cor. 5:21). And it is significant that the apostle, in this same context, can say alternately that to be "in Christ" means to be "a new creation" (II Cor. 5:17). Justification does not just prepare for the new life but already effects it. Reference may also be made to Rom. 5:1 ff. where the situation of "having been rightwised by faith" is further described as "having peace with God," "standing in grace," and "rejoicing" in the hope which the actual presence of God's love in his Spirit makes possible. For Paul, as such texts show, justification means far more than the formal inception of salvation. It has to do with the new life which has presently come to the believer "in Christ."

On the other hand, this specious distinction between justification and sanctification also fails, at least when applied to Paul, to understand the primary significance of "sanctification." [79] In effect this distinction would convert the concept of sanctification into a special "ethical doctrine" having to do with the believer's conduct in the world as contrasted with his relation-

[78] See above, p. 152. See also Gaugler, "Die Heiligung in der Ethik des Apostels Paulus," *IKZ*, XXXIII (1925), 106-7.

[79] The topic as such is too broad to be treated in full here. Notable contributions to it have been made by O. Procksch and K. G. Kuhn, *ThW*, I, 87 ff. [ET: pp. 88 ff.], Gaugler ("Die Heiligung in der Ethik"), and Stalder (*Das Werk des Geistes*).

ship to God ("justification"). The "indicative" aspects of the apostle's thought would thus be regarded as expressive of his doctrine of justification and the "imperative" aspects of it as the result of his doctrine of sanctification.[80] Now it is certainly true that "sanctification" has significant ethical connections and connotations. This is most apparent in I Thessalonians 4. There it is contrasted with "impurity" (vs. 7) and said to involve "abstaining from sexual immorality" and other transgressions (vss. 3 ff.). In this passage, as Stalder also notes,[81] there is no question but that "sanctification" is interpreted in terms of man's concrete moral activity.

Yet the moral aspect of sanctification is secondary to its primarily "soteriological" reference,[82] and this is also apparent in I Thessalonians 4. It is significant that there sanctification is identified *first of all* with God's will and God's call: "For this is the will of God, your sanctification" (vs. 3 RSV); "For God has not called us for uncleanness, but in sanctification" (vs. 7 RSV). God's call is in itself sanctification, for it means being "made holy" to God, that is, being "set apart" for his service. This is why even the Corinthians can be addressed as "sanctified in Christ Jesus" (I Cor. 1:2 RSV); their "call to be holy" (ἅγιοι) presupposes nothing about their moral worthiness, but only that they *belong* to the Lord ("those who . . . call on the name of our Lord Jesus Christ, both their Lord and ours," RSV). Sanctification consists not in a particular moral quality which has been attained, but in a particular relationship to God which has been given. This is in keeping with the originally cultic application of the concept "holiness"—as in the Old Testament passages where anything or anyone who stands in a positive relationship to the cult is described as "holy" ("devoted to service").[83] The specifically ethical demands which sanctification involves are derivative from this central point. The "call" of God, the "being made holy" by him, at the same time expresses his "will" for

---

[80] This distinction is analogous to that between "kerygma" and "didache" which has already been criticized (above, pp. 106 ff.).

[81] *Das Werk des Geistes*, pp. 211 ff.

[82] Cf. G. Stählin, *RGG* (3rd ed.), III, cols. 179-80.

[83] Procksch, *ThW*, I, 88 ff. [ET: pp. 89 ff.].

those who are called (I Thess. 4:3). From the gift arises the demand.[84] Far from being the "ethical" counterpart to the "theological" doctrine of justification, the doctrine of sanctification in and of itself displays the unity of indicative and imperative.

One more passage has to be considered. In Rom. 6:19 ff. the terms "righteousness" and "sanctification" are both used. Paul exhorts, "For just as you once yielded your members to impurity and to greater and greater iniquity, so now yield your members to righteousness for sanctification" (vs. 19 RSV). Does not this suggest that sanctification is the "working out" of justification, the attainment of an ever fuller measure of "righteousness"? But such a neat formulation is complicated by vs. 22, for there "sanctification" is used where one might have expected to find "righteousness" ("But now that you have been set free from sin and have become slaves of God, the return you get is sanctification and its end, eternal life," RSV). Some light is shed on the question when it is noted, first, that, considering the wider context, Paul uses "God" and "righteousness" as parallel terms (vs. 13, "present yourselves to God"; vs. 19, "present yourselves to righteousness"). The same parallelism is implicit in vss. 20 and 22 (slavery to sin means "freedom" from righteousness, vs. 20; freedom from sin means "slavery" to God, vs. 22). Even further, it becomes clear that "sanctification" and "righteousness" can also be used similarly: present yourselves to God and thus become instruments of righteousness (vs. 13); present yourselves to righteousness "for sanctification" (vs. 19). This is even more striking when comparing vss. 13 (surrender to God means righteousness) and 22 (slavery to God means sanctification).

It would be too much to say that righteousness and sanctification are here identified. On the other hand, a clear distinction between them is not easily drawn. In fact, the phrase "instruments of righteousness [God]," vs. 13, is an appropriate description of what is meant by the call to sanctification—to be set aside for God's service. Yet there is also a special additional nuance in the concept of sanctification, as implied by the "tri-

[84] Stählin, RGG, III, cols. 179-80; also Bultmann, Theology, I, 338-39.

umphant climax" of vs. 19b.[85] What this nuance is can be detected by noting the parallelism within the verse itself: the believer is no longer to yield his members "to impurity and *to lawlessness for ever repeated lawlessness* [τῇ ἀνομίᾳ εἰς τὴν ἀνομίαν]" but *"to righteousness for sanctification* [τῇ δικαιοσύνῃ εἰς ἁγιασμόν]." The RSV translation of the first phrase is misleading ("to impurity and *to greater and greater iniquity*") insofar as Paul may be misinterpreted to mean that there are successively more serious stages of iniquity (or "lawlessness"). In that case the parallel εἰς ἁγιασμόν could be taken in the same way, yielding the idea that sanctification is the highest level of righteousness. But Stalder rightly criticizes this exegesis (Lipsius and Lagrange are cited as examples) on the grounds that neither "lawlessness" nor "sanctification" is regarded by Paul as a static condition.[86] He does not view the sinner as one who falls successively from one "level" of sin to another. Rather, the sinner is *enslaved* to sin in such a way that he cannot break out of its bonds, and it is in that sense that he "goes on sinning." He has given himself up to impurity "for *ever repeated* lawlessness."

This is the clue one needs for determining the meaning of sanctification in the parallel phrase "to righteousness for sanctification." It has to do with the service of righteousness, "slavery" to it (vs. 18)—which means, to God (vs. 22). Sanctification is not the "goal" of justification, if by that is meant an ultimate condition somehow attained. It is, instead, the "ever repeated" service of God, and the *goal* of justification in that it represents the meaning of God's call. Just as slavery to sin means alienation from God and thus "death," so "justification" means reconciliation with God, the "fruit" (καρπός) of which is sanctification (the service of God), the *telos* of which is, in turn, "eternal life" (vs. 22).

c. The law as an instrument of God

Up to this point the law has been discussed only as an "agent of sin," the means by which sin deceives and ultimately kills.

---

[85] Stalder, *Das Werk des Geistes,* p. 228.
[86] Ibid., pp. 227-28.

But now before moving on it must also be emphasized that the polemical application of the Pauline doctrine of justification by faith is by no means directed against the law per se, but against the *works* of the law, the *use* of the law in an effort to achieve righteousness. Paul rejects the law as a way to salvation, but he does not reject the law absolutely.[87] Sin finds its "opportunity" in the law, and thus freedom from sin and death also involves freedom from the law (e.g. Rom. 7:1 ff.). Yet alongside the apostle's frequent "negative" evaluations of the law stand positive statements about it.

This positive assessment of the law is reflected in various ways in the apostle's letters. For one thing he can speak of it unreservedly as "the law *of God*" (Rom. 7:22, 25). For another, he acknowledges that the Jews have an advantage because they are the recipients of the law (Rom. 9:4).[88] Paul, therefore, is not only able to say that the law is *not* sinful (Rom. 7:7) and *not* contrary to the promises of God (Gal. 3:21), but in a yet more affirmative way to declare that the law is "spiritual" (Rom. 7:14) and its commandments "holy, just, and good" (Rom. 7: 12). His gospel does not "overthrow" the law, he says, but actually "upholds" it (Rom. 3:31). How can this be? How can the law be said to have a constructive place in God's plan?

In the first place, the law is regarded as *bearing witness* to God's purposes and God's demands. This is taken for granted when Paul appeals to "the law" as an authority in matters "practical" as well as "theological" (I Cor. 9:8-9; 14:21; Gal. 4:21 ff.).[89] It is no objection to say that such appeals are to scripture in general and not just to the commandments, for the

---

[87] It is therefore much too strong to speak about a Pauline "abolition of the law" (Schoeps, *Paul: The Theology of the Apostle,* pp. 171 ff.) or to say that Paul "abrogated," "repealed," or "did away with" the law of Moses (S. Sandmel, *The Genius of Paul* [1958], pp. 116-17).

[88] It is questionable (Michel, *Römer,* p. 95) whether, in his reference to "the oracles of God" (τὰ λόγια τοῦ θεοῦ), in Rom. 3:2 Paul is referring to the law given on Sinai or the "promises" of God in a more general sense (so Lietzmann, *Römer,* p. 45). If this is to be taken as a reference to, or at least inclusive of, the law itself, then it could be listed under each of these first two points.

[89] I Cor. 14:34 is not listed here, for it is probably a non-Pauline interpolation (see above, p. 70).

very fact that scripture as a whole can be thought of under the category of "law" shows that for Paul the commandments constitute its essential aspect. (Note, e.g. the parallelism of "law" and "scripture" in Gal. 3:21, 22). Moreover, there is the evidence of Rom. 3:21 where "the law" is distinguished from "the prophets" and thus has a narrower meaning: "But now the righteousness of God has been manifested apart from law, although *the law and the prophets bear witness to it*" (RSV).

Secondly, and more important, precisely *in and through* its work as the agent of sin, the law is standing in the service of God! It is this paradox which accounts for the remarkable juxtaposition of negative and positive statements about the law in Paul's letters, a juxtaposition which is especially striking in Rom. 7:11, 12: "For sin, taking advantage of the opportunity afforded it through the commandment, deceived me and through it killed me. *For this reason* [ὥστε!] the law is holy, and the commandment is holy and just and good." The explanation of this surprising conclusion is given in vs. 13. Through the law ("what is good") sin is "shown to be sin" and becomes "sinful beyond measure" (RSV). As sin takes hold in the life of the individual sinner, the extent of its tyrannical power is actually increased,[90] and its sinister intentions unmasked. This unmasking of sin is the first step in its defeat: "Law came in, to increase the trespass; but where sin increased, grace abounded all the more, so that, as sin reigned in death, grace also might reign through righteousness to eternal life through Jesus Christ our Lord" (Rom. 5:20-21 RSV).

The place of the law in God's total redemptive strategy is further illuminated by Gal. 3:23 ff. The law has a pre-eschatological function. *Before* faith came, *until* the time when faith should be revealed (ἀποκαλυφθῆναι), the law served to hold man "in custody" (φρουρεῖν) and to "imprison" him (συγκλείειν). The RSV translation, "confined under the law, kept under restraint," suggests that Paul is viewing the law as a "check" on sin (cf. I Tim. 1:8 ff.), but such a concept is not in keeping with Paul's thought.[91] The participle συγκλειόμενοι

[90] See above, pp. 140 ff.
[91] See above, p. 143.

("restraint," RSV) must be interpreted in accord with the
apostle's use of the same verb in vs. 22 ("The scripture has imprisoned [συνέκλεισεν] all men in disobedience").[92] Paul's characterization of the law as a παιδαγωγός ("custodian," vss. 24,
25 RSV) is in keeping with this. The Greek παιδαγωγός was
not a "tutor" (KJV) but a household attendant (usually a
slave) assigned to care for the minor child. The metaphor is
apparently used here to emphasize the law's temporary service—
only "until Christ" comes (εἰς Χριστόν, vs. 24; in the light of
vs. 23 and the total context, the εἰς must be regarded as temporal [93]). For when Christ comes, the minor child is freed from
his "slavery" and comes into the fullness of his sonship (4:1 ff.).
Thus, the thought of Gal. 3:23 ff. is in accord with that of Rom.
7:13: even the law's negative function of "imprisoning in sin"
serves the ultimate purpose of God.

The discussion of the law in Gal. 3:23 ff. also discloses, however, that it can be regarded as having a positive role in salvation
only when it is viewed in the light of Christ's coming. Only to
the eyes of faith is the real purpose of the law revealed. This
is the implication of Rom. 3:21-22, and it is also this conviction
which allows Paul to speak of "the law of faith" (Rom. 3:27).
Friedrich has argued convincingly that the apostle is not speaking here of "law" in some general sense (cf. RSV, "*principle* of
faith") and that his contrast of "the law of works" with "the law
of faith" is not a reference to two laws. Rather, he is speaking
of the *one* law of God which is only truly understood from the
standpoint of faith.[94] The children of Israel did not succeed in

[92] Cf. Bauer, p. 781.

[93] Thus εἰς is here equivalent to ἄχρις in 3:19. Among those who opt
for the temporal interpretation are P. Bonnard (*L'Épître aux Galates* in
CNT [1953], p. 76) and Schlier (*Galater*, pp. 169-70). Contrast K. Benz (*Die
Ethik des Apostels Paulus* [1912], pp. 64-65) who holds that the εἰς has
also a telic meaning. He views the law as having the "propadeutic purpose" of awakening a desire for the Redeemer (pp. 59, 65). Cf. also Burton,
A Critical and Exegetical Commentary on the Epistle to the Galatians, p.
200.

[94] "Das Gesetz des Glaubens," pp. 404-5, 415. Fuchs makes a similar point
when he argues that Paul is able to say that the law reveals sin (Rom. 3:20)
only because he conceives of the law *sub gratia* (*Die Freiheit des Glaubens:
Römer 5-8 ausgelegt* in *BEvTh*, 14 [1949], 68). Cf. Stalder, *Das Werk des
Geistes*, p. 269.

fulfilling the law and finding righteousness "because they pursued it not on the basis of faith, but as if it were based on works" (Rom. 9:32). In Christ the true righteousness and the true way to righteousness are revealed and made real, and hence also the true function of the law.

If one understands the relationship between the law and Christ in this manner, one may gain some insight into two further problems. First, how is it possible that Paul can speak alternately of dying to the law "through the body of Christ" (διὰ τοῦ σώματος τοῦ Χριστοῦ, Rom. 7:4) and "through the law" (διὰ νόμου, Gal. 2:19)? The answer seems to be that, in Christ's death ("through the body of Christ"), the "curse" of the law is fully vented (Gal. 3:10 ff.) and thus removed from the believer. By this means the "promise" of life which the law had only inchoately expressed and deceptively proffered (Rom. 7:10) is released from its involvement with sin (Rom. 7:11) and given its true and effective basis in the Spirit and faith (Gal. 3:14). Christ defeats the law, but not apart from the law's own complicity. Christ is not sent in order to "correct" God's previous "mistake" in giving the law, but in order to allow the law to become once again an instrument of God.

From this standpoint one is also able to understand better what the apostle means by calling Christ the "end" (τέλος) of the law (Rom. 10:4). The term τέλος here has a double aspect.[95] On the one hand Christ's coming "ends" the law as an advertised way of salvation, writes "finis" to the sorry spectacle of man's vain attempt to achieve life through works of law. On the other hand, in Christ, the law's true function is for the first time accurately appraised and its true "goal" achieved. In Christ it may be seen that the law is an instrument of God and in what sense that is so. Moreover, in Christ the *commandments* of the law, the importance of obedience to which Paul does not question, are seen in a new light, and now the believer can do what was not possible before—he can "fulfill" the law in the highest sense

---

[95] See also Stalder, pp. 351 ff.; R. Bring, "Die Erfüllung des Gesetzes durch Christus," *KuD*, V (1959), 1 ff.; W. Joest, *Gesetz und Freiheit* (1951), pp. 138 ff.

(Rom. 13:8 ff.; Gal. 5:14). But to understand this requires examination of the eschatological event itself and what Paul believes man's participation in that event, through faith, involves.

3. THE EVENT OF GRACE: DEATH AND RESURRECTION

Paul's christology, like his pneumatology and doctrine of
righteousness (justification), has a thoroughly eschatological
orientation. In Pauline thought, Jesus is a figure *in* history but
not *of* history. That is, Jesus' "historicity" is seen as derivative
from his primary role as God's emissary to "the world." Jesus'
status as "Lord" was not won on the basis of historical performance—as a teacher, reformer, miracle worker, or even as a
martyr. Rather, Jesus' "historical" activities are seen to have
meaning and effect because they manifest the power of the age to
come already operative in the present. The Spirit, which the
apostle regards as the "first fruits" of salvation,[96] has its focal
center in Jesus' ministry (which Paul takes for granted) and his
death and resurrection (which he emphasizes) to such an important extent that it can even be said that "the Lord *is* the Spirit"
(II Cor. 3:17 RSV). It is in him that God's power is effective for
the defeat of the powers of "this age," in him that the righteousness of God is revealed, in and through him that God's reconciling love is bestowed. He is the summation of what God gives
and the fullness of what man may receive. He is, in this double
sense, *the event of grace.*

a. Jesus Christ as "crucified" and as "Lord"

It is clear beyond question that Christ's death and resurrection
represent the decisive element in the Pauline gospel. The gospel
is "the word of the cross" (see I Cor. 1:17-18 RSV); among the
Corinthians Paul preached nothing but "Jesus Christ crucified"
(I Cor. 1:23; 2:2), and he boasts in nothing save "the cross of
our Lord Jesus Christ" (Gal. 6:14 RSV). It is in Christ's death
that God's love is shown (Rom. 5:6 ff.), and it is there that the

[96] See above, pp. 126 ff.

divine love is active in rightwising and reconciling men to God (Rom. 5:9 ff.). This "obedience" of Christ (Rom. 5:19; cf. Phil. 2:8) was itself an "act of righteousness" (Rom. 5:18 RSV), the event of redeeming "grace" (Rom. 3:23-24; 5:15 ff.). In Gal. 6:12 and again in Phil. 3:18 the phrase "the cross of Christ" is nothing less than a shorthand reference to the sum total of what the gospel represents.

Yet Christ's is not a martyr's death; the cross is never viewed as an isolated event of world history. It is seen exclusively as an eschatological event, an act of God. As such it is never dissociated from the resurrection power of God (e.g. Rom. 4:17). The Christ who died and was buried is the Christ who was raised (e.g. I Cor. 15:3-4; Rom. 4:25). Where one speaks of "the death of [God's] Son," he must speak also of "his life" (Rom. 5:10). Since the "crucified" one is none other than "the Lord of glory" (I Cor. 2:8 RSV), the preaching of "Jesus Christ and him crucified" is at the same time the preaching of "Jesus Christ as Lord" (II Cor. 4:5; cf. Phil. 2:6 ff.). Both aspects of this Pauline gospel are worthy of examination.

Already in the pre-Pauline church various interpretations of the meaning of Christ's death were being crystallized into "formulations" and taking on the aspect of "traditions." These were influenced primarily by the cultic-juristic categories of Judaism, so that Christ's death could be interpreted as a "propitiatory" or "vicarious" sacrifice cancelling the sinner's guilt. Of such traditional formulations Paul was an heir, and these motifs continue to play a part in his preaching, as Bultmann has shown.[97] But since it was not a part of Paul's own purpose either to evaluate or harmonize the traditional categories, it is dangerous for the interpreter of Paul to attempt this for him. Rather, it is chiefly important to identify the apostle's most characteristic approaches and emphases.

First of all, Christ's death is viewed as an integral part of God's plan and purpose. It was not just a happenstance of history but an act of God, the meaning of which can be found in scripture (e.g. Gal. 3:13). This conviction is also evident when

[97] *Theology*, I, 295 ff.

Paul says that Christ died "at the appropriate time" (κατὰ καιρόν, Rom. 5:6) and when, under the influence of juristic thinking and formulations, he speaks of Christ's being "given up" or "giving himself up" (Rom. 4:25; 8:32; Gal. 1:4; 2:20). This means, in turn, that Christ's death can be viewed as an act of "obedience" and contrasted with Adam's disobedience (Rom. 5:19). There is, moreover, the evidence of the hymn in Phil. 2:6 ff. which speaks of Christ's obedience "unto death" (vs. 8). The apostle's hortatory application of this obedience motif (vss. 12-13) shows that it is at least partially for this reason that the hymn is used in this context.

Secondly, Christ's death is an act of God, or alternately, an act of obedience to God, *for us,* for the sake of God's people. This is constantly emphasized with a variety of expressions. Christ died "on our behalf" (ὑπὲρ ἡμῶν, Rom. 5:8; cf. "on their behalf" [ὑπερ αὐτῶν], II Cor. 5:15), "for us" (περὶ ἡμῶν, I Thess. 5:10); God gave up his Son "for us all" (ὑπὲρ ἡμῶν πάντων, Rom. 8:32); Christ died "for all" (ὑπὲρ πάντων, II Cor. 5:14, 15); he "became poor on account of you" (δι᾽ ὑμᾶς, II Cor. 8:9). The significance of Christ's death may be even further concretized, as when Paul mentions "the brother for whom Christ died" (I Cor. 8:11; Rom. 14:15) and when he says that Christ "gave himself up for me (ὑπὲρ ἐμοῦ, Gal. 2:20). But why "for me," "for my brother," "for us," "for all"? Because "all" are sinners and stand in bondage to the powers of this age. Christ therefore "gave himself up for our sins [ὑπὲρ τῶν ἁμαρτιῶν ἡμῶν] in order to rescue us from the present evil age" (Gal. 1:4); he was "given up on account of our trespasses" (διὰ τὰ παραπτώματα ἡμῶν, Rom. 4:25). This is a central part of the confessional tradition Paul had received from the earliest church (I Cor. 15:3, "Christ died for our sins," [ὑπὲρ τῶν ἁμαρτιῶν ἡμῶν]) and of course involves thinking of the crucifixion as a sacrificial, atoning act. But, as Bultmann notes, in Paul's thought the perspective is broadened, and the significance of Christ's death is not limited to the idea of the removal of guilt or its punishment.[98]

[98] *Ibid.,* p. 297.

This is most readily appreciated by inquiring into the meaning of "redemption from sin" in Paul's thought. The image which this concept evokes is that of *freedom* through the payment of a sum of money, as, for example, the release of a prisoner through payment of a ransom, or the release of a man from his debt through paying off a mortgage. Although the apostle himself never speaks explicitly of a "ransom" (λύτρον; the only New Testament occurrences are in Matt. 20:28; Mark 10:45), rarely employs the noun "redemption" (ἀπολύτρωσις, Rom. 3:24; 8:23; I Cor. 1:30) and never the cognate verb, the image of freedom through a payment is not absent from his thinking. Twice he says to the Corinthians, "You were bought with a price" (ἠγοράσθητε γὰρ τιμῆς, I Cor. 6:20 RSV; τιμῆς ἠγοράσθητε, 7:23), and in each case the plea is that men so ransomed remain in the freedom they have been given in Christ. To be redeemed from sin means to be freed from its power, to be delivered from the demonic forces which control "the present evil age" (Gal. 1:4 RSV). It therefore means freedom from the flesh and the law, sin's host and sin's agent. Christ himself was "born under the law" (Gal. 4:4 RSV), assumed "the likeness of sinful flesh" (Rom. 8:3 RSV), was "made to be sin" though he was not a sinner (II Cor. 5:21 RSV), and thereby met sin in its own kingdom and effectively broke its power (Rom. 8:3).

It has already been shown that Paul views sin as slavery to worldly values, alienation from God, reliance on "the flesh," and seeking for life apart from God's purpose and power.[99] If this interpretation is valid, then one would expect a reappearance of these themes in connection with the apostle's preaching of the death of Christ. This is indeed so, as seen in I Corinthians 1. When identifying the cross as God's "power" for those who believe ("are being saved," vss. 17-18 RSV) Paul acknowledges that, in the eyes of "the world," it is sheer "foolishness" (μωρία, vss. 18, 21, 23; μωρός, vs. 25; cf. the verb in vs. 20). Yet God has deliberately *chosen* what is foolish in the world (μωρός, vs. 27), what is weak, low, despised—even

[99] Above, pp. 135 ff.

things that "are not" (τὰ μὴ ὄντα, vs. 28) —"so that no man
might have grounds for boasting before God" (ὅπως μὴ καυχήση-
ται πᾶσα σάρξ ἐνώπιον τοῦ θεοῦ, vs. 29). The world measures
life in terms of human achievement—that is its "wisdom."
But in God's sight this reliance on things human and worldly
is really "foolishness" (I Cor. 3:19) because it is seen to estrange
man from the true source of his life and only assure his continuing bondage to sin. Man's "boast," therefore, is not to be
in himself but in "the Lord" (I Cor. 1:31, citing Jer. 9:24).
From the context of this remark, one must infer that Paul views
the cross as the supreme instance of God's "foolishness," and
that the cross stands over against the world's powers because it
contradicts the idea that "achievement" leads to life in any
meaningful sense. To "boast in the Lord" means, then, to
"boast . . . in the cross of our Lord Jesus Christ, by which the
world has been crucified to me, and I to the world" (Gal. 6:14).

The nerve of Paul's thinking about Christ's death has not
been located, however, until one sees that he views it preeminently as an expression of God's love. This is the apostle's
own characteristic category for interpreting the cross, and three
thoroughly Pauline passages make the point well. There is,
first, Gal. 2:19 ff. which speaks of crucifixion with Christ and
thus "death" to the law. Such is possible, says Paul, "by faith
in the Son of God *who loved me* and *gave himself up for me*"
(vs. 20). Christ's giving himself up to death is an act of love
by which the believer is freed from the law (sin and death) and
granted life.

Of yet greater importance is Rom. 5:6 ff. Here the death of
Christ is interpreted primarily in terms of reconciliation.[100]
Christ's death, it is shown, has the character of grace because it
is for those who are ungodly (vs. 6), sinners (vs. 8), and even
enemies (vs. 10). It is something which occurs entirely apart
from man's own strength, piety, or worthiness. By acting in
this way God is motivated by nothing other than his own
purpose to save. Therefore, Christ's death is above all a *demonstration* of God's love ("But God demonstrates his love for

[100] See above, pp. 148-49.

us in that while we were still sinners Christ died on our behalf,"
vs. 8). This declaration is parallel not only to that of vs. 5,
which speaks of God's love being given to men through his
Spirit, but also to that of Rom. 3:5. There Paul had been
speaking with a touch of irony, and the unfaithfulness ("wickedness") of the Jews to the covenant was described as the means
by which God's faithfulness to it (his "righteousness") is
"demonstrated" (συνιστάνειν). In Rom. 5:8 the same verb
(συνιστάνειν) is used, except now there is no interest in irony,
and God himself is its subject. But the point is the same:
God's nature is to meet wickedness with righteousness and
enmity with love. His purpose is to redeem from sin and
restore to life ("rightwise," "reconcile"). Christ the crucified
Lord is the demonstration of God's love and thus becomes
"wisdom, righteousness, sanctification, and redemption for us"
—our only true "boast" (I Cor. 1:30-31). Because it is an event
of love, Christ's death is an event of *grace,* and the believer's
whole life is aptly called a "standing in grace" (Rom. 5:2).

A third text which speaks to this matter is II Cor. 5:14 in
which Paul declares that "the love of Christ controls us [συνέχει
ἡμᾶς], because we are convinced that one has died for all"
(RSV). Here again Christ's death is associated with a deed of
love. The question is only what precise meaning is to be
assigned to the verb. Does it mean to "impel" or "urge on"
(Bauer) or to "hold within bounds" or "control" (RSV)?
Yet another possible meaning is to "sustain," [101] and it is in
fact this interpretation which best fits with Paul's view of
God's love as the redeeming, reconciling, rightwising power
for life. "Standing in grace" (Rom. 5:2) means being supported by Christ's love for us,[102] which not only forgives but

[101] Bauer, p. 796, cites examples.

[102] The genitive τοῦ Χριστοῦ is thus interpreted as subjective (as also,
e.g., Bultmann, *Theology,* I, 305). This is supported not only by the context which is speaking of Christ's death and its effects for men ("for all,"
vss. 14, 15; "for their sake," vs. 15), but also by the apostle's emphasis
in other places on Christ's love for men, most notably Gal. 2:20 ("who
loved me and gave himself up for me") and Rom. 8:35 ff. (where "the love
of Christ" [vs. 35] is unambiguously identified by a subsequent reference
[vs. 37] to "him who loved us").

also renews and sustains. The "demonstration" of God's love
in the cross is not just its passive disclosure, but its active
coming and working for man's salvation.

The "power of the cross," however, is not intelligible apart
from Christ's resurrection. Paul preaches not only "Jesus Christ
crucified," but also "Jesus Christ as Lord," for coordinate with
the demonstration of God's love in Christ's death is the demonstration of his sovereignty in Christ's resurrection. God's grace
is not a weak, indulgent love, but "reigns" with power (Rom.
5:21). "Standing in grace" means freedom from sin's domain
and "standing *under* [the power of] grace" ("Sin will no
longer exercise its sovereignty over you, for you are not under
law [ὑπὸ νόμον] but under grace [ὑπὸ χάριν]" Rom. 6:14). This
is the power of the new age itself, God's power bringing the
dead to life (cf. Rom. 4:17). Christ was "crucified in weakness,
but lives by the power of God" (II Cor. 13:4 RSV). Just as
"God raised the Lord, so will he raise us up by his power"
(I Cor. 6:14), and the believer's hope of being raised with
Christ is a hope to know "the power of his resurrection" (Phil.
3:10 RSV). Christ's resurrection is, therefore, an act of God
himself (see also Rom. 6:4; 10:9, etc.), and as a powerful
demonstration of God's sovereignty in creation and redemption
it constitutes the decisive entry of the "coming age" into the
present.[103]

Paul is no more inclined to regard Christ's resurrection as
an event of "world history" than he is to view Jesus himself
as a figure of world history or his death simply as a datable
tragedy of world history. The decisive point in Paul's preaching
of the resurrected Christ is just this: God's victory over the
powers of this age, his conquest of sin and death (e.g. I Cor.
15:54 ff.). The cross has power not because it is an example,
or even the supreme instance, of heroism, for heroism is a
worldly phenomenon from which Christ's obedience is in principle to be distinguished (cf. Rom. 5:7). Rather, there is power
in the cross because it is "the *Lord*" who is crucified there
(I Cor. 2:8); it is "the *Lord's* death" (I Cor. 11:26) which Paul

[103] See above, p. 134.

proclaims. As the demonstration of God's love, Christ's death is one vital part of the inbreaking of God's redeeming power. If Paul's "boast" is only in the cross (Gal. 6:14), if the cross cuts away the ground for reliance on anything worldly or human, that is so, finally, because it points to "God who raises the dead" (II Cor. 1:9).

There are various aspects of Christ's lordship unfolded in Paul's preaching, but of first importance is the eschatological. It is true that the expectation of the future *parousia* of the Messiah who will judge and redeem is still alive in Paul, and that the title "Lord" is characteristically applied in this connection (see esp. I Cor. 4:4-5; 11:26, 32; Phil. 4:5; I Thess. 4:6, 15 ff.; cf. II Cor. 5:11; 10:18; I Thess. 3:13). But primarily the lordship of Christ is seen as already operative, and his death and resurrection are seen to constitute the eschatological event. Through his death-resurrection he has been enthroned in power to exercise his dominion already in the present age: "For to this end Christ died and lived, that he might reign [κυριεύσῃ] over the dead and the living" (Rom. 14:9). The hymn of Philippians 2 expresses the same function when it sings of Christ's exaltation and the bestowal of his name, "Lord." Christ's lordly rule with God is also implied in the reference to Christ Jesus "who died, indeed was raised, who is at the right hand of God" (Rom. 8:34 [104]). Since Christ is Lord only because the title and power have been given him by God, the ultimate *goal* is that the sovereignty (βασιλεία ["kingdom," RSV]) should be delivered to God after the demonic powers of the present age have been completely destroyed (I Cor. 15:24, 28). In the meantime, however, Christ himself continues to reign, for God has put all things in subjection to him (vss. 25, 27).

The total claim which Christ's lordship lays upon the believer is a basic and pervasive element of Pauline thought and is implied in almost every paragraph he writes. In two special instances, however, it is expressed with particular effectiveness.

---

[104] This motif in the preaching of the early church was influenced by Ps. 110, as many other New Testament passages also reveal. See Foerster, *ThW*, III, 1088-89 [ET: pp. 1089-90].

One of these is when the apostle seeks to correct the Corinthian slogan, "All things are lawful" (I Cor. 6:12 ff. RSV), by emphasizing that even material things—for example, the stomach and food—stand within God's dominion and thus under his judgment (vs. 13a). The Christian has not "transcended" the world, as the Corinthian spiritists evidently held, but still stands within it. He is, then, precisely in his worldly relationships, subject to the sovereignty of God. His body (σῶμα) is representative of his whole being, and what he does with it is representative of his response to God's claim. Thus, the body "is not meant for sexual immorality but for the Lord, and the Lord for the body" (vs. 13b). The claim which the Lord thereby lays upon "the body" absolutely excludes that it should be given to a prostitute (vs. 15 ff.); it is the Lord's alone (vs. 17).

Later in I Corinthians the absoluteness of God's sovereignty is expressed in even grander fashion: "Even if there are so called gods in heaven or on earth—and there are in fact many lords—nevertheless for us there is but one God, the Father, from whom are all things, and we live for him; and one Lord, Jesus Christ, through whom are all things, and we live through him" (8:5-6). Paul does not deny that other powers, good and evil, inhabit the cosmos, but he does deny that they have any legitimate claims upon men. Two expressions in vs. 6 are decisive and nicely exhibit the significance of the divine sovereignty: "*for us*" (ἡμῖν) there is one God, and we are "*for him*" (εἰς αὐτόν).

At its center, then, Paul's gospel of the *Lord* Jesus who lives and reigns is a declaration concerning *the believer's relationship to Christ as Lord*. Paul regards ministers of the gospel as "servants" of the Lord (I Cor. 3:5) engaged in the Lord's "work" (I Cor. 16:10), the authority and power for which (ἐξουσία) comes from the Lord (II Cor. 10:8; 13:10). In his own life the apostle is attentive to the "will" of the Lord (I Cor. 4:19; cf. 16:7), views what admonitions of Jesus he does have as commands of the Lord (I Cor. 7:10; 9:14; 14:37; cf. I Thess. 4:2, 15),[105] and believes that the concern to "please the Lord"

[105] See above, p. 56.

should have the highest priority in the Christian's life (I Cor. 7:32).

As Kramer's investigation has shown, Paul's own characteristic application of the title "Lord" (κύριος) comes principally in contexts which have to do with the believer's concrete activities and responsibilities.[106] But before this topic can be pursued, one other essential aspect of Christ's death-resurrection must be discussed.

b. Dying and rising with Christ

Never far removed from Paul's preaching of the cross and resurrection is the proclamation that the believer is one who is *united with him* in his death and resurrection (e.g. I Cor. 6:14; II Cor. 4:14; Phil. 3:10; Gal. 2:20). Since Christ died for all, "therefore all have died" and live as he lives (II Cor. 5:14-15). The Spirit of God who raised Christ from the dead can also give life to those in whom it dwells (Rom. 8:11). This emphasis on the believer's participation with Christ in death-resurrection is also determinative for Paul's interpretation of Christian baptism. The primary text for a consideration of these related topics is Rom. 6:1–7:6.[107]

The contention that the law through the multiplication of sin is actually promoting God's plan by opening the way to grace (Rom. 5:20-21) is bound to radicalize a question which had been posed earlier in Romans: "And why not do evil that good may come?" (3:8 RSV). That question, newly formulated,

---

[106] *Christ, Lord, Son of God*, pp. 169 ff. (Section 47).

[107] The important and illuminating monograph by Robert C. Tannehill, *Dying and Rising with Christ, a Study in Pauline Theology* in BZNW, 32 (1967), was published just as the results of my own work were being put in final form. Insofar as I can tell, Tannehill's findings are in every respect supportive of my analysis of the Pauline ethic, and where possible this is indicated in the following sections. Tannehill and I, working completely independently (although each dependent upon and influenced by some of the same scholars, notably Käsemann), have really produced two mutually complementary studies.

For a recent discussion of the possible ideological backgrounds of Rom. 6:1–7:6 see G. Wagner, *Pauline Baptism and the Pagan Mysteries*, trans. J. P. Smith (1967). For the purposes of the present discussion, however, this may be left open.

introduces the discussion of 6:2–7:6: "What shall we say then?
Are we to continue in sin that grace may abound?" (6:1 RSV).
For Paul an affirmative answer is unthinkable, for the declaration that grace "reigns" (5:21) is at the same time a declaration
that sin's power has been broken. This is the meaning of the
statement that the Christian has "died to sin" (6:2). The
point is that the power of sin (which is the law, I Cor. 15:56)
is incompatible with the power of grace, and further on in
his argument the apostle specifically says that "sin will exercise
no dominion over you [ὑμῶν οὐ κυριεύσει], for you are not under
[the power of the] law [ὑπὸ νόμον] but under [the power of]
grace [ὑπὸ χάριν]" (vs. 14). The event of grace, as the whole
of this portion of Romans shows, is the event of Christ's death-
resurrection *and* the believer's participation in it.

While baptism itself is not the "subject" of Rom. 6:1–7:6,
Paul uses the common acceptance and practice of baptism
among Christians as the point of reference for answering the
question of vs. 1. Baptism is "into [Christ's] death" (vss. 3-4)
and is representative of a union with him "in a death like his"
(vs. 5 RSV). Parallel ideas, without specific reference to baptism, appear in Phil. 3:10 ("participation in his sufferings, being
conformed to a death like his") and II Cor. 4:10 ("always
carrying in the body the death of Jesus," RSV). Since Christ's
death is God's way of meeting and overcoming sin,[108] it may
be said that Christ himself "died to sin, once for all" (Rom.
6:10 RSV). As an act of obedience to God (5:19) and thus
righteousness (5:18), Christ's death is the actualization of God's
power and puts an effective check on sin's tyrannical hold.
"For he who has died is freed [δεδικαίωται] from sin" (vs. 7
RSV). The believer's death *with* Christ has the same result.
The Christian too has "died to sin" (vs. 2) because his old
sin-dominated self ("the old man" [ὁ παλαιὸς ἄνθρωπος]) has
been "crucified" with Christ (vs. 6). To this even bolder description of what the Christian's death with Christ means, there
are also parallels elsewhere in the letters (but again without
specific reference to baptism): "And those who belong to Christ

[108] See above, pp. 163 ff.

Jesus have crucified the flesh with its passions and desires"
(Gal. 5:24 RSV), and "I [have been crucified] to the world"
(Gal. 6:14 RSV).

Three points are worth noting here. First, Paul speaks of
the Christian's death with Christ as having already occurred,
just as his baptism itself is something in his past upon which
he may look back. In these cases the verbs are all aorist or
perfect (past tense): ἀπεθάνομεν ("we died," vss. 2, 8); ἐβαπ-
τίσθημεν ("we have been baptized," vs. 3); συνετάφημεν ("we
were buried," vs. 4); γεγόναμεν ("we have been [buried]",
vs. 5); συνεσταυρώθη ("was crucified," vs. 6). This means that
the *effects* of death to sin have also taken place (cf. δεδικαίωται
["has been freed"], vs. 7; ἐλευθερωθέντες ["have been freed"],
vss. 18, 22). Freedom from sin is not just a possibility but a
fact. In this much Wernle, for example, was correct.[109]

But a second point was not appreciated by Wernle. Nowhere
does Paul say that sin has, as such, been abolished. It is not
sin but the *sinner* who has "died" (vss. 2, 10, 11; cf. 7:4, death
to the law). To speak of being "freed" from sin (vss. 7, 18,
22) implies that sin still seeks to enslave, even though, being
"dead" to it, one no longer stands under its dominion (vs.
14). The same thing can be said of death. Christ has in effect
"died to death" so that it no longer exercises its dominion over
him (vs. 9). But this does *not* mean, as I Cor. 15:25 ff. shows,
that death has ceased to exist. Its power has been broken, but
the final triumph over it is still to come. Similarly, one may
say that Paul speaks not of the Christian's freedom from *sinning,*
but of his freedom from the power of sin.[110] There is no speculation here about the abstract question whether sin still "reigns"
in general. It is only with the existential question of sin's power
over the believer that Paul deals. And he says that living under

[109] See below, pp. 245 ff.
[110] Contrast Whiteley (*The Theology of St. Paul*, p. 168) who, with
reference to I Cor. 6:11, says: "St. Paul clearly supposed that those who
had been through the purifying waters would have ceased from the
practice of sinning." Such an interpretation of the verse cited ("But you
were washed . . . sanctified . . . rightwised") misunderstands not only
Paul's view of baptism, but also his views of sanctification and justification
(see above, pp. 146 ff., 153 ff.).

the reign of sin ("in it" [ἐν αὐτῇ,], vs. 2) is absolutely excluded
for the believer who "reigns in life" (ἐν ζωῇ, 5:17). The believer
has a new Sovereign whose dominion has been revealed and
made real in the death and resurrection of Christ.

In the third place, it should be observed that baptism itself
is not the "saving" event. Sin's power is not broken by baptism
but by Christ's death and resurrection, his "obedience" and
"righteousness" (5:18-19). In Romans 6 "we have been bap-
tised" is not parallel with "we have died" or "we have been
crucified" but with "we have been buried" (vs. 4). Baptism
is always "into Christ Jesus" (vs. 3), into *his* death for *us*.
The priority here is with what God has accomplished through
Christ.[111] Baptism as such does not constitute the "event of
grace" but is one aspect only of the whole event. It is only *the
believer* who is baptized, and so baptism as "burial" presumes
that the "death" has already occurred! To carry the burial
metaphor a step farther, baptism into Christ's death means one's
committal to him as Lord. To be baptized means to "put
Christ on" (Gal. 3:27). It stands for a change of dominion,
from that of Adam (the reign of the law, sin, death) to that
of Christ (the reign of grace, Rom. 5:20; 6:14; cf. 5:17).[112]

While baptism, in keeping with Christ's own death on the
cross (vs. 10), is a "once for all" event in the life of the Christian and something on which he looks *back,* like every other
major Pauline theme it has also an important eschatological
dimension. In Rom. 6:1 ff. it is connected with Christ's resurrection as well as with his death. The Christian has been baptized into Christ's death and thus into the *hope* for resurrection
from the dead. The future tenses of vss. 5, 8 must not be overlooked: "we *shall be* united in his resurrection" (ἐσόμεθα, vs.
5); "we *shall* also live with him" (συζήσομεν, vs. 8). Baptism
itself is always an event of the Christian's past life, but it repre-

[111] Note, in this connection, the comment of Hans von Soden ("Sakrament und Ethik bei Paulus," *Urchristentum und Geschichte,* I, 27): "The
death of Christ is the sacrament." The point is also repeatedly stressed in
various ways by Tannehill, *Dying and Rising with Christ;* see esp. p. 41.

[112] Similarly Lohse, "Taufe und Rechtfertigung bei Paulus," pp. 316 ff.;
Käsemann, "God's Righteousness in Paul," pp. 104 ff.; and esp. Tannehill,
e.g. pp. 14 ff., 41-42.

sents his receipt of a hope concerning the full manifestation of life (salvation) in the future. Insofar as Paul, like the earliest church in general, may have associated baptism with the coming of the Spirit (see Gal. 3:3 ["Having begun with the Spirit," RSV]; Rom. 8:15-16; Gal. 4:6), it is conceived of as baptism into an eschatological community, the receipt of a certified promise, participation in what is already the "first fruits" of salvation.

What baptism into the hope of Christ's resurrection means for the believer is indicated by Paul in vs. 4: "We were buried therefore with him by baptism into death, so that as Christ was raised from the dead by the glory of the Father, *we too might walk in newness of life*" (RSV, italics added). It is important to observe that, while the apostle regards the believer's own resurrection with Christ as something to come in the future, the power of that future life is even now at work renewing the present. The reference in this verse to "newness of life" is to the *present* life of the Christian. Paul's verb περιπατεῖν ("to walk") makes this certain, for he always uses it with reference to a particular mode of conduct in the world. A man may, on the one hand, "walk" *according to the flesh* (Rom. 8:4-5; II Cor. 10:2-3), *according to man* (I Cor. 3:3), *in various vices* (Rom. 13:13), *in evil cunning* (II Cor. 4:2), *by sight* (II Cor. 5:7), or *as an enemy of the cross of Christ* (Phil. 3:18). On the other hand, the "new life" of the Christian is characterized as "walking" *according to* [or *by*] *the Spirit* (Rom. 8:4-5; Gal. 5:16; cf. I Thess. 4:12), *according to love* (Rom. 14:15), *by faith* (II Cor. 5:7), *in a way appropriate to the day* (Rom. 13:13), *worthily of God and in keeping with his call* (I Thess. 2:12; I Cor. 7:17), and *in a way pleasing to God* (as that has been exemplified in the lives of the apostles and other Christians; I Thess. 4:1; Phil. 3:17). Paul's reference to the Christian's baptism into "newness of life" (Rom. 6:4) is, then, the corollary of his declaration that baptism stands for the Christian's "death to sin" (vs. 2) and is in continuation of his answer to the question posed in vs. 1.

The "newness" of the Christian's life consists in the fact that it is no longer in bondage to the law, sin, and death, but is

yielded to God (righteousness) for obedience (vss. 11 ff.).[113]
The Pauline dialectic of freedom and slavery which is emergent
in these verses is illustrated in 7:1 ff. by the case of the widow
who, because of her new situation, is free to marry another
(7:3). This theme merits special attention.

c. Belonging to Christ

The believer's participation in Christ's death and resurrection
is misinterpreted if it is conceived as a "mystical union" with
Christ. The believer retains his identity *as* a believer; his being
is not merged with Christ's but rather belongs to Christ. The
categories used to describe the believer's association with Christ
are all *relational,* not *mystical* categories. So must the com-
pound words with the prefix συν ("with") in chap. 6 be interpreted: συνθάπτεσθαι (to be buried with Christ, vs. 4);
σύμφυτος (to be united with him in his death and resurrection,
vs. 5); συσταυροῦσθαι (to be crucified with him, vs. 6; also Gal.
2:19 [RSV, vs. 20]); συζῆν (to live with him, vs. 8). Closely
related are συνπάσχειν and συνδοξάζεσθαι in 8:17 (to "suffer"
and "be glorified" with Christ—and thus to be a "co-heir"
[συνκληρονόμος] with him)—and σύμμορφος in 8:29 and Phil.
3:21 (to be "conformed" to the "image" or "glory" of God's Son).

An alternate way, within Romans 6, of saying that the Christian "belongs" to Christ is to speak of him as being "alive to
God in Christ Jesus" (ζῶντας δὲ τῷ θεῷ ἐν Χριστῷ Ἰησοῦ, vs.
11), in which perspective the idea of being brought from
death to life (ἐκ νεκρῶν ζῶντας) in vs. 13 is surely to be interpreted. The Christian "lives" insofar as he "presents" himself
to God for obedience (vss. 13 ff.) and places his "members"
at the disposal of God so that they might become instruments
(ὅπλα, perhaps specifically "weapons") of righteousness (vs.
13). It is important, then, that this Pauline emphasis on the
believer's freedom *from* sin (vss. 7, 18, 22) not be isolated from
the simultaneous emphasis on his being bound over *to* the
service of God. When in vss. 18, 22 Paul speaks of being freed
from bondage to sin (ἐλευθερωθῆναι), he also speaks of be-

[113] This theme is discussed below, pp. 182 ff.

coming "slaves" (δοῦλοι) of righteousness (vs. 18; of God, vs. 22). For Paul, freedom does not mean detachment from all commitments and disengagement from all claims. That would have seemed to him a naïve misunderstanding of the realities of man's life. In his view man does not live apart from commitments; his life is never finally his "own," and so the question only is *to whom* it should be given, *to whom* it should belong: to sin or to righteousness. For him the answer is plain because sin leads to death, but righteousness to life (vss. 20 ff.).

That freedom from sin has no meaning apart from bondage to righteousness, that dying and rising with Christ means belonging to him as one who has been called to obedience is the chief point of the metaphor with which the discussion of Rom. 6:1 ff. is concluded (7:1-6). The metaphor is developed in several different ways (vss. 1, 2-3, 4 ff.), but its point is clear enough. In vss. 2-3 the apostle refers to the married woman's legal obligation to her husband. "As long as he lives," she is bound to him, and marrying another would be adultery. But the moment he dies (it would probably be pressing the terms of the metaphor too far to claim that Paul is here thinking of *Christ's* death), she *is* free to marry another. The law is still in effect; it still forbids adultery. Because, however, the woman's situation is changed and she has become a widow, the law concerning adultery no longer applies to her. The point here is evident: the Christian, like the widow, stands in an entirely new relationship to the law; he is no longer under its jurisdiction (ὑπὸ νόμον, 6:14-15). Because in Christ's death he has died to the law (vs. 4a), it is no longer binding on him (cf. vs. 1b). In vs. 4b, however, a new dimension of the problem is considered, and the metaphor is given an additional twist. The Christian (= the widow; but now the original terms of the metaphor are left behind) is *not* free for any and all kinds of new alliances. He is free for one only. He has been given freedom for a specific reason: "in order that [he] might belong to another" (εἰς τὸ γενέσθαι [ὑμᾶς] ἑτέρῳ). That "other" is Christ "who has been raised from the dead."

This metaphor obviously holds a fascination for Paul. It also appears in II Cor. 11:2-3 where the apostle casts himself as

the Christian's father (cf. I Cor. 4:15) who has betrothed his
daughter to Christ as a bride is presented to her husband. It
is not only the image of the Christian as Christ's "bride" which
links this passage to Rom. 7:4, but also the interpretation of
what this relationship means. As a bride the Christian is pledged
(cf. the use of παριστάναι [to "present" or "yield"] in II Cor.
11:2 and Rom. 6:13, 16, 19) to her husband (Christ) "for
sincere and pure devotion" to him (cf. II Cor. 11:3 RSV).
She belongs only to him (Rom. 7:4b). The metaphor is carried
even a step farther when, in Rom. 7:4b, Paul speaks of "bearing
fruit for God." The "issue" of this marriage between Christ
and the Christian is obedience ("fruit of the Spirit," Gal. 5:22).
Thereby it is shown that life, not death (Rom. 7:5), is at
work in the Christian; that he has been released from captivity
to the "old written code" and given over to serve (δουλεύειν,
"to be a slave to") "the new life of the Spirit" (Rom. 7:6
RSV). Thus it is clear that, in 7:4-6, Paul applies the metaphor
in such a way as to recapitulate and reemphasize his answer to
the query of 6:1: Because the Christian has died with Christ
and lives in hope of resurrection with him, he has a new
"Lord" ("husband") and is committed to a new life of obedience.

There are many additional texts which emphasize or imply
the importance of the Christian's "belonging" to Christ. When,
for example, Paul refers to "the marks of Jesus" which he
bears on his body (Gal. 6:17), is he not describing his sufferings
as an apostle as the signs of his belonging to Christ, just as a
slave bears the identifying mark of his earthly master? Paul
indeed thinks of himself and other apostles as "slaves of
Christ" (δοῦλος, δοῦλοι, Rom. 1:1; Gal. 1:10; Phil. 1:1; cf.
also "servants" [διάκονοι], II Cor. 11:23; "underlings" [ὑπηρέται],
I Cor. 4:1; a "priestly servant" [λειτουργός], Rom. 15:16), an
expression which may be applied to any Christian (I Cor. 7:22b).
Furthermore, when it is said that the man who seeks to be justified by the law is "severed" from Christ (Gal. 5:4 RSV), that
implies that the man who lives by faith "belongs" to him.
This is also implicit when Christians are referred to as "members of Christ" (I Cor. 6:15) or as those who have been "taken
over" by him (Phil. 3:12). In baptism they have "put Christ

on" (Gal. 3:27) and now live only because he lives "in" them (Rom. 8:10; II Cor. 13:5; Gal. 2:20; 4:19) or—alternately expressed—because they live "in Christ." [114] Nor must the Pauline "genitive of belonging" be overlooked, for it is frequent and characteristic: κλητοὶ 'Ιησοῦ Χριστοῦ ("summoned to belong to Jesus Christ," Rom. 1:6); Χριστοῦ εἶναι ("to belong to Christ," II Cor. 10:7); οἱ [δὲ] τοῦ Χριστοῦ ['Ιησοῦ] ("those who belong to Christ [Jesus]," I Cor. 15:23; Gal. 5:24); ὑμεῖς [δὲ] Χριστοῦ ("you belong to Christ," I Cor. 3:23; Gal. 3:29) .[115]

Finally, it is in connection with the Christian's belonging to a new Sovereign that the full significance of Paul's preaching of Christ as Lord (κύριος) is disclosed.[116] When the Christian is thought of as a "slave" (δοῦλος), then the thought of Christ as "Master" or "Lord" (κύριος) is not far away. As the slave is completely subject to and dependent upon his master, so the Christian's whole life is lived "in the Lord" (ἐν κυρίῳ), in utter dependence upon the one to whom he rightfully belongs. He was "called in the Lord" (I Cor. 7:22); he is to "stand fast in the Lord" (Phil. 4:1); all his daily activities and responsibilities are conducted "in the Lord" (e.g. I Cor. 7:39; I Thess. 5:12); he trusts "in the Lord" (Gal. 5:10); and he is to "rejoice in the Lord" (Phil. 3:1; 4:4). His single concern is to be— not for "the things of the world" (τὰ τοῦ κόσμου), but—for "the things of the Lord" (τὰ τοῦ κυρίου, I Cor. 7:32 ff.). He is to "give" himself to the Lord (II Cor. 8:5) for service to him (κυρίῳ δουλεύειν, Rom. 12:11), so completely that nothing is allowed to distract him (I Cor. 7:35). And the Lord who reigns as Sovereign over the life of each individual who belongs to him is also sovereign over the life of the community as a whole, commissioning its members for various types of service (διακονία, I Cor. 12:5). The admonition to "stand fast in the Lord" (στήκετε ἐν κυρίῳ, Phil. 4:1) is really nothing else than the appeal to "be steadfast, immovable, always abounding in

[114] On the often examined expression ἐν Χριστῷ see F. Neugebauer, *In Christus. Eine Untersuchung zum paulinischen Glaubensverständnis* (1961), and Kramer, *Christ, Lord, Son of God,* pp. 141 ff. (Section 36).

[115] See Kramer, p. 137 (Section 33b).

[116] See above, pp. 168 ff.

the work of the Lord [τὸ ἔργον τοῦ κυρίου], knowing that in the Lord [ἐν κυρίῳ] your labor is not in vain" (I Cor. 15:58 RSV).

d. Summary

Paul believes man's bondage to the powers of this age is so complete and complex that only the transcendent power of God can suffice to effect his release. In the death and resurrection of Christ this redeeming, reconciling, rightwising power of the coming age has already broken in and through the Spirit is even now at work for man's salvation. It is an event of grace, for it depends on nothing man is of himself or can do for himself, but springs alone from God's love. By his obedience unto death the "Lord of glory" enters into the enemy kingdom of sin and death, and by his resurrection from the dead shows that those alien rulers are ultimately subject to God. The event of grace is, then, an event of power by which the believer who shares in Christ's death and resurrection is released from his slavery to sin. The believer is no longer under sin's power (the law), but under the power of God (grace). He has a new Master whose power is sovereign without being tyrannical, for in the service of God, in bondage to his Lord, he is free to receive the promised inheritance of life.

Finally, then, the themes of Paul's preaching have to be elucidated in terms that speak to man's own life and experience. It is, after all, to *him* that the gospel is addressed. This gospel speaks of the sovereignty of God's love in creation and redemption. It declares that, because man's life is a gift from God (cf. I Cor. 4:7), his life is to be found only "in God" (cf. Rom. 5:11) and not in himself. In Christ, supremely in his death and resurrection, God's sovereign love is at work making new the lives of those who "believe" in him and "give" themselves to him. These ideas are particularly well summarized in Rom. 14:7 ff. No one, says Paul, lives or dies "to himself" (ἑαυτῷ, vs. 7). One's life as well as one's death is "to the Lord" (τῷ κυρίῳ, vs. 8*a*); that is, both bear witness to the sovereign power of God and man's utter dependence on him. Whether one "lives or dies," he "belongs to the Lord" (τοῦ κυρίου ἐσμέν, vs. 8*b*). The purpose and goal (εἰς τοῦτο) of Christ's death and resur-

rection are to demonstrate to whom man "belongs" and to
effect a lifegiving reconciliation (vs. 9). Now it is clear what
Paul means by "freedom" from sin's power, "death" to the
law and the "crucifixion" of the old man, the "desires" of the
flesh and of "the world." All these expressions refer to man's
release from the tyranny of a life turned in upon itself, pre-
occupied with its own ambitions and accomplishments, and
thus alienated from its true destiny. What else than this does
the apostle have in mind when he writes the Corinthians that
Christ "died for all in order that [ἵνα] those who live might live
no longer for themselves [ἑαυτοῖς] but for the one who died and
was raised for their sake" (II Cor. 5:15)?

4. FAITH, LOVE, AND OBEDIENCE

Coordinate with all the themes of the Pauline preaching so
far discussed is the apostle's emphasis on faith (πίστις) and
believing (πιστεύειν). The gospel is God's power for salvation
to those who "believe" (Rom. 1:16), and it is to believers
that God's righteousness is revealed (vs. 17; cf. 3:22). Justification comes by way of "faith" (e.g. Rom. 3:28; 5:1); it is by
faith that the Spirit (Gal. 3:2, 5) and the promise (Gal. 3:14)
are received. The Christian's total situation as a Christian
may be described as a "standing" in faith (e.g. II Cor. 1:24),
so that Timothy is sent to the Thessalonians to find out about
their "faith" (I Thess. 3:5). And Christians in their relationships
with one another are described as "the household of faith"
(Gal. 6:10).

Paul's conception of faith is particularly crucial for an understanding of his ethic, for it is faith which characterizes the
mode of man's life in the world. This is seen not only from
such a statement as II Cor. 5:7 that "we walk by faith, not
by sight," [117] but also by Gal. 2:20b: "And the life which I
now live in the flesh [ἐν σαρκί] I live by faith in the Son of
God." The ethical significance of the concept is also apparent
when one notes the parallelism of "standing in faith" with

[117] On Paul's use of the verb περιπατεῖν ("to walk") see above, p. 175.

the expressions "standing in the Lord [ἐν κυρίῳ]" (I Thess. 3:8)
and "standing in grace" (Rom. 5:2). As already emphasized, to
be "under grace" means to be transferred into a new dominion,[118]
and to be "in the Lord" means to be subject to the sovereign
power of God.[119] It is not surprising, then, that the apostle's
conception of faith is closely allied with his conception of
obedience, as when in Rom. 1:5 he speaks of "faith's obedience"
(ὑπακοὴ πίστεως) and in I Thess. 1:3 of "faith's work" (τὸ
ἔργον τῆς πίστεως). This latter passage shows that he also couples
the ideas of faith and *love,* for along with "faith's work" is
"love's labor" (ὁ κόπος τῆς ἀγάπης). Moreover, Timothy is to
find out about the Thessalonians' "faith and love" (I Thess.
3:6); and it is in love that faith operates (Gal. 5:6). No wonder
that Paul, because he has heard of Philemon's "faith" and
"love" (Philemon 5), can have confidence in his "obedience"
(vs. 21). While each of these themes—faith, love, and obedience—has its own particular prominence within Paul's overall
message, it is their vital interrelationship which is most striking
and most characteristic. They are therefore best examined
together.

a. Faith as obedience

Grace, as demonstrated above all in the death and resurrection
of Christ, is the mode of God's giving of himself to men for
their justification and salvation. It is therefore possible to say
that man is rightwised "by his grace" (τῇ αὐτοῦ χάριτι, Rom.
3:24). It is more usual, however, for Paul to speak of justification "by faith" (ἐκ πίστεως, διὰ πίστεως, ἐπὶ τῇ πίστει, or
πίστει[120]). Thereby he designates man's openness to and recep-
tion of God's grace. Grace, to be sure, has a "power" of its
own, quite apart from man's acceptance or rejection of it.[121]
Yet the reign of grace is not really separable from its reign
in the life of the believer, for only there is it specifically and

---

[118] Above, p. 174.

[119] Above, pp. 169 ff.

[120] Instances of each of these varied constructions are given by Bultmann,
Theology, I, 316-17.

[121] See above, pp. 168, 172.

concretely operative for salvation. That is why it can be said that "those who receive the abundance of grace and the free gift of righteousness" *themselves* "reign in life through the one man Jesus Christ" (Rom. 5:17 RSV). Here, broadly conceived yet compactly expressed, is Paul's own definition of what faith and believing means. Believers are "those who receive" (οἱ λαμβάνοντες) God's grace and righteousness by virtue of their belonging to the one in whom grace and righteousness have been bestowed.

Paul, however, does not attempt a formal definition of faith, but prefers to offer the example of Abraham (Rom. 4:1 ff.; cf. Gal. 3:6 ff.; Rom. 9:6 ff.). It is interesting to observe the profile of "Abraham the believer" which emerges from Romans 4. In vs. 5 it is said that the patriarch "believes in the one who rightwises the ungodly." On the one hand this anticipates the discussion of 5:6 ff. (Christ died for the "ungodly"), and on the other hand it echoes the description of God's righteousness in 3:3 ff. There, God's righteousness had been presented as his persistent "faithfulness" and "truth" to his covenant and his covenant people. In spite of their wickedness and apostasy he remains their covenant God.[122] Now in 4:5 Paul goes a step further and describes God's righteousness as actively expressed in his "rightwising the ungodly." Abraham's faith involves trust in this redemptive purpose of the righteous God.

In Rom. 4:17 the God of Abraham's faith is further described as one "who makes the dead to live and summons into being things which do not exist." God's redemptive purpose is here more precisely expressed as resurrection from death to life. As God is the one who first gave life, so is he the one who constantly restores it. This is the essence of the promise which Abraham and Sarah have received (vss. 19-20). Abraham's faith is not only trust, but hope (vs. 18).

But it is, finally, God's *power* which permits Abraham to trust and to hope. Abraham's faith is in a God who "is powerful also to do what was promised" (vs. 21). Since God's power is decisively present and active in Christ, Paul says in Gal. 3:16 ff.

[122] See above, p. 144.

that God's promise of life to Abraham finds its fulfillment in Christ, the patriarch's one true "offspring." The true spiritual sons of Abraham are therefore those who have faith as he had faith (Rom. 4:16; 9:6 ff.) and whose faith has as its object and center the redemptive work of God fulfilled in Christ Jesus (Gal. 3:16 ff.). Because it is above all in his death and resurrection that God's power is manifested (cf. Rom. 4:17), it is in these terms that Abraham's exemplary faith is applied to the apostle's Roman readers (4:23 ff.). Righteousness is reckoned to those who believe in the God who "raised from the dead Jesus our Lord, who was put to death for our trespasses and raised for our justification" (vss. 24b-25 RSV). In its own way, then, Paul's portrayal of Abraham's faith illustrates the fundamental motif of the Pauline conception: faith means openness to and finally participation in the redemptive power of God operative in Christ's death and resurrection. Through faith the believer "dies" to sin and death as Christ died to them and lives in hope of resurrection with him.

Bultmann's keen analysis of "the structure of faith" in Pauline thought shows that it has many components in addition to those of hope and trust.[123] It is unnecessary to duplicate Bultmann's efforts or even to report all his results here.[124] It will be useful, however, because of the special theme of the present investigation, to elaborate on the one aspect of faith which Bultmann has correctly identified as "primary" in the apostle's thought, viz. faith as *obedience*.[125] For it is precisely the obedi-

---

[123] *Theology*, I, 314 ff. Cf. also his article in *ThW*, VI, 218 ff.

[124] Bultmann should perhaps be criticized for undervaluing trust (confidence) as a constituent of faith, although more attention is given to this in his *Theology* than in the *ThW* article. Approaching the topic of Paul's view of faith in an entirely different way, Ljungmann lays primary emphasis upon its "trust" character in *Pistis: A Study of Its Presuppositions and Its Meaning in Pauline Use* (1964), pp. 14, 79, 107.

[125] Whiteley, who admits that faith in Paul "can . . . carry overtones of the notion of obedience," believes nevertheless that Bultmann's assertion is too "sweeping" and not supported by the evidence (*The Theology of St. Paul*, p. 162). But Whiteley's attempted refutation is not successful, for he ignores several of the major texts Bultmann cites in support of his point (e.g. I Thess. 1:8 compared with Rom. 15:18; Rom. 1:5; 10:3; 11:30 ff.; II Cor. 10:15).

ence character of faith which makes it the means of the believer's
participation in Christ's death and resurrection and which
discloses how this is at the same time a "walking in newness of
life" (Rom. 6:4).

If, as the character of Abraham's faith has itself suggested,
faith's reference is first of all to the God who has raised Jesus
from the dead (cf. Rom. 10:9*b*) and if such saving faith is coordinate with the confession that Jesus is "Lord" (Rom. 10:9*a*),
then the obedience character of faith is already made clear.
The acknowledgment of Jesus as "Lord" is not possible apart
from the acknowledgment that one resides in the sphere of
his sovereign power and is bound over to his service. Faith,
therefore, is the acknowledgment that one "belongs" to Christ.
and as such it is an act of commitment to him. This is why
the apostle can speak of "faith's obedience" (Rom. 1:5), why
the unbelieving Jews can be described as not having "submitted"
(obediently) to God's righteousness (Rom. 10:3), and why
the idea of "obeying" the gospel can stand parallel with that of
"believing" the preached word (Rom. 10:16-17). The concept
of "obedience to" Christ, doubtless implied in the metaphor
of the Christian as Christ's bride (Rom. 7:4; II Cor. 11:2-3),
is explicitly formulated in II Cor. 10:5-6: "We destroy arguments and every proud obstacle to the knowledge of God, and
take every thought captive to obey Christ, being ready to punish
every disobedience, when your obedience is complete" (RSV).
The thought here is certainly not of obedience to precepts or
commandments (e.g. of the earthly Jesus), but of "belonging"
to him (cf. "to be Christ's" [Χριστοῦ εἶναι] and "of Christ"
[Χριστοῦ], vs. 7) totally and unconditionally. The "obedience"
to Christ which faith involves implies such a radical "belonging
to" him that Paul finds it appropriate to speak not only of
the Christian's actual *being in Christ* (e.g. II Cor. 5:17), but
of Christ's being *in him,* in full "possession" of him, absolutely
sovereign in his life (II Cor. 13:5; Gal. 2:20).

But what does "faith's obedience" involve? How is it expressed? These questions are best examined by looking com-
prehensively at the concept of obedience itself as it is found in
the Pauline letters.

Two different word groups must come under consideration here: (1) the nouns ὑπακοή and παρακοή, with the related verb ὑπακούειν and adjective ὑπήκοος; (2) the verbs πείθειν (in passive forms) and ἀπειθεῖν, with the related noun ἀπείθεια and adjective ἀπειθής. The first group connotes *subjection* (or lack of subjection) *to,* as its formation from ὑπό (or παρά) and ἀκούειν suggests ("to be under [or "against"] what is heard"). In the second group the passive forms of the verb πείθειν, when they refer to obedience, connote following by reason of having been *persuaded.* These subtle distinctions, however, are not important in Paul's usage, where the second group is employed mainly when *dis*obedience is under discussion. This is perhaps influenced by the LXX usage of ἀπειθεῖν ("to disobey") as, for example, in Isa. 65:2, cited by the apostle in Rom. 10:21. Considering the first and second groups together, the following picture emerges.

Twice Paul refers to the obedience of Christ himself. One instance is in Rom. 5:19 where Christ's obedience (ὑπακοή) is contrasted with Adam's disobedience (παρακοή). Adam's disobedience was his transgression (παράπτωμα, vss. 15, 17, 18, 20; cf. vs. 16; παράβασις, vs. 14) of the commandment of God. Presumably, then, Christ's obedience would be his *following* God's commandment. Since Gal. 1:4 suggests that God's will for Christ was that he should "give himself" for man's sins, one may presume that Christ's "obedience" would be his *obedience to death.* This is, of course, made explicit in Phil. 2:8, the second reference to Christ's own obedience. The possibility that at this exact point the apostle is himself interpolating an idea into a hymn which he quotes[126] makes the reference even more noteworthy.

Elsewhere the concept of obedience refers to Christians, those who, by faith, belong to Christ and hence participate in his

---

[126] So Lohmeyer, *Der Brief an die Philipper* in *KEK* (19th ed., 1954), p. 96. Also E. Käsemann, "Kritische Analyse von Phil. 2, 5-11," *Exegetische Versuche und Besinnungen,* I (1960), 82; F. W. Beare, *A Commentary on the Epistle to the Philippians* in *HNTC* (1959), p. 85; G. Strecker, "Redaktion und Tradition im Christushymnus, Phil. 2:6-11," *ZNW,* LV (1964), 70-71.

obedience. In a number of cases the object of obedience is specified. In II Cor. 10:5-6 the object of the Christian's obedience is Christ himself; in Rom. 10:16 it is "the gospel"; and in Rom. 2:8 and Gal. 5:7 it is "the truth," presumably meaning "the truth of the gospel" (cf. Gal. 2:14). If the genitive in the phrase ὑπακοὴ πίστεως (Rom. 1:5) is interpreted as objective ("obedience to faith"), then this passage should also be listed here; but it is probably preferable to interpret the genitive subjectively, thus: "faith's obedience," "the obedience which faith is." [127] The references in Rom. 6:16-17 to obeying "obedience" and obeying "the pattern of teaching" present their own difficulties, discussed below.[128] While Paul never specifically speaks of "obeying God," this is implied when he speaks of those who "*dis*obey" him (Rom. 11:30, 31, 32; cf. Rom. 10:21 [LXX]). Also on the negative side, he speaks of obeying "sin" (Rom. 6:16), "wickedness" (Rom. 2:8), and the "evil desires" (ἐπιθυμίαι) which sin stirs to life (Rom. 6:12).

In an equally impressive number of instances the Christian's "obedience" is referred to in general, without naming a specific object. Paul characterizes his whole mission as the attempt to win "obedience" from the Gentiles (Rom. 15:18) and on the other hand speaks of "the disobedient in Judea" (οἱ ἀπείθουντοι, Rom. 15:31; RSV translates, "the unbelievers"). He writes the Corinthians in order to find out whether they are "obedient in everything" (II Cor. 2:9) and refers to Titus' memory of their obedience (7:15). Paul himself remembers how the Philippians "obeyed" when he was with them (Phil. 2:12) and also expresses confidence in the obedience of Philemon (Philemon 21).

This survey of passages shows, surprisingly, that the apostle nowhere speaks directly about obedience to "the law" or its "commandments," or to God's "will." Why are these conceptions lacking? An examination of these matters will go far in clarifying his total concept of Christian obedience and the relationship he presupposes between obedience, faith, and love.

---

[127] So Bultmann, e.g. *Theology*, I, 314.
[128] Pp. 196 ff.

b. The "will of God"

There are, altogether, sixteen clear references to God's "will" (θέλημα) or his "willing" (θέλειν) in the Pauline letters. The majority of these may be classified fairly readily under three main headings.

1. References to God's "general will" in his role as Sovereign over man's life: God has mercy on whom he wills (Rom. 9:22), and he has arranged the organs of the body and given to each seed its own type of body according to his will (I Cor. 12:18; 15:38). Perhaps here one should also list the reference of Phil. 2:13 to God's "willing" (and working) for each man's salvation.

2. References to God's will for Christ. The only instance is Gal. 1:4 where Christ's "giving" of himself (unto death) for man's sins, his deliverance of believers "from the present evil age," is said to have been "according to the will of our God and Father."

3. References to God's will in calling Paul as an apostle and directing his activities. In I Cor. 1:1 and II Cor. 1:1 he refers to his apostleship as being "through the will of God." Moreover, he looks to God's will for the direction of his apostolic ministry. If he is able to come to the Romans, it will be by God's will (Rom. 1:10; 15:32), and he will soon return to Corinth "if the Lord wills" (I Cor. 4:19). (It is questionable whether θέλημα in I Cor. 16:12 should be regarded as God's will [RSV] or the will of Apollos himself [RSV margin]. If the former, then this would be a seventeenth reference by Paul to God's will, and the passage should be listed here.)

The remaining five references are more diverse. In Rom. 2:18, addressing the Jew, Paul characterizes him as *knowing* "God's will" and approving "what is excellent" because he is "instructed in the law." Although, in this same context, the apostle is critical of the Jew for "relying" on the law, using it as an occasion for "boasting" (vs. 17) and then "breaking" the law (vs. 23), he does not deny that the law may mediate the will of God. Nowhere, however, does he speak of the *Christian* as having God's will available in the law. For the Christian, the will of God is not *possessed* but—as Rom. 12:2 implies—ever newly sought and found. As the Christian's whole life is "transformed" and his critical faculties of ethical discernment and decision are "renewed" (contrast the "reprobate mind" [ἀδόκιμος νοῦς], Rom. 1:28, with "the renewal of the mind" [ἡ ἀνακαίνωσις τοῦ νοός], 12:2), he is enabled to "find out what the will of God is, what is good and acceptable and perfect." [129] Moreover, this discovery of and dedication to God's will is not separable from the Christian's total "presentation" of himself to God, for which Paul had appealed in the preceding verse. God's "will" is that one should put his whole being at God's disposal. In this total "belonging" to him he is to apply himself unto what is good. In this light Paul's remark about the churches of Macedonia takes on special significance. Their *specific* act of obedience, their liberal contribution to the offering for Jerusalem, was "of their own accord" (αὐθαίρετος, II Cor. 8:3). Yet their unexpected liberality was but a specific manifestation of a more basic and total obedience. Their chief (or "first" [πρῶτος]) obedience was to *give themselves* (ἑαυτοὺς διδόναι; the ἑαυτούς is first and emphatic) to the Lord and to the Lord's apostles. And this "giving of themselves" was "through the will of God" (vs. 5).

Only two passages remain for consideration, both in I Thessalonians, each employing the demonstrative pronoun (τοῦτο ["this"]) in such a way as to suggest that the specific content of God's will is being described. This expectation is not realized, however, at least in I Thess. 5:16 ff. There Paul concludes the threefold admonition to "rejoice always, pray constantly, give thanks in all circumstances" with the observation that "this is the will of God in Christ Jesus for you" (RSV). For Paul, rejoicing, prayer, and thanksgiving are aspects of the believer's total relationship to God in Christ. Because the Christian's rejoicing is "in the Lord" (Phil. 4:4, 10; perhaps also 3:1) and "before God" (I Thess. 3:9), it characterizes his whole life even in the midst of adversity (e.g. II Cor. 6:10). Similarly, the Christian's whole life is described as a "thanksgiving" to God, so completely yielded to God that "whatever" he does is to be done thankfully and to God's "glory" (e.g. Rom. 14:6; I Cor. 10:30-31; II Cor. 4:15). The refusal to give God "glory" and "thanks-

[129] See above, pp. 104-5.

giving" is what constitutes the disobedience of the Gentiles
(Rom. 1:21) whose "obedience" Paul is intent on winning
(Rom. 15:18). And finally, the obligation of constant prayer
(I Thess. 5:17; cf. Rom. 12:12) makes sense only when prayer,
too, is conceived of as a continuing openness and attentiveness
to God's will. This is why references to prayer can be coupled
with references to rejoicing (Rom. 12:12) or thanksgiving (Phil.
4:6) or—as in I Thess. 5:16 ff.—with both of these. Prayer, like
these other two, is expressive of the believer's total surrender to
God and his freedom from worldly care (Phil. 4:6). *This* relationship is "God's will" for his people (I Thess. 5:16 ff.).

In I Thess. 4:3 the reference to God's will is specified as the
believer's "sanctification," and introduces admonitions to abstain
from sexual immorality (vss. 3, 5-6) and to take a wife "in holiness and with honor" (vs. 4). This is as close as the apostle
ever comes, except in the passages relating to apostolic activities
(above, 3), to identifying specific acts as in accord with the will
of God.[130] Yet even here it should be noted that the concept of
God's will is not limited to specific ethical requirements, for the
admonitions in question are concluded with a reference to God's
"call" which has not been for impurity but "in sanctification"
(vs. 7). God's "will" is "sanctification" in that it means a "call"
to a total way of life, a "call," as the apostle has said earlier
in this same letter, to "walk worthily" of (=obey!) the "kingdom and glory" into which he has been called (2:12).[131]

[130] Numerous commentators have held that the ethical admonitions of
Rom. 12:3 ff. represent a spelling out of what God's will (Rom. 12:2) involves. Barrett, e.g., commenting on 12:1-2, says that "even the renewed
mind needs a good deal of instruction: hence the detailed advice and exhortation of the following paragraphs" (*A Commentary on the Epistle to the
Romans*, p. 233). So also Bradley, who claims that general teachings like
those of Romans 12-15 "answer the need for a clear statement of the
ethical content of Christianity," and that in his exhortations Paul "defines and makes explicit the will of God for men. The Christian is called
to a new life, and Paul says in no uncertain terms what this new life
is to be" ("The Origins of the Hortatory Materials," p. 219). His admonitions
are thus selected "excerpts" of God's will (*ibid.*, p. 20). But while it is
not to be denied that Paul's exhortations can be very specific and concrete (see above, pp. 72 ff.), there is certainly no evidence to warrant the conclusion that he would have regarded them (e.g. those in Rom. 12:3 ff.)
as a specific unfolding of the "content" of God's will.

[131] See also above, p. 155.

This investigation has confirmed Wahlstrom's conclusion that Paul seldom speaks of God's will in terms of "any specific act or line of conduct." [132] Insofar as he relates the concept to the believer's own responsibility, it has to do with the *total* sovereign claim God lays upon him, the claim to "give" or "present" himself to God for obedience. Since obedience thus conceived is deeper and broader than formal adherence to prescribed statutes, Paul is critical of the Jew who thinks the will of God is something which is *possessed* in the law and fulfilled when the law's commandments are observed (Rom. 2:17 ff.). For the apostle, God's will is the object of a constant and repeated seeking, finding, and doing, a quest which is at the same time a "rejoicing" and a "thanksgiving" because the believer is *himself* "possessed" by the Lord. In Paul's view, God's will is not "obeyed" in the same way that the Jew "obeys" the law; and it is probably in order to avoid any such misunderstanding that admonitions to "obey God's will" never occur in his letters.[133]

c. The "law of faith"

Paul also avoids speaking of obedience to *the law*. The law is something which one "does" (ποιεῖν, Rom. 2:14; Gal. 5:3; πράσσειν, Rom. 2:25 [the RSV translation "obey" is misleading]; οἱ ποιηταὶ νόμου, Rom. 2:13), "carries out" (τελεῖν, Rom. 2:27), "keeps" (φυλάσσειν, Rom. 2:26; Gal. 6:13), "serves [as a slave serves]" (δουλεύειν, Rom. 7:25), "submits to" (ὑποτάσσειν, Rom. 8:7), and "pursues" (διώκειν, Rom. 9:31), but nowhere does the apostle suggest that it is something one "obeys." The reason for this is clear: as long as the law is conceived as a formal code of moral obligations, it demands no more than formal adherence to specific requirements. This is something far less radical than what Paul has in mind when he speaks of obedience as the surrender of one's whole life to God.

This is illustrated, first of all, by the criticism of the Jews implicit in the apostle's description of them as those who "rely upon the law" (Rom. 2:17) and the discussion which follows (esp.

---

[132] *The New Life in Christ,* p. 162.
[133] Similarly Wahlstrom, *ibid.*

through vs. 29). Conceiving the law as the full and final disclosure of God's will (vs. 18), the Jews presume that their mere possession of it ("hearing" of it, vs. 13) is proof of a unique relationship to God which affords them special security. Boasting in the law (vs. 23), they boast of their relationship to God. But their boasting turns out to be "blasphemy" when the law is transgressed (vss. 23-24).

To understand the point being made, it is necessary to notice the distinction Paul makes in vs. 27 between "the law" (ὁ νόμος) and the "written code" (RSV; τὸ γράμμα). To keep the law in the latter sense, as a *pro forma* matter, means nothing. The reference to circumcision and uncircumcision shows this well (vss. 25 ff.). The "circumcised" are those who have a formal relationship to the law; their circumcision signifies that they "have" the law as a written code. Their relationship to the law is external, "apparent" (ἐν τῷ φανερῷ, vs. 28), but not necessarily real. On the other hand the "uncircumcised," those who can claim no formal relationship to the law as a written code and who therefore have no "apparent" relationship to God, *may* nevertheless "keep the law" (τὸν νόμον τελοῦσα) in the truest sense (vs. 27). The apostle's meaning is plain: true obedience is not to be identified with a merely formal keeping of the law. Rather, it is the commitment of the *whole man* to God, expressed in this passage by speaking of true circumcision as something "hidden" in the "heart" (vs. 29). One might paraphrase as follows: Physical circumcision signifies only that God's law in its formal aspects belongs to this man; but what really matters is whether this man belongs to God, whether his whole life ("heart") has been given over to the sovereign Lord.

The point being made in Rom. 2:25 ff. is almost epigrammatically stated in I Cor. 7:19: "For neither circumcision nor uncircumcision amounts to anything, but only keeping the commandments of God." This last phrase calls attention to Paul's conviction that there *is* something to be "kept," as also the discussion in Romans 2 presupposes (vss. 23, 25 ff.; cf. vs. 13). This "something" is described in I Cor. 7:19 as "commandments" (ἐντολαί) and in Rom. 2:25 ff. as the "law." However, it is important that Paul's distinction between "law" and "written code" be borne in mind. This distinction is more clearly made in II Cor. 3:6 ff. where the "written code" is identified with the old "ministry" (διακονία) of death and condemnation. Such a description fully agrees with what Paul has to say about the law as the agent and power of sin.[134] With the law viewed in this way, however, Paul contrasts the life-giving "Spirit." This he identifies with the new covenant and therefore with "Christ." The "ministry of the Spirit" is at the same time the "ministry of righteousness." A similar distinction is made in Rom. 7:6 where it is said that the one who belongs to Christ serves "not under the old written code but in the new life of the Spirit" (RSV). These passages afford a significant commentary on the remark in Rom. 2:29 that true circumcision is "in Spirit not letter" (ἐν πνεύματι οὐ γράμματι). The law is not really kept by those whose obedience is measured in terms of their formal adherence to a collection of statutes, but only by those whose obedience consists in their new life in the Spirit, in their *belonging* as whole persons ("secretly," "in their heart," i.e. inwardly), to the Lord.

Paul's conception of obedience is further illustrated in his polemic against "works of the law" (ἔργα νόμου). When the concept of obedience is formalized and externalized, the effect is to limit its meaning to the performance of specified, measurable, and visible deeds. Thereby the obedient acts are regarded as possessing value in and of themselves, quite independently of the one who performs them. It is precisely this formalization and externalization of the concept of obedience which Paul understands "works of the law" to represent. They are acts regarded as having meritorious value for the one who does them,[135] *accomplishments* by which the doer presumes to establish and make secure his relationship to God. When Paul rejects the view that justification is something earned in this way, he is rejecting the superficial conception of obedience which it presupposes. When, in its place, he claims that justification is on the basis of faith apart from works (e.g. Rom. 3:28), he is presuming that faith

---

[134] See above, pp. 135 ff.
[135] Cf. Bultmann's comment that "in a true deed the doer himself is inseparable from it, while in a 'work' he stands side by side with what he does" (*Theology*, I, 316).

means the surrender of every supposed claim the doer has on
God, and acknowledgment of and surrender to the total claim
God makes on him.

Once more Abraham's faith provides a relevant example. Had
Abraham been rightwised by works, says Paul, he would have
had "something to boast about, but not before God" (Rom.
4:2 RSV). His praise would have been only from men (cf. Rom.
2:29), and his "righteousness" would have been illusory; his life
would have been tyrannized by the "law of works" and thus held
captive in sin.[136] But because Abraham quite totally yielded his
life to God, trusting and hoping in his power alone, he received
righteousness as a gift (Rom. 4:2 ff.). His faith was obedience
to God radically, not just formally, conceived. His covenant
with God was based on God's grace (the "promise," Rom. 4:
13 ff.; Gal. 3:16 ff.). By his faith he was freed and opened to
receive that promise, even as it was manifested in the law (cf.
Rom. 7:10). The law did not tyrannize him, for by his faith
in Christ, to whom the law itself bears witness (Rom. 3:21 ff.;
Gal. 3:6 ff., etc.), it ceased to be "the law of works" and became "the law of faith" (Rom. 3:27). The believer, because his
whole life is given to God for obedience, is freed *from* the law's
works and *for* the law's fulfillment in a new sense.[137]

d. Romans 6:12 ff.

Before asking in what sense the believer "fulfills" the law,
we must deal with one further text in which the Pauline conception of obedience is articulated, Rom. 6:12 ff. As one who
belongs to Christ, the Christian is bound over to his service.[138]
Paul finds the metaphor of slavery appropriate to his topic not
only because it helps him to make vivid the captivity of one
who obeys only his own passions (vs. 12), but also because it
expresses the scope of the obedience which God claims from
men. The believer is to put himself at God's disposal (παριστά-

---

[136] See the discussion of sin as "boasting," above, pp. 137 ff.

[137] For additional comments on the meaning of "the law of faith" in
Rom. 3:27, see above, pp. 160-61.

[138] On this, see above, pp. 176 ff., and also the similar treatment of these
themes by Tannehill, *Dying and Rising with Christ*, pp. 8 ff.

ναι, vss. 13, 16, 19) just as completely and obediently as the slave is to put himself at the disposal of his master.

Two particular points are worth noting. First, the Christian's obedience is inseparable from the event of God's grace which makes it possible. God's grace constitutes not just the summons to obedience but the possibility of obedience. Vs. 14 makes this clear when it speaks of sin's power being displaced by the power of grace. Even more suggestive is the way in which the appeal of vs. 13 is formulated: "Put yourselves at God's disposal *as those who from death have been brought to life* [ὡσεὶ ἐκ νεκρῶν ζῶντας]." The present participle here cannot refer to the Christian's resurrection with Christ, for that is still to come, as the future tenses in vss. 5, 8 clearly show. The reference can only be to the "walking in newness of life" of which Paul had spoken in vs. 4. The believer who has been baptized into Christ's death and has therefore died to his own past does not stand in some shadowy limbo waiting for the resurrection life. He now stands "in" and "under" grace (Rom. 5:2; 6:14) which gives his hope a special character (Rom. 5:2, 5). While the object of his hope is not yet "seen" (Rom. 8:24-25), its power is already operative through the Spirit (Rom. 5:5) which gives life to those in whom it dwells (Rom. 8:9 ff.). This is why the Christian's "newness of life" (ἐν καινότητι ζωῆς, Rom. 6:4) is also described as "new life of the Spirit" (Rom. 7:6 RSV), "walking by the Spirit" (Rom. 8:4; Gal. 5:16), or "being led by the Spirit of God" (Rom. 8:14). The Christian already has a new life because he already has a new Lord, but the Lord exercises his power redemptively and not tyrannically. That is the difference between standing under the power of the law and under the power of grace. For Paul, obedience means surrender to God's power but not abject capitulation to it; the new Lord not only asks all, but gives all.

In the second place, it is clear from Rom. 6:12 ff., as from other passages already discussed, that Paul does not equate obedience with the performance of "righteous deeds" moralistically or legalistically conceived. When believers are exhorted to commit themselves to God as "instruments" (ὅπλα) of and "slaves" to righteousness (vss. 13, 18), then it is apparent that righteousness is not something under their control. Instead, it is

that by which *they* are *to be* controlled. Righteousness is not in
their power to "do," but righteousness is the power of God in
whose service they stand. Righteousness is not the goal of obedience but its presupposition. This is seen in another way in
vs. 16 where obedience to sin is contrasted with obedience "to obedience."[139] Obedience to sin is "unto death" (εἰς θάνατον), for
to be under sin's power is to be alienated from the life of God
which is man's true destiny. On the other hand, the Christian's
obedience is "unto righteousness" (εἰς δικαιοσύνην), for to stand
under the power of grace means to be "rightwised" and thus re-
oriented ("reconciled") to life's true meaning and ground. The
RSV translation, "obedience, which *leads to* righteousness," unfortunately imports the suggestion that the believer's obedience
either produces or guides him to righteousness. But for Paul,
faith's obedience neither achieves nor attains righteousness, but
receives it as a gift. Christian obedience is not the sum total
of one's good works, nor is righteousness thereby produced.
Righteousness is, rather, the "fruit" (in Gal. 5:19, 22 Paul distinguishes between "works" and "fruit") which is given through
Jesus Christ (καρπὸν δικαιοσύνης τὸν διὰ 'Ιησοῦ Χριστοῦ, Phil.
1:11 [140]). Righteousness is *received* by the believer who gives
himself entirely to the Lord.

There is one more verse in Romans 6 which requires attention
in connection with the Pauline view of obedience. What is
meant by the exhortation in vs. 17 to become "obedient from

[139] The idea of "obeying obedience" is of course arresting, but it is
doubtful whether any particular significance can be found in it. The
rhetorical parallelism which is characteristic of this half of chap. 6 sometimes gets out of hand (note, e.g., the whole middle section of vs. 13 which
destroys the otherwise neat parallelism, "members to sin as instruments
of wickedness," "members to God as instruments of righteousness"), and
this peculiar idea may be another instance. If, on the other hand, this
particular formulation is to be taken seriously, it might be viewed as a
further reflection of Paul's conviction that obedience (to God) is, as it
were, an "end" in itself.

[140] Paul's expression contrasts markedly not only with Epictetus' view
that there are degrees of righteousness (implied in his comment that "the
greatest fruit of righteousness" is "calm disinterest" [cited above, p. 87,
n. 32]), but also with the LXX phrase "fruits of righteousness" (Prov. 13:2).
Textual evidence for the plural in Phil. 1:11 is weak (but see the RSV
translation).

the heart to the standard of teaching to which you were committed [ὑπηκούσατε δὲ ἐκ καρδίας εἰς ὃν παρεδόθητε τύπον διδαχῆς]"?

Dodd, in keeping with his thesis about an early Christian didactic tradition, takes this as a Pauline admonition to obey the particular moral "pattern" for life which was commonly promulgated by Christian teachers.[141] Stalder, on the other hand, argues that the expression τύπος διδαχῆς should here be translated, "object and content of teaching." As such, he concludes, it refers to Jesus Christ.[142] A different kind of solution is proposed by Bultmann, who regards the whole clause in question as a "stupid interpolation" by some later hand. He judges this to be so, first, because the "clearly antithetical" structure of the sentence is thereby destroyed, and second, because the intrusive clause contains two decidedly un-Pauline expressions: ἐκ καρδίας ("from the heart") and τύπος διδαχῆς ("pattern of teaching"). By the latter the glossator must certainly have intended a reference to "the specifically Pauline teaching." But the glossator's idea that this is to be "obeyed" represents, particularly in the context of Rom. 6:12 ff., a trivialization of Paul's own understanding of obedience. The insertion, according to Bultmann, has nothing in common with the thought of the passage into which it has been set.[143]

The problem here is complicated by the fact that this reference to a "pattern of teaching" is unique in Paul. The one expression which comes closest to being parallel is in Rom. 16:17: "the teaching which you have been taught" (τὴν διδαχὴν ἣν ὑμεῖς ἐμάθετε). But there the concept of *obedience* is not specifically

[141] "The Primitive Catechism," p. 108. He lists as the probable "table of contents" of this "pattern": the holiness of the Christian calling, the repudiation of pagan vices and their replacement by the Christian law of charity, certain eschatological motives, and special duties within (and perhaps outside) the Christian church.

James Moffatt once argued that the τύπος διδαχῆς was actually the predecessor of the church's "Rule of Faith," and thus "one of the primitive expressions for that germ of the creed or standard of faith and morals which ruled the practice of the churches" ("The Interpretation of Romans 6:17-18," *JBL*, XLVIII [1929], 237).

[142] *Das Werk des Geistes*, pp. 220-21, n. 77.

[143] "Glossen im Römerbrief," col. 202.

applied, and in any case that passage too is suspect of being of non-Pauline origin.[144] Bultmann's point that the problem clause of Rom. 6:17 is rhetorically disruptive may be conceded (as Stalder does) but is not by itself decisive. Stalder, for instance, contends that the intrusion results from Paul's own employment of a traditional formulation; and as already noted, there are other disruptive phrases in this context. The major one (in vs. 13) is clearly of Pauline origin.[145] On the other hand, Bultmann's point that the intrusive clause in vs. 17 reflects a completely un-Pauline view of obedience *is* decisive. Stalder's attempt to find in the expression τύπος διδαχῆς a reference to Christ himself is artful but not persuasive. It is certainly a reference to a "pattern of teaching," either Paul's own (Bultmann) or some other commonly acknowledged as authoritative (Dodd). Thus, if we follow Bultmann, Rom. 6:17*b* is probably to be treated as a gloss and excluded from consideration as evidence for the apostle's own view of Christian obedience.

[144] Rom. 16:17-20 contains a great many un-Pauline features, the more important of which may be summarized as follows: (1) Nowhere else does Paul use the verb σκοπεῖν (RSV: "take note") as a warning to pay attention to troublemakers (contrast Phil. 3:2, βλέπειν) ; (2) διχοστασία ("dissension") occurs in only one other Pauline (or New Testament) passage, and that is the traditional vice list of Gal. 5:20. Paul's own words for dissension and division are σχίσμα and αἵρεσις; (3) only here does the plural τὰ σκάνδαλα (RSV: "difficulties") appear in Paul's writings; (4) διδαχή ("teaching") here, as in Rom. 6:17*b*, refers to a *tradition,* whereas in the only unquestionably Pauline passage where the noun is employed (I Cor. 14:6, 26) the reference is not to a tradition but a *spiritual gift;* (5) only here in the Pauline letters is the verb μανθάνειν ("to learn") used to refer to learning a specific body of material (a "teaching"; contrast I Cor. 4:6; 14:31, [35]; Gal. 3:2; Phil. 4:9, 11) ; (6) the only other Pauline occurrence of the verb ἐκκλίνειν (RSV: "avoid") is in the LXX citation in Rom. 3:12; (7) only here in the New Testament does εὐλογία occur with the negative meaning "fair and flattering words" (RSV) ; (8) the expression, "our Lord Christ" is unique in Paul, who elsewhere does not use the titles "Lord" and "Christ" in immediate juxtaposition (see Kramer, *Christ, Lord, Son of God,* p. 214, n. 744 [Section 65]) .

In his commentary on Romans (*IntB,* IX, 367-68) John Knox proposes the hypothesis that the whole of Romans 16, not just the demonstrably late doxology (vss. 25 ff.), is a second-century appendix originating in the church at Rome. The hypothesis deserves serious consideration.

[145] See n. 139 above.

e. Obedience in love

While Paul nowhere speaks of "obeying" the law, he does presume that its commandments are to be kept, even by the believer (e.g. I Cor. 7:19). But in what sense is the believer, now freed from the law's power, still bound to it? It is clear that the apostle rejects the law as the way to salvation. As a written code promulgating a series of moral duties which, when performed, can be regarded as achievements, the law has come to an "end" in Christ. Yet the law has, in another way, been fulfilled in Christ, for the life it promised but could not deliver has been bestowed in his death and resurrection. Moreover, insofar as the commandments of the law are in accord with the meaning of God's grace as it has been revealed in Christ, they are still, indeed especially, binding upon the believer. How this can be is suggested by the two texts in which Paul speaks about the "fulfillment" (πλήρωμα) of the law, Rom. 13:8 ff. and Gal. 5:13-14.

In both of these passages the law's relevance for the Christian is defined in terms of its command to love the neighbor. There are, to be sure, some interesting differences in details. In Rom. 13:8 the apostle says that "he who loves the other has fulfilled the law," [146] and the subject of the verb πεπλήρωκεν ("has fulfilled") is thus the Christian. In vs. 10, however, ἀγάπη ("love") itself is the acting subject: *"Love* works no wrong against the neighbor, therefore *love* is the law's fulfillment." A comparison with I Corinthians 13 is appropriate, for there too "love" is itself the subject which is longsuffering, kind, etc. One may conclude that for Paul love is not just an aspect of the Christian's new life, but its whole content and mode. The believer *is* "love"; he has been made love in his resurrection to newness of life in Christ. As one "under grace" he has been "overtaken" by Christ (Phil. 3:12) in whom God's own love has been bestowed (Rom.

---

[146] The construction of this remark has been variously analyzed. E.g. Gutbrod (*ThW*, IV, 1063, 1069) and W. Marxsen ("Der ἕτερος νόμος Röm. 13, 8," *TZ*, XI (1955), 230 ff.) construe ἕτερος with νόμος, hence, "he who loves has fulfilled *the other law*." But the usual construction which understands "the other" as the object of the verb "love" is to be preferred, as Cranfield (*Romans 12-13*, pp. 83-84) has successfully demonstrated.

5:8). Therefore, as he shares in that event by dying and rising with Christ, he himself becomes the recipient of that love through the Spirit (Rom. 5:5). Thereby he is brought "from death to life" (Rom. 6:13). Just as Paul views faith as the means by which *grace* is received, so can he speak of faith as that which receives *the Spirit* (e.g. Gal. 3:2, 5). Because the gift of the Spirit is the gift of love, faith is itself the recipient of love (cf. Gal. 2:20). Faith's obedience is therefore the surrender to love. To be "obedient" in the Pauline sense means to yield one's whole self—remade in love—to the controlling power of that love (cf. II Cor. 5:14). The dominion of grace is the dominion where love is given and where it (i.e. the "lover," the believer) is claimed. As a new man in Christ, the believer *is* love; that is the total meaning of his life and the reason why his obedience is the yielding of his whole life to God.

If this exposition of Paul's thought is valid, then it follows that one must be cautious in stating the apostle's position on the fulfillment of the law. It is not the Christian as a *performer* or *achiever* who fulfills the law. It is fulfilled by the power of God active as love in the life of the believer. Paul himself is cautious here. Only in Rom. 13:8 does he refer to the believer as a "fulfiller" (perhaps because the believer as *doer* had been the object of the preceding exhortations). Gal. 5:13-14 requires no qualification of this point: "For the whole law is fulfilled in the one sentence, 'You shall love your neighbor as yourself.'" Thus πεπλήρωται ("is fulfilled") in Gal. 5:14 is synonymous with ἀνακεφαλαιοῦται ("summarized") in Rom. 13:9. For Paul the commandments of the law are all seen as expressions of the one all-encompassing command to love. Nowhere does he indicate that, from this standpoint, some of the law's commandments are invalid. Speculation on such a point would probably have seemed to him but a new kind of casuistry, a return to dealing with the law as a written code. The decisive point is what Rom. 13:8 ff. and Gal. 5:13-14 presuppose: that the law has no value as a norm independent of the believer's new life in Christ, under the dominion of grace and the control of love.

This point can be summarized by examining the parallelism of the three important Pauline epigrams: I Cor. 7:19; Gal. 5:6;

6:15. Each begins with the assertion that neither circumcision nor uncircumcision has value in itself. (A discussion of this occurs in Rom. 2:25 ff.,[147] itself summarized in the statement of Rom. 3:30; "[God] will rightwise the circumcised on the basis of faith and the uncircumcised through faith.") However, each of these three parallel epigrams specifies what *does* matter in a different way. In I Cor. 7:19 it is "keeping the commandments of God" (RSV); in Gal. 5:6, "faith active in love"; and in Gal. 6:15, "a new creation" (RSV). (If, as seems appropriate, one may consider Rom. 3:30 along with these, "faith" as such would constitute yet a fourth variation.) The correspondence of the three epigrams is not just rhetorical but also material.[148] As the recipient of God's grace, put right by God's power and reconciled by God's love, the believer has been raised to newness of life. His whole situation has been so radically transformed that he is a "new creation." When Paul uses this expression in Gal. 6:15, he is obviously thinking of the believer's dying and rising with Christ; through the cross the world has been "crucified" to the believer, and with it the "I" of the old man himself (Gal. 6:14; cf. Rom. 6:6). The "new creation" is thus a *being in Christ* (II Cor. 5:17), and this alone is what matters (Gal. 6:15). It is significant that the related epigram of Gal. 5:6 is introduced with the phrase ἐν Χριστῷ Ἰησοῦ: "*in Christ Jesus* nothing matters but. . . ."

Since it is by faith that one participates in Christ's death and resurrection and thus lives "in" him, it is clear why, in Gal. 5:6 (and Rom. 3:30), Paul can say that *faith* is what really matters. But what is the precise significance of the phrase "faith active in love" (πίστις δι' ἀγάπης ἐνεργουμένη)? The participle ἐνεργουμένη may be taken as either middle ("working," RSV) or passive ("inspired," NEB margin). Is the primary reference thus to the believer's *loving* (the expression of his faith) or to his

---

[147] See above, pp. 192-93.

[148] Schrage, critical specifically of Lietzmann (see *Korinther*, p. 32), has urged that these three ought not to be too closely identified (*Die konkreten Einzelgebote*, p. 100). (Schrage has subsequently, however, changed his opinion on this matter and—as indicated to me in conversation—would now himself interpret each of these verses in the light of the other two.)

being loved (God's love as the "inspiration" for faith)? Most commentators (and virtually all the English translations) have opted for the former, but there is much to be said for the latter, or at least for the judgment that "the two renderings are complementary." [149] It has become evident that for Paul faith's obedience is an obedience in love, but an obedience which has the *character* of love because its ground is God's own love by which the sinner has been claimed by and thus reconciled to God. The Christian is summoned to love in a double sense: to be *loved* and to be *loving*. Within the precincts of Pauline theology these two are not separable. The translation of Gal. 5:6*b* as "faith rendered active through love" [150] is appropriately suggestive: faith is a response to the event of grace and in that sense constituted by it; but as *obedience* to the Lord faith has its own "work" which, as the "labor of love," is expressive of the believer's new life in Christ (τοῦ ἔργου τῆς πίστεως καὶ τοῦ κόπου τῆς ἀγάπης, I Thess. 1:3).

Now the meaning of I Cor. 7:19, "keeping the commandments of God" (RSV), may be readily determined. As Rom. 13:8 ff. and Gal. 5:13-14 have shown, the law's commandments have meaning and force insofar as they express the commandment to love. The commandments are to be kept, *not* because the law requires them (in that case their observance would be "works"), but because they are in accord with God's own way with men. It is perhaps significant that the apostle speaks not of "keeping the commandments of *the law*," but "the commandments of *God*." Christian obedience is neither prompted by nor directed toward a written code. It is obedience to God, who himself has made obedience possible.

So much is now clear: In the vocabulary of Pauline theology faith is obedience, and obedience is love. But since obedience radically conceived means belonging to the Lord, being a "slave" of God, is it not strange that the apostle rarely (Rom. 8:28; I

---

[149] A. E. Garvie, "Suggestive Variants," *ET*, LV (1943–44), 97.

[150] John Ross, "ΕΝΕΡΓΕΙΣΘΑΙ in the New Testament," *Exp.* VII (series VII, 1909), 76; cf. J. B. Mayor, *ibid.*, pp. 191-92. Similarly, C. Spicq, *Agape in the New Testament*, trans. Sisters M. McNamara and M. Richter (1965), II, 218 ff.

Cor. 8:3 [151]) speaks of God as the object of the believer's love? Nygren's answer corresponds with the findings of the present study. God's love is revealed in the cross to be an event of pure grace, spontaneous and unmotivated, from man's side unmerited. Therefore, man's "giving of himself to God is never more than a response. At its best and highest, it is but a reflex of God's love, by which it is 'motivated.' " For this reason obedience to God is "given another name: not ἀγάπη, but πίστις ["faith"]." [152] How, then, is faith's obedience in love expressed? Rom. 13:8 ff. and Gal. 5:13-14 leave no doubt: in one's love of the neighbor.

f. The "household of faith"

The conception of salvation as an individual matter between man and God is utterly foreign to Paul's preaching. It is true that the gospel he proclaims is a summons of individual men to God in the sense that it is the individual who stands addressed and confronted by God's word. And yet the individual does not stand apart from the whole *people of God*. The call to men to belong to their Lord is at the same time a call to belong to one another. Incorporation into Christ's death and resurrection does not occur apart from participation in the household of faith; baptism and the Lord's Supper are both *corporate* acts (e.g. Gal. 3:27 ff.; I Cor. 10:16-17). To be in Christ, in the Lord, in the Spirit means to be in the *community* of Christ, the Lord, and the Spirit. Yet "the church" as such is not to be listed as one of the themes of Paul's preaching (Ephesians, of course, being regarded as the work of another writer). The ecclesiological dimensions of Paul's gospel emerge in other ways, principally in his emphasis on faith as obedience in love.[153]

[151] Cf. also Philemon 5 ("I hear of your love and of the faith which you have toward the Lord Jesus and all the saints" [RSV]); and the LXX quotation in I Cor. 2:9.

[152] *Agape and Eros*, pp. 125-26.

[153] Cf. the remarks of Michel Bouttier who emphasizes that for Paul the two tasks of preaching the word and building up the churches are really only one, that "no dividing line appears between the missionary and the pastoral ministries, just as there is no frontier marking out ecclesiology from ethics" and that "ethics are bound up with the most intimate aspect

It has been demonstrated in many different ways that Paul regards faith's obedience as a radical surrender of one's self to God, a giving of one's self to belong to him as a slave belongs to his master. The same categories are employed when he describes the character of Christian love. It is a radical *giving up* of one's self and a radical *being given over* into the service of others. "Standing fast" in the freedom which Christ's death and resurrection have bestowed means nothing else than freedom *from* one's self and *for others*. Paul exhorts: "Through love be bound in service to one another" (διὰ τῆς ἀγάπης δουλεύετε ἀλλήλοις, Gal. 5:13). The Christian's "slavery" to God finds concrete expression in his serving other men. Only in this one respect, but *always* in this one respect, is he to be in their "debt" (Rom. 13:8). The neighbor to whom the Christian is bound in love is in the first instance the brother in Christ. Yet Paul's appeal to the Galatians to "do good" (="love"; note the parallelism of I Cor. 14:1 [διώκετε τὴν ἀγάπην] and I Thess. 5:15 [τὸ ἀγαθὸν διώκετε]) *"especially* to those of the household of faith" (6:10*b*) defines only the minimum of love's responsibility, not its farthest extent. This exhortation presupposes that love's scope is not restricted and that love does not have the character of love except that it is "for all" (πρὸς πάντας, 6:10*a*). That the household of faith designates only the beginning point of love is also, and perhaps more clearly, the implication of Paul's wish that the Thessalonians may "abound in love to one another and to all [εἰς ἀλλήλους καὶ εἰς πάντας]" (I Thess. 3:12).

The nature of Christian love matches that of faith itself. This is seen best of all in I Cor. 13:4 ff.: love means the *giving* of one's self, the abandonment of all private claims, privileges, and boasts, and constructive concern for others. But love's "giving" and "giving up" have a particular character. Philanthropy, even martyrdom, is not to be equated with love (I Cor. 13:3). Love is not a "virtue," not even when virtuous deeds assume heroic proportions. Love presupposes not that "value" resides in the lover or in the deed of love, but that as the object of love the

---

of life in Christ; they cannot be dissociated from the life of the community" (*Christianity According to Paul*, trans. F. Clarke, in *SBTh*, 49 [1966], 106).

beloved himself becomes "valuable." Love, therefore, does not have to do with "value" or "virtue" in the usual sense. Just as for Paul love is representative of the total being of God as his being for others, so is the believer's love representative of his total life in faith as a life for others. Love always assumes the form of "service" (δουλεία, Gal. 5:13-14; διακονία, I Cor. 12:5—"for the common good" [vs. 7 RSV; πρὸς τὸ συμφέρον]). Love is not a quality of one's own character or one's own activity, but the power of God present with him (e.g. Rom. 5:5; cf. II Cor. 5:14), turning him from the concerns of self to the concern for others. Love's "work" is defined by the neighbor's needs, radically conceived as his one great and continuing need to *be* loved. Since love's work is always before it and never "finished," it has no reason to boast (I Cor. 13:4-5). Paul's appeal, then, is to *abound* in love "more and more" (Phil. 1:9; I Thess. 3:12; 4:10; cf. II Cor. 2:4; 8:7; I Thess. 4:1). This is also the meaning of his exhortation in I Cor. 14:12 to "abound in building up the church," for he knows that it is love alone which "builds up" (I Cor. 8:1).

It is apparent that the nature of that love which is to characterize faith's obedience is determined by the nature of God's love (his grace) to which faith is the response. This is doubtless what Paul has in mind when he writes to the Thessalonians that they have no need of a learned essay "concerning brotherly love" (περὶ τῆς φιλαδελφίας) because they have been "taught of God" (θεοδίδακτοι) about love (I Thess. 4:9).[154] Specifically, the Christian's love is to have the character of Christ's own. He is love's "encouragement" and "incentive" (Phil. 2:1 RSV); the love which brethren in Christ are to share (Phil. 2:2) is thus rooted in God's love bestowed in Christ and received by faith in him. In being reconciled to God by his love, the believer is himself entrusted with the ministry of reconciliation (II Cor. 5:18 ff.). Those who in and through Christ are reconciled to God are reconciled to one another, and their brotherhood consists in their joint receipt of the saving love of God. The radical

---

[154] Cf. Nygren, *Agape and Eros*, p. 116. Contrast, e.g., Plutarch's treatise, "On Brotherly Love" (περὶ φιλαδελφίας), Moralia 478-92. For Paul love's character is determined by theological, not humanitarian considerations; not by reflection, but by revelation.

depth and breadth of God's love have been revealed in Christ's
death (Rom. 5:6 ff.) which, at the same time, shows what the
Christian's own love is to be like (cf. Rom. 14:15; I Cor. 8:11-
12). Christ's death and resurrection was for others, and those
"others," who have died with him, are raised to newness of life
even in the present (Rom. 6:4, 13 [155]), insofar as through him
they themselves have learned how and have been enabled to
live for others (II Cor. 5:15). "Let each of us," writes Paul,
"please his neighbor for his good, to build him up" (Rom.
15:2). It is important to observe that love's "pleasing" of the
neighbor is not in order to win his praise (cf. Rom. 2:29*b*), but
for his own good. It is also significant that this admonition is
grounded in Christ's own obedient, others-regarding love: "For
Christ did not please himself" but "became a servant [διάκονος]"
(vss. 3, 8).

---

[155] See above, p. 195.

IV
The Character
of the Pauline Ethic

INTRODUCTION

Because the indicative and imperative aspects of Paul's preaching
are so vitally interrelated, it is an exceedingly difficult task to
single out and summarize the peculiarly "ethical" aspects of
his gospel. In an important sense the exposition of the themes
of Paul's preaching has already, and in the most appropriate
way, revealed the character of the Pauline ethic. Nevertheless,
it is worthwhile, in conclusion, to attempt a somewhat more
systematic analysis and discussion of that ethic in order to emphasize its salient features. In the first place, its general character as a *theological* ethic must be examined, with a special
concern to illumine the key problem of indicative and imperative. And secondly, a few somewhat more "practical" implications of Paul's ethic for concrete problems of Christian ethical
action must be explored. How is the believer able to discover
what is "right" or "good"? How is he enabled to do it? Has the
concept of "moral progress" a place in this ethic? It must be
granted that Paul himself has not posed or answered such questions in any systematic way; yet it must also be recognized that
important elements of the answers are present, both implicitly
and explicitly, in the apostle's letters.

1. THE THEOLOGICAL STRUCTURE OF THE ETHIC

a. Is there a "Pauline ethic"?

The question of the propriety of speaking of a Pauline ethic has been deferred until now in order that the investigation of Paul's concrete exhortations and the central themes of his preaching could proceed with as few preformulated notions as possible.[1] In retrospect, however, this question can and must be posed: In what sense, if any, is it possible to speak of a Pauline ethic? This requires, to begin with, some consideration of the possible meanings of the term "ethics" itself.

Lying behind the term "ethics" are the Greek words ἔθος and ἦθος, each of which refers, in the most elemental sense, to action which is customary, usual, or habitual. However, insofar as such usual or habitual action may be considered "normal" in a given society or group, the way is prepared for regarding it also as norma*tive*—that is, actually "required" for the members of that society or group, more or less rigorously binding upon them. The Greek terms, in fact, came also to carry this additional meaning, as certain instances of ἔθος in the New Testament itself clearly indicate.[2] In Acts 28:17, for example, Paul is represented as addressing a group of Jewish leaders in Rome: "I have done nothing, brethren, in opposition to the people or contrary to the customs [ἢ τοῖς ἔθεσι] of the fathers, yet I was given over prisoner from Jerusalem into the hands of the Romans." Here the "customs of the fathers" are regarded as normative and binding, ways of living which are not to be opposed. In Paul's own letters, however, the word ἔθος never appears, and the single occurrence of ἦθος (I Cor. 15:33: "Bad company ruins good morals [ἤθη χρηστά]," RSV) is in a familiar proverb Paul is only quoting.[3] Moreover, it must be noted that nowhere in the New Testament is any member of this family of Greek words employed with reference to any particular pattern of conduct or any particular set of moral principles.

---

[1] See above, pp. 10-11.
[2] See Preisker, *ThW*, II, 370-71 [ET: p. 372].
[3] See above, p. 45.

In current popular usage the English adjective "ethical" is applied to concrete actions deemed by the speaker to be "good," so that "ethics" as such is identified with morality in the practical affairs of life (one may thus speak of "ethics" in government). To refer, in this connection, to an individual's "ethics" is to refer to the pattern of conduct which characterizes his day-to-day living, his "conclusions," as it were, about "right" and "wrong" as these are expressed in his life.

"Ethics," however, conceived as a particular subject for systematic study and reflection, has a more precise meaning. As one department of philosophical and religious inquiry, the term is applied to the special consideration of the nature, forms, principles, and goals of "right" or "good" conduct. Thus, it may be said that "ethics aims to give a systematic account of our judgments about conduct, in so far as these estimate it from the standpoint of right or wrong, good or bad." [4] In performing his task, the ethicist inquires not only into the matter of norms, but is concerned also with the *subject* of ethical action (the *actor* or *agent*) and the *object(s)* of ethical action.[5] As usually understood, then, "ethical" reflection involves systematic and critical consideration of the various modes and motives of human conduct. As Karl Barth has put it, the "ethical question" has to do with

the basis and possibility of the fact that in the multitude and multiplicity of human actions there are certain modes of action, i.e., certain constants, certain laws, rules, usages or continuities. It is the question as to the rightness of these constants, the fitness of these laws. It is the question as to the value which gives any action the claim to be the true expression of a mode of action, the fulfilment of a law—the right to be repeated and in virtue of its normative character to serve as an example for the actions of others.[6]

It is readily apparent that Paul has as little concern for ethics in a *systematic* sense as he has for a "systematic theology." Nowhere

---

[4] John Dewey and James H. Tufts, *Ethics* (1908), p. 1. Cf. William Frankena who describes ethics as "primarily concerned with providing the general outlines of a normative theory to help us in answering problems about what is right or ought to be done" (*Ethics* [1963], p. 5).

[5] Cf. H. van Oyen, *RGG* (3rd ed.), II, cols. 708-9.

[6] *Church Dogmatics*, trans. G. W. Bromiley *et al.*, II, 2 (1957), 513.

in his letters does he deal in a deliberative, reflective, critical way with the questions which an *ethicist* per se must always examine. The apostle himself seems not to have conceived of any special "ethical" side to his message or mission[7] and certainly never attempts appraisal or even presentation of ethical principles, norms, or theories. As virtually every interpreter of Paul has emphasized, his letters offer no self-conscious, systematic analysis of the ground, motives, forms, or goals of Christian conduct. It is inappropriate to speak of a "Pauline ethic" in this sense.[8]

On the other hand, if one employs the term "ethics" in its everyday sense, it is obviously possible to speak of "the ethics of Paul." The apostle most certainly does have his *own* ideas, at least, about right and wrong, good and bad. These he applies not only to himself but often to his churches. Yet even here one must be cautious. While Paul does exhort, instruct, admonish, and advise his readers, this is almost always done in *ad hoc* fashion in relation to specific situations and cases. No single practical ethical pattern or "Christian code of conduct" is ever promulgated. He sponsors no particular ethical program, and his various specific ethical injunctions taken together are not intended to provide a comprehensive portrait of "the Christian man." The attempt to wrest from the apostle's letters a pattern of ethics in the practical sense is as futile as the attempt to find there ethical theories or the systematic presentation of ethical norms and principles.

[7] The present investigation has uncovered no substantial basis for the assertion that Paul's thought and ministry had distinctive "kerygmatic" and "didactic" aspects. The two passages which could conceivably be used as evidence for some self-consciously and specifically "ethical" concern in the strictest sense (Rom. 6:17; 16:17) have been shown to be, probably, and for other reasons, deutero-Pauline (above, pp. 196 ff.) .

[8] One can go even farther than this and say, with D. Mackenzie: "There is no formal science of Ethics in the NT" (*ERE*, V, 468) . The Roman Catholic scholar, John L. McKenzie, wishes to say even more—that "there cannot be a Christian ethics," for he defines ethics restrictively to be "a theory of moral obligation in general and a system of moral obligations in particular based on a rational consideration of nature" ("Natural Law in the New Testament," p. 12) .

Is it necessary, then, to reduce the idea of "Pauline ethics" to mean only Paul's practical ethical concern and his *ad hoc* exhortations and instructions? Is the apostle, after all, only a practical moralist whose concern for morality is so tied to concrete circumstances and problems that it holds interest only for the historian who wants to reconstruct the antique ethical ideas and customs of a bygone era? [9] On the contrary, while it is true that Paul does not reflect critically and systematically upon the problems of ethics, and that his exhortations and instructions are for the most part directed to specific situations, his concern for the practical conduct of Christians is inseparably related to the central themes of his preaching. This has been demonstrated in many different ways during the course of this present investigation.

Undoubtedly, Paul's own personal background in Judaism and his experiences as a Jew, the general moral climate of his age, and the specific moral problems he encountered in his congregations—all helped to determine the direction of and give shape to his concrete ethical teaching. But the decisive factor behind this teaching is the apostle's understanding of what it means to be "in Christ" and to "belong" to him. Paul himself does not deliberate on the ways in which his ethical concerns are related to his basic theological convictions, but significant relationships between these do exist, and it is one of the important tasks of the interpreter of Paul to identify and exposit them. Precisely by tracing and understanding these relationships, the character of his ethic may be clarified. It is in this connection that one may indeed speak of a "Pauline ethic." Never raised to the level of critical examination by the apostle himself, never self-consciously formulated or presented by him, it is present, nonetheless, in the dynamic of indicative and imperative which lies at the center of his thought.

The study of the Pauline ethic, therefore, is not the study of

[9] Such is maintained, e.g., by Mary Andrews who declares that for Paul "circumstances rule" and that he "simply did the best he could in the immediate situation, and when conflict arose he attempted to justify his course of action or his judgment" (*The Ethical Teaching of Paul*, p. 171).

his ethical theory, for he had none, nor of his code for Christian living, for he gave none. It is the study, first of all, of the theological convictions which underlie Paul's concrete exhortations and instructions and, secondly, of the way those convictions shape his responses to practical questions of conduct.

b. Three basic motifs of the Pauline ethic

Because the Pauline ethic cannot be equated with any clearly definable ethical theory or moral code, all attempts to give it some particular label are bound to be at best misleading, at worst deceiving. Many proposals have been made. It has been called an "ethic of gratitude" or a "telos-ethic"; "sacramental," or "pneumatic," or "charismatic," or "eschatological," or "christological." There have also been attempts to capture its essence in a formula—for instance: "Love, and do as you then please." Each of these contains some measure of truth, and yet no single term or simplistic formula is able to do justice to the complexity of (a) Paul's own ethical judgments and exhortations and (b) the relationship between his theological and ethical perspectives. It is in fact the interaction of many factors and most especially the dynamic integrity of theological and ethical concerns, which has given to the Pauline ethic its own distinctive structure.

It is equally impossible to single out any one Pauline doctrine as having to do specifically with "Christian ethics" or the Christian's moral life. This has been attempted very often, especially by appealing to the doctrines of the Spirit and of sanctification. While there are important relationships between each of these and ethical judgments and actions, neither can be legitimately reduced to the status of a "doctrine of ethics" per se. Paul's view of the Spirit is by no means isolable from his eschatology,[10] and his understanding of sanctification is quite inseparable from his doctrine of justification.[11]

Any study of the ethic of Paul must, as the whole previous discussion has indicated, acknowledge that *multiple* theological

[10] See above, pp. 129 ff.
[11] See above, pp. 153 ff.

motifs have left their mark upon that ethic. If one seeks to analyze the structure of Paul's ethic in terms of its absolutely fundamental components, then the following formulation can perhaps be defended: radically conceived, the Pauline ethic is compounded of the apostle's *theological, eschatological,* and *christological* convictions. These are the three inseparably related root-motifs of his preaching and thus, also, of his ethic. For it has become crystal clear that Paul's ethic has its place only *within* the circumference of his total gospel.

The Pauline ethic is first of all radically *theo*logical because it presupposes that man's whole life and being is dependent upon the sovereign, creative, and redemptive power of God. This is the basis, for instance, upon which Paul pointedly asks the Corinthians, "What do you possess that was not given you? If then you really received it all as a gift, why take the credit to yourself?" (I Cor. 4:7 NEB). The theme of God's power has been seen to pervade the whole of Pauline theology: the "transcendent power" is God's alone (II Cor. 4:7), and it is God's power to create and redeem which enables faith to be faith, as in the case of Abraham (Rom. 4:16-21). This is why the apostle may describe his gospel of justification as "the power of God for salvation to all who believe" (Rom. 1:16), thereby making it a gospel of justification through God's grace received by *faith* (believing). The Spirit which God bestows (Rom. 5:5) is God's power at work within and among believers (e.g. Rom. 15:13, 19; cf. II Cor. 13:3). But most of all God's gracious saving power is revealed in Christ (I Cor. 1:24; 5:4; II Cor. 12:9), in his death (I Cor. 1:17-18) and resurrection (Rom. 1:4; II Cor. 13:4; cf. Rom. 6:4 where "glory" stands for "power"). It is, moreover, the believer's hope to share in this resurrection power (or "glory") of God (Phil. 3:10; Rom. 5:2). The power of God which raised Christ will also raise up those who are in Christ (I Cor. 6:14; cf. 15:43).

As previously shown,[12] Paul sees hostile worldly powers set over against the power of God, exerting their own claims on man's life. Here the apocalyptic aspects of Pauline theology

[12] See above, pp. 115 ff.

and ethics are especially clear. As a creature *of God,* man's true destiny and fulfillment are found only within the precincts of his power. But as a *creature* of God (a man like Adam), he is susceptible to the competing claims of rival powers. To yield to their power, thus rejecting the sovereignty of God's claim, is to live "according to the flesh" rather than "according to the Spirit," and to allow "sin" and "death" to take over. The only redemption from this bondage to sin and death (which exercise their power through the law) is in Christ, by whose death and resurrection God's power achieves its victory. So at last, those who are Christ's will share in the kingdom he delivers to the Father, all hostile powers, even death, having been finally conquered, and God alone reigning with undisputed sovereignty over all things (I Cor. 15:20-28). At the "end," everything is God's and his alone, even Christ (cf. I Cor. 3:23).

Along with this radical theocentrism of Paul [13] goes the basically and thoroughly *eschatological* orientation of his whole gospel. The Pauline eschatology is not just one motif among numerous others, but helps to provide the fundamental perspective within which everything else is viewed.[14] The absolute priority and sovereignty of God's power are expressed not only in the spatially conceived mythology of God's dwelling in "heaven" (e.g. Rom. 1:18; I Cor. 15:47 ff.; Phil. 2:10; I Thess. 1:10), but also in the temporally conceived mythology of God's future triumph over all hostile powers (e.g. I Cor. 15:20 ff). In both cases it is God's *transcendence* of the world and history which struggles to find expression, and therefore his "otherness," which both Old and New Testament writers identify as his "holiness." Both of these mythologies are involved in the apostle's insistence that believers are citizens of another realm ("heaven") from which shall come the Savior whom they "await" (Phil. 3:20).

Yet Pauline eschatology is not totally futuristic. As Wendland

---

[13] The implications of this Pauline theocentrism for a total theological program are briefly explored by Schubert M. Ogden, *Christ Without Myth* (1961), pp. 141 ff.

[14] This point is made with particular effectiveness by H.-D. Wendland, "Ethik und Eschatologie," esp. p. 800. See also above, p. 114.

appropriately remarks, the contrast between what is "present"
and what is "eschatological" is not representative of Paul.[15] For
him the eschatological action of God (that is, God's transcendent
power) has also a *present* dimension. In this crucial respect
Paul's preaching breaks through the traditional categories of
Jewish apocalypticism.[16] The meaning and reality of the ultimate
triumph of God's power are already manifested in the present.
Side by side with Paul's statements regarding the future salvation
go his emphatic assertions that "now is the day of salvation"
(II Cor. 6:2) and that "if any one is in Christ he *is* a new creature" (II Cor. 5:17).[17] It is important to give full weight to
the seriousness with which the apostle affirms this. It is not just
a matter of rhetoric, an attempt to emphasize the importance
of what is to come. Nor does he just mean that salvation which
will be *fulfilled* in the future has been *initiated* already in the
present. Rather, Paul's thought at this point is genuinely dialectical. He sees no easy chronological continuity between past,
present, and future. The future is totally *God's* future, and it
does not progress or develop from the past and present (which
is man's).[18] The salvation which is already present is not, therefore, somehow qualitatively preliminary or second-rate. What is
given is present in its *fullness* (although there is still something
not given—namely resurrection from the dead and the final cosmic triumph of God's power over death).

The importance of the eschatological orientation of Pauline
theology for the apostle's ethic in particular is well exhibited
in Romans 12–13. The exhortations of these chapters (12:3–

---

[15] *Ibid.*, p. 797.

[16] As do also, perhaps—but only in part—the psalms of the Jewish
sectarians at Qumran. See the discussion of Qumran eschatology by Helmer
Ringgren in *The Faith of Qumran* (1963), pp. 152 ff.; esp. p. 154.

[17] See above, pp. 126 ff.

[18] This point is made very well by Paul Schubert: "It would be an un-
Pauline reductionism . . . to reduce this dialectic to a mere chronological
sequence: partial or even relatively decisive fulfilment now—consummation
later." ("Paul and the New Testament Ethic in the Thought of John
Knox," *Christian History and Interpretation*, ed. W. R. Farmer, C. F. D.
Moule, and R. R. Niebuhr [1967], p. 379). Cf. also Tannehill, *Dying and
Rising with Christ*: "The new dominion is not an epoch of world history,
which could be superseded in the course of historical development, but
something which is hidden within history" (p. 40).

13:10) are framed by an introduction (12:1-2) and conclusion (13:11-14), both of which emphasize the genuinely eschatological existence of those exhorted. The appeal not to be "conformed to this age" (12:2) presupposes the believer's belonging to another age in which, through faith, he already participates. In 13:11 ff. the terminology differs, but the perspective is the same: the believer is not to give himself over to "the flesh" and its "passions" (vs. 14="this age," 12:2); but because he belongs to "the day" (vss. 12-13; cf. I Thess. 5:8), he is to "put on the Lord Jesus Christ" (vs. 14="be transformed in the renewal of the mind," 12:2). Here the Pauline dialectic of present and future is closely tied to the dialectic of indicative and imperative (cf. "Put on the Lord Jesus Christ," 13:14, with the indicative," "[you] have put Christ on" in Gal. 3:27). The exhortations are not designed for some "interim" before the future comes; they are rooted precisely in the future as it is already present to faith, though still hidden within this age.

Because Paul regards Christ's death and resurrection as the decisive event of grace through which God's power is active in the present,[19] it is necessary to consider, along with his theology and eschatology, also his *Christology.* Faith in God's power is focused and defined in commitment to Christ. Through his death and resurrection God's power has been operative in man's history, and those who belong to him, who participate in his body,[20] have been freed from sin's dominion and set within the dominion of God. To be thus redeemed and reconciled is to be justified, placed "under [the power of] grace" (Rom. 6:14-15).[21] When Paul speaks of life "in Christ," he is speaking of life made new by the love of God bestowed in Christ (e.g. II Cor. 5:17) and by that very fact *claimed* by God, "held in custody" by God's love given in Christ (cf. II Cor. 5:14, "Christ's love holds us in custody").

Romans 6 is one of the crucial passages for determining the christological dimensions of Pauline theology in general and

[19] See above, p. 162.
[20] See above, pp. 171 ff., 176 ff.
[21] See above, pp. 168 ff.

the Pauline ethic in particular.[22] Baptism is the sign that the believer has already died with Christ; it is baptism "into death in order that, just as Christ was raised from the dead through the glory [=power] of God, so we too might walk in newness of life" (vs. 4). As Bornkamm has noted, it is significant that Paul does *not* say: "so we too might be *raised from the dead.*" [23] The believer's resurrection with Christ is as such still in the future (vss. 5, 8). But the resurrection power of God in Christ is already operative in the believer's present life. In belonging to Christ, he belongs to a whole new order, and thus the "style" of his life (περιπατεῖν) is also entirely new. When in vs. 13 Paul exhorts his readers to surrender themselves to God "as [ὡσεί] those who from death have been brought to life," the thought is essentially the same. The life of faith is a life which already bears the marks of God's redeeming power. The believer's life is not just "analogous to" the future resurrection life, but already shows it forth. Thus, ὡσεί should by no means be translated: "*as if* [you have been raised from death to life]." [24] Barrett, to be sure, thinks that ὡσεί means *both* "as if you were" and "as in fact you are." This can be, he argues, because when Christians are raised "by faith," they are *in that sense* already raised; but because they are not yet raised up "at the last day," they live now only "as if" they were raised.[25] Such an interpretation, however, fails to do justice to the genuinely dialectical character of Paul's thought. Moreover, it obscures the essential Pauline insight that the power of God to which faith is a response and by which faith is nourished is nothing else than the power which created and resurrects (Rom. 4:17, 19 ff.).

Paul's understanding of the quality or character of the new life in Christ given already to the believer is also derived from his Christology. As shown eloquently by Rom. 5:6 ff. Christ's death is regarded by the apostle as the showing forth of God's rightwising, reconciling love (esp. vs. 8). The death of Christ

---

[22] Various points in this passage have already received special attention; esp. pp. 105-6, 194 ff. above.

[23] "Taufe und neues Leben bei Paulus," *Das Ende des Gesetzes*, p. 38.

[24] Correctly Michel, *Römer*, p. 157.

[25] *Romans*, p. 128.

was "for us" (cf. "for all," II Cor. 5:14), a pure act of grace
to be received by faith (Rom. 5:1-2). By this "one man's obedience" (Rom. 5:19) those who belong to him by believing
in him are given life and righteousness. That the obedience of
Christ has the character of humble, selfless love and service is
made clear by the context into which Paul draws the hymn of
Phil. 2:6-11. Christ's "obedience unto death" (vs. 8, probably
Paul's own interpolation[26]) is regarded as the ultimate expression of humble concern for others (vss. 3-4). Moreover, the
apostle intends Christ's obedience to be paradigmatic for the
believer. What he has done becomes an "incentive of love" (vs.
1 RSV), a "paraclesis" (vs. 1 RSV: "encouragement") in the
double sense of gift and demand.[27] The believers' obedience—
to which Paul summons them in vss. 12-13—is made both possible and imperative by God's working within and among them
(vs. 13), and its character is to be that of Christ's own obedience.

Consideration of the so-called *imitatio Christi* passages will
help to show the way in which and extent to which Paul regards
Christ's obedience as paradigmatic for the believer's new life in
Christ.[28] The apostle himself only once appeals for a direct
"imitation" of Christ, and even in that instance the appeal is
appended to an initial admonition to imitate the apostolic
leaders (I Thess. 1:6).[29] The passage is, however, of no little
importance, as is also the exhortation of I Cor. 11:1: "Be imita-

[26] See above, p. 186.

[27] See above, p. 109.

[28] Among recent studies of the general topic of *imitatio Christi* are
W. P. de Boer, *The Imitation of Paul: An Exegetical Study* (1962); E.
Lohse, "Nachfolge Christi," *RGG* (3rd ed.), IV, cols. 1286 ff.; Anselm Schulz,
*Nachfolgen und Nachahmen. Studien über das Verhältnis der neutestament-
lichen Jüngerschaft zur urchristlichen Vorbildethik* in *SANT*, VI (1962);
D. M. Stanley, " 'Become Imitators of Me': The Pauline Conception of Apos-
tolic Tradition," *Bibl*, XL (1959), 859 ff.; E. J. Tinsley, *The Imitation of
God in Christ* (1960), and Hans Dieter Betz, *Nachfolge und Nachahmung
Jesu Christi im Neuen Testament* in *BHTh*, 37 (1967). The last of these
is particularly important but appeared too late to be taken into account here
or at the other points where it contributes to the discussion of Paul's ethic.

[29] Contrast the deutero-Pauline formulation of Eph. 5:1: "Therefore,
become imitators of God, as beloved children, and walk in the way of love
just as Christ has also loved us and given himself up on our behalf, a
fragrant offering and sacrifice to God."

tors of me, as I am of Christ" (RSV). Nor are those passages in which Paul urges imitation of himself or other Christians, without specific reference to Christ, irrelevant for the topic (I Cor. 4:16; Phil. 3:17; I Thess. 2:14).

The significance and meaning of this Pauline motif have been warmly debated. There are those who believe it calls attention not only to Christ's *obedience* in a general sense, but to the specific traits and characteristics of the earthly Jesus. W. de Boer believes that, for the early church, Jesus "was a pattern to his people and his earthly life was a graphic portrayal for them of the Christian way." [30] W. D. Davies goes so far as to contend that the preservation of Jesus' sayings and stories about him was due largely to the importance his followers attached to imitating his example.[31]

At the other extreme are those interpreters who have sought to take practically all specific content out of the Pauline idea of the *imitatio Christi*. Thus, Michaelis argues that these Pauline appeals are only to *obedience* as such; they are indirect appeals to become obedient to the will of God as Christ was obedient to it. They are appeals to be *followers* of the heavenly Lord, so Paul's word "imitator" (μιμητής) is in a certain sense equivalent to the (non-Pauline) word "disciple" (μαθητής).[32] Less extreme, but strongly influenced by this view, are the views of Wahlstrom[33] and Lohse.[34]

A more moderate and moderating position is taken by Schulz who believes that Michaelis is too one-sided and has not been willing to admit that there are passages in which Paul has the pattern of Jesus' earthly life in mind.[35] A more distinctive approach is represented by Tinsley who wishes to view the whole of Pauline theology as centered on the *imitatio Christi* concept. Although he believes Paul has specific qualities in mind "which unmistakably marked out the imitator of Christ," [36] Tinsley

[30] *The Imitation of Paul*, p. 90.
[31] *IntDB, E-J*, p. 173.
[32] *ThW*, IV, 668 ff.; esp. p. 676.
[33] *The New Life in Christ*, p. 169.
[34] *RGG* (3rd ed.), IV, cols. 1286 ff.
[35] *Nachfolgen und Nachahmen*, pp. 270 ff.; esp. pp. 282-83.
[36] *The Imitation of God in Christ*, p. 150.

rejects the notion that imitation means "a striving to emulate the life of Christ." [37] It signifies, rather, the process of being mystically *"conformed"* to the Lord, a profound "transfiguration." [38]

Since a judgment about the significance of this particular christological motif obviously has a great bearing on the character of the Pauline ethic, it will be worthwhile to examine briefly each of the principal passages.

1. *I Cor. 11:1:* "Be imitators of me, as I am of Christ" (RSV).

The key admonition of this whole context had been expressed already in 10:24: "Let no one be concerned first of all for himself, but for his neighbor." Not rules, but personal relationships are of primary importance in the Christian's deciding what and what not to do. In support of this view, Paul speaks in vs. 33 about his own concern to "please all men" in everything he does. Thus, the subsequent exhortation to "imitate" Paul refers to this concern to "please" or "do good" to all men, to be concerned for all. In this concern Paul himself has been guided by Christ.

These verses have a striking parallel in Rom. 15:1-3: the "strong" are to "bear with" their weaker brethren, concerned first of all to "please" them by working for their "good" and their "upbuilding." The admonition is derived, as Paul himself makes clear ("For Christ also," vs. 3), from Christ's own self-giving ("did not seek to please himself") for the benefit of others (cf. also vs. 7). Those in Christ are to be servants as was Christ himself (vs. 8). This is doubtless the meaning of living "after the manner of Christ Jesus" (vs. 5 NEB [κατὰ Χριστὸν 'Ιησοῦν]) and the meaning likewise of the parallel admonition of I Cor. 11:1 to be "imitators" of Paul as he has been of Christ.

2. *I Thess. 1:6-7; 2:14:* "And you became imitators of us and of the Lord, having received the word in the midst of much affliction, with joy made possible by the Holy Spirit. Thus, you in your own turn became an example for all the believers in Macedonia and Achaia." "For you, brethren, became imitators

[37] *Ibid.,* p. 162.
[38] *Ibid.,* pp. 161 ff.

of the churches of God which are in Judea—and in Christ Jesus. For you yourselves suffered the same things from your own countrymen as they also had from the Jews."

In both these passages the Thessalonians are commended for their faithfulness to the gospel even in the midst of adversity. In 1:6 it is clear that in this respect they have been imitators of the apostles and of the Lord. Moreover, the Thessalonians have in their turn become examples for other Christians to imitate. The thought is not of following the whole pattern of Jesus' life, or that other Christians will imitate the Thessalonians in all relevant respects. There is *one* clear and specific point to be imitated: patient and loyal obedience even in the midst of suffering (cf. Heb. 5:8; 12:1 ff.; 13:12). The same topic is involved in 2:14 where the Thessalonians are reminded that theirs was not the first church to be called upon to endure through tribulation. The Judean congregations had also been persecuted by their own countrymen, thus supplying the Thessalonians another example to imitate.

3. *Phil. 3:17:* "Join together in imitating me, brethren, and give attention to those who live in such a way as to show that they follow our example."

What is the particular point of imitation to which Paul is here exhorting the Philippians? To say that he urges them to imitate his singleminded "pressing on" for the goal of the upward call in Christ Jesus (vs. 12) is true, but this does not go deep enough. The Paul who "presses on" is the Paul who has renounced all past achievements and gains—who has made himself "poor" (cf. vs. 7). He is, in short, the Paul who has shared in Christ's sufferings and has been conformed to his death (vss. 10-11)! *This* is the Paul whom the Philippians are to imitate. Barth's comment on the verse is quite to the point:

What is to be seen in *him,* Paul, as a Christian is in point of fact not anything positive on which *he* could pride himself, but *Christ*—that is, however, the traces of the *dynamis tēs anastaseōs autou* . . . the fellowship of his sufferings, a *gap* so to speak, a lack, a defect: he is *not* holy, *not* righteous, *not* perfect, all for the sake of Christ. This *typos* . . .

he can really without presumptuousness commend to them for imitation.[39]

The point is confirmed by the reference of vs. 18 to those who
live as "enemies of the cross of Christ." In contrast, Paul exhorts
his readers to be *conformed* to that cross—that is, conformed to
the sufferings and death (and resurrection) of Christ.

4. *I Cor. 4:16-17*: "Hence I exhort you, be imitators of me.
For this reason I sent to you Timothy, who is my beloved and
faithful child in the Lord, so that he could remind you about
my ways in Christ, just as I teach them everywhere in every
church."

Since Paul is the spiritual "father" of the Corinthians (vss.
14, 15), he is responsible for their continuing welfare. "Hence"
he can exhort them to imitate his example. The "ways" which
Paul teaches in every church and of which Timothy is to remind
them are Paul's own "ways" (not "the way of Jesus"), the ways
of a man in Christ.[40] Does the context afford any clue as to what
Paul may have specifically in mind? From 3:18 he has been
criticizing false wisdom, the conceit of some Corinthians who
believe that the full benefits of salvation are somehow specially
theirs (e.g. 3:18-21a; 4:7b-c, 8 ff.). Paul seeks to deny this primarily by mimicking the Corinthians and contrasting their
allegedly "kingly" position with the sufferings and hardships
of the apostles. Paul's "ways in Christ" are therefore the ways of
a servant (ὑπηρέτης, οἰκονόμος, 4:1), and his aim is that the
Corinthians should learn by seeing his life what it means to
be in Christ ("that you may learn by us to live according to
scripture," 4:6 RSV).

If these passages are taken together, can any continuity be
discerned in the apostle's concept of *imitatio Christi* and *imitatio
Pauli*? First, it is clear that Paul regards himself not only as a
bearer of *traditions* (e.g. I Cor. 11:2; I Thess. 4:1-2) but also as
a bearer of Christ (e.g. I Cor. 11:1; cf. Phil. 4:9). What this
means is most succinctly indicated by II Cor. 13:4: Paul's suffer-

---

[39] *The Epistle to the Philippians*, trans. James W. Leitch (1962), p. 112.
[40] See above, pp. 55-56.

ing and serving as an apostle are to be regarded as a sort of "parable" of Christ's own saving death and resurrection (see also II Cor. 4:10; cf. II Cor. 12:9, 10; Gal. 6:17). The two themes which bind all these *imitatio* passages together are (1) the need for humble, selfless service, and (2) the almost inevitably attendant need to suffer as Christ suffered in order to be obedient. To imitate Paul and Christ means to be conformed to Christ's suffering and death in the giving of one's self over to the service of others.

Secondly, it is noteworthy that none of these imitation passages singles out any particular qualities of the earthly Jesus with the insistence that they be emulated. Rather, it seems always to be the humble, giving, obedient *love* of the crucified and resurrected Lord to which the final appeal is made. Paul sees the meaning of love (both what God gives and asks) revealed first of all in the grand humiliation of Christ's incarnation and death (Rom. 5:6 ff.; II Cor. 8:9; Phil. 2:6 ff.), not primarily in his earthly deeds of compassion and humility (which are nowhere mentioned by Paul [41]). In this event of God's giving his Son and the Son's giving up of his own life unto death, Paul discerns the decisive redemptive deed of God.

To sum up: the whole of Pauline theology—which includes what may be called the "Pauline ethic"—is eschatologically oriented and radically theocentric. Man's life is viewed consistently as a gift from God whose power and purpose transcend

---

[41] Of course many passages have been cited to try to show that Paul *does* indeed give attention to the qualities of Jesus' earthly life and ministry. Of these, the most impressive is II Cor. 10:1: "I, Paul, myself entreat you, by the meekness and gentleness of Christ" (RSV). But is it not significant that in Paul's Bible (LXX) each of these terms had already been used to describe Yahweh himself ("meekness" [πραΰτης], Sir. 12:7; 45:4; "gentleness" [ἐπιείκεια, ἐπιεικής], Wisd. of Sol. 2:19; 12:18; Apoc. Bar. 2:27; II Macc. 2:22; 10:4; Ps. 85:5)? Is it not more likely, therefore, that Paul's thought is of the "meekness and gentleness" of the *Lord Christ* who, in his incarnation and death, *became* the humble servant of others and obedient to his Father in the fullest measure?

Another passage which sometimes comes in for consideration is Rom. 15:1 ff. which speaks, e.g., of Christ's having become a "servant" to the circumcised (vs. 8). But here again it would seem to be the diaconate of the crucified Savior which is involved. In the whole section, 14:1–15:3, the apostle is appealing for genuinely Christlike love to prevail in the Christian

the lesser powers and purposes of the created order and human history. But the power of God is not just sheer brute force; it is creative and redemptive. God's power is the power of love, and this love is revealed and made real for men in the death and resurrection of Jesus Christ. Those who belong to him (through faith) are thus brought under the dominion of God's power. This is their "justification," by which they are freed from the "worldly powers" which have alienated them from their Creator and are renewed for obedience to their real Lord. Just as Christ's death reveals that God's power is the power of love, so it reveals that love is to be the content of the obedience to which believers are summoned. Christ's death-resurrection *is*, therefore, the eschatological event, God's powerful deed of redemption which justifies, reconciles, and summons to service. Thus, Paul's ethic is radically and pervasively *theo*logical, *eschato*logical, and *christo*logical.

c. Indicative and imperative in Pauline theology

It is now possible to consider the more specific question of the relation between indicative and imperative in Paul's thought. This whole study has documented the fact that indicative statements stand alongside the Pauline imperatives and in the closest connection with them. But how is this to be explained? Do indicative and imperative form an uneasy and ultimately artificial coalition in Paul's thought? Does the first represent Paul the "theologian" and the second Paul the "pastor" confronted with the hard realities of what Christians are "actually" like?

No such conclusions are necessary. Paul understands these two dimensions of the gospel in such a way that, though they are not absolutely identified, they are closely and necessarily

community. The basis of this community, that which makes the believers "brethren" to one another, is their common dependence upon Christ's *death:* "If your brother is being injured by what you eat, you are no longer walking in love. Do not let what you eat cause the ruin of one for whom Christ died" (14:15 RSV). The conclusion of Dibelius is substantially correct: when Paul speaks of following Christ, he is not thinking first of all of the historical person, Jesus of Nazareth, but of the Son of God who emptied himself and lived and died for others (*RGG*, 2nd ed., IV, cols. 395-96).

associated. God's *claim* is regarded by the apostle as a constitutive part of God's *gift*. The Pauline concept of grace is *inclusive of* the Pauline concept of obedience. For this reason it is not quite right to say that, for Paul, the imperative is "based upon" or "proceeds out of" the indicative.[42] This suggests that the imperative is designed somehow to "realize" or "actualize" what God has given only as a "possibility." [43] It leads also to the slogan, "Become what you are!" which Bultmann and many others have proposed in an attempt to formulate the dialectic of indicative and imperative. But such a formula is too easily misunderstood in terms of exactly that non-Pauline ethical idealism which Bultmann himself rightly rejects. The Pauline imperative is not just the result of the indicative but fully integral to it.

How can this be? The answer is found in Paul's view that the believer, who on the basis of his faith has been rightwised, thereby belongs to a new realm. He stands under the aegis and hegemony of a new Sovereign.[44] He has been given not just the *possibility* of a new life, but an actually and totally new existence. This does not mean that the believer suddenly no longer

[42] See, e.g., Bultmann, *Theology*, I, 332-33; Schrage, *Die konkreten Einzelgebote*, p. 28; D. J. Doughty, "Heiligkeit und Freiheit: Eine exegetische Untersuchung der Anwendung des paulinischen Freiheitsgedankens in I Kor. 7" (1965), p. 148, n.1. Similarly Preisker, *Das Ethos des Urchristentums*, pp. 64-65.

[43] See, e.g., Doughty, "Heiligkeit und Freiheit," pp. 150-51, 156, 176, 193. 207, etc., who in this respect is strongly influenced by Bultmann. A somewhat subtler version of this same basic interpretation speaks of obedience as the "appropriation" or "grasping" of what God has done for man. See Hans von Soden, "Sakrament und Ethik bei Paulus," p. 274; H.-D. Wendland, "Das Wirken des Heiligen Geistes in den Gläubigen nach Paulus," *ThLZ*, LXXVII (1952), col. 463; Preisker, *Das Ethos des Urchristentums*, pp. 64-65; Schlier, "Die Eigenart der christlichen Mahnung nach dem Apostel Paulus," *Besinnung auf das Neue Testament: Exegetische Aufsätze und Vorträge*, II (1964), 357; Lohse, "Taufe und Rechtfertigung bei Paulus," pp. 316 ff., 321, 324.

[44] The present attempt to reformulate the nature of the dialectical relationship of indicative and imperative in Paul's thought is significantly though not entirely indebted to the work of Ernst Käsemann, esp. his article "God's Righteousness in Paul," e.g. pp. 105-6. Käsemann's influence is also clear in the formulation of the Pauline indicative-imperative motif strikingly similar to my own presented by Tannehill, *Dying and Rising with Christ*, pp. 77 ff.

"sins," but that, now reconciled to his true Lord, he knows for
the first time what sin means and the potency of its attempt to
claim him. In Christ he has been engaged, renewed, and restored
by the creative and redemptive power of God's love. Moreover,
in Christ he knows that redemption is not just deliverance from
the hostile powers to which he was formerly enslaved, but freedom *for* obedience to God. For Paul, obedience is neither preliminary to the new life (as its condition) nor secondary to
it (as its result and eventual fulfillment). Obedience is *constitutive* of the new life.

The apostle's polemic against Jewish legalism affords him
ample opportunity to refute the notion that obedience is the
condition for salvation. The idea that obedience is, on the
other hand, the result of salvation and the means by which a
"possibility" is "actualized" is equally non-Pauline, though nowhere explicitly refuted by him. Nevertheless, his metaphor of
the believer as Christ's *bride* (Rom. 7:1-6; II Cor. 11:2-3) supplies an appropriate illustration of his conception of the
Christian life. The Christian "belongs" to his Lord in a way
analogous to that in which a wife in Paul's day belonged to her
husband.[45] The husband's care for her and the wife's obedience
to him constitute the essence of their new life together. Their
life as husband and wife consists precisely in the continuing
mutuality of this relationship, to which love constantly brings its
unrelenting gift and claim. The marriage does not "progress"
toward some distant day when the gift need no longer be given
or the claim no longer heeded. The marriage endures in the
ever repeated giving and receiving, claiming and obeying. Just
so for the believer who belongs to Christ. The reality of his
new life is not separable from the powerful claim which Christ's
lordship now effectively exercises over him. He belongs to the
dominion of God's love, to "the day" (e.g. I Thess. 5:4 ff.; cf.
Rom. 13:11 ff.), to the commonwealth of heaven (Phil. 3:20),
and his obedience is the concrete expression of this belonging.[46]

---

[45] For a discussion of this metaphor and its relationship to Paul's conception of "belonging to Christ" see above, pp. 177-78. Cf. also Tannehill, *Dying
and Rising with Christ*, pp. 43 ff.

[46] It is therefore not inappropriate to speak of the Christian life as an

Paul does not, however, presume that the Christian's obedience is a "spontaneous" expression of the new life. The Pauline indicatives and imperatives are *both* to be taken seriously. Indeed, the apostle's exhortations seek to summon believers to that kind of *deliberate response* to God's claim without which faith forfeits its distinctive character as obedience.[47]

2. PROBLEMS OF ETHICAL ACTION

When, as in Paul's case, Christian ethical action is understood in terms of obedience and thus as a deliberate response to God's claim, several practical questions are immediately raised: How is God's claim recognized? Has it an enduring content? Is there more than one kind of response appropriate to that claim? To what extent does man have the ability to respond? Are there distinguishable degrees or qualities of obedience? Is the Christian's style of life distinguishable in content from the life of the nonbeliever? Paul himself neither poses nor directly answers such questions, but it is nonetheless important to see what if any light his letters shed indirectly upon them.

a. Discerning God's will

Paul's conception of the "will of God" has already been given detailed attention. Although the apostle rarely speaks of the divine will as having a specific moral content and refuses to identify God's will absolutely with the statutes of the law, it is clear enough that the believer's life is both supported and guided by the will of God. Thus, the life yielded to God is the life dedicated to the discovery of God's will (Rom. 12:1-2)

"act of confession" (Bekenntnisakt) by which the reality of one's justification is articulated (e.g. Doughty, "Heiligkeit und Freiheit," pp. 151, 176, although he speaks misleadingly of this as "actualizing" within the world the reality of God's salvation).

[47] Tannehill, p. 81, makes this point very well: "The believer is not simply dragged along by the Spirit as if he had no choice. The believer is actively enlisted in the struggle. He is *exhorted* to not let sin reign in his body, and this exhortation is a serious matter, for by sinning the believer can fall back into the old slavery to sin."

and responsive to the divine "call" (cf. I Thess. 4:3, 7; 2:12). Although the apostle never puts the matter so broadly or abstractly, it is probable that he would be willing to speak of "Christian ethical action" in general as "doing the will of God" (as he in fact virtually does in Rom. 12:2). Since, however, Paul seems not to think of God's will as any prescribed and certified code of duties or program of ethical action, the question as to *how* it is to be discerned in specific instances is particularly urgent.

Theoretically, Paul could have insisted that God's will is revealed in the law. But it has already been seen that he refuses to equate absolutely the divine will and the Mosaic statutes.[48] The Jews assume such an equation (Rom. 2:17-18), but Paul does not. The law is by no means irrelevant to the Christian's practical conduct, and the apostle himself appeals to the binding force of the law's command in the Christian's life (Rom. 13:8-10; Gal. 5:14). But the believer understands the content and force of the law in a new way, within the perspective of his new life in Christ. It is for him the "law of faith" (Rom. 3:27), the "law of Christ" (Gal. 6:2), and it does not offer the security of prescribed rules for conduct, but emphasizes the one great imperative to "love." In Christ the law's true intention and commandment is decisively exposed.

Is it proper, then, to say that Paul understands God's will for the Christian's daily life to be revealed in the teachings and example of Jesus? He does on occasion appeal to the authority of Jesus' sayings, but the sparsity of such appeals is itself enough to show that Jesus' teachings by no means become a "Christian law" analogous to the Jewish.[49] Nor is Jesus' life held up as a pattern for the Christian's moral behavior.[50]

What, then, of the believer's "conscience"? Is this perhaps the means by which he is able to discern God's will? Again the answer must be negative. In the first place, Paul's use of the concept was originally polemical in relation to a particular situation in Corinth. He most frequently employs the term in his letters

[48] Above, pp. 104, 188 ff.
[49] See above, pp. 59 ff.
[50] Above, pp. 218 ff.

to Corinth (I, 8:7, 10, 12; 10:25, 27 ff.; II, 1:12; 4:2; 5:11; cf. I, 4:4), and it was probably from the Corinthians themselves that he took over the term.[51] Moreover, the precise meaning of the term as Paul uses it is not always easy to determine, and the fact is that the apostle is not fully consistent in his use of it.[52] One point, however, is relatively certain: the apostle, in keeping with the general current meaning of the concept in the Hellenistic world, thinks of "conscience" basically as the universal (see Rom. 2:15) human capacity to judge one's own actions. Whether, as Enslin holds, Paul regards conscience as functioning totally in retrospect on already completed acts [53] or whether, as Davies believes, he sometimes thinks of it as having also a future reference,[54] he never establishes conscience as a firm principle or guide for moral action.[55] Its chief function is to *evaluate* actions (e.g. Rom. 2:15; I Cor. 8:7 ff.; 10:25 ff.) or persons (e.g. Rom. 9:1; II Cor. 4:2; 5:11), not to identify and define "the good" or "God's will" either abstractly or concretely. Conscience has a strictly limited and provisional place in the Christian's life.

If, for Paul, the "Christian life" is not, on the one hand, "spontaneous," nor, on the other hand, specifically guided by the statutes of the law, the teachings and example of Jesus, or the believer's own "conscience," what possible means for discovering God's will are available? Paul's concrete ethical admonitions and exhortations need to be taken into account here, for these obviously are issued with the intention of providing moral guidance for the Pauline congregations. It has already been pointed out that the apostolic exhortations employ much traditional ethical material of both Christian and non-Christian origin.[56] Celsus, an important second-century opponent of Chris-

---

[51] This point has already been made in connection with the discussion of the Hellenistic background of the concept, above, pp. 47-48.

[52] Correctly, W. D. Davies, *IntDB, A–D,* pp. 674-75.

[53] *The Ethics of Paul,* pp. 99, 101.

[54] *IntDB, A–D,* p. 674.

[55] On the general topic see, besides Davies and Enslin, Bultmann, *Theology,* I, 216 ff.; Pierce, *Conscience in the New Testament;* Maurer, *ThW,* VII, 897 ff.; Schrage, *Die konkreten Einzelgebote,* pp. 153-54; Whiteley, *The Theology of St. Paul,* p. 210.

[56] Above, chapter II.

tianity, sharply criticizes Christian moral teaching because it is "commonplace and in comparison with the other philosophers contains no teaching that is impressive or new." [57] But it is apparent that, for Paul and his churches, what is "right" and "good" may often be discerned in the universal experience of mankind and thereby receive accreditation as in accord with the Christian's new life in Christ. In the same way, as this study has also acknowledged, Paul assumes and appeals to the Christian's own "reasonableness" which may assist in his judging for himself what ought and ought not to be done.[58]

At the same time, however, it must be emphasized that the apostle never endows traditional morality, the Christian's own reason, or his own personal judgments with absolute authority. It has been seen that the traditional ethical materials Paul employs have been selected, modified, and applied in accord with his understanding of what life "in Christ" is all about.[59] Similarly, the presupposition of Paul's appeal to seek out God's will with one's own critical faculties (δοκιμάζειν, Rom. 12:2) is that those faculties (the νοῦς) have been totally renewed and redeemed in Christ (Rom. 12:1-2). Moreover, while Paul's own admonitions are fully "apostolic" and therefore more authoritative than simple friendly "advice," he does not presume to be saying the last word on any given issue. Christian moral conduct is not dependent upon total and uncritical adherence to the letter of the apostle's exhortations. This is easily illustrated from I Corinthians 7 where, in the discussion of marriage, various *different* decisions and actions are seen as allowable for Christians, each of whom has his own charisma from God (vs. 7). Furthermore, this same chapter shows that, insofar as Paul does stress the authoritative weight of his apostolic admonitions, he considers this grounded not in his own moral wisdom, but in the "Spirit of God" which he believes is present and active in his apostolic ministry (vs. 40).

---

[57] Quoted by Origen, *Contra Celsum,* I, 4 (trans. with an introduction and notes by Henry Chadwick [1953], p. 8). Cf. E. R. Dodds, *Pagan and Christian in an Age of Anxiety* (1965), p. 120.

[58] See above, p. 79, where the relevant Pauline passages are also cited.

[59] Above, pp. 81 ff.

Paul's belief that he "has the Spirit," uttered as it is in connection with the concrete instructions of I Corinthians 7, suggests the possibility that the apostle regards the Holy Spirit as a guide for the believer in practical matters of conduct. E. F. Scott, for example, reflecting on this passage and on Paul's scant use of Jesus' teachings overall, comments:

Assured that he possesses the Spirit, Paul can feel that he is independent of the commands of Jesus as they had been verbally transmitted. He knows what Jesus *would* have said on difficulties which in his earthly career he never encountered, or which have now presented themselves in new forms. He is able to judge for himself on all matters of personal and social duty—relying on the Spirit, which offers a new revelation and yet declares the mind of Christ.[60]

Two things, however, must be noted on this point from the outset. First, I Cor. 7:40 is the only place where Paul even implies that the Spirit functions as a moral guide in specific, detailed ways. It is, for example, remarkable that, in the whole of the most extended and concrete hortatory section in the Pauline letters, Rom. 12:1–15:13, there are only three isolated references to the Spirit (12:11; 14:17; 15:13), not one of which suggests the Spirit as the means by which the Christian is led to discover for himself God's will (Rom. 12:2). Second, while Paul apparently does ascribe this function to the Spirit in I Cor. 7:40, he is there speaking of his own apostolic perception and authority, and it would be unwarranted to suggest that he thinks every believer can possess and be aided by the Spirit in this same way.

It is true enough that the Christian's new life in Christ is constantly described also as a new life "in the Spirit" (e.g. Rom. 7:6), that the Spirit is said to "dwell" in him (e.g. Rom. 8:11; I Cor. 3:16), and that he is urged to "live" and "walk" by the Spirit (e.g. Rom. 8:4; Gal. 5:16, 25). These and related texts will be considered in another connection.[61] There are four other passages, however, which at first glance seem to hold even more promise of illumining the present question of how the Christian

[60] *The Spirit in the New Testament* (1923), pp. 172-73.
[61] Below, pp. 238-39.

discerns the will of God in specific instances. Two of these speak of the believer as one who is "led" by the Spirit: "For those who are led by God's Spirit are sons of God" (Rom. 8:14); "If you are led by the Spirit you are not under the law" (Gal. 5:18 RSV). Yet in neither case is Paul thinking of being led into particular patterns of behavior or guided in particular moral actions. In Romans 8 the context shows that he is thinking of the power of the Spirit by which the power of the flesh is broken and the deeds of the body are put to death (vss. 12-13; cf. vs. 11 where the Spirit is representative of God's power by which Christ was raised from the dead). This is confirmed by Gal. 5:18 where the Spirit-led life is contrasted with life lived under the power of the law (ὑπὸ νόμον).

In a third passage the witnessing function of the Spirit is specifically linked with that of the conscience (Rom. 9:1). But here again there is no evidence that either "conscience" or "Holy Spirit" serves to reveal God's will. Rather, both concepts are employed to give solemnity to the apostle's oath that he does not lie when he speaks of his concern for Israel (vss. 2 ff.). His critical capacity for self-evaluation (conscience), informed as it is by God's Spirit, testifies to his anguished compassion for his own kinsmen who have rejected Christ.

A fourth passage is at once more important and more difficult to interpret. In I Cor. 2:9 ff., in connection with a citation from Second Isaiah (vs. 9), Paul says that "God has revealed to us through the Spirit" what otherwise remains unknown (vs. 10 RSV). And in concluding the discussion he affirms that "we have the mind of Christ" (vs. 16 RSV). The exact meaning of the intervening verses is the subject of much scholarly controversy; yet there is no question but that the apostle is here assigning to the Holy Spirit an important function as revealer. Again, however, nothing is said or implied here about the revelation of God's will for the Christian's practical decisions and deeds. In the whole context Paul is contrasting the foolishness of the world with the wisdom of God, and he seeks to distinguish the latter from what has passed for "wisdom" (vs. 5) amongst the spiritists of Corinth. God's wisdom is "secret" and "hidden," he insists (vs. 7), and because "the rulers of this age" (RSV) were not privy to it, they crucified the Lord of glory (vs 8). This true wisdom, therefore, apparently concerns what God has given (τὰ χαρισθέντα, vs. 12) in Christ. Truly "spiritual" wisdom is knowledge of the magnificence and meaning of God's whole redemptive activity. It is this deep knowledge which the Spirit alone can reveal—and even at that, not to "babes in Christ" such as the Corinthians (3:1 ff.), but to those who are genuinely "mature" (τελείοις, 2:6) and "spiritual" (πνευματικοῖς, 3:1). There is no suggestion here that the knowledge brought by the Spirit has to do with good and bad behavior. Indeed, Paul implies that the Corinthians cannot become truly "spiritual" until some reform of their conduct has already taken place (3:2 ff.).

It does not seem to be possible, therefore, to say that Paul thinks of the Holy Spirit as the means by which the individual Christian is enabled to discern God's will in the midst of the various complex decision-situations in which he is daily involved. No *theory* of how one knows "right" and "wrong," "good" and "evil" is ever propounded. At the same time, however, the apostle insists on the urgency of discerning God's will in one's life, and thus presupposes the practical possibility of this. It is possible because the believer is a "new creature," one whose life has been taken over by Christ (Gal. 2:20; Phil. 3:12). Life in Christ is at the same time life in the Spirit (Romans 8) and thus life in a community of "brethren," for each of whom Christ died (Rom. 14:15; I Cor. 8:11) and each of whom shares in the koinonia of the Spirit (II Cor. 13:13; Phil. 2:2). This *communal* context of the believer's life is of the greatest importance for Paul's understanding of how the Christian is able to know what he ought and ought not to do. Paul never pictures the believer as confronting alone the bewildering complexity of various possible courses of action. The believer's life and action are always in, with, and for "the brethren" in Christ. For him, moral action is never a matter of an isolated actor choosing from among a variety of abstract ideals on the basis of how inherently "good" or "evil" each may be. Instead, it is always a matter of choosing and doing what is good for the brother and what will upbuild the whole community of brethren.

The importance of this Pauline motif is easily documented:

in the case of Onesimus the slave who is commended to his master as a "brother," with the assumption that the right course of action will thereby become apparent (Philemon 16); in the case of the "weak" and "strong" in Corinth, where eating or abstaining from meat offered in sacrifice to the idols is to be decided on the basis of how it will affect the brother (esp. I Cor. 8:9, 11 ff.; cf. 10:23 ff.; Rom. 14:1 ff.); and of course in the case of the Corinthian spiritists who are urged to remember that Christ's body is one (I Cor. 12:12) and that the gifts of the Spirit, though diverse, are given for "the common good" (τὸ συμφέρον, vs. 7). Since Paul conceives of the Christian community as "God's building" (θεοῦ οἰκοδομή, I Cor. 3:9) wherein his Spirit dwells (e.g. I Cor. 3:16; 6:19), he regards Christians individually as "members of the household" (τοὺς οἰκείους, Gal. 6:10),[62] and the imperative of their life together as a mutual "upbuilding" (οἰκοδομεῖν). The task of "upbuilding" the brethren is central to Paul's own ministry, and he emphasizes that it was for that purpose alone that apostolic authority was given him (II Cor. 10:8; 12:19; 13:10). Moreover, this is the urgent imperative within each of his congregations and the subject constantly of his earnest exhortation: "Build one another up!" (I Thess. 5:11 RSV); "Let us then pursue the things that make for peace and build up the common life" (Rom. 14:19 NEB); "Let everything be done with a view toward building up" (I Cor. 14:26). For Paul mutual upbuilding is a central aspect of the church's life (e.g. I Cor. 14:5, 12). Within this context and standing under this claim the Christian is called to discover and do the will of God.

There is something further to be said, however, about this task of "building up the church." It is performed as one abandons concern for self and lives for the sake of others. "Each of us must consider his neighbor and think what is for his good and will build up the common life" (Rom. 15:2 NEB; cf. I Cor. 10:23-24). This the Corinthians in particular need to learn, and Paul urges the point with them repeatedly when discussing the

[62] The church as the "household of faith" is discussed further above, pp. 203 ff.

differing values of the several spiritual gifts: to prophesy is better than to speak in tongues, for while the latter builds up the speaker, the former builds up the hearer (I Cor. 14:3 ff., 17). In other words, Paul's appeal is to *love* in the full Christian sense of surrendering one's self to the claim of God encountered in the neighbor. That is what the concern for "building up" amounts to: "love builds up" (I Cor. 8:1); and therefore what Paul has to say about love in I Corinthians 13 is the presupposition of the exhortations to "build up" the church which immediately follow in chap. 14 (vss. 3, 4, 5, 12, 17, 26). Indeed, chap. 14 itself opens with the admonition to "strive after love" (διώκετε τὴν ἀγάπην, vs. 1; cf. the parallels τὸ ἀγαθὸν διώκετε ["Strive after the good"] in I Thess. 5:15 and τὰ τῆς εἰρήνης διώκωμεν καὶ τὰ τῆς οἰκοδομῆς τῆς εἰς ἀλλήλους ["Let us strive after the things which make for peace and for mutual upbuilding"] in Rom. 14:19).

It is, therefore, the Pauline concept of love which supplies the key to the apostle's thinking about the discernment of the divine will in the various "normal crises" of daily conduct. God's redemptive activity in Christ is an expression of his love, and Christ's own act of obedience unto death for the sake of others is commended as exemplary for all who belong to Christ. To "imitate Christ" means to give one's self in love for others as he gave himself.[63] Love is therefore the "law of Christ" (Gal. 6:2) and the sum and substance of the law of Moses (Rom. 13:8 ff.; Gal. 5:14).[64] The new life in Christ is an "abounding" in love (I Thess. 3:12; 4:10; Phil. 1:9; II Cor. 8:7; cf. II Cor. 2:4), a phrase which in the context of Paul's thought looks in two directions: to the gift of God's love by which the believer lives and to the task of love to which the believer is himself called.

The command to "abound in love" does not, of course, carry with it specific directions for the various modes of action love will have to assume in specific instances. But it does seem to be Paul's conviction that "abounding in love" provides the sufficient context within which specific ethical problems can be responsibly

[63] See above, pp. 222-23.
[64] See above, pp. 59 ff., 191 ff.

met. While evidence on this point is limited to a few lines at
Phil. 1:9-10, the thought there accommodates itself so well to
the apostle's preaching as a whole that it can be given considerable weight. He prays that the Philippians' "love may more and
more abound, with knowledge and all insight," and that they
might thus be able to "find out what things are most worthwhile
[εἰς τὸ δοκιμάζειν . . . τὰ διαφέροντα]." The final phrase here recalls
Rom. 12:2 (εἰς τὸ δοκιμάζειν . . . τί τὸ θέλημα τοῦ θεοῦ, etc.), and
it is certainly legitimate to regard "things most worthwhile" as
an expression equivalent to "God's will, what is good, acceptable
and perfect." God's will is finally discerned through the "knowledge" and "insight" of which the member of Christ's body is
capable when he commits himself to the good of others and thus
abounds in love.

Although it is used only here by Paul, the concept of "insight"
(αἴσθησις; RSV: "discernment") is particularly suggestive and
deserves some additional comment. This word already had a
firm place in the vocabulary of Hellenistic ethical literature before Paul's time, where it had to do with the perception of good
and evil in particular instances. Its meaning is best illumined,
as Werner Jaeger shows, from the way it was employed in medical
texts of the Hippocratic school, from which the ethicists borrowed the concept.

The sick man can be hurt by eating too little, just as he can be hurt
by eating too much. The real doctor is recognized by his power to
estimate what is appropriate for each individual case. He is the man
who has the sure judgment to pick the right quantity for everyone.
There is no standard of weight or measure by which one could fix
quantities on a general basis. That must be done wholly by feeling
(αἴσθησις), which is the only thing that can compensate for the lack
of such a rational standard.[65]

Nor does Paul have any "rational standard" to propose by
which the demands of love (God's will) can be ascertained in

[65] *Paideia: The Ideals of Greek Culture,* trans. Gilbert Highet (1945), III,
18. Jaeger is here summarizing the argument of the anonymous fourth century B.C. medical tractate *On Ancient Medicine,* and proceeds to show how
Aristotle's concept of the "mean" is "borrowed directly from medicine"

particular instances. That is finally a matter for the Christian himself to discern and decide, a matter of "insight" into the given situation. It would be quite wrong, however, to conclude that Paul regards the Christian's αἴσθησις as some vague moral "intuition" or "instinct." For one thing he does not divorce "insight" from "knowledge" (Phil. 1:9-10), and for another he constantly presupposes that both are nurtured by life in the community of faith whose very existence is an "abounding in love." Believing in Christ means the acknowledgment that one belongs not to one's self but to him, and belonging to him means belonging to the body of Christ, the community of brethren who have been redeemed and claimed by the one Lord. This belonging to Christ and hence to one another is the presupposition and crucial preorientation of all the believer's choosing and doing. The believer is not on his own in matters of conduct, nor is he, on the other hand, in possession of prescribed requirements for life in Christ. What is to be done must be discerned and decided in the individual case but always with reference to God's gift of love as it has been met in Christ and God's demand of love as it is repeatedly met in the neighbor.[66]

b. Doing God's will

Peeping out from behind a tree, Peer Gynt watches a village boy sneak into the woods and chop off one of his own fingers in

---

(p. 25). Unfortunately, Delling's article on αἴσθησις (*ThW*, I, 186 ff. [ET: pp. 187-88]) does not touch on this aspect of its background.

[66] Cf. E. Käsemann, "Grundsätzliches zur Interpretation von Römer 13," *Exegetische Versuche und Besinnungen,* II, who also calls attention to the concept of αἴσθησις in Phil. 1:9-10. He translates it, however, "feeling" (*Gefühl*, p. 220), which perhaps subjectivizes the concept to a greater degree than Paul would have himself allowed. See also Spicq's comments on Phil. 1:9 which are in some ways similar to my own (*Agape in the New Testament,* II, esp. pp. 278 ff.). Spicq refers to the use of αἴσθησις in the LXX, where it is employed primarily in Proverbs. There, however, the term (often parallel to σύνεσις, σοφία, and ἔννοια) connotes the sort of prudential wisdom and social discretion which can be *taught* and *learned*, e.g. 23:12: "Give your mind to instruction [παιδεία] and keep your ears attentive to the words of wisdom [λόγοι αἰσθήσεως]." Paul's use of the term, then, does not really correspond at all with the LXX usage (see also Prov. 1:4, 7, 22; 2:3, 10; 3:20; 5:2; 8:10; 10:14; 11:9; 12:1, 23; 14:6, 7, 18; 15:7, 14; 18:15; 19:25; 22:12; 23:12; 24:4).

order to avoid conscription into the army. "He must be mad."
exclaims Peer. "The thought, perhaps—the wish—the will—
Those I could understand; but really to *do* the deed! Ah, no—
that beats me!" [67] It is one thing to resolve to carry out a certain
course of action and quite another thing actually to do it. What
has Paul to say about the Christian's actual ethical *performance*?
Three specific questions deserve some comment in the light of
the whole preceding examination of Paul's ethic: To what extent
is the Christian able to respond to God's summons to "abound
in love"? Is he able to "progress" in the extent and quality of
his obedience? How, if at all, does the Christian's actual conduct
differ from that of the non-Christian? The answers to these
questions have been implicit in what has been said in earlier
sections of this study; yet some further direct, though brief,
attention to them is now appropriate.

First, what is Paul's view of the believer's ability to obey?
This, of course, is not a question which would have occurred to
Paul. His concrete ethical exhortations have a real and specific
intent. They are not merely rhetorical flourishes but presuppose
the necessity for response. Yet "ability" as such is not a Pauline
concept. His ethic does not proceed from an evaluation of man's
capabilities but from a recognition of the divine imperative.
And Paul understands man's response to be an expression of
God's power to redeem and transform, not of man's power to
comply and perform. The life the believer has was given him
by God; it is a life empowered by the Holy Spirit, poured out
into his heart as love (Rom. 5:5), setting him free (Rom. 8:2;
II Cor. 3:17) to serve (Rom. 7:6). The Christian's new life in
the Spirit is not "new" because it has been *reformed* but because
it has been *redeemed*—set free for obedience, now made possible
because the divine call and claim has been acknowledged. Here,
as always in Paul's thought, what God gives is inseparably tied
to what he asks; where the command is heard, the power to
obey is also received. This is most profoundly expressed in the
famous appeal of Phil. 2:12-13 to "work out your own salvation

[67] Henrik Ibsen, *Peer Gynt* ("Everyman's Library" ed.) , pp. 80-81.

with fear and trembling; for God is at work in you, both to will and to work for his good pleasure" (RSV) .

This is what is meant by being "led" by the Spirit (Rom. 8:14; Gal. 5:18) and by "living" and "walking" by the Spirit (Rom. 8:4-5; Gal. 5:16, 25; cf. II Cor. 3:6) . Belonging to Christ means being subject to his power in the double sense of one who is both dependent upon and responsible to a sovereign Lord. In its own way the metaphor of "sowing to" and "reaping from" the Spirit (Gal. 6:8) expresses this central Pauline conviction. The apostle's reference to the "fruit of the Spirit" is therefore fully deliberate (Gal. 5:22) . The various modes of action he thus describes are not regarded as expressions of the Christian's own performing or achieving, but as products of his life in the Spirit; expressions not of his own moral astuteness and ability, but of God's power and grace by which he lives. That Paul, in the same passage, warns his readers about the "works of the flesh" (Gal. 5:18) shows, however, that he does not believe the Christian is exempt from the hostile powers of the world. Indeed, his decision *for* God always requires a decision *against* that which opposes the divine will. The paradox involved in speaking of the Spirit's "fruit" and the "works" of man's own "flesh" is clear: insofar as one concretely acknowledges his dependence upon God's power, he is free to respond in obedience to God's claim; and insofar as one persists in relying on his own power to perform, he is bound in sin to the "works of the flesh."

This suggests already the first point which must be made in answering the question about the possibility of "progress" in the extent or quality of Christian obedience. If "progress" is to include the idea of increasing "achievement," then Paul allows no progress. The idea of progressive achievement supposes that there is some program of action which can be ultimately accomplished, such as full compliance with a law or full correspondence to a pattern or example. But nothing of this sort exists for Paul. Moreover, such could not be appropriated to his preaching, which constantly insists that fullness of life is not attained but given, and that Christian obedience is not an expression of man's effort gradually to realize his own innate potentialities, but an ever repeated response to the ever newly repeated summons of

God. It has been seen that this is precisely the meaning of the
"sanctified" life—a life given over ever anew to the service of
God.[68] The idea of a progressive moral achievement is hardly
compatible with the apostle's insistence that every past accomplishment is to be cast aside (Phil. 3:3 ff.) and that the life
lived on the basis of faith excludes all boasting (Rom. 3:27).

W. A. Beardslee's attempt to document "progress" and
"growth" motifs in Paul's letters is not very successful.[69] He
himself admits that these are not "central conceptions" in the
apostle's thought, but argues nevertheless that they indicate "his
recognition of the necessity for moral development in the individual." [70] Beardslee's evidence, however, is meager and uncon-
vincing. Paul's insistence in Phil. 3:3 ff. that his past accomplishments as a Jew totalled up to something worse than nothing
certainly prevents the reference in Gal. 1:14 to his own past
"progress" in Judaism from being used as evidence for a positive
idea of progress.[71] The only other Pauline reference to the
progress of individuals is in Phil. 1:25. There he speaks of his
own remaining with the Philippians "for [their] progress and
joy in the faith" (RSV). But the thought is not of progress in
the sense of increasing moral achievement. Rather, as the subsequent exhortations show, Paul is thinking of *maintaining* the
unity of the Spirit and *continuingly* striving for the gospel even
in the face of unsettling opposition (vss. 27-28). Nor are the
Pauline athletic, "conflict," or military metaphors designed to
illustrate the need for moral progress or "growth of character." [72]
They illustrate instead the need for *persistent* devotion to the
task in spite of all hardship and danger. The most elaborated
of these metaphors (Phil. 3:3 ff.) makes the point most emphatically that it is precisely *not* the cumulative effect of the
Christian's achievements which adds up to life.[73] And the

----

[68] Above, pp. 156-57.

[69] *Human Achievement and Divine Vocation in the Message of Paul* in
SBTh, 31 (1961), esp. Chap. IV.

[70] *Ibid.*, p. 75.

[71] As Beardslee does, *ibid.*, p. 67.

[72] *Ibid.*, p. 68. Beardslee discusses these metaphors on pp. 68 ff.

[73] Beardslee's own conclusions on the point are not completely clear. At
one place he affirms that "Paul continues the typically Hebraic concern that

"growth" metaphors are even "somewhat less sharply defined," [74] and thus also fail as evidence for a Pauline conception of successively greater degrees of moral achievement.

Finally, the question must inevitably come whether Paul conceives of the Christian's mode of conduct as being distinctive and thus distinguishable from that of the non-Christian. If by "distinctive" one has reference to modes of conduct completely *unique* to Christians, then the answer must obviously be negative. The apostle does not strive for uniqueness in his exhortations and does not hesitate to commend universally accredited morality to his Christian congregations.[75] If, on the other hand, one has reference to some sort of *characteristic* Christian style of life, the answer can be clearly affirmative, for love is without question the hallmark and urgent imperative of Christian existence. This, however, does not mean that the various forms Christian love assumes are exclusively "Christian," for the modes by which love is expressed must always accord with the realities and possibilities of human history. The range of moral possibilities open to the Christian is thus in no way different from the range of possibilities available to the nonbeliever, and Paul's own exhortations always take account of this fact. Yet in *meeting* these various worldly possibilities for action, the Christian operates as one whose life is claimed by a higher Sovereign whose call is ever to selfless, serving love. The believer's difficult yet glorious task is to attempt the translation of that "excellent way" of love (I Cor. 12:31) into the most appropriate of the *many* ways open to him in the world. In Paul's view, the uniqueness of the Christian's new life in Christ does not consist in the forms his concrete actions take in the world, but in the nature and the power of the word by which he has been redeemed from sin and death and re-created for righteousness and life.

---

a man's activity be in such relation to God that it may have a permanent cumulative result" (p. 49). But then later he says that Paul's comments about growth lack "any conviction that the results which are to be expected will be in any significant way permanently cumulative in this world" (p. 77).

[74] *Ibid.*, p. 70.

[75] See above, pp. 69 ff.

A SURVEY OF NINETEENTH- AND
TWENTIETH-CENTURY
INTERPRETATIONS OF PAUL'S ETHIC

Each new generation of scholars inevitably and properly profits from the accomplishments and mistakes of its predecessors. The present writer's indebtedness to many who have tackled the questions of Pauline theology and ethics has been acknowledged throughout. But all the scholarly footnotes, taken collectively, are still too fragmentary and unorganized to reveal the interesting course which scholarly research on the special topic of Pauline ethics has followed. There has been no recent, general survey of the literature available; thus, the following review and summary may have a useful bibliographical function. But more than that, it helps to disclose where the most crucial issues lie and what the questions of greatest urgency are in studying the Pauline ethic.

NINETEENTH-CENTURY INTERPRETERS

A survey of interpretations of Paul's ethic need begin only with the nineteenth century, for only then were the tools of critical biblical scholarship beginning to be honed with sufficient precision and employed with sufficient maturity to yield lasting results. Moreover, only in the nineteenth century did interpreters begin to focus on the "ethics" of Paul per se as a suitable topic for independent investigation. Indeed, one of the earliest discussions of Paul's ethic, the third section of Immanuel Berger's *Versuch einer moralischen Einleitung ins Neue Testament für Religionslehrer und denkende Christen* (1798), is little more than a collation of the various Pauline statements and exhortations relevant to the moral life.[1] Even in F. C. Baur's two-volume work on Paul, first published in 1845,[2] there is no discussion as such of the apostle's ethical concerns, exhortations, or presuppositions. The closest Baur comes to this is in his remarks on faith, love, and hope as "the three momenta of Christian consciousness" (II, 228 ff.). But his treatment of these Pauline themes is too schematic and superficial, and he never relates them to the ethical issues Paul is constantly addressing or the ethical exhortations he is constantly issuing.

Credit for publishing the first critical study of Paul's ethic handled as a topic worthy of full-scale, independent treatment must go to *H. Fr. Th.L. Ernesti,* the first edition of whose monograph appeared in 1868.[3] For Paul, he argues, the ethical life is founded upon the insight that men as children of God are called to righteousness, which means obedience to the "absolute" and "unconditional norm" of the Christian's moral life, God's will (pp. 6, 57). It is claimed that Paul views God's will as having both a "general" and a "special" content, the former involving the general purpose or goal of life (pp. 58-59), and the latter having to do with the concrete tasks and duties of the Christian life. Even after his conversion Paul continues to regard the law as the revelation of God's special will (p. 62).

What, then, is distinctive about the apostle's ethic? Ernesti believes its uniqueness lies in the fundamentally new idea of *freedom* (pp. 2 ff.) and the identification of this as a gift of the *Spirit,* the principle of the Christian ethical life and that in which the Christian lives (pp. 10 ff.). Through baptism and the word the Spirit is given and a new birth effected, the essence of which is described as "a real community-of-life [*Lebensgemeinschaft*] with Christ" in which the believer is granted forgiveness (p. 55). Those who have the Spirit are freed from the "outward authority of the law" and are able to know inwardly the truth about life's ultimate goal, as well as the specific requirements of God's will (pp. 64-65). Ernesti quotes with apparent approval Vilmar's contention that *formally* works done in obedience to the law

---

[1] This book itself has not been available to me, and I am acquainted with it only through the comments of A. Juncker, *Die Ethik des Apostels Paulus,* I (1904), 8.

[2] F. Chr. Baur, *Paul,* trans. A. Menzies (2 vols.; I, 1876; II, 1875).

[3] *Die Ethik des Apostels Paulus in ihren Grundzügen dargestellt.* Citations are from the 3rd rev. ed. of 1880.

and those which are done as a result of the "new birth" are identical,
but that *substantially* and *essentially* they belong to different categories.
The first are done out of fear in order to avoid harmful consequences,
but the others proceed as "necessary expressions" of the new life, "out
of the life of God in us," the love of God which we bear (pp. 78-79, n.).
Ernesti himself wishes to speak of the "true interpenetration [*Ineinan-
dersein*] of divine and human activity," which Paul views the Spirit
as accomplishing (p. 25), and concludes that the new life is a "spontaneous" consequence of faith's acceptance of forgiveness (p. 105).

Imputation to Paul of the view that there is a "spontaneous" character to the Christian's new life creates certain difficulties, and Ernesti
recognizes some of these. If, for example, the Spirit creates such an
interpenetration of the human and divine that obedience to God's
will is a "necessary" and "spontaneous" expression of the new life,
why must Paul spend so much time addressing admonitions and exhortations to his "Christian" congregations? Ernesti's answer would
seem to be that the new life really only "begins" with conversion as
"the center of the personality" is renewed. Hence, the fulfillment of
holiness occurs "only through an inner progressive process" by which
the victory over sin which has been accomplished in the "center" of
the Christian's life is extended daily farther toward the "periphery."
To this process, claims Ernesti, Paul applies the term "sanctification"
(p. 73). Thus, the apostle's commands, prohibitions, exhortations, and
warnings do not at all contradict his teaching about "the liberating
power of the Spirit," for he recognizes that the Christian life is only
sound when the Christian's task (which is to achieve holiness in freedom) is ever before him as a duty (p. 79).

It must be granted that Ernesti succeeds in identifying some of the
Pauline themes most important for an understanding of his ethic:
the Spirit, freedom, law, sin, righteousness, the new life, etc. But it is
perhaps a special weakness of his exposition that he tends to thrust
into the center concepts and categories, which in Paul's own letters
have only a secondary place, and to give too little emphasis to Paul's
own pivotal themes. Thus, on the one hand, Ernesti lays great stress
on forgiveness of sins; on the other, his discussion of Paul's concept
of faith is curiously brief and the Pauline eschatological motifs, save
for a few references to "hope," are almost totally neglected.

There are other questions which need to be raised with respect to
Ernesti's interpretation: Is Paul's polemic against the law directed
solely to the fact that it represents an "outward authority" rather than
an "inward" one? Is there within Paul's own thought the systematic

distinction between justification and sanctification which Ernesti's exposition involves? Can such texts as II Cor. 4:16 be made to support the notion of a daily moral "progression" in the Christian life? Is Paul's emphasis on the believer's participation in Christ's death and resurrection best described as an "interpenetration of divine and human activity"? Finally, it is worth noting that Ernesti often, and sometimes in crucial matters, employs evidence found in Colossians, Ephesians, II Thessalonians, and the Pastoral Epistles which—despite the questions being raised already in his own day—he takes as indisputably authentic.

Briefer treatment is accorded Paul's ethic in an article by *Hermann von Soden*,[4] and many of the themes of Ernesti's book are also present here. This interpreter also identifies freedom in the Spirit as the crucial aspect of Paul's ethical ideal (p. 121); and where Ernesti had spoken of an "interpenetration" of the human and divine, von Soden now speaks of a "fusion" of God's power with the human personality, through which morality issues forth freely of itself (Ernesti had said "spontaneously") (p. 145). Thus, the power for the moral life is not in man but in God, by whose mercy man is called to a new life and a "walking worthily" of the God who calls him (p. 177). The emphasis in von Soden's article is upon the inseparability of "religion" and "ethics" in Paul's thought, no less than in the preaching of Jesus (p. 111). God's character is the motive, his Spirit the power, and his will the norm for all ethical action (pp. 114-15). The Christian is thus moved to ethical action from "within," not from something "outside" himself (p. 125). More than Ernesti, von Soden interprets Paul's ethic from within the context of the apostle's own major categories, and he assigns more importance to the Pauline christological and eschatological theologoumena. Moreover, the weight of his evidence is drawn from those parts of the Pauline Corpus whose authenticity cannot be seriously questioned.

The tendency observed in both Ernesti and von Soden to speak of the new life as "spontaneously" resultant from an "interpenetration" or "fusion" of the divine power and man's will is carried to extreme lengths by *Paul Wernle*. Wernle was licensed as a docent at the University of Basel in 1896 after the presentation of a monograph on Paul's concept of sin which was then published the following year.[5] His participation in the discussion of Paul's ethic is remarkable, first, because of the radical views he set forth in his monograph of 1897, and

---

[4] "Die Ethik des Paulus," *ZThK*, II (1892), 109 ff.
[5] *Der Christ und die Sünde bei Paulus* (1897).

second, because in a book published only four years later[6] he moderated
and qualified those views to such an extent that his critics (who in the
intervening period had been numerous) were no longer sure what
Wernle himself really believed. Nevertheless, the main aspects of
Wernle's work need to be noted here, if only because they are important background for many of the subsequent investigations.

In *Der Christ und die Sünde bei Paulus*, Wernle maintains that
Pauline theology as a whole is best described as "enthusiast," governed
by an overriding expectation of the imminent parousia (p. 119). "The
Pauline piety," he says, "is above all a walking in the Spirit, therefore
a restlessness, an enthusiasm, an intermingling[7] of future and present"
(p. 25). From this basic "enthusiasm" Paul developed during the
course of his missionary activity his theory of the Christian life (p. 79).
Paul's theory is that, with the death of the Messiah, the Spirit is free
"to inundate like an unleashed stream the hearts of all believers" (p.
87) who are thus transposed to the coming age (p. 23). Since sin is
a phenomenon of "this world," the Christian is entirely freed from
sin (pp. 15-16, 24-25, *et passim*), and the law becomes "simply superfluous; the 'enspirited' [*Begeisterte*] does it of his own accord" (p. 88).
Wernle insists that this doctrine of Christian sinlessness is a central
and essential tenet of Pauline theology; for Paul himself, after his
conversion, sin was no longer a factor (p. 15), and he subsequently
projected this experience on to every Christian (pp. 103-4). According to Wernle, "all gnostic and methodistic sects which have striven
for the sinlessness of the reborn, only exaggerate a correct Pauline
tradition" (p. 24). Wernle concludes on a similarly provocative note:
"One can say that Paul thought worse of man and better of the
Christian than Jesus. Both are foreign to Jesus, the theory of inherited
sin and of the flesh, as well as the teaching that the Christian sins no
more" (p. 127).

As Wernle's critics quickly pointed out, this interpretation of Paul
not only ignores a great deal of evidence contradictory of the thesis,
but also involves some naïve and superficial conclusions about the
evidence that is discussed. (Wernle himself notes in his foreword and
introduction that this interpretation was heavily influenced by the
theology of Albrecht Ritschl.) How, for example, in the light of I

---

[6] *The Beginnings of the Christian Religion*, trans. G. A. Bienemann (2
vols., 1903; German ed., 1901).

[7] Wernle's word here is *Ineinandermengung;* cf. Ernesti's use of *Ineinan-
dersein* and von Soden's description of God's power as "fused" (*verschmolzen*)
with man's personality (see above).

Corinthians 15, can Wernle hold that for Paul death has been abolished *already* at baptism, thus assuring the Christian's perfectly sinless post-baptismal life (p. 23)? Paul himself clearly indicates that the conquest of death is yet to come "in its own order" (I Cor. 15:20-28). And it is also certainly wrong to cite Paul's μὴ γένοιτο in Rom. 6:2 as evidence that, for him, sin (among Christians) constituted no real problem (p. 103). Clearly, the *whole* of chap. 6, not just the initial, rhetorical μὴ γένοιτο, is addressed to that problem!

Moreover, for Wernle's interpretation even more than for Ernesti's, the presence in Paul's letters of ethical exhortations and warnings poses a serious difficulty. The variety of ways in which Wernle himself refers to these hortatory aspects of Paul's preaching indicates that his interpretation of Paul's ethic is, already with respect to them, seriously defective. In some places he refers only to the "disorders" or "excesses" among Christians, for example in Thessalonica (p. 29) and Corinth (p. 38), apparently distinguishing these from "sinful" acts. He categorically denies any ethical dimension to Paul's theology, claiming that his preaching "was purely the preaching of faith, no morality" (p. 35; cf. pp. 26-27), since in the Pauline view baptism frees the Christian completely from the possibility of sinning. Paul could therefore regard all disturbances in his churches as merely "superficial episodes" (p. 45).

In other contexts, however, Wernle is more willing to acknowledge certain tensions or even contraditions within Paul's thought. Sometimes, he says, Paul refers to the Spirit as a supernatural power which grasps men and transfers them into a higher order (the "indicative" aspects of the apostle's preaching), whereas at other times Paul refers to the Spirit as a high, divine potentiality in man which the Christian himself can help to victory (the apostolic imperatives). "An ethic of miracle and an ethic of the will," concludes Wernle, "here quite abruptly merge into one another" (p. 89). But then again, the insoluble contradiction which Wernle finds between Paul's theory of righteousness and his missionary practice of preaching about God's judgment of works is accounted for by ascribing the latter to the apostle's heritage from the primitive Christian community (p. 99). Though Paul "indeed placed religion far above all else," he did not entirely forget morality (p. 100). To this extent Wernle's monograph touches upon the problem of indicative and imperative in Pauline theology, but without any attempt to discern whether these two aspects of the apostle's preaching may have been already significantly related for Paul himself.

Perhaps as an indirect response to the sharp and widespread criticism levelled against his monograph of 1897, Wernle very shortly modified his views. In his Basel lectures delivered in the summer of 1900[8] there is not one reference to his earlier interpretation of Paul as an enthusiast who discounted the possibility of sin in the Christian's life. Now Wernle says that for Paul the Spirit does *not* work freely but is bound "inwardly" to faith and "outwardly" to the word, the church, and the sacraments (*Beginnings*, p. 156). Man must help the Spirit by restraining the lusts and the passions, by work and discipline. Here, Wernle now admits, the imperative enters into Paul's thought whether or not it has a "theoretical" place there alongside his doctrine of the Spirit (p. 168). The Christian no longer stands under the law but under an *inner* requirement whose content is love (p. 191). However, Wernle still feels constrained to add that the apostle's vigorous polemic against Jewish legalism precludes his expressing very well this ethical aspect of the Christian life (p. 192). Thus, when read over against von Soden's insistence that "religion" and "ethics" were inseparable for Paul, Wernle's interpretation of Pauline theology, which even in its modified form ascribes to the apostle little theoretical or practical ethical concern, raises a provocative issue which is of fundamental importance.

Hermann Jacoby[9] rejects the description of Paul as an enthusiast and the attendant imputation to him of the view that the Christian's life is totally free from sin (pp. 324 ff.). But he acknowledges an essential element of truth in Wernle's interpretation, namely, that for Paul the Christian's life manifests the divine victory over sin and that "the key-note of [Paul's] creed is not the *Kyrie eleison,* but rather the *Hallelujah*" (p. 327).

Although, like Wernle, Jacoby stresses the importance of Paul's doctrine of the Spirit, and, like Ernesti, wishes to describe Paul's ethic as "an ethic of freedom," he pointedly distinguishes this from an "ethic of choice," from enthusiasm or antinomianism. To be sure, Paul regarded Jesus as having set the old law aside by fulfilling it (pp. 398-99), but in its place the law of the Spirit exercises its own rule (pp. 301, 399). Through the Spirit the exalted Christ himself governs within each individual Christian and within the corporate life of the community "as the ethically enlivening principle" (p. 399). Hence, "the Christian fulfils the law of God as ἔννομος Χριστοῦ (I Cor. 9:21)" (p. 402).

[8] *The Beginnings of the Christian Religion.*
[9] *Neutestamentliche Ethik* (1899).

It has been noted that Ernesti, von Soden, and Wernle characterize
in different but related ways Paul's view of the Spirit's working
within men: Ernesti as an "interpenetration," von Soden as a "fusion,"
Wernle as an "intermingling." But now Jacoby uses other expressions which, judged from the standpoint of Paul's own vocabulary,
are more appropriate and potentially more illuminating: "communion
[Gemeinschaft] with God" (p. 291), "being in Christ" (p. 401), and
"faith-communion [Glaubensgemeinschaft] with Christ" (p. 397). Indeed, more than preceding interpreters, Jacoby emphasizes and analyzes
the place of faith as a structural part of Paul's ethic. As "trust" in God's
grace bestowed in Jesus Christ, it is the means by which the Christian enters into the "invisible, heavenly world" and opens himself
to the presence and working of God; through the agency of faith
"God in Christ becomes the determinative principle of the inner life,
Gal. 2:20" (p. 291). Paul regards baptism as an act of confessing
faith, through and in which the Holy Spirit is received into the believer's life (pp. 292, 299). These two together, man's act of faith
and God's gift of the Spirit, thus constitute the Pauline basis of
the new life (p. 299).

Although Jacoby, in sharp contrast with Wernle, amply documents
the ethical aspects of Paul's theology, one may question whether he
has yet come to grips carefully enough with two special issues—the
place of "law" in the Christian's life and the dialectic of indicative
and imperative in Paul's thought. Regarding the first, Jacoby clearly
wants to interpret Paul's doctrine of freedom in such a way as to
make the Spirit of Christ constitutive of a new law (of love) obeyed
in response to an inner, not an outer, authority. Whether such an
interpretation does justice to the apostle's full criticism of the old
law is a question already raised with respect to Ernesti's views. And
one may also wonder whether Jacoby has given enough weight to
the passages in which Paul exercises his apostolic authority by admonishing, encouraging, exhorting, and warning.

But this first issue is only preludial to the second: Does Jacoby
provide a satisfactory interpretation of the Pauline dialectic of indicative and imperative? For Paul, he says, the Spirit's abiding
presence with the believer makes it possible for him "to live according
to the impulses of the Spirit and to fulfill the just demands of the
law" (p. 301). The Christian community thus constitutes "in principle the people of God; yet the individual Christian is obligated to
let the principle of holiness" take ever greater effect in his life (p. 311).
Jacoby interprets the Pauline imperatives as exhortations to accom-

plish in fact what God's grace has already—but *only*—accomplished "in principle." Paul views the new life as a joint enterprise of God and man, grounded in what God does but actually brought about by what man does as he allows himself to be guided by the Spirit. Jacoby contends that Paul firmly believes in an "ethical process" in the Christian life during the course of which "the Christians actually become what they already are in principle, τέκνα θεοῦ ἄμωμα, ἄμεμπτοι καὶ ἀκέραιοι" (pp. 316-17).

Is this formulation of the function of the Pauline imperatives adequate? Is the distinction between the realization of the new life "in principle" and "in fact" true to Paul's thought? Is one to conclude, then, that the apostolic imperatives have only an *expedient* function, that they are necessary only, so to speak, in the "interim" between God's inauguration of the "ethical process" in the Christian's life and its ultimate completion? Moreover, has Jacoby accorded enough, or even the correct, significance to the eschatological dimensions of Paul's ethic? He regards the Pauline eschatology as relevant for ethics only insofar as it includes hope for a future, other-worldly "moral perfection," and devotes only three pages to the topic (pp. 396 ff.). Insofar as the Christian stands in the service of God, there is formed in him "an ethical quality which issues in ἁγιασμός and has as its end result eternal life" (p. 396). And even though the "ideal, ethical blessings for which he strives" are beyond the Christian's earthly attainment, they are present in "the personality of the glorified Savior" and through an "inner faith-communion" with him may become finally the Christian's possession as well (p. 397). Can this portrayal of the Christian's ethical responsibility be documented from Paul's own writings? Would the concept of an "ethical quality" formed in the Christian have meaning for him? Or the notion that obedience is essentially a striving for future blessings?

Nineteenth-century interpreters of Paul were beginning to reckon with the specifically ethical dimensions of his thought. The apostle's ethic was now regarded by some as an appropriate topic for special investigation, and interest was generally centered upon Paul's view of the Spirit as the ground and power of the new life. In this connection some interpreters began to raise the question of the relation between Paul's preaching of God's gift of grace and his ethical exhortations. Most often, attempts were made to define this relationship by making distinctions between what God establishes "in principle" and what man accomplishes "in fact," or between what occurs at the "center" of man's personality and what takes effect progressively toward the "periphery" of his life. However, this problem of the Pauline indicative and imperative did not stand at the center of the nineteenth-century discussion; its varied aspects were not yet fully exposed, and numerous interpreters frankly regarded it as due to an insoluble contradiction between Paul's theory and practice. Typical of many, the American writer *Orello Cone*[10] expresses his continuing puzzlement at the inconsistency between Paul's doctrine of "supernatural imputed righteousness" and the ideal of "practical righteousness" which he held before the Christian as worthy of his ethical striving (pp. 384-85). To this paradox Cone believes there is no resolution and concludes that Paul's "contribution to practical righteousness [especially in his social ethics] *despite* the paradox of grace and works remains one of the permanent achievements of his genius" (p. 397, italics added).

JUNCKER, WEISS, SCHWEITZER, *ET AL.*

Most of the early twentieth-century interpretations of Paul's ethic belong really to the nineteenth century, with respect to their approach, methodology, and results. *Ernst von Dobschütz*, in a book published first in German in 1902, deals primarily with the actual moral life of the earliest Christians and discusses Paul's ethic only insofar as it provides a relevant introduction to the broader topic.[11] Paul presents Christ as "the founder of the new law of love," and through a "mystical union with the exalted Lord" the Christian is enabled to attain "the ideal of Christian morality" (p. 8). Since most of Paul's converts had had no schooling in morality, the apostle was obliged to teach "the elements of morality, that God's will is sanctification." Von Dobschütz suggests that Paul is reluctant to go beyond this, for he "trusted the working of the Holy Spirit to develop therefrom a steadfast moral conscience which could, in all cases, give correct guidance" (p. 372).

In 1904 *H. Weinel* published a volume on Paul in which substantial attention was paid to his ethics.[12] According to him Paul's

---

[10] *Paul—The Man, the Missionary, and the Teacher* (1898).

[11] *Christian Life in the Primitive Church*, trans. Geo. Bremner; ed. W. D. Morrison (1904).

[12] *St. Paul: The Man and His Work*, trans. G. A. Bienemann; ed. W. D. Morrison (1906).

two great ethical insights were, first, that a moral life is only possible
when the whole man has undergone a religious transformation, and
second, "that morality cannot even be presented in the shape of
law, but is something entirely individual, something that has always
to be created afresh by every single man from his own heart" (p.
329). Although Weinel insists that morality has no independent
significance in Paul's religious theory (p. 330), he does not seek
to minimize the apostle's moral teaching. Paul, he holds, was "compelled to become an ethical legislator and to form a regular system
of ethics"; he had "to go into details" (pp. 329-30).

Present in this interpretation are several ideas which, though
they had been advanced previously by others, are so articulated
by Weinel that they come to play an increasing role in subsequent
interpretations. First, Weinel holds that for Paul the ruling presence
of the Spirit (Christ) in the Christian's life assures that that life
can be no other than moral in correspondence with the heavenly
being" (p. 341, italics added). Second, he notes that this conviction
of Paul has not resulted from his attempt to find a theoretical sanction
for an ethic but is an outgrowth of his own "personal religion" (p.
341). In these two instances Weinel sounds, except for his calmer
rhetoric, very much like the "early Wernle," but on a third point
he is more in accord with Wernle's modified position. For Weinel
acknowledges that, while sinlessness was the apostle's "ideal," he
recognized that the Christians in his own congregations "were still
very 'carnal' " (p. 344). Thus, even though Paul holds to the theoretical conviction that "the religious man 'ought' not to be moral,
he is moral," in practice the apostle must resort to the invocation
of traditional ethical sanctions and admonitions (p. 343). In this
connection an important proposal is made by Weinel: Paul himself
for the most part failed to develop a "new ideal of life" (p. 346);
his ethical sanctions are modifications of the Jewish doctrine of
rewards and punishments (Paul individualizes this doctrine and
balances it with an equal emphasis on "inner sanctions," p. 339);
and in setting up his concrete ethical demands, Paul was dependent
upon Hellenistic models as well as the law (pp. 345-46). Weinel
thus becomes one of the first to suggest that Paul's ethic may have
important Jewish and Hellenistic antecedents, although it is left for
others, most of all Martin Dibelius,[13] to investigate this possibility
in detail.

[13] See below, pp. 259 ff.

The first full-length interpretation of Paul's ethic in English was published by *Archibald B. D. Alexander* in 1910[14] and shows the influence of Ernesti's work, to whom Alexander specifically refers (p. v.). Alexander proposes to treat not only the background of Paul's ethic but also the "principles" and the concrete "virtues and duties" which he inculcated (p. vi.). He does more than assert the inseparability and internal consistency of Paul's religious and ethical teaching; these two, he says, "perfectly coincide" (p. 364), and he quotes with approval Edward Caird's contention that for Paul the ethical principle begets the theological, not the reverse (p. 8). Alexander speaks, even more boldly than Ernesti, of Paul's view that "the hidden life of God passes into the Christian's personality" and becomes such "an integral part of the man that his moral character, instead of being merely an adjunct of faith or an external requirement . . . becomes the spontaneous outflow, the automatic expression of the new germ of life within the soul" (p. 354). It is the fusion of the vision of an ideal with the actual appropriation of a power within one's personality which distinguishes the Pauline ethic (p. 356).

But what is the "ideal" of the Christian life? Here Alexander emphasizes the christological dimension: Christ himself is the ideal, for in him the perfect life is seen, and from him comes the power for its realization (p. 352). Paul viewed "all practical questions in the light of Christ's life and teaching" (p. 358). Alexander, in fact, defines "Pauline ethics" as "Paul's interpretation of the ethics of Christ" (p. 23). To be sure, this emphasis on the virtual identity of Jesus' ethic and Paul's is polemically directed against Wrede's thesis that between Jesus and Paul there was a radical discontinuity (p. 10),[15] but this does not minimize the significance of the issue here raised: To what extent and in what way does the Pauline ethic structurally and/or materially have a "christological" dimension? And what is the relationship between Jesus' teaching and Paul's?

One of the most ambitious and detailed expositions of Paul's ethic appearing about this same time is the two-volume work of *Alfred Juncker* published in two halves fifteen years apart.[16] The second half is devoted entirely to a systematization of Paul's concrete ethical teachings but—as Martin Dibelius noted in his unfavorable

---

[14] *The Ethics of St. Paul.*
[15] On this question see my article, "The Jesus-Paul Debate," pp. 342 ff.
[16] *Die Ethik des Apostels Paulus* (1904, 1919).

review of volume II [17]—Juncker ignores the question of possible
non-Christian sources of these teachings, does not deal adequately
with the way Paul applies them in concrete situations, and at least
in the view of Dibelius, falsely makes the apostle out to be a very
proper, unoffending, bourgeois moralist. Since it is in the first volume
that Juncker seeks to discern the basic structure and principles of
the Pauline ethic, only that earlier part need be considered here.

Juncker is critical of most previous discussions of the ethics of
Paul: Ernesti's is superficial; von Soden's, although good, is too brief;
and Jacoby's is effective in tracing the progress of Paul's thought
but ineffective in expositing its basic meaning (11 ff.). Nevertheless,
most of the key points in Juncker's own study had already been
made by these men and others. He claims that Paul sees the Christian's new life as resultant from a "wedding" of God's Spirit with
man's whereby the tyrannous power of the flesh is broken, man's
God-related powers are "mobilized" for action, and his mind, conscience, and heart are inwardly renewed (p. 143). Man's Spirit is
thus to be regarded as the "lodging and work place" of the divine
Spirit, and although Paul does not view this as a *unio absorptiva*,
it is fair to say that for him the human spirit functions like a
"mother's lap" (or womb, *der empfangende Mutterschoss*) for God's
Spirit (pp. 148-49). Hence, in describing Paul's conception of the
new life, Juncker follows a line laid down already by Ernesti,
Jacoby, and others: the Christian life is not just adherence to a sum
of virtues but "the direct outflow of a general bent of the soul
effected through the unity of God's Spirit with man's" (p. 32).

Does this mean that Paul excludes the possibility of sin in the Christian's life? Juncker is emphatic in his rejection of Wernle's statement of such a view. Paul is aware of the moral defects of the
Christians in his churches (pp. 209 ff.) ; he speaks of a war within
the Christian between flesh and spirit (pp. 212 ff.) ; and he presupposes and encourages "development," "growth," and "progress"
in the Christian life (pp. 215-16). While it may sometimes *appear*
that the apostle speaks of the Christian life as sinless, Juncker
believes that this is due to Paul's need in his apologetic to emphasize
the radical break in the life of one who has been converted and
baptized, and to his conviction that Christ had decisively broken the
power of Satan (pp. 216 ff.).

Like others before him, then, Juncker believes that Paul distinguishes between what is *ideally* true and what is *actually* so; while

[17] *ThLZ*, XLVI (1921), cols. 149 ff.

the Christian is inwardly and in principle free from sin, the victory over various specific points in his outer life is not yet complete (pp. 179-80). Man's ethical task is to help God's power attain its full effect in his life and to confirm by his own actions what God has already made of him (p. 32). This means that the Christian must be continually admonished and stimulated to ethical action and that he must be given certain moral directives for the conduct of his life (p. 180). Juncker sees no inconsistency in Paul here, for the apostolic exhortations seek only to make clear what the Christian already knows implicitly and "in principle" in his conscience, and do not represent a Christian casuistry (pp. 180-81). Paul's ethical teaching is to be viewed as an "awakening and educating of the conscience" by which man's "mind" is renewed (Rom. 12:2) and his whole nature morally transformed (p. 187).

In thoroughness and scope Juncker's interpretation surpasses its predecessors, but he answers most of the basic questions in ways which are already beginning to sound conventional. His chief contribution is an emphasis upon the relevance for ethics of Paul's interpretation of Christ's death and resurrection, and the Christian's baptism and faith. For Paul, he insists, the ultimate ground of the new moral life is Christ's death and resurrection, by which sin has been conquered (p. 88). As the second Adam, Christ stands at the beginning of a new creation (p. 107) which becomes a reality for the individual through receipt of God's Spirit in baptism (p. 109). Baptism enables the believer to participate "personally" in Christ's death and resurrection. The "objective" act of salvation thereby has a "subjective" effect (pp. 113-14): to free the believer from guilt and the power of sin. This is "justification," and Juncker argues that for Paul it was not principally a *moral*, but a *forensic* concept (pp. 121-22). While rooted in his own conversion experience, Paul's concept of righteousness as "amnesty" (p. 126) took its distinctive shape in the course of the apostle's polemic against Judaism and Jewish Christianity and his defense of a gospel freed from the law (p. 122).

Juncker's predecessors had not given much attention to Paul's doctrine of justification as a vital part of his ethic. This is now partially corrected in Juncker's study, although it must be acknowledged that he still lays primary stress upon the Pauline doctrine of the Spirit and regards the doctrine of justification as having chiefly a polemical role. Indeed, since Juncker believes what he does about Paul's view of the Spirit's actual working and effect within man's life, it is really necessary for him to hold that Paul's concept of justification, defined simply as "amnesty," is a less central, even adjunct, doctrine.

Karl Benz is one of the first Roman Catholic scholars to produce a monograph on the Pauline ethic.[18] Like Juncker's it is divided into two sections, one on the principles of Paul's ethic and another on the apostle's concrete ethical teachings. Unlike Juncker, Benz rejects the notion that Paul conceived justification as a purely forensic act. In most cases, he argues, the verb δικαιοῦν means actually to "make righteous" (pp. 29 ff.), and the apostle sees righteousness and holiness as closely related (pp. 36 ff.). Benz, therefore, believes that Paul's concept of the Spirit's presence and working within the Christian is a constituent part of the total Pauline doctrine of justification. Here an important issue in the interpretation of Pauline theology and ethics comes to the fore.

In other respects, however, Benz's interpretation of Paul's ethic follows familiar lines: through the gift of the Spirit received by faith at baptism the Christian becomes mystically united with Christ (pp. 31 ff.) and an heir of the life God bestows in the Son's death and resurrection (pp. 38 ff.); his life renewed, the Christian is able to "unfold his moral personality" (p. 29) in service to God and Christ (pp. 71 ff.); in the Spirit he is freed from a multiplicity of minor commandments and bound only to the commandment to love (pp. 74 ff.); and Paul's detailed ethical advice, given only as a concession to the human weaknesses of Christians who are still struggling to attain the goal of perfection, has its basis not in the apostle's ethic as such but in his practical work as a missionary and pastor (pp. 80-81).

Benz, acknowledging that Paul was no systematic theologian and that he framed no detailed moral code, nevertheless believes it possible to construct a perfectly "harmonious" picture of the foundations of Paul's ethic (p. 6) and to gather into a serviceable whole and catalog (albeit with certain lacunae) the scattered moral admonitions and advice of his letters (pp. 137-38). But it is problematic whether Benz's minutely detailed systematization of Paul's ethic would be recognizable to the apostle himself.

This error of oversystematization is not made by *Johannes Weiss*[19] who finds little system in Paul's ethic and cautions against expecting

[18] *Die Ethik des Apostels Paulus* (1912).

[19] "The Pauline Ethics," chap. XIX in *The History of Primitive Christianity*, trans. F. C. Grant (1937; German ed., 1917).

"unity and consistency everywhere" (II, 546). Nor does Weiss feel compelled to make Paul a representative of modern, bourgeois morality. Although he does not describe Paul as an "enthusiast" and hence does not go as far as Wernle, he does speak of Paul's "enthusiastic mode of thought" (II, 554) and does apply to him the term "pneumatic" (II, 555). For it is also characteristic of Weiss's treatment that Paul's ethic is seen first of all in connection with his doctrine of the Spirit; Paul's concepts of justification, righteousness, and faith are not brought into the discussion of his ethic at all—not even when Weiss speaks about Paul's view of the law. According to Weiss, the apostle believes that the Christian, living "under the impulse of the Spirit," already possesses salvation and *can* only be moral (II, 553). The bestowal of the Spirit at baptism "means an inner connection with God and the Spirit" (II, 564) so that "even as an ethical teacher Paul is primarily a Spirit-filled man" and "expects the new life to shape itself out of the religious impulse" (II, 576-77). Yet Paul *is* an "ethical teacher"; Weiss does not deny this. Even though Paul sees no meaning for a Christian confession of sins, the Christian is not removed from temptation (II, 574-75) and is always under the obligation to "maintain" the "condition of purity" which he has been granted (II, 564). In spite of his "ideal," then, the apostle, faced with the "realities" of life within his churches, must provide moral directives and "fixed rules of conduct" for them. This means that already in Paul one may see the beginnings of a "transition from the uncontrolled morality of spiritual men to obedience toward statutes" (II, 558).

Weiss discusses Pauline eschatology as one of several motives in his ethic (II, 559 ff.) and finds here at least part of the basis for the apostolic imperatives. "His ethic, inasmuch as it moves in the imperative, is the alarm-cry of the last hour: still one more mighty, final exertion of strength—then comes the end!" (II, 577). Moreover, Weiss believes that it is Paul's pneumatic-eschatological perspective which gives his ethic the character of a "highly tensioned religious idealism" and alienates it from the world (II, 593). Thus, this interpreter's final judgment is that Paul "lacks a feeling for that which adorns and transfigures life," is "a stranger in the world," and should be expected to present "no ethic which could show us how, living in the midst of the world . . . we may at the same time satisfy the world's demands and the demands of God without becoming unfaithful to one or the other" (II, 594).

Albert Schweitzer,[20] even more than Weiss, emphasizes the controlling place of eschatology in Paul's ethic which, he says, is "born . . . of the eschatological expectation" (p. 309). While Schweitzer believes that this eschatological basis gives Paul's ethical principles and advice a temporary, "interim" character (p. 300), he does not assent to the notion that an ascetic, world-denying ethic results (p. 311). The apostle's "spirituality" (p. 312) raises his ethic above the level of a mere outward asceticism. Paul does not renounce the earthly but stresses man's "inner freedom" from it and is thus "far removed from Jesus' prohibition of having any care for earthly things!" (pp. 312-13; cf. p. 332). The ideal of the Pauline ethic is "to live with the eyes fixed upon eternity, while standing firmly upon the solid ground of reality" (p. 333).

The distinctiveness of Schweitzer's interpretation of Paul's ethic comes, however, at another point. He argues that the doctrine of justification by faith is not only a "fragment" and minor aspect of the apostle's total gospel, but that it is logically impossible to derive from it an ethic of any kind (pp. 225, 294-95). Rather, it is in Paul's "mysticism," in his doctrine of the Christian's dying and rising with Christ, that the ethic is theologically grounded (pp. 294 ff.). As one whose being is "in Christ," the Christian possesses the Spirit of Christ "as the life-principle of the supernatural state of existence on which he has now entered" (p. 294). Ethics is "a natural function of the redeemed state" (p. 295) and is for Paul "the necessary outward expression of the translation from the earthly world to the super-earthly, which has already taken place in the being-in-Christ" (p. 333).

In Schweitzer's interpretation of the Pauline ethic ideas which are implicit in the work of many other interpreters are articulated with special force and followed to their extreme, perhaps logical, conclusions. Here the notion that Paul views God's Spirit as somehow "interpenetrating" man's (Schweitzer himself speaks of the Spirit's "union with the spiritual part of man's personality," p. 342, or with "the psychic side of man's nature," p. 374) is elaborated into the concept of a Pauline "mysticism." Schweitzer believes this doctrine is the key not only to Paul's ethic but to his theology as a whole. Moreover, where other interpreters, by focusing attention on Paul's concept of the Spirit, tend to neglect the doctrine of

[20] *The Mysticism of Paul the Apostle,* trans. William Montgomery (1931). The first German ed. was published in 1930, but Schweitzer remarks in his Preface that a first draft of the study had been completed already in 1906.

justification by faith, Schweitzer now rejects this latter entirely, regarding it as a subsidiary theme in Paul. In any case, he holds, the doctrine of justification allows no room for the development of an ethic. It is, of course, extremely doubtful whether the doctrine of justification can be assigned such a minor role in the apostle's thought, and at least debatable whether it precludes the development of an ethic. But the virtue of Schweitzer's discussion is that these questions are now exposed and posed clearly and provocatively. For this reason it is possible to say that Schweitzer summarizes and closes one chapter in the history of the interpretation of the Pauline ethic.

DIBELIUS, BULTMANN, ENSLIN, *ET AL.*

Decisive new chapters in the interpretation of the Pauline ethic are written by *Martin Dibelius*. He comes to the Pauline letters with the interests and methods of *Formgeschichte* (form-history), in which he is a pioneer,[21] and insists that the first task is to determine the origin and form of Paul's moral teaching.[22] Dibelius sees this as urgent because, in his view, the eschatological expectations of the earliest church precluded the development of any peculiarly Christian ethic. But as these eschatological hopes faded and Christians were confronted with an extended pilgrimage in the world, the need for ethical directives became apparent. Jesus' sayings which had presupposed a much simpler cultural situation were no longer sufficient for guidance in the complex Hellenistic society. To meet this need, Dibelius argues, the church turned to the Hellenistic world itself, and from the ethical traditions of Hellenistic Judaism and contemporary popular philosophy borrowed materials for the practical direction of its own life in the world.[23]

Consequently, Dibelius interprets the ethical teachings and exhortations in the letters of Paul against the background of the Greek

[21] Dibelius discusses the application of form-historical methods to the New Testament epistolary literature in his article "Zur Formgeschichte des Neuen Testaments (ausserhalb der Evangelien)," *ThR*, n.F., III (1931), 207 ff.

[22] This point is made by Dibelius in his review of Jacob Kooy, *De Paranese van den Apostel Paulus* (1926) published in *ThLZ*, LIII (1928), cols. 413 -14.

[23] This thesis is developed in Dibelius' *Urchristentum und Kultur* (1928). See esp. p. 18, and cf. his *Fresh Approach to the New Testament and Early Christian Literature* (1936; German ed., 1926), p. 224.

"parenetic tradition," drawing heavily upon the conclusions reached
about Greek parenesis by Rudolf Vetschera.[24] Dibelius himself defines
"parenesis" as "a text which strings together one after another
exhortations having a general moral content." Usually, he says,
the parenesis is directed to some specific individual or group, real
or fictitious, or at least has the form of a command or appeal.[25]
Dibelius also notes that the parenetic writer is inclined to draw
his materials from a great variety of sources, to give little thought to
their inner coherence once assembled, to be fond of linking the
separate advisories together by catch words, to be repetitious, and
to strive to make his exhortations as broadly applicable as possible.[26]
All these features Dibelius finds in the ethical teaching of Paul and
elsewhere in the New Testament. He holds that the "Pauline parenesis"
consists of materials appropriated from the Hellenistic world and
then "Christianized" by the apostle.[27] This is described as a "phenomenon of the first rank in the history of religion," for it meant that
earliest Christianity, following Paul's example, looked to the ethical
treasury of the ancient world (popular philosophy, the wisdom of
the rabbis, etc.) as the source for determining the content of the
moral life.[28]

If these judgments about the form, character, and sources of Paul's
ethical teaching are correct, then some important new conclusions
about the ground and structure of his ethic result. Dibelius himself
does not hesitate to draw these conclusions. Paul's ethical admonitions, he insists, "are not formulated for special churches and concrete cases, but for the general requirements of earliest Christen-
dom." [29] Moreover, Paul's ethical teaching bears no essential relationship to his theological point of view. The hortatory sections
with which the apostle's letters customarily close stand apart from
the doctrinal sections not only in form and style but also in content;
these ethical sections "have nothing to do with the theoretic foundation
of the ethics of the Apostle, and very little with other ideas peculiar to
him." [30] Since the parenetic form provides no place for the unfolding or
working out of religious ideas, the parenetic sections of the Pauline

[24] *Zur griechischen Paränese* (1912).

[25] *Der Brief des Jakobus* (8th ed.) , p. 4. The first ed. appeared in 1921.

[26] *Ibid.,* pp. 6 ff.

[27] "Das christliche Leben (Eph. 4, 17–6, 9) ," *ThBl,* IX (1930) , col. 342.

[28] "'Ἐπίγνωσις ἀληθείας," *Botschaft und Geschichte,* II, 5. The essay was
first published in 1914.

[29] *From Tradition to Gospel* (1935; German ed., 1919) , p. 38.

[30] *Ibid.,* pp. 238-39.

letters can yield a "theology" only with difficulty and, in any event, not the theology of Paul.[31] Dibelius, then, prefers to speak of a "Christian ethos" in the New Testament rather than of a "Christian ethic." The content of this ethos is faith, hope, and love, and "it consists in radical obedience, superhuman love, and treating everything that exists as relative and provisional." Christians of every succeeding generation must learn anew what specific ethical actions are appropriate to this basic ethos.[32]

The importance of Dibelius' contribution to an understanding of Paul's ethic cannot be ignored, and its influence upon the work of other scholars is readily apparent.[33] He succeeds in demonstrating the necessity of a formal analysis of Paul's ethical teaching and the relevance of an inquiry into its background. As a result of his efforts, it seems undeniable that this teaching has both a formal and material kinship with the Hellenistic parenetic tradition. Dibelius makes it clear that one must learn to distinguish between concepts unique to and specially distinctive of Paul, and those which he shares with the Hellenistic world in general.

However, to acknowledge the use of traditional materials by Paul is not yet to say in what *way* he has used them or for what purpose he has drawn them into a particular context. The presupposition implicit here, that that which is not *distinctively* Pauline is therefore not integral to his thought, is surely unwarranted. The effect of Dibelius' work is to suggest that, so far as the specific ethical exhortations are concerned, the apostle was somehow at the mercy of the parenetic tradition on which he drew. Sufficient attention is not given to the context into which these materials have been drawn or to the possibility that they are made to serve in Paul's letters a function different from that in the parenetic tradition. Is it true that the

---

[31] *Jakobus,* p. 19.

[32] "Das christliche Leben," col. 342.

[33] E.g. Dibelius' own student, Karl Weidinger, who employs form-historical methods to analyze the New Testament "household codes" (*Die Haustafeln. Ein Stück urchristlicher Paränese*). See also the monograph of Mary E. Andrews, *The Ethical Teaching of Paul,* and the unpublished doctoral dissertations of two Americans, both submitted in 1947: David G. Bradley, "The Origins of the Hortatory Materials in the Letters of Paul" (Yale), and Alfred J. Gross, "The Development of Pauline Paraenesis on Civil Obedience" (Chicago). The concerns and approach of Dibelius are given a British accent in the books of Philip Carrington, *The Primitive Christian Catechism,* and Archibald M. Hunter, *Paul and His Predecessors* (1940; rev. ed., 1961), and in a whole series of articles and books by C. H. Dodd (see below, pp. 272 ff.).

essential points of Paul's theology have no determinative effect on his concrete ethical admonitions? The strength of Dibelius' work is the freshness and thoroughness of his inquiry into the form and origins of Paul's ethical teaching; its weakness lies in his tendency to underestimate both the ethical impulse already present in Paul's doctrine and the apostle's ability to adapt traditional materials to the service of distinctive ends.

Unlike Dibelius, with whom however he shares a common form-historical methodology, *Rudolf Bultmann's* chief interest is with the theological aspect of Paul's ethic, in particular the problem of indicative and imperative.[34] In his article "Das Problem der Ethik bei Paulus," [35] he opposes the view that there is a logical contradiction between the apostle's indicative and imperative statements. For Paul, he argues, the imperative is grounded precisely in the fact of justification and is "derived from" the indicative: *"Because* the Christian is freed from sin through justification, he ought to wage war against sin" (126). Bultmann rejects the attempt to define this relationship along the lines of ancient or modern rationalism or idealism, as if the imperatives are designed to urge the "realization" of the "good" (p. 127). Paul does not regard righteousness as a general ethical norm toward which, as in Stoicism, "progress" can be made. Rather, his doctrine of righteousness "characterizes the situation of the particular concrete man before God" (p. 131).

This interpretation of Paul's view of *righteousness* is the necessary place to begin in understanding Bultmann's interpretation of Paul's ethic. He seeks to demonstrate that righteousness is an "eschatological" not a "moral" concept, that Paul regards it as an "otherworldly" *(jenseitige)* phenomenon (p. 135). By this Bultmann means that, according to Paul, righteousness is not rooted in man's accomplishments, moral or otherwise, but solely in God's action and judgment. This is what gives justification the character of an "event"; it is an "event" of God's grace directed toward man in his concrete situation (p. 135)). The old question whether the justified man is only "regarded" as righteous by God or actually "made" righteous may be dismissed, says Bultmann. For in Paul's view, whomever God regards

---

[34] Oden's recent discussion of Bultmann's work as it relates to ethics *(Radical Obedience)* criticizes Bultmann's views almost exclusively on *systematic* grounds. But Bultmann's work must be evaluated first of all *exegetically*, as should be particularly apparent to Oden himself who believes that one symptom of the "malaise of current Protestant ethics is the stubborn and inflexible *divorce between ethics and exegesis"* (p. 18, italics his).

[35] *ZNW*, XXIII (1924), 123 ff.

as righteous *is* thereby righteous (p. 136, n. 9). But—and here is Bultmann's crucial point—this is not righteousness in an "ethical" sense, for it is not that sense in which, according to Paul, God regards man as righteous (p. 136). Against Wernle, Bultmann argues that Paul does not hold righteousness or "sinlessness" to involve a change in the "moral quality" of man or to be something perceptible in his life. As an "occurrence" of grace, justification is only perceptible to faith and can only be believed (p. 136). Just as, for Paul, man's sin is not an empirical commodity perceptible to other men but rather the human condition seen, as it were, from God's side, so with righteousness. Bultmann emphasizes the "continuity" between the old and the new man in Paul's thought. "The δικαιωθείς is the concrete man who bears the burden of his past, present and future, who therefore also stands under the moral imperative" (p. 137). Bultmann's solution of the problem of indicative and imperative in Pauline thought is thus based on his particular interpretation of the apostle's concept of righteousness.

The implications Bultmann draws from this for the Christian's practical ethical actions are no less provocative. Seen in Paul's perspective, he argues, God's grace is the decisive moral act, not faith (pp. 128-29); faith is an act of *obedience* (p. 137). Man's ethical actions are not "works" by which righteousness is actualized, but concrete expressions of that more radical obedience to which he is called: putting his whole being at the disposal of God (pp. 137-38). For Paul this obedience has no special content, and the moral conduct of the believer differs from that of the unbeliever only in that it has the character of obedience (p. 138). Although the believer indeed possesses the Spirit which is the power of the new moral life, it is not correct to say that the decisive difference is visible in his conduct; for what is decisively different cannot be seen except by the "eyes of faith" (p. 139).

These themes are accorded a fuller and more systematic treatment in Bultmann's *Theology of the New Testament*.[36] Bultmann describes in more detail the apostle's concept of righteousness as "forensic-eschatological" (pp. 270 ff.). It denotes not a new ethical quality, but a transformed relation to God (p. 277) effected by God's grace, the "paradox" of which is that it is the sinner to whom it applies (p. 282). Grace comes to him "not as approval of his striving and a prop for his failing strength, but as the decisive question: Will you surrender,

---

[36] Vol. I. The sections dealing with Pauline theology were first published in German in 1948.

utterly surrender, to God's dealing—will you know yourself to be a
sinner before God?" (p. 285). Man's response to this grace is faith,
defined primarily as obedience (pp. 314 ff.), and Bultmann stresses
the freedom which is thus gained since the believer no longer "belongs
to himself" (p. 311). But this freedom binds one over to a new servi-
tude—to righteousness—and opens for him the "possibility, once flung
away, of realizing the commandment's intent to bestow life" (p. 332).
Here, then, the indicative of justification gives rise to the imperative,
for faith is constantly summoned to express itself in obedience which
is the "appropriation of grace," a "laying hold" of the Spirit which
God has already given (pp. 332-33). According to Bultmann this
understanding that the indicative "calls forth" the imperative is the
key to the Pauline ethic. "The indicative gives expression to the new
self-understanding of the believer, for the statement 'I am freed from
sin' is not a dogmatic one, but an existential one. It is the believer's
confession that his whole existence is renewed. Since his existence includes his will, the imperative reminds him that he is free from sin,
provided that his will is renewed in obedience to the commandment
of God." [37]

Bultmann's interpretation of Paul raises to a new level of prominence
a number of issues and themes which he succeeds in demonstrating to
be crucial for an understanding of the apostle's ethic: the character of
grace, the meaning of justification and righteousness, faith as a laying
hold on grace and the Spirit, freedom as liberation for a new obedience,
etc. At the same time there are questions which have to be raised.
Is justification properly regarded as a "forensic-eschatological" concept?
Is, perhaps, the "event" of grace seen by Paul to have more of a
transforming effect in the believer's empirical life than acknowledged
by Bultmann? Has Bultmann paid enough attention to the concrete
ethical exhortations within the Pauline letters, and may these require
some modification of the judgment that for Paul the new life in Christ
has no new "content" as such? Has Bultmann accorded enough importance to the sacramental passages in Paul? To the apostle's doctrine
of the Spirit? And is there no sense in which the apostle would speak
of a "realization" of righteousness or "progress" toward it in the
Christian life?

Some of these questions are raised already by *Hans Windisch* in his
response to Bultmann's article on the indicative and imperative.[38]
Windisch believes that Bultmann overlooks Paul's sacramental perspec-

---

[37] Bultmann, *Jesus Christ and Mythology* (1958), pp. 76-77.
[38] "Das Problem des paulinischen Imperativs," *ZNW*, XXIII (1924), 265 ff.

tive, especially as expressed in the idea of baptism in Romans 6. Underlying this whole passage, says Windisch, is the apostle's conviction that man's will can be moved to action only when the "divine deed" which baptism effects in him has occurred (p. 269). Paul's sacramentalism, regarded by Windisch as independent of his doctrine of justification (p. 268), is thus the key to his ethic. Paul's imperative urges that "what has become real in the invisible sphere of the divine activity" must be made visible in the earthly sphere, and in this sense the apostle does speak in terms of an ethical "realization" in the Christian's life (p. 271). Moreover, this sacramental teaching does include—here again Windisch counters Bultmann—the idea that a qualitative change is effected in the believer and that this is both experienced and visible among Christians (p. 272). Hence, the continuity of the old and new man is destroyed, and the Christian is freed from the burden of his past (p. 273). Windisch, like many earlier interpreters but unlike Bultmann, also thinks Paul conceives of a close alliance of divine and human factors in the working out of the new life (p. 278), and concludes that, putting aside Paul's doctrine of justification, the apostle after all does know an "ethic of sinlessness." His imperatives urge the realization of this sinlessness, and his teaching about baptism and the Spirit shows how this realization of sinlessness has been made possible (pp. 280-81).

In 1931 *Hans von Soden,* son of Hermann von Soden whose article on Paul's ethic had appeared in 1892,[39] himself published a study on the same topic.[40] A comparison of these articles by father and son demonstrates the increasingly greater theological sophistication with which the subject of Paul's ethic is being approached. The younger von Soden now shows that the sacramental motifs of the pre-Pauline church have been reinterpreted by the apostle and invested with a historical meaning of crucial importance. For Paul the wine of the Lord's Supper becomes symbolic of death, and drinking the wine means sharing in Christ's death, just as eating the bread means participating "in the spiritual life of Christ" (pp. 262-63). Emphasizing the importance of this union of the believer with Christ's death and resurrection, von Soden concludes that "the ethic of Paul is itself sacramental (in his sense), i.e. that it is historically, christologically,

[39] See above, p. 245.

[40] "Sakrament und Ethik bei Paulus," *Marburger Theologische Studien,* I, (1931), 1 ff. Page citations here are to *Urchristentum und Geschichte,* I, in which the article was reprinted in 1951.

and eschatologically bound, a specifically theological ethic and ethical theology" (p. 271).

Defined theologically, says von Soden, man's real "ethical decision" does not concern the inner form and motivation of an act or the "value" or "good" toward which an act is directed. Much more, it has to do with a particular understanding (*Erfassung*) of history, namely, that which is presented in the event of Christ's death (p. 273). This "decision" involves man's acknowledgment of God as himself the truth and also his affirmation of the reality of God's working in the present (p. 274). For Paul, then, the "crisis" of this deciding is a "passive" one; the Christian's decision is whether to accept the decision which has already been made concerning him. The apostle employs the sacraments (I Corinthians 10; Romans 6) to illustrate the insight that in Christ's death and resurrection the believer is already "pre-engaged" and "pre-justified"; "we cannot, we are not able 'not to do' this, or 'to do' that; but rather only this and absolutely nothing else" (p. 274). It is precisely at this point that von Soden's interpretation of the Pauline ethic brings him to the crucial issue, the relation of indicative and imperative. He acknowledges this (p. 274, n. 49) but, unfortunately, declines to discuss the matter.

While the interest of German writers (e.g. Bultmann, Windisch, von Soden) turns increasingly to the theological aspects of Paul's ethic, these are almost totally ignored in the work of the American *Morton Scott Enslin*.[41] It is true that Enslin constantly emphasizes the indissoluble unity of "morals and religion" in Paul (pp. xiii., 53, etc.), but his study presupposes distinctions between "practical morality" and "theoretic ethics" on the one hand (p. 134), and "religion" and theological "doctrine" on the other. By "religion" Enslin would seem to mean the believer's religious experience of his "mystical union with Christ" through which "the new life is revealed and made possible, we might almost say inevitable, for him" (p. 107). But Enslin does not mean that Paul's moral teaching is "indissolubly united" with his *theology*, either his doctrine of justification (Bultmann) or his sacramental teaching (Windisch). Indeed, considering Paul's emphasis on salvation by faith, he says, we might expect a *neglect* of morals; that

[41] *The Ethics of Paul* (1930). In a special introduction to the 1962 reprinting of this book, Enslin avers that, except for a few matters like the use of II Thessalonians and Ephesians, he is not inclined to alter "materially" his views of 1930 and that he is fully satisfied to let the book reappear still "quite devoid of references either to the kerygma . . . or to the Dead Sea scrolls" (pp. xxv-vi.). References herein are to this 1962 reprint.

these are not neglected shows how "moral integrity ofttimes surpasses logic" (p. 50). Enslin makes a similar judgment when he claims that, though Paul regarded baptism as making the believer holy, he persisted in pointing out the necessity to refrain from sinning. This, says Enslin, "was a flaw in logic, but a glorious one" (p. 58). Twice he refers approvingly to Percy Gardner's judgment that, though the apostle occasionally "drifts into a doctrinal discussion," he returns to his ethical exhortation "with obvious relief." [42]

In short, one might characterize Enslin as emphasizing a *sociological* over against a *theological* origin and context for Paul's ethical teaching. Although Enslin himself never puts the matter this sharply, his approach and results would seem to support such a judgment. For example, he believes that it was Paul's *heritage* as a moral Jew, his pre-Christian experience, which enabled him to see the importance of morality in spite of the logical implications of his own doctrine (p. 58), and that this same heritage gave him a special horror of sexual laxity (p. 89). Along with this background in Jewish morality Enslin stresses the pressure of actual moral problems in the churches as a stimulus for the formation of ethical teaching: "Taking the specific case, he would develop the general principle involved" (p. 244). Moreover, Enslin describes the "ultimate ideal for Christian conduct" as anything which promotes true fellowship (κοινωνία) with the Lord—which means also "with the brethren" (p. 127). "Love" and "forbearance," two of Paul's most important themes, are thus referred to here as "social virtues" (p. 74), and it is claimed that when the apostle declares that all things should "edify" (οἰκοδομεῖν), he means that they should serve to promote "another's growth in the Christian graces" (p. 231).

Enslin, then, more than any previous interpreter of the Pauline ethic, takes into account the sociological context in which Paul's teaching developed and to which it was addressed.[43] Moreover, and partly for

[42] *The Religious Experience of St. Paul* (1911), cited by Enslin on pp. xii and 77.

[43] A few years later Mary E. Andrews, also attempted a social-historical approach to Paul's ethic, focusing attention on the apostle's "behavior" and "the more warmly human" aspects of his teaching (pp. 6 ff.). She differs from Enslin not only in emphasizing Paul's Hellenisitc background and minimizing the influence of Judaism upon him, but also by contending that "Paul's ethical judgments were much more conditioned by the contemporary social situation than they were conditioned by any heritage from his past" (*The Ethical Teaching of Paul*, pp. 167-68). But the position taken here is that also in Enslin the elements of a "sociological" approach may be seen.

this reason, his discussions of individual ethical terms employed by Paul are often particularly illuminating. He also succeeds in locating a great number of materials from other ancient sources which help in shedding light on Paul's world and, by comparison and contrast, on the apostle himself.

But there are important points on which Enslin needs to be challenged. The criticism that he has interpreted Paul too exclusively against the background of Judaism[44] is to be taken seriously. Enslin, who describes Paul as "a Jew to the finger tips" (p. xxiv.), consistently minimizes Hellenistic aspects of his thought. While Dibelius surely goes too far in assuming that what Paul borrows from Hellenistic sources he only slightly modifies, Enslin also goes too far—in the opposite direction—when he claims that the individual terms Paul appropriated he transformed "regardless" of their previous meaning (p. 43) and with "entire unconcern" for it (p. 102). It is also significant that Enslin does not often ask whether Paul may also have reinterpreted *Jewish* terms and concepts which he employs. And what of Enslin's evaluation of the meaning and ethical significance of Pauline eschatology? Is this only that the apostle has projected the "sphere of happiness beyond this life" (pp. 200, 300) as a time of glorious victory (pp. 217, 227, 296 ff.) which would more than compensate for present hardships (p. 199), thereby infusing Paul with a "contagious optimism" (p. 298)? Is it really accurate to say that *"though* he expected this world to end on the morrow, he taught as if it would last forever" (p. 308, italics added)? And is it true that the overriding moral concern of Paul was for sexual purity (pp. 190, 195, etc.)?

The most serious limitation of Enslin's work is, however, the author's total and intentional disregard of any *theological* dimensions of Paul's ethic. Dare one dismiss so arbitrarily the possibility of significant relationships between Pauline "doctrine" and ethical teaching? Is Paul's ethic so completely "practical" (in Enslin's sense) as is here claimed? In fact, there are "theological" problems and questions which emerge even within the avowedly "nontheological" precincts of Enslin's own discussion, but because they are not explicitly acknowledged as such, they are handled quite naïvely. There is, for example, the emphatic but unexamined statement that for Paul the ultimate moral authority was "the light within" and that "the standards he set were his own standards of conduct" (p. 130); there is, also, the several times repeated

[44] *Ibid.,* esp. chap. V.

but never developed thought that it is from a "mystical union" with Christ that morality springs and the associated suggestion that under the "influence of the Spirit" and through the power of love the Christian is "impelled" to a new life which might "almost" be described as an "inevitable" consequence (pp. 88, 107, cf. 236). Finally, the suggestion that Paul's polemic against the law was prompted not by theological convictions but by practical exigencies (pp. 85-86), itself highly debatable, leads Enslin to ignore many of the passages in which the apostle's most subtle and original thinking about the law is expressed.

GOGUEL, DODD, SCHRAGE, ET AL.

Between 1930 and 1950 several volumes were published dealing with the topic of "New Testament ethics" as a whole, but none contributes in a substantial or original way to an understanding of Paul's ethic in particular. *C. A. Anderson Scott* [45] interprets Paul's ethic as essentially an application to new conditions and problems of Jesus' ethical principles (p. 76), although at the same time he believes that most of the apostle's ethical regulations and ideals are held in common with the non-Christian world and that his greatest originality is in the motives he employs (pp. 96 ff.). *Ernest F. Scott* [46] endeavors to show that the New Testament is not concerned for social problems as such but for the individual soul, the individual "human personality." [47] Sounding very much like Enslin, *L. H. Marshall* [48] stresses both the "practical" character of Paul's ethic (p. 218) and the indissoluble union of religion and morals in the apostle's thought (pp. 232 ff., 316, etc.). Marshall depends heavily on the distinction between "moral" and "religious" reality (e.g. p. 262), speaks often of "the secret of the good life" (a "living experience of the power of God at work in the heart") which Paul shares with Jesus (e.g. pp. 230-31, 247-48, 270), and attempts to wrest Paul's conception of "the good man" from the series of ethical terms employed in Galatians 5 and Philippians 4 (p. 308). *Lindsay Dewar* [49] believes that the concept of God's

[45] *New Testament Ethics: An Introduction* (1930).
[46] *Man and Society in the New Testament* (1946).
[47] A few years earlier Holmes Rolston had published a relatively unenlightening study of *The Social Message of the Apostle Paul* (1942).
[48] *The Challenge of New Testament Ethics* (1946).
[49] *An Outline of New Testament Ethics* (1949).

righteousness as found in the Jewish law is the basic presupposition of Paul's ethic (p. 122), that Paul's quarrel was not with the ethical precepts of the law (which remained "of cardinal significance" to him) but with one's inability to obey them, and that faith in Christ "became for him the primary ethical requirement" because it did bring the power for obedience to the commandments (p. 123).

Worthy of more serious attention is the contribution, both original and provocative, of *Maurice Goguel* [50] who identifies the fundamental problem of the Pauline ethic as the relationship of the apostolic indicatives and imperatives (p. 426). Although he claims that they constitute an "antinomy," not an "antithesis" (p. 440), he explains them by saying that "Paul placed two ethics side by side which are not in perfect harmony with each other" (pp. 446 ff.). One of these is the ethic of the imperatives, "the ethic of law and judgment" inherited, at least in its fundamentals, from Judaism. Even as a Christian Paul remains attached to "the nomistic principle," viewing the moral life in terms of obedience to God's law. His ethical imperatives result from this. But, partly under the influence of the teaching of Jesus, Paul radicalizes the demand of the law to include the obedience of the whole person and sees that man himself is incapable of fulfilling the demand thus conceived. Goguel also argues, however, that Paul comes to see God's law as coincident with that of "the inner man," in concord with man's true nature and therefore not just something formal (p. 447).

It is exactly here that Goguel believes Paul's ethic of law and judgment "interpenetrates" (p. 449) his *second* ethic, "the ethic of the justified man." This ethic of indicatives derives from Paul's experience of forgiveness and assurance of future redemption. The Christian who "has in fact (although not completely) become a spiritual being" experiences salvation as "the expansion of the inner man"; for him the law ceases to be an external, formal rule and becomes "an inner reality and a spiritual power which helps him to realize the programme it has drawn up for him. It gives what it imposes" (p. 447).

The ultimate origin of this dual ethic, Goguel suggests, is the very nature of religion itself, "which associates two disparate elements [the divine and the human] with each other and integrates the eternal into the transitory and ephemeral" (p. 450). Pauline eschatology is a concrete manifestation of this antinomy (p. 452) and is therefore of

---

[50] "Paul's Ethic" in *The Primitive Church,* trans. H. C. Snape (1964; French ed., 1947), pp. 425 ff. Goguel also includes a few pages on "Paul's moral teaching" in his chapter on "Ethical Education" (pp. 507 ff.).

further help in explaining Paul's two ethics. The Christian is subject to them both because, so long as he lives in the present world, "he is a double being, half flesh and half spirit" (p. 453). Sin is a reality in the sphere of the flesh and requires Paul's ethic of law; salvation is a reality in the sphere of the Spirit and enables an ethic of justification. This juxtaposition of the two ethics is a result of the "eschatological dissonance" in Paul's thought (p. 455).

It is unquestionably a virtue of Goguel's interpretation that the problem of indicative and imperative is so forcefully stressed as the key to understanding Paul's ethic, and it is a further virtue that in dealing with this problem he takes serious account of the concrete ethical exhortations which constitute such a large part of the Pauline letters. But has he yet succeeded in resolving or explaining this problem? Do not remnants of older, more conventional "answers" remain in his interpretation, as when he distinguishes between holiness as a "reality" and an "ideal" (pp. 440, 441), when he ascribes to Paul the view that justification and sanctification are two separate aspects of the Christian life (p. 438), when he suggests that Paul's ethic had to be adopted to meet the fundamental contradiction between ideals and reality (p. 428), and when he claims that for Paul, although the liberating act had already occurred, its full consequences had not yet been worked out (p. 432)?

Must it not also be acknowledged that the point which is most crucial in Goguel's interpretation of Paul's ethic is also the point about which most serious question can be raised: Paul's view of the law and its significance for the Christian. Goguel would have us believe (a) that the apostle consistently distinguishes between the ethical and ceremonial aspects of the law (p. 443); (b) that he retains "the nomistic principle" as the basis for morality; (c) that he regards the law as "an inner reality and a spiritual power" which "gives what it imposes"; and (d) that now as a Christian Paul can describe the Old Testament law also as "the law of God" or "the law of Christ" (p. 516). The crucial question is whether Paul retained and interpreted the Jewish conception of the law in just this way, whether, more specifically, one can support exegetically the view that the law (e.g. as "an inner reality and a spiritual power") has such a central and decisive role in the apostle's doctrine of salvation as is here claimed. If not, then Goguel's entire analysis of the indicative and imperative aspects of Pauline theology needs to be overhauled. For Goguel's conclusion, stated plainly, is just this: the Christian, anticipating the eschatological fulfillment of a salvation already made partially real by

God's working in the Spirit, needs still to battle against sin because he is still partly ("half") in the flesh; and the power and guidance for this fight are provided by the law which, despite certain changes in perspective, Paul regards as identical with the law of the Old Testament in its nomistic function.[51]

Although *C. H. Dodd* had already published an article on "The Ethics of the Pauline Epistles" in 1927,[52] his greatest influence on the discussion of the early Christian ethic in general, and thus Paul's in particular, has been in his systematic distinction between preaching (κήρυγμα) and teaching (διδαχή) within the New Testament. The first of a series of lectures he published in 1936 [53] opens with the assertion that "the New Testament writers draw a clear distinction between preaching and teaching" (p. 7), and for Dodd this distinction corresponds to that between "theology" and "ethics" or "gospel" and "law." Without specific reference to Dibelius' views of New Testament parenesis, Dodd nevertheless approaches the subject in essentially the same way: "For the earliest church, to preach the Gospel was *by no means the same thing* as to deliver moral instruction or exhortation" (p. 8, italics added). Dodd does not go so far as to say, with Dibelius, that the early Christian eschatological expectation precluded an ethic. Rather, he regards that expectation as expressing "a sense of transience" and a keen awareness of a new age which has already dawned. The sense of transience "enables us to contemplate the ulti-

---

[51] An even more emphatic assertion of the nomistic structure of Paul's ethic is present in the book by a conservative Protestant: John Murray, *Principles of Conduct: Aspects of Biblical Ethics* (1957). Nowhere in the Bible, he argues, does one find "that the renewed heart is allowed spontaneously to excogitate the ethic of the saints of God." Rather, "there are objectively revealed precepts, institutions, commandments which are the norms and channels of human behavior" (p. 24). Respecting Paul in particular, "it is futile to try to escape the underlying assumption of [his] thought, that the concrete precepts of the decalogue have relevance to the believer as the criteria of that behavior which love dictates" (p. 192). Murray's book, however, is too dogmatically oriented to deserve much serious attention as a critical historical and exegetical investigation.

[52] In *The Evolution of Ethics*, ed. E. H. Sneath, pp. 293 ff. Although in this early essay Dodd affirms that "the basis of Paul's ethics is in his religion, and the one cannot be fully understood without the other," there is no real discussion of the theological dimensions of his ethic, e.g. virtually no reference to the sacraments and no reference to the "problem of indicative and imperative" which had several years before been so sharply posed by Bultmann.

[53] *The Apostolic Preaching and Its Developments*. Citations are from the new ed. of 1944.

mate ethical demand as absolute claim upon us," [54] while the awareness of a new age now present "is the recognition that an unattainable
ideal lays infinite obligations upon us; that the best we can do lies
under the judgment of God; but that the judgment of God carries
forgiveness within it." [55]

With reference to Paul specifically, Dodd claims that the apostle's
letters, because "they expound and defend the implications of the
Gospel rather than proclaim it," must be regarded as essentially didactic, not kerygmatic. [56] In fact, Paul himself is viewed by Dodd as the
promulgator of a new law, a Christian pattern for conduct which
"can be stated in the form of a code of precepts to which a Christian
man is obliged to conform." [57] For while Paul theoretically held that
the Christian should be led by the Spirit, in fact he doubted the prac-
ticality of this and thus expounded the "law of Christ" (I Cor. 9:21;
Gal. 6:2), "a comprehensive and somewhat detailed scheme of ethical
teaching" [58] which was "in some sort analogous to the Torah." [59] Dodd
further holds that such a new law enjoined upon the Christian the
responsibility for carrying out, although "in altered circumstances,"
"the precepts which Jesus Christ was believed to have given to His
disciples, and which they handed down in the Church." [60]

Similarities to Goguel's position are apparent here: Goguel speaks
of "two ethics" in Paul, and Dodd refers to the juxtaposition of "gospel
and law"; they both think of the Pauline ethic as having an essentially
nomistic structure; and both regard Paul's references to "the law of
Christ" as reflecting this Christian nomism. [61] Yet Dodd's extraordinarily
sharp distinction between doctrine and ethics prevents him from raising, at least in as subtle a fashion as Goguel, the vexed problem of
their possible relationship. Moreover, it is questionable whether he
succeeds any more than Goguel in demonstrating the nomistic character of Paul's ethic. And it is perhaps especially questionable whether
Paul does in fact refer to the church's tradition of Jesus' sayings when

[54] *Gospel and Law*, p. 30.
[55] *Ibid.*, p. 32.
[56] *The Apostolic Preaching*, p. 9.
[57] "ΕΝΝΟΜΟΣ ΧΡΙΣΤΟΥ," p. 100.
[58] *Gospel and Law*, p. 72.
[59] "ΕΝΝΟΜΟΣ ΧΡΙΣΤΟΥ," p. 103.
[60] *Ibid.*, p. 109.
[61] Goguel and Dodd differ as to the specific reference of "the law of
Christ." Goguel believes it describes the Old Testament law known to the
Christian as an inner power, while Dodd takes it as descriptive of a moral
pattern for Christian conduct derived from the teaching of Jesus.

he speaks of being ἔννομος Χριστοῦ (I Cor. 9:21) and when he employs the phrase ὁ νόμος τοῦ Χριστοῦ (Gal. 6:2).

Dodd's position is taken up and carried even farther by his student, W. D. Davies.[62] Faced by the delay of Christ's second coming and the tension of being "in the flesh" and "in Christ" at the same time, Paul was forced, for the sake of his churches, to become a teacher (διδάσκαλος) (p. 112). In fact, Davies thinks it is not too much to say that Paul became a catechist after the fashion of the rabbis (p. 129) and, in framing "rules for the moral guidance" of the church, "drew upon certain Jewish codes or regulations" (p. 130), notably the *derek 'eretz* literature (pp. 132 ff.). But most of all Davies stresses Paul's reliance upon the words of Jesus, the "primary source in his work as ethical διδάσκαλος" (p. 136), and offers a catalog of Pauline passages in which these words are used (pp. 137 ff.) Davies is even bolder than Dodd in discussing the meaning of Paul's references to "the law of Christ." Paul, it is claimed, "regarded Jesus in the light of a new Moses" and "recognised in the words of Christ a νόμος τοῦ Χριστοῦ which formed for him the basis for a kind of Christian Halakah." Indeed, "he meant that the actual words of Jesus were for him a New Torah" (p. 144).

If Goguel, Dodd, and Davies all tend to emphasize the nomistic aspects of the Pauline ethic, *Eric H. Wahlstrom*[63] is even more emphatic in declaring that law plays no role whatsoever in that ethic. Paul, he claims, "never appealed to the law as a standard of conduct, and never even directed his people to learn from the law what moral conduct should be" (p. 137). Wahlstrom rejects the notion that Paul regarded the sayings of Jesus as a "new law" (cf. Dodd, Davies) and believes this identification does not occur before the second century (p. 165). The Christian is not under "law" of any kind, but under grace; and because he is in Christ, "he needs no code of morals" (p. 152). Ernesti was perhaps the first interpreter of the Pauline ethic to speak of the Christian's "spontaneous" morality; now Wahlstrom

---

[62] *Paul and Rabbinic Judaism.* The first ed. appeared in 1948. With only slightly different emphases and minor modifications Davies takes the same approach to Paul's ethic in his article "Ethics in the New Testament." The influence of Dodd is also apparent in the remarks of T. W. Manson who argues that the early church "held as one of its most treasured possessions the *corpus* of teaching which laid down the law of Christ and which showed ways in which its principles could be applied to human affairs in all their variety and complexity" (*Ethics and the Gospel,* p. 69). See also Richard N. Longenecker, *Paul: Apostle of Liberty,* esp. chap. VIII.

[63] *The New Life in Christ* (1950).

uses the term repeatedly to describe Paul's view, meaning by it "a voluntary disposition of the new man, an identity of willing between God and the new man" (pp. 106-7; cf. 107-8, 144, 157, etc.). In his exposition of Paul's thought Wahlstrom depends heavily on the apostle's reference to God's working within man both "to will and to do" his good pleasure (Phil. 2:13), and he takes this to mean that "between the Spirit and the new man there is an identity of purpose and direction" (p. 149). The Christian, so far as ethical action is concerned, is therefore "Christ-autonomous" (p. 152) or "pneuma-autonomous" (p. 165). "What the new man does as a man in Christ is *ipso facto* good," says Wahlstrom, "for the nature of the new man is love" (p. 185).

But if Paul's ethic is so radically pneumatic as Wahlstrom believes, how are the ethical exhortations of his letters to be interpreted? Wahlstrom's comments on this question are brief and not too persuasive. Referring again to Phil. 2:13, he says that "what the 'doing' implies is not given with the 'willing'" (p. 107), and therefore the apostle must advise and exhort his congregations (p. 108); but this statement is never reconciled with Wahlstrom's contention in another place that "the Christian, by virtue of the indwelling Christ, knows of himself what is right and proper" (p. 152). In still another connection he refers to the "immaturity" of Paul's converts which sometimes made it necessary to offer them "tangible standards" in the form of personal examples (p. 158). But Wahlstrom definitely minimizes the specifically imperatival aspects of Paul's thought: Paul employed ethical standards "very sparingly" (p. 159); his references to the will of God in relation to specific conduct are "very few" (p. 162); and his ethical commands "are removed from the sphere of legal enactments" (p. 173). In a sense Wahlstrom's solution of the problem of indicative and imperative in Pauline theology is to eliminate the imperative altogether! It is "the old man" who lives under the imperative, he says; the "new man" lives under the indicative. But then, almost parenthetically, he adds a qualification of this judgment which shows that the basic problem of indicative and imperative is still present even for him: "This was Paul's *ideal* and he strove to *realize* it among his converts" (p. 195, italics added).[64]

[64] Cf. the position of James T. Cleland, "The Religious Ethic of St. Paul" (unpublished dissertation). Although the Christian is under the control of the Spirit (p. 377) and there is thus a "spontaneity" in the Christian life (p. 378), Paul's "theory" of salvation "did not work in practice" (p. 388). Therefore, in his missionary work he "pleads, argues, scolds and encourages" (p. 406).

An all-out attack on the view that Paul's ethic is wholly pneumatic
and lacks concrete "norms" of any kind is launched by *Wolfgang
Schrage*.[65] He examines the specific ethical admonitions of the Pauline
letters and argues persuasively that these cannot be dismissed as due
only to a weakening of the eschatological hope (Paul's ethical teaching existed side by side with his eschatology from the beginning, pp.
13 ff.), as a compromise between the ideal and the actual (pp. 26 ff.),
as of only temporary validity but in the long run superfluous (pp.
29 ff.), or as valid only in very specific circumstances (pp. 37 ff.).
Schrage does not dispute the grounding of the new life in the Spirit
(p. 71), nor that God's demand is a total claim on man (pp. 49 ff.),
nor that the love-commandment is the highest and most comprehensive
of all norms for the life in Christ (pp. 249 ff.). But he does dispute
the conclusion that the Christian is thereby released from all objectively
definable standards and criteria for conduct. He points out that there
is no evidence Paul ever distinguished between God's demand as an
"inner" and "outer" word (p. 76), that the phrase ἐν Χριστῷ is given
by the apostle not a mystical but an eschatological-ecclesiological significance (p. 80), and that Paul never identifies the Christian's will
with the will of God, Christ, or the Spirit (p. 84). Attacking Wahlstrom's view in particular, Schrage argues that Paul does not understand the indwelling Spirit (or Christ) as an "inward monitor" of
ethical action, "but rather he exhorts in, with and by 'outer' exhortation, and precisely this is a charismatic function." The means of this
"outer exhortation" may be scripture or the apostolic admonitions
themselves (p. 86).

God's "total claim" on man, the all-encompassing exhortation to love,
is manifested and concretized *in* Paul's admonitions and exhortations
(p. 60), says Schrage. The apostle does not just proclaim "abstract
ethical principles of a basic kind," but shows that the Christian's
new obedience is "formed and unfolded in concrete deeds and duties."
Paul does not leave his congregations unclear as to what these are
(p. 67). While Paul was not a "systematic" ethicist, neither was he
a purely "practical" moralist or "improvisor" who admonished different things from day to day (p. 123). He utilized norms and commandments which have a consistent and enduring force, "which remain the
same though times and situations change and which are to be followed
by Christians in all the congregations" (p. 135; cf. pp. 210 ff.). Love,

---

[65] *Die konkreten Einzelgebote in der paulinischen Paränese: Ein Beitrag
zur neutestamentlichen Ethik* (1961).

like faith, despite all variations, has a continuing "structure and content"; and although it is not expressed in stereotyped ways, "it is also not irregular and arbitrary, always improvising and different" (p. 267). Yet this does not mean that Paul was a legalist or that his ethic is basically nomistic: "True obedience cannot be measured, weighed and added up, but it is nonetheless concrete. Concreteness is thus to be distinguished from legalism and an ethic of achievement" (p. 69). In Paul's view freedom from the law means freedom from slavery to it, not freedom from concrete demands (p. 96); he rejects the law as a way of salvation (*Heilsweg*) but not as a norm for life (*Lebensnorm*) (pp. 232, 238).

Schrage succeeds in showing that Paul's ethic cannot without substantial qualification be characterized as "situational" or "improvisational"; and along the way he deals suggestively with numerous related themes and issues (the place of reason and conscience in discerning God's will, the Christian community as the context for ethical decision, Paul's critical selection and reshaping of traditional ethical materials, etc.). He effectively challenges those interpretations of Paul's ethic which dismiss the specific ethical commandments as essentially unrelated to the Pauline gospel as a whole ("God's demand meets man . . . not alongside of or separately from the apostolic preaching, but precisely in it," p. 103). The effect of Schrage's study is thus to raise with even more urgency the question of the relation of the concrete commandments to Paul's basic theological perspective and in particular to his doctrine of justification by faith. For while this matter is touched on here in various ways, it is not the subject of any extended discussion.

Other recent attempts to define the character of Paul's ethic do not significantly depart from or amplify earlier approaches. *John Knox*[66] repeats the old complaint that Paul's doctrine of justification is an unfortunate distortion of Jesus' preaching of forgiveness and sets law and grace so firmly against one another (p. 75) that no theoretical ground is left for an ethic (p. 97).[67] *R. Newton Flew's* chapter on the

[66] *The Ethic of Jesus in the Teaching of the Church: Its Authority and Relevance* (1961).

[67] Two contributors to the Festschrift honoring Knox (*Christian History and Interpretation: Studies Presented to John Knox,* ed. W. Farmer, C. F. D. Moule, R. R. Niebuhr [1967]) have provided needed and instructive critiques of his interpretation of the Pauline ethic. See C. F. D. Moule, "Obligation in the Ethic of Paul" (pp. 389 ff.), and Paul Schubert, "Paul and the New Testament Ethic in the Thought of John Knox" (pp. 363 ff.).

ethical teaching of Paul [68] discusses "grace" as "the cardinal conviction of the Christian Church" (p. 86) and sees the Pauline ethic as structured according to the threefold response to grace: faith, hope, and love (pp. 86 ff.). But Flew's discussion proceeds without much reference to the most important preceding treatments of Paul's ethic, and he himself does not seem to be bothered by any problem of indicative and imperative. Although *William Baird,*[69] like Schrage, denies that Paul's was a "situational" ethic (pp. 213-14), his own characterization is also undercut by Schrage's work (with which Baird is evidently unfamiliar). God's righteousness, he argues, lays an "absolute" demand upon the Christian (pp. 211 ff.), but the Christian's responsibility is to make decisions which are "relatively right" (p. 80; cf. p. 78, *et passim*). Baird holds that the "problematic" character of this ethic is partly overcome by the availability of certain principles, the most basic of which, "grounded in the character of the absolute," still makes only an "elusive demand: Do all to the glory of God" (p. 207). Like so many others, then, Baird in general ignores Paul's *concrete* exhortations when he comes around to a formulation of the structure of the apostle's ethic.

D. E. H. Whiteley's [70] treatment of the Pauline ethic involves the view that the apostle himself distinguished between justification and sanctification; although baptism effects certain perceptible results in the believer's life (p. 168), really only a "beginning" has been made (p. 208), and thus one can say that morality bears an integral relationship to Paul's dogmatic theology (pp. 205-6). Not significantly different, although with more of an emphasis on the eschatological dimension of Paul's ethic, is the interpretation of the Roman Catholic *Rudolf Schnackenburg.*[71] Through baptism the Christian shares in God's gift of salvation and thus receives the divine life (pp. 269-70). But this life will be revealed in its plenitude only "at the last day," and "it is the tension between what we already possess and what we do not yet possess which demands so imperiously our ethical probation" (p. 270). Specifically, the Christian is called upon to struggle against the world's evil powers which have not yet submitted to the rule of God (pp. 278 ff.). Paul's ethic therefore is seen to have two focal points: "the

[68] In *Jesus and His Way: A Study of the Ethics of the New Testament* (1963), pp. 82 ff.
[69] *The Corinthian Church—A Biblical Approach to Urban Culture* (1964).
[70] *The Theology of St. Paul* (1964).
[71] In *The Moral Teaching of the New Testament,* trans. J. Holland-Smith and W. J. O'Hara (1965), pp. 261 ff. The original German ed. appeared in 1954, and this English trans. is from the 2nd rev. ed. of 1962.

redemption already given us by God impelling us towards the sanctification of our way of living, and the salvation we have not yet
attained demanding the exertion of all our own powers if we are to
achieve it" (p. 278). Finally, then, Schnackenburg's solution of the
problem of indicative and imperative is to speak of the need for the
Christian, after his baptism, to "co-operate with the grace of God" (p.
281). But the question remains whether the apostle himself would
have found this a meaningful clarification of his gospel.[72]

CONCLUSION

Viewing overall the course of nineteenth- and twentieth-century research into Paul's ethic, two things are clear. First, the fact of Paul's
ethical concern, his concern for the moral life, individual and corporate,
of the members of his congregations may be amply documented. There
have been attempts to minimize this concern, to accord it a secondary
status, or to explain it away, but the manifest presence in the apostle's
letters of ethical warnings, prohibitions, exhortations, and concrete
moral teaching must be reckoned with seriously. Second, a survey of
the various attempts to interpret Paul's ethic exposes as the central
and decisive problem *the relation of these concrete ethical materials
to the apostle's preaching as a whole, especially to his basic theological
presuppositions and convictions.* Otherwise stated, it has become apparent that no interpretation of the Pauline ethic can be judged
successful which does not grapple with the problem of indicative and
imperative in Paul's thought.

[72] It has not been possible in this survey of the literature dealing with
the Pauline ethic to comment on or even mention all the contributions.
Some have had to be omitted, and several different criteria have been employed in determining which to include, e.g. originality, influence, an especially
lucid or provocative statement of the issues. A particularly good bibliography
of nineteenth-century works will be found in K. Benz's *Die Ethik des Apostels
Paulus,* pp. ix-xii. The most complete recent bibliography (although not
always accurate in detailed data) is W. Schrage's *Die konkreten Einzelgebote
in der paulinischen Paränese,* pp. 277-301.

Bibliography
of Major Works Cited

I. TEXTS AND TRANSLATIONS

The Apocrypha, Revised Standard Version. New York: Thomas Nelson & Sons, 1957.

Charles, R. H., ed. *The Apocrypha and Pseudepigrapha of the Old Testament in English.* 2 vols. Oxford: The Clarendon Press, 1913.

————, ed. *The Greek Version of the Testaments of the Twelve Patriarchs.* Oxford: The Clarendon Press, 1908.

Easton, Burton S., trans. "Pseudo-Phocylides," *AThR,* XIV (1932), 222-28.

Goodspeed, Edgar J., trans. *The Bible: An American Translation—The New Testament.* Chicago: The University of Chicago Press, 1931.

The Holy Bible, Revised Standard Version. New York: Thomas Nelson & Sons, 1952.

The Loeb Classical Library, Classical Greek and Latin Texts with Parallel English Translations. Cambridge, Mass.: Harvard University Press, various dates.

Moffatt, James, trans. *The New Testament: A New Translation.* New York: Hodder & Stoughton, 1913.

Nestle, Erwin, and Aland, Kurt, eds. *Novum Testamentum Graece.* 24th ed. Stuttgart: Privileg. Württ. Bibelanstalt, 1960.

The New English Bible: New Testament. Oxford and Cambridge: The Oxford and Cambridge University Presses, 1961.

Origen of Alexandria, *Contra Celsum,* trans. with an intro. and notes by Henry Chadwick. Cambridge: Cambridge University Press, 1953.

Rahlfs, Alfred, ed. *Septuaginta, id est Vetus Testamentum Graece Iuxta LXX Interpretes.* 2 vols. 5th ed. Stuttgart: Privileg. Württ. Bibelanstalt, 1952.

II. STANDARD REFERENCE WORKS

Bauer, Walter. *A Greek-English Lexicon of the New Testament and Other Early Christian Literature.* Trans. and adapt. W. F. Arndt and F. W. Gingrich. Chicago: University of Chicago Press, 1957.

Billerbeck, Paul, and Strack, Hermann L. *Kommentar zum Neuen Testament aus Talmud u. Midrasch.* 5 vols. München: Beck, 1922–56.

Blass, F., and Debrunner, A. *A Greek Grammar of the New Testament and Other Early Christian Literature.* Trans. and rev. Robert W. Funk. Chicago: University of Chicago Press, 1961.

Buttrick, George A., ed. *The Interpreter's Bible.* 12 vols. Nashville: Abingdon Press, 1952–57.

———, ed. *The Interpreter's Dictionary of the Bible.* 4 vols. Nashville: Abingdon Press, 1962.

Galling, Kurt, ed. *Die Religion in Geschichte und Gegenwart.* 3rd ed. 7 vols. plus an index vol. Tübingen: J. C. B. Mohr (Paul Siebeck), 1957–65.

Hastings, James, ed. *Encyclopedia of Religion and Ethics.* 13 vols. New York: Charles Scribner's Sons, 1928.

Hennecke, Edgar, ed. *New Testament Apocrypha.* Rev. Wilhelm Schneemelcher. Eng. trans. ed. by R. McL. Wilson. 2 vols. Philadelphia: The Westminster Press, 1963, 1965.

Kittel, G., ed. *Theologisches Wörterbuch zum Neuen Testament.* Stuttgart: Verlag von W. Kohlhammer, 1933 ff. Eng. trans. ed. by G. Bromiley. Grand Rapids, Mich.: Wm. B. Eerdmans Publishing Co., 1964 ff.

Moulton, James H. *A Grammar of New Testament Greek.* Completed by Nigel Turner. 3 vols. Edinburgh: T. & T. Clark, 1908–63.

Singer, Isidore, ed. *The Jewish Encyclopedia.* 12 vols. New York and London: Funk & Wagnalls, 1901 ff.

III. BOOKS, COMMENTARIES, ARTICLES, DISSERTATIONS

Alexander, Archibald B. D. *The Ethics of St. Paul.* Glasgow: James Maclehose & Sons, 1910.

Althaus, Paul. *Der Brief an die Römer* (*NTD*, 6). 7th ed. Göttingen: Vandenhoeck & Ruprecht, 1953.

Andrews, Mary Edith. *The Ethical Teaching of Paul. A Study in Origin.* Chapel Hill: University of North Carolina Press, 1934.

Baird, William. *The Corinthian Church—A Biblical Approach to Urban Culture.* Nashville: Abingdon Press, 1964.

Bandstra, Andrew J. *The Law and the Elements of the World. An Exegetical Study in Aspects of Paul's Teaching.* Kampen: J. H. Kok N.V., 1964.

Barclay, William. *Flesh and Spirit: An Examination of Galatians 5:19-23.* Nashville: Abingdon Press, 1962.

Barrett, C. K. *A Commentary on the Epistle to the Romans* (*HNTC*). New York: Harper & Brothers, 1957.

Barth, Karl. *Church Dogmatics.* Trans. G. W. Bromiley, *et al.* Vol. II, Pt. 2. Edinburgh: T. & T. Clark, 1957.

———. *The Epistle to the Philippians.* Trans. James W. Leitch. Richmond, Va.: John Knox Press, 1962.

———. *The Epistle to the Romans.* Trans. from the 6th German ed. Edwyn C. Hoskyns. London: Oxford University Press, 1933.

Baur, F. Chr. *Paul: The Apostle of Jesus Christ.* Trans. from the 2nd German ed. and ed. by Eduard Zeller. Vol. I, 2nd ed. rev. A. Menzies; Vol. II, trans. A. Menzies. London: Williams & Norgate, 1875–76.

Beach, Waldo, and Niebuhr, H. Richard, eds. *Christian Ethics.* New York: The Ronald Press Company, 1955.

Beardslee, William A. *Human Achievement and Divine Vocation in the Message of Paul* (*SBTh*, 31). Naperville, Ill.: Alec R. Allenson, 1961.

Beare, Frank W. *A Commentary on the Epistle to the Philippians* (*HNTC*). New York: Harper & Brothers, 1959.

———. "New Testament Christianity and the Hellenistic World," *The Communication of the Gospel in New Testament Times.* ("SPCK Theological Collections.") London: SPCK, 1961. Pp. 57 ff.

Benz, Karl. *Die Ethik des Apostels Paulus.* ("*Bibl. Stud. 17, 3-4.*") Freiburg im Breisgau: Herdersche Verlagshandlung, 1912.

Betz, Hans Dieter. *Nachfolge und Nachahmung Jesu Christi im Neuen Testament* (*BHTh*, 37). Tübingen: J. C. B. Mohr (Paul Siebeck), 1967.

Bonhöffer, Adolf. *Epiktet und das Neue Testament.* ("Religionsgeschichtliche Versuche und Vorarbeiten, x.") Giessen, 1911.

———. "Epiktet und das Neue Testament," *ZNW*, XIII (1912), 218 ff.

Bonnard, Pierre. *L'Épître de Saint Paul aux Galates* (*CNT,* IX). Neuchatel and Paris: Delachaux and Niestlé S.A., 1953.

Bonsirven, Joseph. *Exégèse rabbinique et exégèse paulinienne* ("Bibliothèque de théologie historique.") Paris: Beauchesne et ses fils, 1939.

Bornkamm, Günther. *Das Ende des Gesetzes, Gesammelte Aufsätze,* Bd. I (*BEvTh,* 16). München: Chr. Kaiser Verlag, 1952.

————. "Faith and Reason in Paul," *NTS,* IV (1958), 93 ff.

————. "Gesetz und Natur," *Studien zu Antike und Urchristentum,* pp. 93 ff.

————. "Glaube und Vernunft bei Paulus," *ibid.,* pp. 119 ff.

————. "Der Lohngedanke im Neuen Testament," *ibid.,* pp. 69 ff.

————."Die Offenbarung des Zornes Gottes, Röm. 1–3," *Das Ende des Gesetzes,* pp. 9 ff.

————. *Studien zu Antike und Urchristentum, Gesammelte Aufsätze,* Bd. II (*BEvTh,* 28). München: Chr. Kaiser Verlag, 1963.

————. "Taufe und neues Leben bei Paulus," *Das Ende des Gesetzes,* pp. 34 ff.

————. "Die Vorgeschichte des sog. zweiten Korintherbriefes," *SAH,* 1961.

Bouttier, Michel. *Christianity According to Paul* (*SBTh,* 49). Trans. Frank Clarke. Naperville, Ill.: Alec R. Allenson, 1966.

Bradley, David G. "The Origins of the Hortatory Materials in the Letters of Paul." Unpublished Doctoral dissertation, Yale University, 1947.

Brandenburger, Egon. *Adam und Christus, exegetisch-religionsgeschichtliche Untersuchung zu Röm. 5:12-21 (1. Kor. 15)* (*WMANT,* 7). Neukirchen Kreis Moers: Neukirchener Verlag, 1962.

Bring, Ragnar. "Die Erfüllung des Gesetzes durch Christus, Eine Studie zur Theologie des Apostels Paulus," *KuD,* V (1959), 1 ff.

Brunner, Emil. *The Divine Imperative: A Study in Christian Ethics.* Trans. Olive Wyon. London: Lutterworth Press, 1937.

Bultmann, Rudolf. "Adam and Christ According to Romans 5," *Current Issues in New Testament Interpretation.* Ed. W. Klassen and G. Snyder. New York: Harper & Row, 1962. Pp. 143 ff.

————. "Allgemeine Wahrheiten und christliche Verkündigung," *ZThK,* LIV (1957), 244 ff.

————. *Existence and Faith: Shorter Writings of Rudolf Bultmann.* Selected, trans., and introduced Schubert M. Ogden. New York: Living Age Books, 1960.

————. "Glossen im Römerbrief," *ThLZ,* LXXII (1947), cols. 197 ff.

———. *Jesus Christ and Mythology*. New York: Charles Scribner's Sons, 1958.

———. "Das Problem der Ethik bei Paulus," *ZNW*, XXIII (1924), 123 ff.

———. "Das religiöse Moment in der ethischen Unterweisung des Epiktets und das Neue Testament," *ZNW*, XIII (1912), 97 ff., 177 ff.

———. "Romans 7 and the Anthropology of Paul," *Existence and Faith*, pp. 147 ff.

———. *Der Stil der paulinischen Predigt und die kynisch-stoische Diatribe* (*FRLANT*, 13). Göttingen: Vandenhoeck & Ruprecht, 1910.

———. *Theology of the New Testament*. Trans. Kendrick Grobel. 2 vols. New York: Charles Scribner's Sons, 1951–55.

Burrows, Miller. *More Light on the Dead Sea Scrolls*. New York: The Viking Press, 1958.

Burton, Ernest DeWitt. *A Critical and Exegetical Commentary on the Epistle to the Galatians* (*ICC*). New York: Charles Scribner's Sons, 1920.

Carrington, Philip. *The Primitive Christian Catechism, A Study in the Epistles*. Cambridge: Cambridge University Press, 1940.

Cleland, James T. "The Religious Ethic of St. Paul." 2 vols. Unpublished Doctoral dissertation, Union Theological Seminary (New York), 1954.

Cone, Orello. *Paul—The Man, the Missionary, and the Teacher*. New York: The Macmillan Company, 1898.

Corssen, R. "Paulus and Porphyrios," *ZNW*, XIX (1919–20), 2 ff.

Cranfield, C. E. B. *A Commentary on Romans 12–13*. ("*SJTh* Occasional Papers," 12.) Edinburgh: Oliver & Boyd, 1965.

Daube, David. *The New Testament and Rabbinic Judaism* (Jordan Lectures, 1952). London: The Athlone Press, 1956.

———. "Participle and Imperative in I Peter," in E. G. Selwyn, *The First Epistle of St. Peter*. London: The Macmillan Company, Ltd., 1955.

Davies, William D., "Ethics in the New Testament," *IntDB*, E–J, pp. 167 ff.

———. "Paul and the Dead Sea Scrolls: Flesh and Spirit," *The Scrolls and the New Testament*, ed. K. Stendahl. New York: Harper & Row, 1957. Pp. 157 ff.

———. *Paul and Rabbinic Judaism: Some Elements in Pauline Theology*. 2nd ed. London: SPCK, 1955.

———. *Torah in the Messianic Age and/or the Age to Come* ("*JBL* Monograph Series," VII), 1952.

DeBoer, Willis P. *The Imitation of Paul: An Exegetical Study.* Kampen: J. H. Kok N. V., 1962.

Deissmann, Adolf. *The Religion of Jesus and the Faith of Paul.* Trans. William E. Wilson. London: Hodder & Stoughton, 1923.

DeJonge, M. *The Testaments of the Twelve Patriarchs: A Study of Their Text, Composition and Origin.* ("Van Gorcum's Theologische Bibliotheek, XXV.") Assen: Van Gorcum & Comp. N.V., 1953.

Dewar, Lindsay. *An Outline of New Testament Ethics.* Philadelphia: The Westminster Press, 1949.

Dewey, John, and Tufts, James H. *Ethics.* New York: Henry Holt & Company, 1908.

Dibelius, Martin. *Botschaft und Geschichte.* In Verbindung mit Heinz Kraft, hrsg. von G. Bornkamm. 2 vols. Tübingen: J. C. B. Mohr (Paul Siebeck), 1953, 1956.

————. *Der Brief des Jakobus (KEK).* Hrsg. von H. Greeven. 8th ed. Göttingen: Vandenhoeck & Ruprecht, 1957.

————. "Das christliche Leben (Eph. 4, 17—6, 9)," *ThBl,* IX (1930), cols. 341-42.

————. " Ἐπίγνωσις ἀληθείας," *Botschaft und Geschichte,* II, 1 ff.

————. "Zur Formgeschichte des Neuen Testaments (ausserhalb der Evangelien)," ThR, n.F. III (1931), 207 ff.

————. *A Fresh Approach to the New Testament and Early Christian Literature.* New York: Charles Scribner's Sons, 1936.

————. *From Tradition to Gospel.* Trans. from the rev. 2nd ed. by Bertram Lee Woolf. New York: Charles Scribner's Sons, 1935.

————. *An die Kolosser, Epheser, An Philemon (HNT).* 3rd ed. rev. H. Greeven. Tübingen: J. C. B. Mohr (Paul Siebeck), 1953.

————. *Studies in the Acts of the Apostles,* ed. H. Greeven. Trans. Mary Ling and Paul Schubert. London: SCM Press, 1956.

————. *An die Thessalonicher I, II, An die Philipper (HNT).* 3rd ed. Tübingen: J. C. B. Mohr (Paul Siebeck), 1937.

————. *Urchristentum und Kultur.* Heidelberg: Carl Winters Universitäts-buchhandlung, 1928.

Dinkler, Erich. "Zum Problem der Ethik bei Paulus," *ZThK,* XLIX (1952), 167 ff.

Dobschütz, Ernst von. *Christian Life in the Primitive Church.* Trans. Geo. Bremner and ed. W. D. Morrison. London: Williams & Norgate, 1904.

Dodd, Charles Harold. *The Apostolic Preaching and Its Developments.* New ed. London: Hodder & Stoughton, 1944.

————. "ΕΝΝΟΜΟΣ ΧΡΙΣΤΟΥ," *Studia Paulina, in honorem Johannis deZwaan, septuagenarii.* Haarlem: De Erven F. Bohn N.V., 1953. Pp. 96 ff.

―――. *The Epistle of Paul to the Romans (MNTC).* New York and London: Harper & Brothers, 1932.

―――. "The Ethics of the Pauline Epistles," *The Evolution of Ethics,* ed. E. H. Sneath. New Haven: Yale University Press, 1927. Pp. 293 ff.

―――. *Gospel and Law: The Relation of Faith and Ethics in Early Christianity.* New York: Columbia University Press, 1951.

―――. *New Testament Studies.* Manchester: Manchester University Press, 1953.

―――. "The Primitive Catechism and the Sayings of Jesus," *New Testament Essays. Studies in Memory of Thomas Walter Manson,* ed. A. J. B. Higgins. Manchester: Manchester University Press, 1959. Pp. 106 ff.

Dodds, E. R. *Pagan and Christian in an Age of Anxiety: Some Aspects of Religious Experience from Marcus Aurelius to Constantine.* Cambridge: Cambridge Press, 1965.

Doughty, D. J. "Heiligkeit und Freiheit. Eine exegetische Untersuchung der Anwendung des paulinischen Freiheitsgedankens in 1 Kor. 7." Unpublished Doctoral dissertation, Georg-August-Universität (Göttingen), 1965.

Drower, E. G. "ADAMAS—humanity: ADAM—mankind," *ThLZ,* LXXXVI (1961), cols. 173 ff.

―――. *The Secret Adam, A Study of Nasoraean Gnosis.* Oxford: The Clarendon Press, 1960.

Ellis, E. Earle. *Paul's Use of the Old Testament.* Edinburgh: Oliver & Boyd, 1957.

Enslin, Morton Scott. *The Ethics of Paul.* New York: Harper & Row, 1930. Reprinted with an additional intro. as an Apex Book; Nashville: Abingdon Press, 1962.

Ernesti, H. Fr. Th. L. *Die Ethik des Apostels Paulus in ihren Grundzügen dargestellt.* Göttingen: Vandenhoeck & Ruprecht's Verlag, 1868 (rev. ed., 1880).

Farmer, William R., Moule, C. F. D., and Niebuhr, Richard R., eds. *Christian History and Interpretation: Studies Presented to John Knox.* Cambridge: The University Press, 1967.

Farrar, A. M. "On Dispensing with Q," *Studies in the Gospels. Essays in Memory of R. H. Lightfoot,* ed. D. E. Nineham. Oxford: B. Blackwell, 1955.

Filson, Floyd V. *St. Paul's Conception of Recompense (UNT, 21).* Leipzig: J. C. Hinrichs'sche Buchhandlung, 1931.

Fitzer, Gottfried. " 'Das Weib schweige in der Gemeinde' ": Über den unpaulinischen Charakter der mulier-taceat-Verse in I Korinther 14," *ThEx*, n. F. 110, 1963.

Fletcher, Joseph. *Situation Ethics: The New Morality.* Philadelphia: The Westminster Press, 1966.

Flew, R. Newton. *Jesus and His Way. A Study of the Ethics of the New Testament.* London: The Epworth Press, 1963.

Frankena, William. *Ethics.* ("Foundations of Philosophy Series.") Englewood Cliffs, N. J.: Prentice-Hall, 1963.

Friedrich, Gerhard. "Das Gesetz des Glaubens, Röm. 3:27," *ThZ*, X (1954), 401 ff.

————. "Ein Tauflied hellenisticher Judenchristen, I Thess. 1:9 f.," *ThZ*, XXI (1965), 502 ff.

Fuchs, Ernst. *Die Freiheit des Glaubens. Röm. 5-8 ausgelegt (BEvTh, 14).* München: Chr. Kaiser Verlag, 1949.

————. "The Theology of the New Testament and the Historical Jesus," *Studies of the Historical Jesus (SBTh, 42).* Trans. A. Scobie. Naperville, Ill.: Alec R. Allenson, 1964. Pp. 167 ff.

Furnish, Victor Paul. "The Jesus-Paul Debate: From Baur to Bultmann," *BJRL*, XLVII (1965), 342 ff.

————. "*Kerygma* and *Didache* Reconsidered," *Perkins School of Theology Journal,* XIV (1961), 31 ff.

————. *Paul's Exhortations in the Context of His Letters and Thought.* ("Microcard Theological Studies, XXXVI.") Washington, D.C.: The Microcard Foundation for the American Theological Library Association, 1960.

Gardner, E. Clinton. *Biblical Faith and Social Ethics.* New York: Harper & Row, 1960.

Garvie, A. E. "Suggestive Variants," *ET*, LV (1943–44), 95 ff.

Gaugler, E. "Die Heiligung in der Ethik des Apostels Paulus," *IKZ*, XV (1925), 100 ff.

Goguel, Maurice. *The Primitive Church.* Trans. H. C. Snape. New York: The Macmillan Company, 1964.

Goppelt, L. "Tradition nach Paulus," *KuD*, IV (1958), 213 ff.

Grafe, Eduard. "Das Verhältnis der paulinischen Schriften zur Sapientia Salomonis," *Theologische Abhandlungen,* 1892. Pp. 251 ff.

Gross, Alfred J. "The Development of Pauline Paraenesis on Civil Obedience." Unpublished Doctoral dissertation, University of Chicago, 1947.

Gustafson, James M. "Christian Ethics," *Religion,* ed. Paul Ramsey. Englewood Cliffs, N.J.: Prentice-Hall, 1963. Pp. 287 ff.

Haenchen, Ernst. *Die Apostelgeschichte (KEK)*. 13th ed. Göttingen: Vandenhoeck & Ruprecht, 1961.

Hamilton, Neill Q. *The Holy Spirit and Eschatology in Paul.* ("*SJTh* Occasional Papers, 6.") Edinburgh: Oliver & Boyd, 1957.

Harnack, Adolf von. "Das alte Testament in den paulinischen Briefen und in den paulinischen Gemeinden," *SAB*, 1928. Pp. 124 ff.

――――. *The Mission and Expansion of Christianity in the First Three Centuries.* Trans. ed. James Moffatt. New York: Harper Torchbooks, 1961.

Harris, J. Rendel. "Pindar and St. Paul," *ET*, XXXIII (1921–22), 456-57.

――――. "St. Paul and Aeschylus," *ET*, XXXV (1923–24), 151 ff.

――――. "St. Paul and Aristophanes," *ET*, XXXIV (1922–23), 151 ff.

――――. "St. Paul and Epimenides," *Exp*, 8th series, IV (1912), 348 ff.

――――. "Did St. Paul Quote Euripides?" *ET*, XXXI (1919–20), 36-37.

Hunter, Archibald M. *Paul and His Predecessors.* Rev. ed. Philadelphia: The Westminster Press, 1961.

Hurd, John Coolidge, Jr. *The Origin of First Corinthians.* New York: The Seabury Press, 1965.

Jacoby, Hermann. *Neutestamentliche Ethik.* Königsberg i. Pr.: Verlag von Thomas & Oppermann, 1899.

Jaeger, Werner. *Paideia: The Ideals of Greek Culture.* Trans. Gilbert Highet. 3 vols. Oxford: B. Blackwell, 1939–45 (Vol. I, 4th ed., 1954).

Joest, W. *Gesetz und Freiheit: Das Problem des Tertius usus legis bei Luther und die neutestamentliche Paränese.* Göttingen: Vandenhoeck & Ruprecht, 1951.

John, D. "St. Paul and Empedocles," *ET*, XXXIX (1927–28), 237-38.

Johnson, Sherman E. "Paul and the Manual of Discipline," *HThR*, XLVIII (1955), 157 ff.

Juncker, Alfred. *Die Ethik des Apostels Paulus.* 2 vols. Halle: Max Niemeyer, 1904, 1919.

Kadushin, Max. *Worship and Ethics: A Study in Rabbinic Judaism.* Evanston, Ill.: Northwestern University Press, 1964.

Kamlah, Erhard. *Die Form der katalogischen Paränese im Neuen Testament (WUNT, 7).* Tübingen: J. C. B. Mohr (Paul Siebeck), 1964.

Käsemann, Ernst. "Die Anfänge christlicher Theologie," *Exegetische Versuche und Besinnungen*, II, 82 ff.

――――. *Essays on New Testament Themes (SBTh, 41).* Trans. W. J. Montague. Naperville, Ill.: Alec R. Allenson, 1964. Pp. 169 ff.

———. *Exegetische Versuche und Besinnungen.* 2 vols. Göttingen: Vandenhoeck & Ruprecht, 1960, 1964.

———. "God's Righteousness in Paul," *JThC,* I (1965), 100 ff.

———. "Grundsätzliches zur Interpretation von Römer 13," *Exegetische Versuche und Besinnungen,* II, 204 ff.

———. "Kritische Analyse von Phil. 2:5-11," *ibid.,* I, 51 ff.

———. "Zum Thema der urchristliches Apokalyptik," *ibid.,* II, 105 ff.

Knox, John. *The Ethic of Jesus in the Teaching of the Church.* Nashville: Abingdon Press, 1961.

Kramer, Werner. *Christ, Lord, Son of God (SBTh,* 50). Trans. Brian Hardy. Naperville, Ill.: Alec R. Allenson, 1966.

Kümmel, Werner G. *Römer 7 und die Bekehrung des Paulus (UNT,* 17). Leipzig: J. C. Hinrichs, 1929.

Lietzmann, Hans. *An die Korinther, I, II (HNT).* 4th ed. enlgd. by W. G. Kümmel. Tübingen: J. C. B. Mohr (Paul Siebeck), 1949.

———. *An die Römer (HNT).* 3rd ed. Tübingen: J. C. B. Mohr (Paul Siebeck), 1928.

Lightfoot, J. B. *Saint Paul's Epistle to the Philippians.* London: Macmillan & Company, 1896.

Ljungmann, Henrik. *Pistis: A Study of Its Presuppositions and Its Meaning in Pauline Use.* Lund: C. W. K. Gleerup, 1964.

Lohmeyer, Ernst. *Der Brief an die Philipper (KEK).* 19th ed. Göttingen: Vandenhoeck & Ruprecht, 1954.

Lohse, Eduard. "Paränese und Kerygma im 1 Petrusbrief," *ZNW,* XLV (1954), 68 ff.

———. "Taufe und Rechtfertigung bei Paulus," *KuD,* XI (1965), 308 ff.

Longenecker, Richard N. *Paul, Apostle of Liberty.* New York: Harper & Row, 1964.

Lowe, John. "An Examination of Attempts to Detect Development in St. Paul's Theology," *JThS,* XLII (1941), 129 ff.

Manson, Thomas Walter. *Ethics and the Gospel.* New York: Charles Scribner's Sons, 1960.

Marshall, L. H. *The Challenge of New Testament Ethics.* London: Macmillan & Company, 1946.

Marxsen, Willi. "Der ἕτερος νόμος, Röm. 13:8," *ThZ,* XIII (1955), 230 ff.

McArthur, Harvey K. "Computer Criticism," *ET,* LXXVI (1965), 367 ff.

McKenzie, John L. "Natural Law in the New Testament," *Biblical Research,* IX (1964), 3 ff.

Michel, Otto. *Der Brief an die Römer* (*KEK*). 13th ed. Göttingen: Vandenhoeck & Ruprecht, 1966.

————. *Paulus und seine Bibel* (*BFChTh*, 18). Gütersloh: C. Bertelsmann, 1929.

Moffatt, James. "The Interpretation of Romans 6:17-18," *JBL*, XLVIII (1929), 233 ff.

Moore, George Foot. *Judaism in the First Centuries of the Christian Era.* 3 vols. Cambridge: Harvard University Press, 1927–30.

Morton, A. Q. "The Authorship of the Pauline Corpus," *The New Testament in Historical and Contemporary Perspective. Essays in Memory of G. H. C. Macgregor,* ed. H. Anderson and W. Barclay. Oxford: B. Blackwell, 1965. Pp. 209 ff.

————, and McLeman, James. *Paul: The Man and the Myth.* New York: Harper & Row, 1966.

Moule, C. F. D. "Obligation in the Ethic of Paul," *Christian History and Interpretation: Studies Presented to John Knox,* ed. W. R. Farmer, C. F. D. Moule, and R. R. Niebuhr, Pp. 389 ff.

Murray, John. *Principles of Conduct: Aspects of Biblical Ethics.* Grand Rapids, Mich.: Wm. B. Eerdmans Publishing Co., 1957.

Nauck, Wolfgang. "Das οὖν-paräneticum," *ZNW*, XLIX (1958), 134-35.

Nepper-Christensen, P. "Das verborgene Herrnwort, Eine Untersuchung über I Thess. 4:13-18," *StTh*, XIX (1965), 136 ff.

Neugebauer, F. *In Christus: Eine Untersuchung zum paulinischen Glaubensverständnis.* Göttingen: Vandenhoeck & Ruprecht, 1961.

Niebuhr, Reinhold. *The Nature and Destiny of Man: A Christian Interpretation.* 2 vols. New York: Charles Scribner's Sons, 1941.

Nygren, Anders. *Agape and Eros.* Rev. ed. trans. P. S. Watson. Philadelphia: The Westminster Press, 1953.

————. *Commentary on Romans.* Trans. Carl C. Rasmussen. Philadelphia: Muhlenberg Press, 1949.

Oden, Thomas C. *Radical Obedience: The Ethics of Rudolf Bultmann.* Philadelphia: The Westminster Press, 1964.

Ogden, Schubert M. *Christ Without Myth.* New York: Harper & Row, 1961.

Pierce, C. A. *Conscience in the New Testament* (*SBTh*, 15). Naperville, Ill.: Alec R. Allenson, 1955.

Preisker, Herbert. *Das Ethos des Urchristentums.* 2nd ed. Gütersloh: C. Bertelsmann, 1949.

Ramsey, Paul. *Basic Christian Ethics.* New York: Charles Scribner's Sons, 1950.

Reitzenstein, Richard. "Zu Porphyrius und Paulus," *Historia Mona-chorum und Historia Lausiaca, (FRLANT*, 24). Göttingen: Vanden-hoeck & Ruprecht, 1916. Pp. 242 ff.

Resch, Alfred. *Der Paulinismus und die Logia Jesu in ihrem gegen-seitigen Verhältnis untersucht (TU*, xxvii). Leipzig: J. C. Hin-richs'sche Buchhandlung, 1904.

Ringgren, Helmer. *The Faith of Qumran: Theology of the Dead Sea Scrolls.* Trans. E. T. Sander. Philadelphia: Fortress Press, 1963.

Roloff, Jürgen. *Apostolat—Verkündigung—Kirche. Ursprung, Inhalt und Funktion des kirchlichen Apostelamtes nach Paulus, Lukas und den Pastoralbriefen.* Gütersloh: Gütersloher Verlagshaus (Gerd Mohn), 1965.

Ross, John. "ΕΝΕΡΓΕΙΣΘΑΙ in the New Testament," *Exp*, 7th series, VII (1909), 75 ff.

Russell, D. S. *The Method and Message of Jewish Apocalyptic, 200 B.C.–A.D. 100.* ("The Old Testament Library.") Philadelphia: The Westminster Press, 1964.

Salom, A. P. "The Imperatival Use of the Participle in the New Tes-tament," *ABR,* XI (1963), 41 ff.

Sanday, William, and Headlam, Arthur C. *A Critical and Exegetical Commentary on the Epistle to the Romans (ICC).* 5th ed. New York: Charles Scribner's Sons, 1902.

Sandmel, Samuel. *The Genius of Paul.* New York: Farrar, Straus and Cudahy, 1958.

———. "Parallelomania," *JBL,* LXXXI (1962), 1 ff.

Schlier, Heinrich. *Der Brief an die Galater (KEK).* 13th ed. Göttingen: Vandenhoeck & Ruprecht, 1965.

———. "Die Eigenart der christlichen Mahnung nach dem Apostel Paulus," *Besinnung auf das Neue Testament: Exegetische Aufsätze und Vorträge, II.* Freiburg: Herder, 1964. Pp. 340 ff.

———. "Vom Wesen der apostolischen Ermahnung nach Röm. 12:1-2," *Die Zeit der Kirche.* 2nd ed. Freiburg: Herder, 1956. Pp. 74 ff.

Schnackenburg, Rudolf. *The Moral Teaching of the New Testament.* Trans. J. Holland-Smith and W. J. O'Hara from the 2nd rev. ed. Freiburg: Herder, 1965.

Schoeps, H. J. *Paul: The Theology of the Apostle in the Light of Jewish Religious History.* Trans. Harold Knight. Philadelphia: The Westminster Press, 1961.

Schrage, Wolfgang. *Die konkreten Einzelgebote in der paulinischen Paränese.* Gütersloh: Gütersloher Verlagshaus (Gerd Mohn), 1961.

———. "Die Stellung zur Welt bei Paulus, Epiktet und in der Apokalyptik. Ein Beitrag zu 1 Kor 7:29-31." *ZThK*, LXI (1964), 125 ff.

Schubert, Paul. *Form and Function of the Pauline Thanksgivings BZNW*, 20). Berlin: A. Töpelmann, 1939.

——. "Paul and the New Testament Ethic in the Thought of John Knox," *Christian History and Interpretation: Studies Presented to John Knox*, ed. W. R. Farmer, C. F. D. Moule, and R. R. Niebuhr. Pp. 363 ff.

Schulz, Anselm. *Nachfolgen und Nachahmen* (*SANT*, VI). München: Kösel-Verlag, 1962.

Schürer, Emil. *Geschichte des jüdischen Volkes im Zeitalter Jesu Christi*. 4 vols. 3rd and 4th ed. Leipzig: J. C. Hinrichs'sche Buchhandlung, 1901-11.

Schweitzer, Albert. *The Mysticism of Paul the Apostle*. Trans. Wm. Montgomery. London: Adam and Charles Black, 1931.

Scott, C. A. A. *New Testament Ethics: An Introduction*. New York: The Macmillan Company, 1930.

Scott, Ernest F. *Man and Society in the New Testament*. New York: Charles Scribner's Sons, 1946.

——. *The Spirit in the New Testament*. London: Hodder & Stoughton, 1923.

Scroggs, Robin. *The Last Adam: A Study in Pauline Anthropology*. Philadelphia: Fortress Press, 1966.

Shires, Henry M. *The Eschatology of Paul in the Light of Modern Scholarship*. Philadelphia: The Westminster Pres, 1966.

Sittler, Joseph. *The Structure of Christian Ethics*. Baton Rouge: Louisiana State University Press, 1958.

Soden, Hans von. "Sakrament und Ethik bei Paulus," *Urchristentum und Geschichte*, I. Tübingen: J. C. B. Mohr (Paul Siebeck), 1951. Pp. 239 ff.

Soden, Hermann von. "Die Ethik des Paulus," *ZThK*, II (1892), 109 ff.

Spicq, Ceslaus. *Agape in the New Testament*. Trans. Sister Marie Aquinas McNamara and Sister Mary Honoria Richter. 2 vols. St. Louis: B. Herder Book Co., 1963, 1965.

Stalder, Kurt. *Das Werk des Geistes in der Heiligung bei Paulus*. Zürich: EVZ-Verlag, 1962.

Stanley, David M. " 'Become Imitators of Me,' " *Bibl*, XL (1959), 859 ff.

Strecker, Georg. "Redaktion und Tradition im Christushymnus, Phil. 2:6-11," *ZNW*, LV (1964), 63 ff.

Stuhlmacher, Peter. *Gerechtigkeit Gottes bei Paulus* (*FRLANT*, 87). Göttingen: Vandenhoeck & Ruprecht, 1965.

Tannehill, Robert C. *Dying and Rising With Christ, A Study in Pauline Theology (BZNW, 32)*. Berlin: A. Töpelmann, 1967.

Thomas, George F. *Christian Ethics and Moral Philosophy*. New York: Charles Scribner's Sons, 1955.

Thyen, Hartwig. *Der Stil der jüdisch-hellenistischen Homilie (FRLANT, n. F. 47)*. Göttingen: Vandenhoeck & Ruprecht, 1955.

Tinsley, E. J. *The Imitation of God in Christ, An Essay on the Biblical Basis of Christian Spirituality*. London: SCM Press, 1960.

Vetschera, Rudolf. *Zur griechischen Paränese* (Sonderabdruck aus den Jahresberichten des k. k. deutschen Staatsgymnasiums in Smichow, 1911 und 1912). Smichow: Druck von Rohlíček und Sievers in Prag. Im Selbtsverlage, 1912.

Vielhauer, Philipp. "On the 'Paulinism' of Acts," *Studies in Luke-Acts*, ed. L. E. Keck and J. L. Martyn. Nashville: Abingdon Press, 1966. Pp. 33 ff.

Vincent, Marvin R. *A Critical and Exegetical Commentary on the Epistles to the Philippians and to Philemon (ICC)*. New York: Charles Scribner's Sons, 1906.

Wagner, Günter. *Pauline Baptism and the Pagan Mysteries. The Problem of the Pauline Doctrine of Baptism in Romans VI:1-11, in the Light of its Religio-Historical "Parallels."* Trans. J. P. Smith. Edinburgh: Oliver & Boyd, 1967.

Wahlstrom, Eric H. *The New Life in Christ*. Philadelphia: Muhlenberg Press, 1950.

Wegenast, Klaus. *Das Verständnis der Tradition bei Paulus und in den Deuteropaulinen (WMANT, 8)*. Neukirchen: Neukirchener Verlag, 1962.

Weidinger, Karl. *Die Haustafeln. Ein Stück urchristlicher Paränese (UNT, 14)*. Leipzig: J. C. Hinrichs'sche Buchhandlung, 1928.

Weinel, Heinrich. *St. Paul: The Man and His Work*. Trans. G. A. Bienemann; ed. W. D. Morrison. London: Williams & Norgate, 1906.

Weiss, Johannes. *Der erste Korintherbrief (KEK)*. 10th ed. Göttingen: Vandenhoeck & Ruprecht, 1925.

———. *The History of Primitive Christianity*. (Completed Rudolf Knopf; trans. Four Friends; ed. Frederick C. Grant.) 2 vols. New York: Wilson-Erickson, 1937.

Weizsäcker, Carl von. *The Apostolic Age of the Christian Church*. Trans. from the 2nd rev. ed. by James Millar. 2 vols. London: Williams & Norgate, 1894.

Wendland, H.-D. "Ethik und Eschatologie in der Theologie des Paulus," *NKZ*, XLI (1930), 757 ff.

———. "Das Wirken des Heiligen Geistes in der Gläubigen nach Paulus," *ThLZ*, LXXVII (1952), cols. 457 ff.

Wernle, Paul. *The Beginnings of the Christian Religion*. Trans. G. A. Bienemann. 2 vols. London: Williams & Norgate, 1903.

———. *Der Christ und die Sünde bei Paulus*. Freiburg i. B. und Leipzig: Akademische Verlagsbuchhandlung von J. C. B. Mohr (Paul Siebeck), 1897.

Whiteley, D. E. H. *The Theology of St. Paul*. Philadelphia: Fortress Press, 1964.

Wibbing, Siegfried. *Die Tugend und Lasterkataloge im Neuen Testament (BZNW, 25)*. Berlin: A. Töpelmann, 1959.

Windisch, Hans. "Das Problem des paulinischen Imperativs," *ZNW*, XXIII (1924), 265 ff.

Index of
Biblical References

(In the Pauline homologoumena [see p. 11] only the principal references are indexed. References to footnotes are italicized.)

Index of
Subjects and Authors

(Principal references are in bold type; references to footnotes are in italic; all other references are in Roman type.)